MICROHISTORIES OF THE HOLOCAUST

War and Genocide

General Editors: Omer Bartov, Brown University; A. Dirk Moses, European University Institute, Florence, Italy

In recent years there has been a growing interest in the study of war and genocide, not from a traditional military history perspective, but within the framework of social and cultural history. This series offers a forum for scholarly works that reflect these new approaches.

"The Berghahn series Studies on War and Genocide has immeasurably enriched the English-language scholarship available to scholars and students of genocide and, in particular, the Holocaust."—**Totalitarian Movements and Political Religions**

Volume 1
The Massacre in History
Edited by Mark Levene and Penny Roberts

Volume 2
National Socialist Extermination Policies: Contemporary German Perspectives and Controversies
Edited by Ulrich Herbert

Volume 3
War of Extermination: The German Military in World War II, 1941/44
Edited by Hannes Heer and Klaus Naumann

Volume 4
In God's Name: Genocide and Religion in the Twentieth Century
Edited by Omer Bartov and Phyllis Mack

Volume 5
Hitler's War in the East, 1941–1945
Rolf-Dieter Müller and Gerd R. Ueberschär

Volume 6
Genocide and Settler Society: Frontier Violence and Stolen Indigenous Children in Australian History
Edited by A. Dirk Moses

Volume 7
Networks of Nazi Persecution: Bureaucracy, Business, and the Organization of the Holocaust
Edited by Gerald D. Feldman and Wolfgang Seibel

Volume 8
Gray Zones: Ambiguity and Compromise in the Holocaust and Its Aftermath
Edited by Jonathan Petropoulos and John K. Roth

Volume 9
Robbery and Restitution: The Conflict over Jewish Property in Europe
Edited by M. Dean, C. Goschler and P. Ther

Volume 10
Exploitation, Resettlement, Mass Murder: Political and Economic Planning for German Occupation Policy in the Soviet Union, 1940–1941
Alex J. Kay

Volume 11
Theatres of Violence: The Massacre, Mass Killing and Atrocity in History
Edited by Philip G. Dwyer and Lyndall Ryan

Volume 12
Empire, Colony, Genocide: Conquest, Occupation, and Subaltern Resistance in World History
Edited by A. Dirk Moses

Volume 13
The Train Journey: Transit, Captivity, and Witnessing in the Holocaust
Simone Gigliotti

Volume 14
The "Final Solution" in Riga: Exploitation and Annihilation, 1941–1944
Andrej Angrick and Peter Klein

Volume 15
The Kings and the Pawns: Collaboration in Byelorussia during World War II
Leonid Rein

Volume 16
Reassessing the Nuremberg Military Tribunals: Transitional Justice, Trial Narratives, and Historiography
Edited by Kim C. Priemel and Alexa Stiller

Volume 17
The Nazi Genocide of the Roma: Reassessment and Commemoration
Edited by Anton Weiss-Wendt

Volume 18
Judging "Privileged" Jews: Holocaust Ethics, Representation, and the "Grey Zone"
Adam Brown

Volume 19
The Dark Side of Nation-States: Ethnic Cleansing in Modern Europe
Philip Ther

Volume 20
The Greater German Reich and the Jews: Nazi Persecution Policies in the Annexed Territories 1935–1945
Edited by Wolf Gruner and Jörg Osterloh

Volume 21
The Spirit of the Laws: The Plunder of Wealth in the Armenian Genocide
Taner Akçam and Ümit Kurt

Volume 22
Genocide on Settler Frontiers: When Hunter-Gatherers and Commercial Stock Farmers Clash
Edited by Mohamed Adhikari

Volume 23
The Making of the Greek Genocide: Contested Memories of the Ottoman Greek Catastrophe
Erik Sjöberg

Volume 24
Microhistories of the Holocaust
Edited by Claire Zalc and Tal Bruttmann

MICROHISTORIES OF THE HOLOCAUST

Edited by

Claire Zalc and Tal Bruttmann

berghahn
NEW YORK • OXFORD
www.berghahnbooks.com

Published in 2017 by
Berghahn Books
www.berghahnbooks.com

© 2017, 2019 Claire Zalc and Tal Bruttmann
First paperback edition published in 2019
This book has received the support of TransferS (laboratoire d'excellence, program "Investissements d'avenir" ANR-10-IDEX-0001-02-PSL* and ANR-10-LABX-0099).

All rights reserved.
Except for the quotation of short passages for the purposes
of criticism and review, no part of this book may be reproduced in any form
or by any means, electronic or mechanical, including photocopying, recording,
or any information storage and retrieval system now known or to be invented,
without written permission of the publisher.

Library of Congress Cataloging-in-Publication Data

Names: Zalc, Claire, editor. | Bruttmann, Tal, editor.
Title: Microhistories of the Holocaust / edited by Claire Zalc and Tal Bruttmann.
Description: New York ; Oxford : Berghahn Books, [2017] | Series: War and genocide ; volume 24 | "The international conference "Exploring the microhistory of the Holocaust," which took place in Paris in December 2012 … was the origin of this work"—Introduction. | Includes bibliographical references and index.
Identifiers: LCCN 2016026106 | ISBN 9781785333668 (hardback : alk. paper)
Subjects: LCSH: Holocaust, Jewish (1939–1945)—Congresses. | Holocaust, Jewish (1939–1945)—Historiography—Congresses.
Classification: LCC D804.18 .M53 2017 | DDC 940.53/18—dc23
LC record available at hcps://lccn.loc.gov/2016026106

British Library Cataloguing in Publication Data

A catalogue record for this book is available from the British Library.

ISBN 978–1–78533–366–8 hardback
ISBN 978-1-78920-054-6 paperback
ISBN 978–1–78533–367–5 ebook

Contents

List of Illustrations and Tables	viii
Acknowledgments	x
Introduction Toward a Microhistory of the Holocaust *Claire Zalc and Tal Bruttmann*	1

Part I. Biographies, Groups, Transports, Ghettos: The Scales of Analysis

Chapter 1 An Inconceivable Emigration: Richard Frank's Flight from Germany to Switzerland in 1942 *Christoph Kreutzmüller*	17
Chapter 2 Pursuing Escape from Vienna: The Katz Family's Correspondence *Melissa Jane Taylor*	29
Chapter 3 Moving Together, Moving Alone: The Story of Boys on a Transport from Auschwitz to Buchenwald *Kenneth Waltzer*	44
Chapter 4 Dehumanizing the Dead: The Destruction of Thessaloniki's Jewish Cemetery *Leon Saltiel*	68
Chapter 5 Reconstructing Trajectories of Persecution: Reflections on a Prosopography of Holocaust Victims *Nicolas Mariot and Claire Zalc*	85

Chapter 6
Microhistories, Microgeographies: Budapest, 1944, and Scales
of Analysis   113
Tim Cole and Alberto Giordano

Part II. Face-To-Face: Victims and Perpetrators

Chapter 7
Microhistory of the Holocaust in Poland: New Sources, New Trails   131
Jan Grabowski

Chapter 8
Jewish Slave Workers in the German Aviation Industry   151
Daniel Uziel

Chapter 9
The Devil in Microhistory: The "Hunt for Jews" as a Social Process,
1942–1945   171
Tomasz Frydel

Chapter 10
On the Persistence of Moral Judgment: Local Perpetrators in
Transnistria as Seen by Survivors and Their Christian Neighbors   190
Vladimir Solonari

Chapter 11
Defiance and Protest: A Comparative Microhistorical Reevaluation
of Individual Jewish Responses to Nazi Persecution   209
Wolf Gruner

Chapter 12
The Murder of the Jews of Ostrów Mazowiecka in November 1939   227
Markus Roth

Chapter 13
Échirolles, 7 August 1944: A Triple Execution   242
Tal Bruttmann

Chapter 14
The Beginning—First Massacres against the Jews in the
Romanian Holocaust: Level of Decision, Genocidal Strategy, and Killing
Methods regarding Dorohoi and Galați Pogroms, June–July, 1940   251
Alexandru Muraru

**Part III. The Material for Shifting Scales: Sources between
Testimonies and Archives**

Chapter 15
The Holocaust and Postwar Justice in Poland in Three Acts   267
Andrew Kornbluth

Chapter 16
The Small and the Good: Microhistory through the Eyes of the
Witness—A Case Study   285
Hannah Pollin-Galay

Chapter 17
The Witness against the Archive: Toward a Microhistory
of Christianstadt   300
Jeffrey Wallen

Index   315

Illustrations and Tables

Illustrations

7.1.	Melania Weissenberg (middle) with her mother, Sara, and brother Zygmunt (Zyga), Kraków, 1936(?). Photo from the Weissenberg family archive.	136
7.2.	Sabina Golman, Dąbrowa Tarnowska ghetto, 1941.	138
7.3.	Chaja Rosenblatt (Garn) second from the left, with her parents and sisters. Radomyśl Wielki, 1935(?). Photograph from the Rosenblatt family archive.	141
7.4.	Exhumation of the remains of Hela and Salomea Süss, Dąbrowa Tarnowska, December 1945.	143

Tables

3.1.	Boys on the Buna Transport to Buchenwald in This Microstudy	62
5.1.	Characteristics of Self-declared and Non-declared Jews	96
5.2.	Those Who Left and Those Who Remained: Household Size	99
5.3.	Kinship Network and Arrests of Departed (compared to total number of households)	99
5.4.	Destination as a Function of Time of Departure	100
5.5.	The Effect of Departure Time on Arrest Rates	100
5.6.	Arrest as a Function of Final Destination	101
5.7.	Departing versus Remaining in Lens: Street Addresses and Proximity	103

5.8.	Family Declaration in December 1940 and Deportation	104
5.9.	Nationality and Departure between 1940 and 1942	104
5.10.	Nationality and Arrest	105
5.11.	Nationality and Dates of Departure	105
5.12.	Socioeconomic Status of Jews Who Left Lens between 1940 and 1942	106
5.13.	Socioeconomic Status and Arrest	107

Acknowledgments

We would like to thank all of the institutions and individuals who made the truly collective adventure of this book possible. The international conference "Exploring the Microhistory of the Holocaust," which took place in Paris in December 2012 and was the origin of this work, enjoyed the support of the Ecole normale supérieure, as well as the early and enthusiastic support of three of its directors, Guillaume Bonnet, Michel Espagne, and Christophe Charle. We would also like to thank the Fondation pour la mémoire de la Shoah, the région Ile de France, the Direction de la mémoire, du patrimoine et des archives (DMAP), the Archives nationales, the Mémorial de la Shoah, and the Institut universitaire de France.

Aside from institutions, we have not forgotten the many helping hands who provided support at various moments of this adventure: Ivan Ermakoff and Nicolas Mariot, our associates on the organization committee with whom we developed the first phases, Annette Wieviorka, Maurice Olender, Jan Gross, Dieter Pohl, Omer Bartov, and the anonymous readers of the early versions of this manuscript, whose comments helped to greatly improve it. Our heartfelt thanks to John Angell and Arby Gharibian, who translated and edited the texts with elegance. Last but not least, this book owes a tremendous deal to the invaluable help of Virginie Durand (UMR 8138 Sirice), who assisted us throughout the adventure with energy, rigor, friendship, and incredible good humor. We are deeply grateful to her, from the bottom of our hearts.

Introduction
Toward a Microhistory of the Holocaust

Claire Zalc and Tal Bruttmann

Applying a narrow focus to the study of the "Final Solution" is not, strictly speaking, a new approach. A similar process was adopted even during the conflict itself through early attempts to understand what was taking place. Vasily Grossman, for example, entered Polish territory in the summer of 1944 embedded as a journalist with the Red Army. They traveled to Treblinka, where he undertook a study to help him comprehend the true nature of a place of which virtually nothing remained aside from some debris and a few scattered fragments of human remains. Originally published in 1944, his report, *The Treblinka Hell*,[1] represents a novel effort to compose an immediate history of a killing center. Grossman's study helped him better understand the fate of the Jews walled up in Polish ghettos, as well as the wider fate of most of the Jewish inhabitants of the rest of Europe. Retracing in minute detail the history of this individual—and extremely singular—site allowed Grossman to imagine the fate of the entire continent's Jewish population.

A vast body of historiographical research on the Holocaust has developed since then. The overall framework of this research, which focuses broadly on the devastation of European Jews, was well established beginning with the pioneering studies by Léon Poliakov[2] and Gerald Reitlinger[3] in the early 1950s, whose work was followed by that of Raul Hilberg and Saul Friedländer.[4] Studies conducted in the 1980s and 1990s tended to be smaller scale, focusing on local or regional contexts such as Riga, the Lublin district, or Belarus.[5] These more fine-grained studies provided a better understanding of the mechanisms used to implement the Final Solution and often provided clearer views of a far vaster whole.[6] For the past decade, studies focusing on a single camp or ghetto or a particular roundup, city, convoy, family, or battalion have contributed to a deep renewal of Holocaust studies.[7] It should be acknowledged, however, that the implications and historiographical relevance of this microhistorical shift have not been critically examined. The fundamental question, however, is whether there really are matters of substance to renew in this field. Hasn't everything already been said? How will microhistory enrich the history of the Holocaust?

Our idea of assembling a series of microhistorical approaches to the Holocaust within a single edited volume was inspired by a desire to reconsider the intellectual, heuristic, and archival operations underlying this tectonic shift in the scale at which the destiny of European Jews is currently being studied. The generic expression "microhistory of the Holocaust" designates a multitude of processes that adopt different orientations, ask different questions, and explore a vast and complex history that swept through nearly all of the European continent. The studies approach the field from a variety of angles and utilize a range of methodologies. There is as yet no single agreed-upon definition of this strand of historiographical research, which began in the late 1970s and expanded during the 1980s. Without risking a single definition, it should be remembered that this historiographical movement calls into question the certainties of earlier historiographies, notably the grand explanations based on economic or cultural determinations, by granting renewed importance to individual practices and experiences. It involves criticizing not only the inadequacy of the categories used by a self-styled "total" history, but also emphasizing the importance of the different scales of the phenomena in their own right. It gives increased attention to the categories of actors, the strategies of individuals and small groups, as well as to ways of writing history.

While micro-level studies have proliferated around the world, valid questions can be raised about the effects of this change of scale on the production of knowledge.[8] Indeed, microhistory cannot be reduced to monographs or to local history or histories. What is at issue here is clearly to move away from the metaphor of grand history as a puzzle composed of the accumulation of small monographs focusing on such and such locality or histories centering on specific micro-moments. The change of scale entails a change of paradigm in the way of writing history.

When we refer to microhistory, we are echoing the appeal of the Italian pioneers of the 1980s—Carlo Ginzburg, Giovanni Levi, Carlo Poni, and others—who concentrated on smaller units and spaces. Reducing the level of analysis increases knowledge, because smaller spaces can better elucidate the complexities of decision-making, help reestablish the "space of the possible," show how reality was experienced at the individual level, and ultimately provide more compelling insights into the events that contemporaries faced in their day-to-day lives. Francesca Trivellato has issued a useful reminder to maintain the distinction between *la microstoria,* which was developed by Italian historians, *microhistoire à la française,* and microhistory, as it is understood by Anglophone historiographers:[9] the first is compatible with both empiricism and self-reflexivity; the second, in the tradition of the critical turning point pursued by the journal *Les Annales,* has called for a socioeconomic meaning of changing scales; while the American reception has placed more emphasis on notions of agency and narrative history.[10] Although the disjunctions within this "microhistorical" trend are considerable, the questions raised by the change of scale, as well as its effect on the writing of history, nevertheless take on particular resonance and intensity concerning the historiography of the Holocaust.

In order to reflect on the contributions of changing scale in writing Holocaust history, we organized an international conference at the École normale supérieure entitled "Changer d'échelle pour renouveler l'histoire de la Shoah/Changing Scale: Exploring the Micro History of the Holocaust" (5–7 December 2012).[11] The call for papers aroused a revelatory enthusiasm for these types of approaches: choices had to be made from among the 150 paper proposals from twenty-two different countries. In the end, the conference brought together 47 contributors from eleven countries. After attempting to benefit from the strengths of microhistorical processes, primarily using French examples, the fundamental necessity for us as editors of this volume was to examine various national historiographies by extending the analytical spectrum well beyond French borders.

The contributions that we have selected for this project are engaged in a reflexive process that critically appraises the advantages, as well as the limitations, of their particular contexts; they emphasize questions of source and method in order to promote a reflection on what and how such approaches contribute to the overall historiography of the Holocaust. We decided to give special priority in this volume to texts that make it possible to question the actual effects of a change of scale on the writing of history and the concrete ways in which it can be implemented: What sources lend themselves to this? How can hitherto neglected archives be used to shed light on certain issues? How can quantitative analysis be used in local situations? Is it possible, and if so under what conditions, to adopt the classic methodologies of social history for controversial questions and matters of memory, and more specifically for the Shoah, which is largely defined by its exceptional nature? The selected texts thus entail an overall reflexive dimension, both with regard to sources and methodology as well as to the consequences of variations in focal point. Our intention is not to claim that monographic studies, which can be very provocative, are merely bricks for constructing a "grand historical narrative" of the Holocaust. Quite the contrary—such studies decenter the gaze. Shifting the level, or scale, of analysis reveals the diversity and complexity of processes by deconstructing an entire monolithic approach without limiting oneself to the borders of a particular locality or group. A microhistorical approach systematically involves situating oneself within a broader whole and within relationships to other scales in order to understand the context of a particular case, reproducing "the range of the possible," and placing the emphasis on distortion of the general.

For this reason, assembling the approaches represented in this volume seems promising. By encouraging comparison, casting light on the differences between cases, reminding of the diversity of historiographical approaches, and always interrogating that which is general, the process invariably departs from the most local level by questioning the nature of established boundaries: What is a family? A group? A ghetto? A Jew? By studying the epistolary relations among different members of the Katz family—Jews trying to flee Austria in the late 1930s—Melissa Jane Taylor (chapter 2) shows how family dynamics are redefined by the context of anti-Semitic persecution; the emigration projects that unfolded according to different scales and chronologies redraw the outlines of the family, especially the role of children. The in-depth study of the trajectories of 304 young men under the age of sixteen (including Elie Wiesel, who arrived in Buchenwald from Auschwitz on 26 January 1945) enables Kenneth Waltzer (chapter 3) to reflect on the social firmness of this group, through analysis of the solidarity and social relations present within it.

It must be clearly asserted from the very beginning that the question is not representativeness, but instead the normal exception, which is both difficult and stimulating. The "exceptional normal," to use Edoardo Grendi's expression, is probably one of the most cited and transformed slogans of microhistory: it entails remembering that what is in question is not representativeness but the additional information generated by analysis conducted on the microscale.[12] Focusing attention on an individual, local setting, or situation different from the average or the norm can reveal the dynamics and help us understand them. For instance, the extraordinary case of Richard Frank, studied by Christoph Kreutzmüller (chapter 1), is both exemplary and exceptional. At a time when all emigration was forbidden for Jews (beginning in October 1941), Frank succeeded in December 1942 in officially reaching Switzerland from Germany by way of a succession of circumstances. It nevertheless demonstrates the existence of certain cracks in the Nazi political machine, through which certain rare individuals were able to slip. Similarly, the case of Jews from the city and environs of Lens, studied by Nicolas Mariot and Claire Zalc (chapter 5), is in no way representative of the French situation, for half of the Jewish community was deported, a figure that is significantly higher than the national average of 25 percent. The intention is not to choose a representative or emblematic case, but on the contrary to attempt to understand why the situation in Lens was exceptional. How can one understand the incredible harshness of the persecution there?

Microhistory is not synonymous with local history, disconnected from the whole in which it unfolded. On the contrary, it is a history placed in perspective and linked to the decisions, choices, and deeds that intervened at different levels, from the international to the "grassroots." As a result, we have chosen contributions that specifically consider this dimension. For example, Waltzer's contribution reveals the role of solidarity in the survival process by focusing on the relations between these boys. Places are also explored by the microhistorical approach, notably borders: based on the case of Budapest, where buildings and even isolated apartments became elements of the ghetto, Tim Cole and Alberto Giordano (chapter 6) show that the image of the ghetto, so frequently associated in representations with a space of segregation and concentration enclosed by walls, such as the Warsaw ghetto, was much more malleable and dispersed, and hence more complex to analyze.

Without necessarily summarizing the framework of Italian *microstoria*, we argue in favor of a nondogmatic approach, in which the micro does not suffice unto itself, but is articulated at other levels to create a whole. The contributions presented here are never confined to a limited space. If, for example, a project addresses the Jews of Lens, as does the contribution by Nicolas Mariot and Claire Zalc (chapter 5), it also entails references to Poland, Czechoslovakia, Romania, Germany, the Saar, Paris, and the many other origins of the Jews of a northern French city, as well as their destinations. It also means following their flight through Occupied France to the free zone, to Périgueux, Toulouse, and occasionally to Switzerland, or their arrests in Poitiers, their detentions, their deportations to Auschwitz, and in some cases their return to Lens. The dozens of locations explored in this volume, situated principally if not exclusively in Europe, are in fact highly diverse: Berlin, Vienna, Szczebrzedzyn, Auschwitz, the Buna, Buchenwald, Warsaw, Cologne, Łódź, Pinsk, Bialystok, Budapest, Échirolles, Łuków, Mielec, Ostrów Mazowiecka, Czernowitz, Birkenau, Siedlce, Majdanek, Flossenbürg, Moldova, Parczew, and Lublin, as well as Paris. Studies at the grassroots level can highlight facts that transcend a specific local framework to shed light on the broader context. In his investigation of the execution of three Jews in Échirolles, near Grenoble, for example, Tal Bruttmann (chapter 13) analyzes the specific acts themselves and the motivations of the ultra-collaborators who committed them in order to call attention to the many long-neglected assassinations of Jews that took place on French soil in 1944. His study also demonstrates that the Final Solution cannot be reduced to the arrest-deportation mechanism on which most historiographical studies of the period have focused. It also illustrates certain broader transformations of German policies in France over time.

In other words, the microhistorical focus brings new discoveries to light and humanizes abstract ideas. As Daniel Mendelsohn noted at the conclusion of his study *The Lost*:

> "The Holocaust is so big, the scale of it is so gigantic, so enormous, that it becomes easy to think of it as something mechanical. Anonymous. But everything that happened, happened because someone made a decision. To pull a trigger, to flip a switch, to close a cattle car door, to hide, to betray."[13]

Microhistorical approaches help us bridge the gap between the deeply personal approaches of the Holocaust that sometimes characterize the literary field, including the work of Daniel Mendelsohn, and the collective destiny of vast numbers of communities and immense populations. On one side is embodied history, and on the other, the abstraction of vast numbers. But more than that, these approaches also lead us to reintroduce the individuals, as well as a certain degree of flexibility, into our understanding of the process—both the name and the game, as Ginzburg and Poni put it.[14] As Jeffrey Wallen says in his text (chapter 17), "microhistory has the potential to change the pictures we have of the Holocaust: not only to substitute a finer and more complex understanding for the set of better-known names, places, and events, but to help us rethink the boundaries and oppositions that structure our understanding."

Still, the goal is not exclusively to embody "great history" within individuals or the "local," whether they were the residents of an apartment building, street, or neighborhood. Diving into the details of decision-making processes and revealing the behaviors of a range individuals who were persecuted—or were agents of persecution—allow us to see lively debates in an entirely new light. For instance, the implementation of the measures that made the Dorohoi and Galați pogroms possible, along with their actual execution, is interpreted by Alexandru Muraru (chapter 14) in the broader context of the Romanian-Soviet confrontation by also going down to the regional and local levels, with each shedding light on the others. Leon Saltiel (chapter 4) shows that although the destruction of the cemetery of Thessaloniki took shape during the Nazi occupation, the project had been part of city reorganization plans since the mid-1920s. Local authorities consequently used the German presence to implement their project; one could thus speak of the "opportunity effect" of anti-Semitic policy, which made it possible to disregard the protests of the Jewish community of Thessaloniki, in order to raze and obliterate their graves.

Placing oneself at the level of an Einsatzgruppe, a brigade of gendarmes, or a police battalion, as Christopher Browning did,[15] makes it possible to offer a different interpretation of the mechanisms of obedience and decision-making. It raises the question of conformism, but in a novel way, along with questions about authority, constraint, and the implementation of decisions emanating from various ranks. This involves many perspectives and just as many questions. A similar case reconstructed by Markus Roth (chapter 12) is the massacre conducted by a police battalion in Ostrów Mazowiecka in November 1939, whose early date raises many interesting questions and whose mechanisms are not easy to grasp. Tomasz Frydel (chapter 9) uses the example of the Rzeszów region to show the setting in which violence against Jews, as well as those who came to their aid, took place. The mechanisms of control implemented by the German occupier through the imposition of various responsibilities and burdens on local populations constituted an essential tool in the *Judenjagd*, the hunt for Jews. These mechanisms are interpreted from the point of view of both the executioners and the victims. The interaction of the executioners with the populations from which they came also represents a field of its own, which is highlighted by Vladimir Solonari (chapter 10), whose analysis of southwestern Ukraine extends into the very hearts of households.

The microhistorical level also alters perspectives from the point of view of the victims. Immersing oneself in a ghetto, reconstructing a family's escape and emigration, or following the persecution trajectories of a convoy of deportees step-by-step throughout the genocidal process offers a glimpse into the spectrum of the possible. It is a way of retrieving the "spaces of the possible" as well as "the plurality of possible futures," to invoke fellow microhistorians; or, as the case may be, a way of showing the "spaces of the impossible" or the "plurality of impossible futures" by highlighting the role of the arbitrary, and of nooses as they were cinched ever tighter.[16] These approaches allow us to question the relevance of concepts like strategy and agency at a particular moment in history, which is often understood as being in the grip of an ineluctable determinism. Above all, changing scales compels us to observe specific interactions and face-to-face contacts, which leads us in turn to envision differently the often-cited—and sometimes criticized—triad first mentioned by Raul Hilberg: perpetrators, victims, and "others," that is, bystanders.[17]

Changing scales becomes particularly important, in our opinion, with the history of the Holocaust, as its ending tends to cloud our understanding of the processes underlying how it unfolded. Attempts to exempt oneself from teleological risk, and to some extent relinquish the historical omniscience that knows "the end of history"—along with placing oneself on the ground—thus enable us to consider individuals not as mere pawns on the checkerboard of the Final Solution. Their diverse voices and points of view call into question the many facets of what Marc Bloch called the "historian's craft."[18]

The question of the origins of this change in scales is central. If we ask questions about the historiographical moment in which we find ourselves, we might observe the profound influence of changes of context on the production of sources. For one thing, as time progresses, survivors are no longer present to tell us their itineraries or to offer eyewitness accounts. Furthermore, archives have largely become accessible due to international political changes in the 1990s and the collapse of Communist regimes. National shifts in policy have also played a role, for instance the Matteoli Commission and its repercussions in France, which resulted in the opening up of nearly all archives related to World War II without special permission (the so-called Jospin circular). The culture of memory has also played a significant role. For example, the massive operation to digitize the archives of the International Tracing Service (ITS) has made these documents available for consultation at archive centers in seven countries instead of only at Bad Arolsen. The opening of these archives has made the change in perspectives possible and has consequently encouraged the development of a host of new scholarly approaches. They are used by a number of authors in this volume, including Kenneth Waltzer, Nicolas Mariot, and Claire Zalc.

The stakes are significant for writing and transmitting the history of the Holocaust. But they are also important for the renewal of knowledge brought about by this shift in perspective. Such a shift in perspective is implemented by Daniel Uziel (chapter 8), who shows how the testimonies of Holocaust survivors make it possible to present German industry as seen by those who were reduced to slavery within it.

Restricting the focal point promotes a method based on data and frequently cross-indexed sources—processes long called for by the pioneers of *microstoria* but that are not without their complications. What should be done, for example, with testimonies that diverge from each other? How should the archival sources created by the persecuting authorities be used? The quality, volume, and novelty of sources, archives, and testimonials used by researchers raise such new questions. How can hitherto neglected archives (e.g., administrative forms, newspapers, lists) be used in such a way as to help address particular types of questions? Wolf Gruner's use of a series of documents consisting of previously unexplored archives of the Reich police, corroborated with the oft-used ones of the Ministry of Justice, is one example (chapter 11). It enables him to bring to light a totally underestimated phenomenon, that of individual resistance by Jews in the Reich, from 1933 to the high point of the war. These sources make it possible to understand the attitudes of individuals, which when taken collectively represent a new dimension in the history of the Third Reich's persecution of Jews. Similarly, postwar judicial archives, in this case in Poland, constitute a source whose full importance is revealed by Jan Grabowski (chapter 7). These trials directed at "traitors of the Polish nation" make it possible to reconstitute on the ground—and even on the individual level—the fate of Jews in the General Government, especially those who had escaped from the ghettos with the launch of "Operation Reinhard." Andrew Kornbluth (chapter 15) also examines postwar Polish trials to show, in three specific cases, the evolution of judicial responses to crimes against Jews in Poland. Consequently, it is the connection between the micro level of the trial and the national level of political interpretations of the Holocaust in Poland that is explored.

The change in scale also has its origins in another set of sources, which has undergone important changes in recent years: witness testimonies. Since the 1970s, an important movement collecting witness accounts of persecution has been conducted. These testimonies—initially unheard, then used in a judicial context, and finally collected in large numbers for memorial purposes—have profoundly extended knowledge of the genocidal act.[19] Yet for a number of years, things have changed with the prospect of seeing the survivors disappear. From that point forward, the gathering of testimonies intensified and was the subject of massive and systematic campaigns, such as that conducted by the USC Shoah Foundation Visual History Archive. A number of contributions in this volume dwell on the specificities of using testimonies within a microhistorical approach. Jeffrey Wallen (chapter 17) explores the interrelations between the knowledge stemming from testimonies and those collected by an archival approach, through study of the Christianstadt camp. Hannah Pollin-Galay (chapter 16) demonstrates the importance of the context—and moreover the language—in which these testimonies were gathered, through the example of Lithuanian Jews born between 1918 and 1935 who share similar life stories but who testified to the Holocaust in two different contexts: in English in North America, and in Yiddish in contemporary Lithuania. The microhistorical lens once again calls for a reflexive and, in the best sense, critical use of these numerous and massive sources that offer many new avenues for research.

All of these contributions consequently tend to provide nuanced and diverse answers to the following questions: is it possible, and if so under what conditions, to employ classical social history methodologies to study controversial questions and aspects of memory, and more specifically the Holocaust, which has been defined mostly by its exceptionality? This volume is an initial effort in trying to answer questions such as these, but without claiming to cover every possible angle, approach, or method, because the field is so rich.

Translated from the French by John Angell and Arby Gharibian.

Notes

1. Vasily Grossman's article was published in the USSR in the journal *Znamya* in November 1944 and soon translated and published in French: *L'Enfer de Treblinka* (Grenoble: B. Arthaud, 1945); the English translation appeared thirty-nine years later as *The Treblinka Hell: Photographic Album of Martyrs, Heroes, and Executioners* (Tel Aviv: G. Aharoni, 1984).
2. Léon Poliakov, *Harvest of Hate: The Nazi Program for the Destruction of the Jews of Europe* (Syracuse: Syracuse University Press, 1954; 1st edn in French 1951).
3. Gerald Reitlinger, *The Final Solution: The Attempt to Exterminate the Jews of Europe, 1939–1945* (London: Vallentine, Mitchell, 1953).
4. Raul Hilberg, *Destruction of the European Jews* (Chicago: Quadrangle Books, 1961); Saul Friedländer, *The Years of Extermination: Nazi Germany and the Jews* (New York: HarperCollins, 2008).
5. Dieter Pohl, *Von der "Judenpolitik" zum Judenmord: der Distrikt Lublin des Generalgouvernements, 1939–1944* (Frankfurt am Main, New York: Peter Lang, 1993); Christian Gerlach, *Kalkulierte Morde: die deutsche Wirtschafts- und Vernichtungspolitik in Weissrussland 1941 bis 1944* (Hamburg: Hamburger Edition, 1999); Andrej Angrick and Peter Klein, *The "Final Solution" in Riga: Exploitation and Annihilation, 1941–1944* (New York: Berghahn Books, 2009), originally published as Die "Endlösung" in Riga: Ausbeutung und Vernichtung 1941–1944 (Darmstadt, Wissenschaftliche Buchgesellschaft, 2006).

6. Regarding the contribution of the monographic approach to the analysis of Nazism, see the classic text by William S. Allen, *The Nazi Seizure of Power: The Experience of a Single German Town, 1930–1935* (Chicago: Quadrangle Books, 1965); Henry Huttenbach, *The Destruction of the Jewish Community of Worms, 1933–1945: A Study of the Holocaust Experience in Germany* (New York: Memorial Committee of Jewish Victims of Nazism from Worms, 1981); Klein and Angrick, *The "Final Solution" in Riga*; Pohl, *Von der "Judenpolitik" zum Judenmord*; Gerlach, *Kalkulierte Morde*; Panikos Panayi, "Victims, Perpetrators, and Bystanders in a German Town: The Jews of Osnabrück Before, During and After the Third Reich," *European History Quarterly* 33, no. 4 (2003): 451–92.
7. To cite just a few: Christopher R. Browning, *Ordinary Men: Reserve Police Battalion 101 and the Final Solution in Poland* (New York: HarperCollins, 1992); *Remembering Survival: Inside a Nazi Slave Labor Camp* (New York: WW Norton, 2010); Götz Aly, *Into the Tunnel: The Brief Life of Marion Samuel, 1931–1943* (New York: Metropolitan Books, 2007); Samuel Kassow, *Who Will Write Our History? Emanuel Ringelblum and the Oyneg Shabes Archive* (Bloomington: Indiana University Press, 2007); and Jan Grabowski, *Hunt for the Jews: Betrayal and Murder in German-Occupied Poland* (Bloomington: Indiana University Press, 2013).
8. We have borrowed the term "scale" from Jacques Revel. See Jacques Revel, ed., *Jeux d'échelles* (Paris: Editions de l'EHESS, 1996).
9. Francesca Trivellato, "Microstoria/Microhistoire/Microhistory," *French Politics, Culture, and Society* 33, no. 1 (Spring 2015): 122–134.
10. Among many references, we will cite the key texts for Italy by Giovanni Levi, "On Microhistory," in *New Perspectives on Historical Writing*, ed. Peter Burke (University Park: Pennsylvania State University Press, 1992), 93–113; and Carlo Ginzburg, "Microhistory: Two or Three Things That I Know about It," *Critical Inquiry* 20, no. 1 (1993): 10–35. For France, see "Histoire et sciences sociales. Un tournant critique?" *Annales ESC* 43, no. 2 (1988): 291–93; Jacques Revel, "L'histoire au ras du sol," in Giovanni Levi, *Le pouvoir au village: histoire d'un exorciste dans le Piémont du XVIIe siècle*, trans. Monique Aymard (Paris: Gallimard, 1989), i–xxxiii; and Revel, *Jeux d'échelles*. For the American reception, see Sebouh David Aslanian, Joyce E. Chaplin, Ann McGrath, and Kristin Mann, "How Size Matters: The Question of Scale in History," *American Historical Review* 118, no. 5 (2013): 1431–72, as well as the pioneering work by Natalie Zemon Davies, *The Return of Martin Guerre* (Cambridge, MA: Harvard University Press, 1982).
11. This conference, co-organized with Ivan Ermakoff and Nicolas Mariot, followed on the international study days from June 2011, whose proceedings were published by Seuil in the journal *Le Genre humain* in September 2012: Claire Zalc, Tal Bruttman, Ivan Ermakoff, and Mariot Nicolas, eds, *Pour une microhistoire de la Shoah* (Paris: Editions du Seuil, Series "Le genre humain," 2012).
After this publication, the approach seemed incomplete to us; we noted the need for more comparisons with other parts of Europe where the Shoah was implemented, through an extension of the analytical spectrum. We would like to offer our warm thanks to the members of the Scientific Committee for this conference: Annette Wieviorka, Maurice Olender, Jan Grabowski, Jan Gross, Dieter Pohl, and Omer Bartov, as well as our colleagues from the Organizing Committee, Ivan Ermakoff and Nicolas Mariot, with whom we developed the different stages of this undertaking.
12. Edoardo Grendi, "Micro-analisi e storia sociale," *Quaderni storici* 35, no. 2 (1977): 506–20.
13. Daniel Mendelsohn, *The Lost: A Search for Six of Six Million* (New York: HarperCollins, 2006). The French edition is cited here: *Les disparus* (Paris: Flammarion, 2007), 601.

14. Carlo Ginzburg and Carlo Poni, "The Name and the Game: Unequal Exchange and the Historical Marketplace," in *Microhistory and the Lost People of Europe*, ed. Edward Muir and Guido Ruggiero, trans. Eren Branch, 1–10 (Baltimore: Johns Hopkins University Press, 1991).
15. Browning, *Ordinary Men*.
16. Regarding these expressions, see Jacques Revel, "Micro-analyse et construction du social," in Revel, *Jeux d'échelles*, 15–36; and Pierre-André Chiappori and Maurizio Gribaudi, "La notion d'individu en microéconomie et en microhistoire," in *Le modèle et le récit*, ed. Jean-Yves Grenier, Claude Grignon, and Pierre-Michel Menger, 283–313 (Paris: Editions de la MSH, 2001).
17. Raul Hilberg, *Perpetrators Victims Bystanders: the Jewish Catastrophe, 1933-1945* (New York: Aaron Asher Books, 1992).
18. Marc Bloch, *The Historian's Craft* (New York: Vintage Books, 1964).
19. Annette Wieviorka, *Déportation et génocide. Entre la mémoire et l'oubli* (Paris: Plon, 1992); and *L'ère du témoin* (Paris: Plon, 1998).

Bibliography

Allen, William S. *The Nazi Seizure of Power: The Experience of a Single German Town, 1930–1935*. Chicago: Quadrangle Books, 1965.

Aly, Götz. *Into the Tunnel: The Brief Life of Marion Samuel, 1931–1943*. New York: Metropolitan Books, 2007.

Angrick, Andrej, and Peter Klein. *The "Final Solution" in Riga: Exploitation and Annihilation, 1941–1944*. New York: Berghahn Books, 2009. Originally published as *Die "Endlösung" in Riga: Ausbeutung und Vernichtung 1941–1944* (Darmstadt: Wissenschaftliche Buchgesellschaft, 2006).

Aslanian, Sebouh David, Joyce E. Chaplin, Ann McGrath, and Kristin Mann. "How Size Matters: The Question of Scale in History." *American Historical Review* 118, no. 5 (2013): 1431–72.

Bloch, Marc. *The Historian's Craft*. New York: Vintage Books, 1964.

Browning, Christopher R. *Remembering Survival: Inside a Nazi Slave Labor Camp*. New York: WW Norton, 2010.

———. *Ordinary Men: Reserve Police Battalion 101 and the Final Solution in Poland*. New York: HarperCollins, 1992.

Chiappori, Pierre-André, and Maurizio Gribaudi. "La notion d'individu en microéconomie et en microhistoire." In *Le modèle et le récit*, edited by Jean-Yves Grenier, Claude Grignon, and Pierre-Michel Menger, 283–313. Paris: Editions de la MSH, 2001.

Friedländer, Saul. *The Years of Extermination: Nazi Germany and the Jews*. New York: HarperCollins, 2008.

Gerlach, Christian. *Kalkulierte Morde: die deutsche Wirtschafts- und Vernichtungspolitik in Weissrussland 1941 bis 1944*. Hamburg: Hamburger Edition, 1999.

Ginzburg, Carlo. "Microhistory: Two or Three Things That I Know about It." *Critical Inquiry* 20, no. 1 (1993): 10–35.

Ginzburg, Carlo, and Carlo Poni. "The Name and the Game: Unequal Exchange and the Historical Marketplace." In *Microhistory and the Lost People of Europe*, edited by Edward Muir and Guido Ruggiero, 1–10. Baltimore: Johns Hopkins University Press, 1991.

Grabowski, Jan. *Hunt for the Jews: Betrayal and Murder in German-Occupied Poland*. Bloomington: Indiana University Press, 2013.

Grendi, Edoardo. "Micro-analisi e storia sociale." *Quaderni storici* 35, no. 2 (1977): 506–20.

Grossman, Vasily. *L'Enfer de Treblinka.* Grenoble: B. Arthaud, 1945.
——. *The Treblinka Hell: Photographic Album of Martyrs, Heroes, and Executioners.* Tel Aviv: G. Aharoni, 1984.
Hilberg, Raul. *Destruction of the European Jews.* Chicago: Quadrangle Books, 1961.
Huttenbach, Henry. *The Destruction of the Jewish Community of Worms, 1933–1945: A Study of the Holocaust Experience in Germany.* New York: Memorial Committee of Jewish Victims of Nazism from Worms, 1981.
Kassow, Samuel. *Who Will Write Our History? Emanuel Ringelblum and the Oyneg Shabes Archive.* Bloomington: Indiana University Press, 2007.
Levi, Giovanni. "On Microhistory." In *New Perspectives on Historical Writing,* edited by Peter Burke, 93–113. University Park: Pennsylvania State University Press, 1992.
Mendelsohn, Daniel. *The Lost: A Search for Six of Six Million.* New York: HarperCollins, 2006.
Panayi, Panikos. "Victims, Perpetrators, and Bystanders in a German Town: The Jews of Osnabrück Before, During and After the Third Reich." *European History Quarterly* 33, no. 4 (2003): 451–92.
Pohl, Dieter. *Von der "Judenpolitik" zum Judenmord: der Distrikt Lublin des Generalgouvernements, 1939–1944.* Frankfurt am Main, New York: Peter Lang, 1993.
Poliakov, Léon. *Harvest of Hate: The Nazi Program for the Destruction of the Jews of Europe.* Syracuse: Syracuse University Press, 1954. First published in French 1951.
Reitlinger, Gerald. *The Final Solution: The Attempt to Exterminate the Jews of Europe, 1939–1945.* London: Vallentine, Mitchell, 1953.
Revel, Jacques, ed. *Jeux d'échelles.* Paris: Editions de l'EHESS, 1996.
——. "L'histoire au ras du sol." In *Le pouvoir au village: histoire d'un exorciste dans le Piémont du XVIIe siècle,* by Giovanni Levi, i–xxxiii. Paris: Gallimard, 1989.
Trivellato, Francesca. "Microstoria/Microhistoire/Microhistory." *French Politics, Culture, and Society* 33, no. 1 (Spring 2015): 122–34.
Wieviorka, Annette. *Déportation et génocide. Entre la mémoire et l'oubli.* Paris: Plon, 1992.
——. *L'ère du témoin.* Paris: Plon, 1998.
Zalc, Claire, Tal Bruttman, Ivan Ermakoff, and Mariot Nicolas, eds. *Pour une microhistoire de la Shoah.* Paris: Editions du Seuil, Series "Le genre humain," 2012.
Zemon Davies, Natalie. *The Return of Martin Guerre.* Cambridge, MA: Harvard University Press, 1982.

Part I

Biographies, Groups, Transports, Ghettos
The Scales of Analysis

CHAPTER 1

AN INCONCEIVABLE EMIGRATION
RICHARD FRANK'S FLIGHT FROM GERMANY TO SWITZERLAND IN 1942*

Christoph Kreutzmüller

On 23 October 1941, just after mass deportations from Germany to the ghettos and killing sites in Eastern Europe had started, the Reich Security Main Office decreed in Heinrich Himmler's name that the emigration of Jews was no longer part of official policy and must be stopped. Three months later, the resolution was referred to at the Wannsee Conference:

> As a further possible solution, and with the appropriate prior authorization by the Führer, emigration has now been replaced by evacuation to the East. This operation should be regarded only as a provisional option, though in view of the coming final solution of the Jewish question it is already supplying practical experience of vital importance.[1]

Himmler's decision is usually taken as marking the ultimate end of Jewish emigration from Nazi Germany.[2] Yet more then a year later, on 16 December 1942, the 83-year-old German Jew Richard Frank, wearing a yellow star, was escorted by SS men from his Berlin home to the safety of the Swiss border.[3] At the same time, the murderous deportations from

---

*This essay is dedicated to the late Dietrich Jacob (1922-2015), Berlin, who handled Richard Frank's restitution case and kindly allerted me to it.

the German capital were slowly reaching their devastating peak, with large deportation trains of more than a thousand people going to the extermination sites in the East weekly, and smaller deportations to the ghetto of Theresienstadt twice a week. In fact, the very day Frank was taken to safety, the eighty-first deportation-transport was leaving the city,[4] with one hundred elderly Jews being deported to the Theresienstadt ghetto. Only eighteen of them survived. As the eighty-first transport consisted of two coaches coupled to the regular train to Prague departing from the Anhalter Bahnhof, Berlin's main station, and as the regular trains to Basel departed from that same station, Frank might have actually witnessed the deportation. He might have even known some of those being deported, some of whom were, after all, his age.

After the war, Frank did not comment on the timing of his flight but simply stated it happened in "high time,"[5] while his daughter drily acknowledged that the "circumstances" of her father's emigration had been "unusual."[6] Both remarks are understatements, at the very least. From a macrohistorical perspective, the emigration of a German Jew out of Germany in the midst of systematic mass murder seems incredible. It happened long after the official halt of emigration in the midst of the systematic murder today referred to as the Holocaust. That it was difficult to grasp for contemporaries is shown by the fact that even the Swiss accounting company that filed the compensation claim in Frank's name initially got the date wrong, claiming that their client had emigrated in 1939.[7] Yet was Frank's flight just a freak incident, a minor microhistorical event—or can it help shed light onto hitherto neglected aspects of the Holocaust? Answering this question calls for analyzing the case in greater detail and putting it into a broader framework.

Emigration from Nazi Germany, which turned to outright flight after the November pogrom in 1938, was closely linked both to the expropriation of Jews and, in turn, to the foreign currency crises the Reich was facing. In the aftermath of the international economic depression, bank crisis, and near collapse of the reichsmark, Germany froze its massive foreign debts in summer 1931. While the reichsmark thus stopped being a convertible currency, Germany had neither any international credit nor much foreign currency reserves left. In this situation, the income generated by faltering exports was channeled to pay for food and raw materials. After the Nazis rose to power, foreign currency reserves were increasingly allocated to pay mainly for the raw materials needed for rearmament. This caused much dissatisfaction among the population, giving rise to the rhetorical question of whether the people wanted butter or canons. Under these circumstances, the Nazi regime was also unwilling to allot more then a mere fraction of foreign currency reserves for personal use. Anybody who wanted to move abroad needed special permission to transfer money, one that was not easily granted to Jews, despite the fact that their emigration was the regime's official aim at the time. Furthermore, a so-called Reich Flight Tax was introduced, amounting to 25 percent of all assets of nearly anyone who wanted to leave Germany for good. This decree was initially not directed against Jews but was used for this purpose from 1933 on. Soon, exemption limits were halved, and all Jewish-owned businesses involved in exporting were put under general suspicion of smuggling currency out of Germany.[8]

As it became more and more difficult to transfer money for emigration, the assets that could be transferred were seriously reduced.[9] While in 1935 emigrants had faced losses of eighty pennies to every reichsmark they wanted to take with them, in 1937 the Jewish World Congress estimated that losses amounted up to 95 percent.[10] At the same time, there was a steep drop in the prices that businesses could fetch. As a senior manager of the Dutch-British food and soap multinational Unilever/Lever Brothers told a Jewish banker in Berlin, it was incomprehensible that "Jewish industrialists should be handing over their companies at such knockdown prices."[11] For this reason, many Jewish business owners opted to remain in Germany. Although their future in the German Reich was uncertain, it was apparent that emigration meant forfeiting their assets and starting new lives from scratch.[12]

To make matters worse, in a hitherto overlooked development, the Reichsbank became even more reluctant to allot foreign currency reserves to emigration as German exports faltered in 1938 and the Nazi regime took an even more aggressive course. The Evian Conference showed how earnestly dispossession stood in the way of emigration. Anti-Semitism aside, Jews were not a particularly attractive refugee group because they had been let out of Germany (including occupied Austria) stripped of most of their assets.[13] Moreover, the German bureaucracy itself stood in the way of emigration. In October 1938, even the head of the Foreign Currency Unit (Devisenstelle) of the Central Tax Office complained that overlapping bureaucratic procedures, along with the anti-Semitic zeal of some officials, "had stalled Jewish emigration."[14] Shortly afterward, the situation deteriorated even further when the plunder of the November pogrom led to the final phase of the destruction of Jewish commercial activities and a forced levy on Jews, the so-called *Judenvermögensabgabe*. It was against this background that Reinhard Heydrich was asked by Hermann Göring to build up the system of forced emigration embodied in the Zentralstelle für Jüdische Auswanderung, the Central Office for Jewish Emigration, which in turn served as a springboard for Adolf Eichmann's career.[15]

Of course, Jews reacted to the predicament as well, and it is not surprising that a black market emerged around currency issues and passports in Berlin, and the smuggling of bank notes, coins, and stamps became a sport—albeit a dangerous one—among potential emigrants. By 1938, Jews were regarded as prime suspects for tax evasion and so-called currency crimes.[16] To find loopholes in the system and legally overcome the rising bureaucratic and financial hurdles, ever more intricate transfer schemes were developed by Jewish private banks such as MM Warburg & Co and AE Wassermann, which jointly set up various trust companies, such as the Allgemeine Treuhand-Stelle für jüdische Auswanderung GmbH (Altreu) to manage this difficult business.[17] With the notable exception of the Haavara Transfer,[18] the creators of the transfer schemes sought to locate undiscovered foreign assets connected in some way to Germany and then tried to put Jews in Germany in a position to claim they were the owners of these assets. This in turn would serve as a lever for leaving and earning a living once they were out of Germany. All the transfer schemes were difficult to operate and often took years to prepare and organize. Many failed; some did not. The so-called Turk Transfer Scheme was prepared by MM Warburg & Co as early as 1936. To cut a long story very short, in this scheme one hundred Jewish families from Germany bought, with permission from German authorities, shares of Gas Works in Adana and Ankara via a Dutch holding set up for this purpose in Amsterdam. Having written off 93.5 percent of their "investment," the subscribers became foreign bondholders in the process. This in turn meant they had funds available abroad and could emigrate in the summer of 1940, some even as late as September 1941.[19]

Richard Frank's flight was also part of a transfer scheme, referred to in the files as the "Guatemala Transfer." The Central American country had been regarded as an unlikely location for emigration by the Aid Association of the Jews in Germany; an internal memo from 1938 said that "emigration would only be possible [if at all] for near relatives of people with a permanent residence in Guatemala."[20] Accordingly, only very few Jews from Germany would eventually arrive in this country.[21] Yet in the summer of 1938, the German-born businessman Alfons Herring put his shoe and leather factory in San Cristobal on sale, stating that due to his political convictions as an "upright German," it had become impossible for him to economically thrive in Guatemala. It is an interesting fact that Herring, who had applied for membership to the Nazi Party before returning to Germany, offered his factory to MM Warburg & Co and AE Wassermann, obviously thinking he would get more money from Jewish rather than other investors. Yet even though the Reich Ministry for

Economy had agreed to use the factory for a transfer scheme for Jews in March 1939, it turned out to be hard to sell.[22] Though the shoe factory was of considerable size and employed approximately 140 workers, Herring's terms were anything but lucrative. Turnover and output were mediocre, and living conditions hostile. Furthermore, the Warburg bank feared an investor might face "similar measures in Guatemala [as] Jews faced in Germany"![23] Even Heinrich Klausner, the former Jewish owner of the biggest Berlin shoe-trading company, Leiser, declined the offer in July 1939 while in exile in Amsterdam.[24] As none of their customers were interested, the MM Warburg & Co and AE Wasserman banks asked the other German banks whether their remaining Jewish customers might be interested in the deal but received negative answers. "The remaining Jewish assets" of their customers, one bank wrote, were simply too small for such a big deal,[25] and the procedure came to a standstill. Just before the war, Herring moved from Guatemala to the south German resort Oberstdorf, leaving his factory behind.[26]

By October 1941, the situation had taken a dramatic turn. MM Warburg and AE Wassermann, both taken over by non-Jews in 1938, changed their company names to Brinkmann, Wirtz & Co and Heinz, Tecklenburg & Co, respectively. Against the backdrop of threatening deportation, saving assets had also become much less important as compared to saving people and finding paths to get them out of the rapidly growing danger zone. At the same time, some of those who had previously declined to leave their homes changed their minds. One of them was Richard Frank, a retired merchant born in 1858 in Oschersleben near Magdeburg. Like many other Jews of their generation, Richard Frank and his wife Gertrud, née Munk, had opted to stay in Germany, as they could not envisage leaving their *Heimat*. Only their daughter Elise had emigrated to the United Kingdom. After the pogrom in 1938, the Franks living conditions had deteriorated, and in 1939 they had to pay a 200,000-reichsmark Jew levy, and to sell their stately house in Berlin's fashionable Wannsee district along with their Buick limousine.[27] They were then forced to move from their eleven-room apartment to a much smaller flat on the fourth floor of a *Judenhaus* that they had to share with five other Jewish tenants.[28] Yet Frank only decided to leave after the deportations had started and his seventy-year-old wife, Gertrud, had ended her life after being threatened with arrest for not wearing the recently introduced yellow star on two occasions.[29] Ending your life before the Nazis came to get you was, of course, a last and desperate act of self-assertion.[30] Richard Frank, too, did not let persecution get the better of him and complained about the "brutal malicious and arrogant behaviour" of a German policeman as late as November 1942![31]

It is unknown how Frank heard about the Guatemala Transfer or why he was asked to be part of it. It is not unlikely that Frank was included because he was one of the few Jews in Germany who still had a substantial fortune. In any case, he took over someone's portion and joined a consortium of thirteen people to raise the 650,000 reichsmark Herring had asked for in the summer of 1942. The Reich Ministry also confronted the subscribers with heavy banking fees, and an extra "contribution" of 2.015 million reichsmark for the economy.[32] Richard Frank thus had to pay 220,000 reichsmark for his 5 percent share.[33] On 31 August 1942, Frank received a letter from Heinz, Tecklenburg & Co stating that they had received payment and that he would soon receive detailed information about emigration, including a questionnaire from the Reich Security Main Office he would have to fill out in three copies. The bank also asserted that Frank and all of the other Guatemala associates faced a total expropriation of their remaining assets.[34] The background for this was that in accordance with the eleventh amendment to the Reich Citizenship Law published in November 1941, the treasury would receive all of the assets of every deported person anyway. Not taking everything from a Jew probably seemed an unwelcome change in routine for the German civil servants in charge of the affair. By November 1942, all of Frank's bank assets—amounting to 800,000 reichsmark—were blocked and later transferred to the German treasury.[35] Moreover, his life insurance was confiscated together with all his personal belongings, including a seventeenth-century Dutch painting.[36]

However, with deportation trains constantly departing to the East, being part of a transfer scheme was no longer to guarantee emigration. Yet it seemingly still served as a kind of foot in the door, for the Reichsbank and Reich Ministry for Economics continued the emigration routine but asked for extra foreign funds. Ten years later, Frank told his lawyer what happened next:

> One day a gentleman in an officer's uniform came to me and asked for detailed information about acquaintances of mine. He was particularly interested in people living abroad with whom I had kept personal or business relations. As I did not regard this to be an infringement of personal trust I gave him the names of various respectable people in Zurich. The emissary then went to Zurich himself, visited all these people, and asked for 50,000 Swiss francs to contribute to the permission of my emigration. He did not succeed, however, as most people laughed at him.[37]

At last, in November 1942, an old Swiss friend agreed to pay 6,000 Swiss francs—cloaked as an interest-free loan to Frank.[38] A telegram in the files indicates that the old friend did so on behalf of Frank's son-in-law, who could not officially play a part in the bargaining for his father-in-law's life because was living in the United Kingdom.[39] By the time the money came in via the Zurich banking house Michelis & Co—a Swiss affiliation of Heinz, Tecklenburg & Co—to the Deutsche Golddiskontbank handling the foreign currency affairs for the Reichsbank, the Swiss emigration visa had expired and needed renewal. This new hurdle was eventually overcome, despite the Swiss parliament's decision in August 1942 to limit immigration to an absolute minimum.[40] The old business friend, who paid for Frank's life and emigration out of Germany, probably also guaranteed he would pay for Frank's expenses in Switzerland. By mid-November the luggage Frank wanted to take with him was checked and sealed. As he prepared for his journey to safety, the old man discovered that there "was a[n] unpublished *Verfügung* (ruling) that Jews are not allowed to register more than 30 to 50 kilograms of luggage."[41] Since the necessary papers had not come through, Frank had to contact "his" police department every day, and the uncertainty must have been hard to bear. Richard Frank nevertheless eventually reached Switzerland on 16 December 1942, with one suitcase in hand. Before arriving at the border, the Gestapo confiscated all receipts from the Guatemala Transfer Frank had taken with him and admonished him again to keep absolutely quiet about the circumstances of his emigration.[42]

Three months after Frank reached safety, Martha Liebermann ended her life in Berlin, fearing imminent deportation. The 86-year-old widow of the famous painter had decided to try and emigrate at the end of 1940, but unlike Frank she was neither in a transfer scheme, nor could she gather the foreign funds to be allowed to leave Germany.[43] Yet given that she could have fled if she had had the foreign funds, her example also indicates that Himmler's order of October 1941 was not the complete end of emigration. Even in 1943, some Jews who were protected by the German military intelligence service could leave Germany.[44] Additionally, the general-commissioner for finance and economy in occupied Netherlands, Hans Fischböck, followed the example he had set in Vienna in 1938 by allowing Jews to flee up until 1945 as part of a "ransom racket," on the condition that they could gather enough foreign funds.[45]

"On October 23, the emigration gates officially closed," Christopher Browning states.[46] That certainly holds true; however, some very expensive back doors remained open. The case study of Richard Frank allows us to look through this back door into the multidimensional aspect of the Holocaust. Of course there was extreme violence from the very beginning, but it often went hand in hand with bureaucracy. Racist hatred, blind rage, greed, plunder, manslaughter, and murder were accompanied by cold reasoning, as well as the question of how to make good use of the Jews, their workforce, and their property. Jewish assets were first used to help finance rearmament and later to silence neighbors and corrupt them into becoming fellow perpetrators. In 1944, the SS even tried to swap lives for lorries.[47] This utilitarian approach to murder is somehow mirrored in the word "liquidation"—deriving from the field of economics, meaning literally "to liquefy one's assets"—it was used by the Nazis, among others, to also describe their murder.

Microhistory, as it were, allows for a closer look, describing and eventually grasping the logic of complex bureaucratic and economic circumstances. This in turn enables us both to question familiar knowledge of standard historical teaching, which is so important yet often so blind to exceptions to the accepted macrohistorical narratives. These exceptions are the salt in the soup we call history, adding texture and perspective, and also highlight the shortcomings and blind spots that the big picture of macrohistory naturally must gloss over. Finally, the story of Richard Frank reminds us not to forget the catastrophes hidden in the statistics. After losing his wife and being forced from his home, he died a poor man on 16 March 1953, supported only by his daughter. It took the Berlin compensation office until 1968 to finally settle Frank's claim, filed in March 1947.[48]

Christoph Kreutzmüller studied history and English in Berlin and in the United Kingdom. After finishing his dissertation on German banks in the Netherlands, he coordinated an extensive research project at the Humboldt University (Berlin) on the fate of Jewish-owned businesses in Berlin from 1930 to 1945. Before joining the Jewish Museum in Berlin as a curator for the new permanent exhibition, he worked as a senior historian for the House of the Wannsee Conference. His publications include *Final Sale in Berlin: The Destruction of Jewish Commercial Activity 1930–1945* (2015); *Berlin 1933–1945* (edited with Michael Wildt, 2013); and *Dispossession: The Plundering of German Jewry 1933–1953* (edited with Jonathan Zatlin, Michigan 2017).

Notes

1. Protokoll, in *Akten zur Deutschen Auswärtigen Politik 1918–1945*, Serie E: 1941–1945, Bd. I, Dok. 150 (Göttingen, 1969), 267–75; http://www.ghwk.de/fileadmin/user_upload/pdf-wannsee/dokumente/protokoll-januar1942_barrierefrei.pdf.
2. See Saul Friedländer, *The Years of Extermination. Nazi Germany and the Jews, 1939–1945* (New York, 2007), 284f; Mark Roseman, *The Villa, the Lake, the Meeting: Wannsee and the Final Solution* (London, 2002), 50; Peter Longerich, *Der ungeschriebene Befehl. Hitler und der Weg zur 'Endlösung'* (Munich, Zurich, 2001), 121.

3. Wolf Gruner, *Judenverfolgung in Berlin. Eine Chronologie der Behördenmaßnahmen in der Reichshauptstadt* (Berlin, 2009), 179.
4. Alfred Gottwald and Diana Schulle, *Die "Judendeportationen" aus dem Deutschen Reich 1941–1945. Eine kommentierte Chronologie* (Wiesbaden, 2005), 346.
5. Curriculum Vitae Richard Frank, 24.4.1952, Compensation Office Berlin (EAB) 56661 (Richard Frank).
6. Sworn statement of Elise Bendhem, née Frank, 25.3.1963, EAB 56661.
7. Letter Fides Treuhand Vereinigung to Vermögensverwaltungsstelle Berlin, 18.3.1947, EAB 56661.
8. Christiane Kuller, *Finanzverwaltung und Judenverfolgung. Die Entziehung jüdischen Vermögens in Bayern während der NS-Zeit* (Munich, 2008), 18–23; Martin Friedenberger, *Fiskalische Ausplünderung. Die Berliner Steuer und Finanzverwaltung und die jüdische Bevölkerung 1933–1945* (Berlin, 2008), 67–78; Dorothee Mußgnug, *Die Reichsfluchtsteuer 1931–1953* (Berlin, 1992), 15–20.
9. Adam Tooze, *The Wages of Destruction: The Making and Breaking of the Nazi Economy* (London, 2007), 69–75.
10. Jüdische Weltkongress, ed., *Der Wirtschaftliche Vernichtungskampf gegen die Juden im Dritten Reich* (Paris, Genf, New York, 1937), 82.
11. Letter from Erich Spiegelberg to Fritz Warburg, 17 June 1935, Foundation Warburg Archive, Hamburg (SWA), C-14001.
12. Christoph Kreutzmüller, *Final Sale in Berlin: The Destruction of Jewish Commercial Activities 1930–1945* (New York, Oxford, 2015), 330–38; Frank Bajohr, *"Arisierung" in Hamburg. Die Verdrängung der jüdischen Unternehmer 1933–1945* (Hamburg, 1997), 266–67.
13. See Fritz Kieffer, *Judenverfolgung in Deutschland. Eine innere Angelegenheit? Internationale Reaktionen auf die Flüchtlingsproblematik 1933–1939* (Stuttgart, 2002).
14. Note by the head of the foreign currency unit of the central tax office, 4 October 1938, State Archive Berlin (LAB), A Rep. 092, 281.
15. Eichmann's pride in his "achievement" probably left a mark on the protocol of the Wannsee Conference as well, when he put Austria (Ostmark) separately on the list of Jews to be murdered—even though the country had long become part of "Greater Germany."
16. Kreutzmüller, *Final Sale,* 129–149.
17. See Database of Jewish Businesses in Berlin: www2.hu-berlin.de/djgb.
18. Adam Hofri, "The Legal Structure of the Haavara Transfer-Agreement," in *National Economies, Volks-Wirtschaft, Racism and Economy in Europe between the wars (1918–1939/45),* ed. Christoph Kreutzmüller, Michael Wildt, and Moshe Zimmermann (Newcastle, 2015), 97–107; Avraham Barkai, "German Interests in the Haavara Transfer Agreement," in *Leo Baeck Institute Yearbook* 35, no. 1 (1990): 245–61; Avraham Barkai, *From Boycott to Annihilation: The Economic Struggle of German Jews 1933–1943* (Hanover, 1989), 187–99; Werner Feilchenfeld, "Die Durchführung des Haavara-Transfers," in *Haavara-Transfer nach Palästina und Einwanderung deutscher Juden 1933–1939,* ed. Werner Feilchenfeld, Dolf Michaelis, and Ludwig Pinner (Tübingen, 1972), 37–85.
19. Dorothea Hauser, "Zwischen Gehen und Bleiben. Das Sekretariat Warburg und sein Netzwerk des Vertrauens 1938–1941," in *"Wer bleibt, opfert seine Jahre, vielleicht sein Leben". Deutsche Juden 1938–1941,* ed. Susanne Heim, Beate Meyer, and Francis R. Nicosia (Göttingen, 2010), 115–33.
20. Memo by the Hilfsverein der Juden in Deutschland, 21 October 1938, SWA, Auswanderer, Länderberichte.
21. Susanne Bennewitz, "Vorwort," in *Ein Zimmer in den Tropen. Briefe aus dem Exil in Guatemala 1937–1940,* ed. Susanne Bennewitz (Berlin, 2013), 7–19, here 11.

22. Note by the currency unit (Devisenstelle), 14 March 1939, SWA, Transfer-Projekte, 2. Mappe.
23. Letter Warburg & Co, Amsterdam, to Anton Bermann, 3 July 1939, SWA, Transfer-Projekte, 2. Mappe.
24. Letter Warburg & Co, Amsterdam, to MM Warburg, Hamburg 14 July 1939, SWA, Transfer-Projekte, 2. Mappe.
25. Letter Berliner Handelsgesellschaft to MM Warburg & Co, 4 July 1939, SWA, Transfer-Projekte, 2. Mappe.
26. Note Behrmann, 16 October 1941, SWA, Transfer-Projekte, 2. Mappe.
27. Curriculum Vitae Richard Frank, 24.4.1952, EAB 56661; Letter of Trustee, 13.1.1951, LAB, B Rep. 025–04, 48/51.
28. Sworn statement of Elise Bendhem, née Frank, 25.3.1963, EAB 56661. Susanne Willems, *Der entsiedelte Jude. Albert Speers Wohnungsmarktpolitik für den Berliner Stadtneubau* (Berlin, 2000); Kunstamt Wilmersdorf, ed., *Berlin Wilmersdorf. Die Juden. Leben und Leiden* (Berlin, 1987), 90.
29. Curriculum Vitae Richard Frank, 24.4.1952, EAB 56661. Vgl. Federal Archive, Memorial Book. Victims of the Persecution of Jews under the National Socialist Tyranny in Germany 1933–1945, Gertrud Frank, née Munk, born 8 January 1871. Gertrud Frank was buried in the Jewish Cemetery in Berlin Weissensee: Anna Fischer, *Erzwungener Freitod. Spuren und Zeugnisse in den Freitod getriebener Juden der Jahre 1938–1945 in Berlin* (Berlin, 2007), 122.
30. See Wolf Gruner, "Die Verfolgung der Juden und die Reaktionen der Berliner," in *Berlin 1933–1945*, ed. Michael Wildt and Christoph Kreutzmüller (Munich, 2013), 311–24.
31. Brief Richard Frank to his lawyer Steiniger, 19.11.1942, File Elise Bendhem nach Richard Frank, Private Collection Dietrich Jacob, Berlin (PCDJ).
32. Account Statement Hardy & Co, not dated (1943), EAB 56661.
33. Note Dietrich Jacob, 9.2.1959, EAB 56661.
34. Letter Heinz, Tecklenburg & Co to Richard Frank 31.8.1942, LAB, B Rep. 025-04, 49/51.
35. Note Dietrich Jacob, 9.2.1959, EAB 56661; Letter Heinz, Tecklenburg & Co to Frank, 26.1.1943, LAB, B Rep. 025–04, 50–51.
36. Sworn statement of Elise Bendhem, née Frank, 25.3.1963, EAB 56661. The Central tax authority's (Oberfinanzpräsident) files on this case are lost. See Index card Richard Frank, Brandenburgisches Landeshauptarchiv, Rep. 36A (Oberfinanzpräsident Berlin Brandenburg (II)).
37. Letter Richard Frank to Abraham Horowitz, 8 November 1951, File Elise Bendhem nach Richard Frank, PCDJ.
38. Letter Abraham Horowitz to Wiedergutmachungsamt, 5 December 1951; Heinz, Tecklenburg & Co to Wiedergutmachungsamt, 15 February 1952, LAB, B Rep. 025–04, 49/51. See Christiane Schoenmaker, "The 'Legal' Theft of Jewish Assets: The German Gold Discount Bank (*Dego*), 1933–1945," in *Dispossession: The Plundering of German Jewry 1933–1953*, ed. Christoph Kreutzmüller and Jonathan Zatlin (Michigan, 2016).
39. Telegram by Charlotte Bendham to Richard Ullmann, 12.11.1942, in Elise Bendhem vs. Deutsches Reich, PCDJ.
40. Regula Ludi, "Dwindling Options: Seeking Asylum in Switzerland 1933–1939," in *Refugees from Nazi Germany and the Liberal European States*, ed. Frank Caestecker and Bob Moore (New York, Oxford, 2010), 82–102.
41. Brief Richard Frank to his lawyer Steiniger, 19.11.1942, File Elise Bendhem nach Richard Frank, PCDJ.

42. Letter Abraham Horowitz to Wiedergutmachungsamt, 13 November 1952, LAB, B Rep. 025–04, 50/51.
43. Regina Scheer, *"Wir sind die Liebermanns"*. *Die Geschichte einer Familie* (Berlin, 2006), 364–83. See Christoph Kreutzmüller and Monika Sommerer, eds., *Finding Aids: Traces of Nazi Victims in Berlin Archives* (Berlin, 2014), 32–39.
44. Winfried Meyer, *Unternehmen Sieben. Eine Rettungsaktion für vom Holocaust Bedrohte aus dem Amt Ausland/Abwehr im Oberkommando der Wehrmacht* (Frankfurt am Main, 1993).
45. Thomas Sandkühler and Bettina Zeugin, *Die Schweiz und die deutschen Lösegelderpressungen in den besetzten Niederlanden, Vermögensentziehung, Freikauf, Austausch 1940–1945* (Bern, 1999).
46. Christopher Browning, *The Origins of the Final Solution: The Evolution of the Nazi Jewish Policy, September 1939–March 1942* (London, 2004), 369.
47. Ibid., 270f.
48. Notification Entschädigungsamt, 12 November 1968, EAB 56661. Frank's daughter received 100.000 DM for her father's losses in the Guatemala Transfer: Ibid.

Bibliography

Bajohr, Frank. *"Arisierung" in Hamburg. Die Verdrängung der jüdischen Unternehmer 1933–1945*, Hamburg: Christians Verlag, 1997.
Barkai, Avraham. "German Interests in the Haavara Transfer Agreement", *Leo Baeck Institute Yearbook* 35, no. 1 (1990), 245–61.
———. *From Boycott to Annihilation: The Economic Struggle of German Jews 1933–1943*, Hanover: Brandeis, 1989.
Bennewitz, Susanne. "Vorwort", in *Ein Zimmer in den Tropen. Briefe aus dem Exil in Guatemala 1937–1940*, edited by Susanne Bennewitz, Berlin: Hentrich und Hentrich Verlag, 2013, 7–19.
Browning, Christopher. *The Origins of the Final Solution: The Evolution of the Nazi Jewish Policy, September 1939–March 1942*, Lincoln: University of Nebraska Press, 2004.
Feilchenfeld, Werner. "Die Durchführung des Haavara-Transfers", in *Haavara-Transfer nach Palästina und Einwanderung deutscher Juden 1933–1939*, edited by Werner Feilchenfeld, Dolf Michaelis, and Ludwig Pinner, Tübingen: Mohr Siebeck, 1972, 37–85.
Fischer, Anna. *Erzwungener Freitod. Spuren und Zeugnisse in den Freitod getriebener Juden der Jahre 1938–1945 in Berlin*, Berlin: Textpunkt, 2007.
Friedenberger, Martin. *Fiskalische Ausplünderung. Die Berliner Steuer und Finanzverwaltung und die jüdische Bevölkerung 1933–1945*, Berlin: Metropol Verlag, 2008.
Friedländer, Saul. *The Years of Extermination: Nazi Germany and the Jews, 1939–1945*, New York: Harper Perennial, 2007.
Gottwald, Alfred, and Diana Schulle. *Die "Judendeportationen" aus dem Deutschen Reich 1941–1945. Eine kommentierte Chronologie*, Wiesbaden: Marixverlag, 2005.
Gruner, Wolf. "Die Verfolgung der Juden und die Reaktionen der Berliner", in *Berlin 1933–1945*, edited by Michael Wildt and Christoph Kreutzmüller, Munich: Random House, 2013, 311–24.
———. *Judenverfolgung in Berlin. Eine Chronologie der Behördenmaßnahmen in der Reichshauptstadt*, Berlin: Edition Hentrich Druck, 2009.
Hauser, Dorothea. "Zwischen Gehen und Bleiben. Das Sekretariat Warburg und sein Netzwerk des Vertrauens 1938–1941", in *"Wer bleibt, opfert seine Jahre, vielleicht*

sein Leben". Deutsche Juden 1938–1941, edited by Susanne Heim, Beate Meyer, and Francis R. Nicosia, Göttingen: Wallstein Verlag, 2010, 115–33.

Hofri, Adam. "The Legal Structure of the Haavara Transfer-Agreement", in *National Economies, Volks-Wirtschaft, Racism and Economy in Europe between the Wars (1918–1939/45),* edited by Christoph Kreutzmüller, Michael Wildt, and Moshe Zimmermann, Newcastle: Cambridge Scholars Publishing, 2015, 97–107.

Jüdische, Weltkongress, ed. *Der Wirtschaftliche Vernichtungskampf gegen die Juden im Dritten Reich,* Paris, Genf, New York: Imprimerie et Editions Union, 1937.

Kieffer, Fritz. *Judenverfolgung in Deutschland. Eine innere Angelegenheit? Internationale Reaktionen auf die Flüchtlingsproblematik 1933–1939,* Stuttgart: Franz Steiner Verlag, 2002.

Kreutzmüller, Christoph. *Final Sale in Berlin: The Destruction of Jewish Commercial Activities 1930–1945,* New York, Oxford: Berghahn Books, 2015.

Kreutzmüller, Christoph, and Monika Sommerer, eds. *Finding Aids: Traces of Nazi Victims in Berlin Archives,* Berlin: Haus der Wannseekonferenz, 2014.

Kuller, Christiane. *Finanzverwaltung und Judenverfolgung. Die Entziehung jüdischen Vermögens in Bayern während der NS-Zeit,* Munich: C.H. Beck Verlag, 2008.

Longerich, Peter, *Der ungeschriebene Befehl. Hitler und der Weg zur 'Endlösung',* Munich, Zurich: Piper Verlag, 2001.

Ludi, Regula. "Dwindling Options. Seeking Asylum in Switzerland 1933–1939", in *Refugees from Nazi Germany and the Liberal European States,* edited by Frank Caestecker and Bob Moore, New York, Oxford: Berghahn Books, 2010, 82–102.

Meyer, Winfried. *Unternehmen Sieben. Eine Rettungsaktion für vom Holocaust Bedrohte aus dem Amt Ausland/Abwehr im Oberkommando der Wehrmacht,* Frankfurt am Main: Philo Fine Arts, 1993.

Mußgnug, Dorothee. *Die Reichsfluchtsteuer 1931–1953,* Berlin: Duncker & Humblot, 1992.

Roseman, Mark. *The Villa, the Lake, the Meeting: Wannsee and the Final Solution,* London: Penguin UK, 2002.

Sandkühler, Thomas, and Bettina, Zeugin. *Die Schweiz und die deutschen Lösegelderpressungen in den besetzten Niederlanden, Vermögensentziehung, Freikauf, Austausch 1940–1945,* Bern: Chronos Verlag, 1999.

Scheer, Regina. *'Wir sind die Liebermanns'. Die Geschichte einer Familie,* Berlin, 2006.

Schoenmaker, Christiane. "The 'Legal' Theft of Jewish Assets: The German Gold Discount Bank (*Dego*), 1933–1945", in *Dispossession: The Plundering of German Jewry 1933–1953,* edited by Christoph Kreutzmüller and Jonathan Zatlin, Michigan, 2017.

Tooze, Adam. *The Wages of Destruction: The Making and Breaking of the Nazi Economy,* London: Allen Lane, 2007.

Willems, Susanne. *Der entsiedelte Jude. Albert Speers Wohnungsmarktpolitik für den Berliner Stadtneubau,* Berlin: Edition Hentrich, 2000.

Wilmersdorf, Kunstamt ed. *Berlin Wilmersdorf. Die Juden. Leben und Leiden,* Berlin: Kunstamt Wilmersdorf, 1987.

CHAPTER 2

Pursuing Escape from Vienna
The Katz Family's Correspondence

Melissa Jane Taylor

The story of the Katz family is of three separate attempts to flee Vienna after the *Anschluss,* which is conveyed to readers through an extensive letter collection. Like thousands of other families, the Katzes vigorously pursued every avenue to escape violent anti-Semitism before and during the Holocaust.[1] What is unusual about the Katz family is that its extraordinary correspondence—over nine hundred pages of letters over a three-year period—has survived. These letters provide scholars with an intense look at one family and its desperate attempts to flee Hitler's Germany. In the letters we see the daily lives and struggles of four individuals: Grete Katz; her adult children, Lena Isaacson and Philip Katz; and her son-in-law, Rudolf Isaacson.[2] These letters tell three immigration stories that convey a range of emotion from joy to heartbreak and that provide the gritty details of how lives were reshaped in a changing world. The family members were always anxious to hear from each other, since silence raised so many unanswerable questions. Grete Katz wrote to her children in March 1940, "I have not gotten news from you [for ten weeks], and I am quite desperate. I hope from one day to the next that I will finally get mail.... I am fine, but only wish to be together with you and have a home with my children. I already have a nice traveling valise, even bigger than the one Lena had.... I am curious when it will be my turn."[3] Such a letter was fairly typical of Grete's correspondence. Collections of this type convey considerable information to researchers: from family dynamics to changes in daily life, political developments, and worldview, along with the efforts to emigrate and the struggles associated with resettling. In this essay, I will briefly share with you the contours of the Katz family's emigration stories, in addition to exploring some of the challenges of doing research in a large letter collection. The Katz family's letters contain a variety of invaluable information for researchers, including the changing situation for Jews in Vienna following the *Anschluss*, changes in emigration policies and procedures, the challenges of resettlement, and changing familial and gender dynamics. They also exhibit raw emotion, when words have to substitute for actions because of the distance separating the letter writers.

Most importantly, the Katz family letters allow us to explore two under-studied areas: the role of adult children in a family's emigration from Europe, and the implications of families emigrating separately instead of as a unit. Holocaust historiography and the historiography of Jewish emigration from Europe just prior to the Holocaust have explored the role of children, but only in the context of their youth; yet a child is always someone's child, even as they age. These historiographies have therefore not given adequate attention to how the Holocaust, and the need or desire to emigrate, caused an often premature change in roles for adult children. The Katz family letters illustrate these changing roles and show explicitly how an approximately thirty-year-old Lena began taking the dominant role in providing for her mother's emigration and ensuring her well-being. Furthermore, many families decided, for legitimate reasons, to emigrate separately, with the hope of reuniting in another part of the world. Many adult children left Europe first with the intention of paving a way for their parents and bringing them over later. As immigration policies became more restrictive in the late 1930s and early 1940s, parents were often unable to follow their children, and families were caught divided, in many instances eternally.[4] What seemed a reasonable strategy often proved unsuccessful; these letters show in vivid detail how this plan failed, not for lack of trying, but due to bureaucratic challenges beyond the family's control.

The Katz family was from Vienna, which was Grete's birthplace as well as where she lived with her husband; it is also from where her children eventually emigrated. The family planned for Philip and Lena to emigrate first and initially planned for their parents, and later just their mother, to come separately. While the initial hope was that Philip and Lena would immigrate together to the United States or Australia, in reality each emigrated separately, and neither did so directly to the United States, which was their final destination. And while both hoped that their mother would eventually join them in the United States, that never transpired.

Philip Katz was the first in his family to flee Vienna. This letter collection does not provide us with the specifics, but when the correspondence began in October 1938, Philip was already in Paris, but with no intention of remaining there permanently. While the letter collection provides plenty of information about the immigration plans of Grete and Lena, it provides only the basic contours of Philip's plans and later journey. In late May 1938, Philip had filled out the immigration questionnaire with the Jewish community (Israelitische Kultusgemeinde, or IKG) in Vienna. Therein he stated that his preferences for immigration were to the United States or Australia and that the family preferred that he and his sister emigrate first and their parents follow later, once he and Lena were established.[5] On 8 November, the letters reveal that Philip was pursuing a Bolivian visa, but it was never mentioned again.[6] By January 1939, it appeared that he would ultimately like to go to Britain, where he would remain until he could proceed to the United States or Australia. Philip's sister, Lena, began her immigration journey to Canada in February 1939. Lena desperately wanted to take Philip, but the "fixer" who was arranging her entry into Canada would not allow her to wait for him and delay her own departure.[7] By mid-February it appeared that the prospects for Philip's immigration to Australia had fallen through. In the March correspondence, it seems that Philip had also applied for immigration to Montevideo, Uruguay.[8] By October, Philip had made it to the United States, stopping first in New York, and then proceeding on to Greenwood, South Carolina.[9] Philip's journey is difficult to trace, in part because the collection contains only letters to Philip from his mother and sister, and no letters from Philip himself.[10] Nevertheless, from the evidence available, we can see that Philip's immigration story is not atypical: Philip was the first of his immediate family members to leave, which fit the norms given his age and gender.[11] He also pursued a host of immigration options, exploring immigration possibilities on four different continents. Philip's story is hence that of many young, German-speaking Jewish men seeking to escape.

The story of Philip's sister, Lena, is equally typical. She remained in Vienna after Philip's departure, during which time her father passed away. She pursued immigration and cared for her mother, but after her father's death she initially hesitated to leave her mother. In November 1938, she pleaded with Philip to write to her before he made an immigration decision, as she did not want the entire family to be scattered around the world.[12] By December, Lena planned to go to South America but later wrote that she would prefer Australia.[13] By the end of December, she had obtained visas for Costa Rica but was still pursuing visas for Canada as well.[14] In January 1939, while still declaring that Costa Rica was the ultimate "goal," Lena wrote to Philip that she and Rudolf would attempt to disembark in Vancouver.[15] In February 1939, she married Rudolf Isaacson, and ten days later the two of them departed for Canada. Lena's immigration to Canada is a bit veiled in the correspondence; Canada's immigration during this period was quite restrictive, and it is unclear whether she and Rudolf ultimately entered legally.[16] By working through a fixer, a friend of Rudolf's, they hoped to have someone loan them the landing fee—20,000 Canadian dollars—and provide a guarantor. It is clear from the correspondence that they were uncertain that this would work, but they were willing to take the risk.[17] The day before their departure, they received a telegram from their fixer telling them not to proceed.[18] Lena and Rudolf disregarded the advice and eventually made it to Vancouver. In April, they wrote to Philip expressing unending gratitude for everything that their fixer had done to facilitate their trip and arrival.[19] Grete wrote to Philip explaining the contents of a telegram she had received from Lena, which indicated that someone had provided the substantial landing fee necessary for the Isaacsons to enter Canada, and a guarantor had vouched for them.[20] Lena's immigration story, like Philip's, is typical. Like Philip, she was willing to search the world for refuge and to pursue multiple options, including illegal entry. She was also willing to take substantial risks, such as going to Canada after being told not to and doing so without a visa or any guarantee that she could enter. In her estimation, what did she have to lose? Her decision illustrates how desperate the situation in Vienna must have been if she determined it was worth the risk to proceed after having been told not to. Lena's story is also a gendered story: Lena was initially unwilling to leave her mother, for since men were often the first to flee, adult female children often became the sole individuals responsible for caring for aging parents.[21] This was clearly Lena's need and not Grete's, who still believed that her children should emigrate and become established, and then she would follow.[22] Additionally, Lena made all of the preparations for emigration (legal, logistical, and practical preparations), which was also typical of women during this period.[23] The young women who stayed behind after the men had fled were often pulled in a variety of directions, by competing concerns influenced most often by family and safety. For many young women, like Lena, this was the beginning of a change in family dynamics and potential generational shifts, as these women began to provide increased care and support for their families.

Grete's immigration story shares many similarities with those of her children but is also distinctly different, for she never emigrated. Grete's husband passed away in October 1938 after suffering a stroke. Neither Grete nor her husband had pursued visas or made immigration plans prior to his death, although that is somewhat surprising given that his death was described as sudden and that Philip had registered the family for emigration with the IKG in May 1938.[24] Thus, in November 1938, Grete began to make plans for emigration. Her daughter assisted her with the process, registering her as a "cook" for immigration to Australia, where she could seek employment as a domestic worker. Grete also filed her visa application at the American consulate general. While Grete must have been making some of her own plans, it appears from the letters that initially Lena, and later Philip, were the most proactive in seeking immigration for their mother, even after they left Austria. The children planned for Grete to join one of them once they were settled.

Grete had the possibility to go to England in March 1939, but she hesitated to do so alone. She wrote to Philip, "There is no point in my going alone to England. I had better wait for something definite. Although I would very much like a change of climate. But I must be patient. If you had been in London, I would have gone."[25] Later that month, she wrote again, "People say I should not have missed such a chance such as London. But I didn't want to go alone to a strange country, especially since I don't know the language."[26] It is quite clear that Grete could not fathom being in an unknown country by herself. Given that immigration is especially hard and has different implications for older adults, such as learning a new language and culture, forgoing a pension, and leaving a community, her age (early fifties) has to be regarded as a factor in her decision-making process.[27] What is especially tragic is that it was quite clear from her letters that all Grete wanted was to be reunited with her children. Had she realized that this was her single opportunity for reunification, her decision in all likelihood would have been different.

Perhaps what is most profound in this correspondence is the efforts of Lena and Grete to care for their family despite the thousands of miles separating them, with care conveyed in each of the letters written. Over time, we see Grete's care increasingly expressed in words—often questions regarding her children's welfare. Lena remained focused on emigration plans and reunification of the family, and her care was increasingly expressed through action, through preparations for her mother's immigration. Both of these efforts were clearly exhibited throughout the length of the correspondence. The letters provide insight into the changing family dynamic, but also the struggles and logistics of emigration. Questions posed in the letters about well-being and preparations for emigration illustrate care and concern at a time when what tied these individuals together across the miles were hope and their letters to each other. Caring words in each letter had to suffice for many of the caring actions often prevented by distance.

By late 1939, Grete understood more clearly that she needed to leave, even if she had to make the journey by herself. She wrote to Philip, "My staying here is limited, and I ask you to do everything possible to get me an affidavit as soon as possible."[28] In January 1940, Philip's employer, Mr. Rosenberg, provided Grete with the much-needed affidavit of support.[29] By February 1941, it appears that emigration might have soon been a reality. Grete decided to proceed to one of the few possibilities still available, Shanghai, a potential transit country where she could await her American visa.[30] Not long after having made that decision, Grete was informed that she needed to book a ticket to the United States. This request would have been made only shortly before an American visa would be issued, because the ticket would only be valid for a limited amount of time.[31] In April, Grete received her departure date—January 1942—from the shipping company.[32] Grete eventually managed to have it rescheduled to September 1941 by booking through a different company. Unfortunately, Grete could not have known that after the American consulate general closed in July 1941, it would be much more difficult for her to receive a visa.

After the closing of the consulate general in Vienna, Hatton Sumners, a congressman from Texas, made an inquiry regarding Grete's case with the Department of State. In response, the Department of State said that Grete's case could not be acted upon as long as she was still residing in Greater Germany. She would have to proceed to a country that had an American consulate.[33] In December 1941, the Isaacsons prepaid for a Cuban visa, which they hoped would serve as a transit country for Grete. Three weeks later they received a refund on that deposit, per their request.[34] It is unclear what transpired in those three weeks to change the situation. Despite the heroic efforts made by her family, Grete was never able to emigrate from Vienna. She was deported to Minsk on 2 May 1942.[35]

Grete's story, unfortunately, is also typical. In many instances, families would split, sending their younger members abroad to settle, assuming that the older parents could follow later. Such a plan assumed that the policies of all countries involved in the process would remain static; however, neither American immigration policy nor German policy regarding the Jews was fixed, instead becoming more and more complex as time progressed. American policy grew increasingly restrictionist over time, due in part to fifth column concerns and the eventual closing of consulates in Greater Germany in July 1941. German policy also made it increasingly difficult for Jews to flee Europe, and emigration from Greater Germany become illegal in October 1941. As a result, many of the parents who were left behind never had the opportunity to follow.

Additionally, Grete's story illustrates the shift that transpired in familial roles. Her children took on the primary role, increasingly worrying about the future and making more and more decisions. It is difficult to pinpoint exactly when this took place, but at its earliest, it was probably at the time of the *Anschluss* (March 1938), when the Katz family's lives were thrown into upheaval by Austria's annexation to Germany, and at the latest probably upon the death of Lena's father in October 1938. In the story of the Katz family, as seen through this letter collection, Lena largely played the dominant role, primarily because her mother was unable to do so, and her brother and fiancé were absent. As Grete begins to navigate the emigration process, readers increasingly see Lena adopting the "adult" or "parental" role that traditionally would have been held by Grete.[36]

As such, the tone of Lena's letters to Grete changed, just as the situation changed and the chances for departure diminished. In March 1940, she wrote to her mother, "I already told you in the last letter that you can not simply sit and wait, but you should do something yourself. Most importantly you should be informed about when you can travel."[37] Lena would often urge her mother to be more proactive, and then in a sentence or two, she would encourage her mother on how to proceed. Then she described all that she, Rudolf, and Philip had done and gently asked what information her mother had gathered from the consulate or the IKG in Vienna. The tone of one specific letter from Lena to her mother in mid-1941 illustrates the change in their relationship:

> I infer from your last letter that you are afraid. I do not know why. Eighty-year-old people travel alone to the United States. It comes from the small European circumstances: here [in the United States] a trip of five to six hours is nothing, whereas I remember when we were going to Ischl [in the Salzkammergut region of Austria] you preferred to be at the train station at least three hours prior to the departure of the train. The whole thing is now far more complicated than if you had received the [American] visa in Vienna. We have the intention of bringing you to us, and you also want to come, so put your nervousness aside. You can speak with each consul just as you would speak to any other person; no one will bite you. While I hope that in the meantime you have undertaken something, I want to again write down everything exactly for you. In contemporary times one must use five senses and one's elbows, and again, don't have any fear, but consider everything exactly and objectively. We can only do so much for you. We cannot do everything; you also have to help.[38]

The tone in this letter is stronger and more urgent than in any of the others. While many of the themes are the same as those of earlier letters, the length of this passage shows that Lena had reached a point of desperation, and the tone indicates that she was clearly trying to motivate her mother. The reader must also consider the role played by hope and the changing circumstances here. Up until then, Lena had largely been hopeful that Grete would be able to emigrate, but did Grete remain hopeful as the situation changed in Vienna? It is often difficult to tell. Did the change in visa policies make Lena lose hope that her mother would emigrate, thus contributing to the tone of this letter? Quite possibly, as her letter also demonstrates how completely she had taken over the role of adult protector. In the strongest possible terms, she implored her mother to actively engage in the process and not give up. In a July letter, Lena guiltily admonished herself for not having taken Grete to Canada with her and Rudolf.[39] As Grete's situation changed and her chances of obtaining a visa significantly diminished, Lena's frustration was apparent in the tone and demands of her letters.

The letters are essentially a family dialogue, providing an intimate microcosm of what was happening to so many Jewish families in Greater Germany.[40] Letter collections such as these give scholars a better understanding of daily life in Europe and abroad, the challenges of emigration and immigration, as well as insight into changing family dynamics and roles forced by war, transition, chaos, and persecution. Immigration stories are certainly most prominent here, but readers also learn, especially in Grete's letters, how Jews in Vienna responded to changing conditions. Grete accepted renters, probably because of both financial necessity and the extreme Aryanization in the wake of Germany's annexation of Austria.[41] When Jews had their property confiscated by the Nazi regime, they would have sought a new and temporary residence while awaiting their immigration prospects. Grete was savvy enough to augment the income from her pension by renting her extra space. She described selling personal effects from her house in preparation for her departure and alluded to the fact that this was common.[42] In addition, Grete discussed the classes she was taking, both to learn English and to make the leather flowers she hoped to sell. These classes were offered by the IKG, and participation in them was quite common for those awaiting visas or immigration possibilities. Tragically, Grete also briefly mentioned the first deportations to Poland, although it remains unclear if she was fully cognizant of what was transpiring.[43]

From Philip and Lena we learn about efforts to maintain or establish normalcy in their new locations. And Grete worried about this too. Philip swam competitively, clearly a hobby he brought from Vienna.[44]

Lena discussed establishing her new business knitting wares in Canada.[45] Grete worried about day-to-day practicalities, such as who was darning Philip's socks,[46] a question she asked more than once. Grete wanted nothing more than to join her children, and it is for that reason I believe she would have gone to London without them if she had known it was her only chance of escape. The example I shared at the beginning of this essay was typical of most of Grete's letters, essentially inquiring when she could come, thanking her children for their hard work toward her immigration, and expressing both her love for them and her loneliness. The letters were Grete's only connection to her absent children. It is clear that as more and more of her friends emigrated from Vienna, she was desperately awaiting letters from her children. She coped with the challenges and was not deterred by her English lessons. In a moment of either self-realization or utter desperation, she articulated that she knew no one would understand her with her accent but remained determined to learn the language, one she would never use on a daily basis.[47] Lena's determination and commitment to immigration are further illustrated in her inclusion of English vocabulary in one of her letters.[48] In efforts toward normalcy or to occupy her time, Grete made a tablecloth with multicolored flowers for the kitchen in South Carolina[49] and worried about her children maintaining an Austrian culture in their new environments, especially pertaining to food. Each year she would promise to celebrate their following birthday, after her arrival, by making *Gugelhupf,* an Austrian cake.[50]

Yet, the letters are an incomplete dialogue. First, Philip's letters to his mother and sister are absent. Second, it is clear that some letters never made it to their destination.[51] Third, there are obvious omissions in some letters, probably to avoid redaction by the censors. For instance, Lena wrote Philip a lengthy letter from the Panama Canal, which she never could have sent from Vienna,[52] in which she gave a detailed description of what happened to them and their friends during *Kristallnacht* and of Rudolf's initial incarceration in Vienna and later deportation to Dachau. Of Rudolf's incarceration Lena wrote:

> I cannot describe what Rudolf took part in [as a result of his incarceration]. In Vienna he was in the worst prison on the Keniengasse [?] and during his six days of imprisonment received nothing to eat. He could not sleep because at night the SS came and thrashed people.... Then he was taken to Dachau in a cattle car and had to do drills everyday in his pajamas for fourteen hours in eighteen-degree weather.[53]

Rudolf's absence had certainly been alluded to in other letters, but this letter provides the context and much of the previously missing information. Lena implored Philip to burn the letter after reading it, in order to protect their family still living in Greater Germany. Fourth, as readers of these letters, we are following a family dialogue with incomplete information, for we do not know either the friends referred to or certainly the family dynamics involved. How did Lena, Philip, Rudolf, and Grete get along under normal circumstances when they were not trying to flee their homeland? We simply do not know.

This collection differs from two other traditional Holocaust sources, namely oral histories and diaries. In contrast to oral histories, letter collections provide a different and more immediate perspective, as letters are documents of the moment, whereas many oral histories are produced years after the fact.[54] Additionally, letter collections are meant to convey information, perhaps private or at least personal information, to a few select individuals, while oral history, lest we forget, is often conducted as a legacy piece to tell one's story. Letter collections are usually not written to be saved or shared and as a result provide a different perspective than oral histories, with different objectives from the outset. Unlike diaries, which are also written in the moment, letters are interactive, asking questions and awaiting responses from the recipient, whereas a diary is a private communication often to oneself. In the case of the Katz letters, the writers had a vested interest in the correspondence and eagerly awaited a response.

In this essay, I have sought to describe some of the day-to-day challenges and struggles of this family, but also the intricacies of their lives, journeys, and transitions. These letters describe in detail the ever more restrictive immigration procedures that destroyed the family's initial plan of emigrating separately and then reuniting and ultimately prevented Grete from emigrating at all. This collection also shows the rapidity with which the generational caretaking roles reversed, with Lena providing increasing care for her mother. The story of the Katzes is one of perseverance in the face of the Nazi regime, a changing society, and difficult relocations. It requires scholars to ask tough questions, use the collection wisely, and explore what it means to closely examine the lives of a few in order to better understand the situation. This story is less about reams of statistics or the weighty enormity of sweeping issues and instead gives names and stories to the horrible events of the Holocaust: Lena, Rudolf, Philip, and Grete. It has shown us three distinct emigration stories, with all of their anxieties, apprehensions, and uncertainties. It has illustrated changes in Vienna and new beginnings in North America. As a result, this letter collection has provided us with a complex and exceedingly personal story of a single family. Moreover, it has given us insight into the shifts in gender, generational, and familial dynamics, along with the details of the daily struggles, successes, failures, and changes that took place for the Katzes as they sought to escape and establish new lives outside of Austria. In this instance, the story of the Holocaust and the efforts to flee Europe transcend numbers and abstractions to become personal and real.

Melissa Jane Taylor is a historian in the Office of the Historian at the U.S. Department of State. She received her Ph.D. from the University of South Carolina. Taylor is interested in many facets of the Jewish refugee experience in the 1930s and 1940s. Her scholarship explores the interaction between Jewish visa applicants in Europe and American diplomats and has been published in *Holocaust and Genocide Studies, Diplomatic History,* and *Journal of Social History.*

Notes

The views expressed in this chapter are the views of the author and do not necessarily reflect the views of the Office of the Historian, the U.S. Department of State, or the U.S. government.

1. For the historiography of Jewish emigration from German-speaking Europe to the United States, see Richard Breitman and Alan M. Kraut, *American Refugee Policy and European Jewry, 1939–1945* (Bloomington: Indiana University Press, 1987); Henry L. Feingold, *The Politics of Rescue* (New Brunswick, NJ: Rutgers University Press, 1970); Arthur Morse, *While Six Million Died* (New York: Random House, 1967); Melissa Jane Taylor, "Bureaucratic Response to Human Tragedy," *Holocaust and Genocide Studies* 21, no. 2 (Fall 2007): 243–67; Melissa Jane Taylor, "Diplomats in Turmoil: Creating a Middle Ground in Post-Anschluss Austria," *Diplomatic History* 32, no. 5 (November 2008): 811–39; David S. Wyman, *Paper Walls: America and the Refugee Crisis 1938–1941* (Amherst: University of Massachusetts Press, 1968); and Bat-Ami Zucker, *In Search of Refuge: Jews and US Consuls in Nazi Germany 1933–1941* (London: Vallentine Mitchell, 2001).
2. Lena Katz Isaacson is the pseudonym of the person who donated the collection. Per her request, all the members of the family have been given pseudonyms. Lena Isaacson Papers, AR7173 (hereafter AR7173), Leo Baeck Institute, New York, New York (hereafter LBI). Courtesy of the Leo Baeck Institute. The collection has been digitized and is available online at this address: http://findingaids.cjh.org/?pID=482035 (accessed 11 October 2015). Lena Katz Isaacson donated the entirety of this collection to the Leo Baeck Institute in 1980. All translations, unless otherwise stated, are my own.
3. Grete Katz to her children, 31 March 1940, folder 1, AR7173, LBI. Courtesy of the Leo Baeck Institute. Translated by Kurt Heinrich.
4. For additional information on the challenges of emigrating as an elderly individual, see Melissa Jane Taylor, "Family Matters: The Emigration of Elderly Jews from Vienna to the United States, 1938–1941," *Journal of Social History* 45, no. 1 (2011): 238–60.
5. Philip Katz, Grete's son, registered himself, his sister, and his parents with the IKG in May 1938. Philip Katz's Emigration Questionnaire, #21747a, reel 993, RG-17.017M, United States Holocaust Memorial Museum, Washington, DC (hereafter USHMM).

6. Lena Isaacson to Philip Katz, 8 November 1938, folder 3, AR7173, LBI. Courtesy of the Leo Baeck Institute. It is unclear from the language used whether Philip simply applied or had already received a visa, but it is best to assume that Lena is referring to his application here.
7. Lena Isaacson to Philip Katz, 1 February 1939, folder 3, AR7173, LBI. Courtesy of the Leo Baeck Institute. A "fixer" was someone whom the émigré hired to help them navigate the immigration process. Each fixer provided different services, and these could include, but were not limited to, deciding preferable routes, completing paperwork, providing guarantors, and even securing loans to pay the landing fees, if required.
8. Grete Katz to Philip Katz, 30 March 1939, folder 1, AR7173, LBI. Courtesy of the Leo Baeck Institute. Translated by Kurt Heinrich.
9. Grete Katz to Lena and Rudolf Isaacson, 27 October 1939, folder 1, AR7173, LBI. Courtesy of the Leo Baeck Institute. Translated by Kurt Heinrich.
10. It is clear from the correspondence that Philip wrote to his mother. Perhaps he did not make carbon copies of his letters before sending them off. Since his mother's letters were often addressed to both him and his sister, they must have been passed from one to the other once the letters made it to North America. It is fair to assume that since two lines of the correspondence were maintained, that had a third line been available, it too would have been retained.
11. Trude Maurer, "From Everyday Life to a State of Emergency: Jews in Weimar and Nazi Germany," in *Jewish Daily Life in Germany, 1618–1945,* ed. Marion A. Kaplan (New York: Oxford University Press, 2005), 355–60.
12. Lena Isaacson to Philip Katz, 5 November 1938, and Lena Isaacson to Philip Katz, 16 November 1938, both in folder 3, AR7173, LBI. Courtesy of the Leo Baeck Institute.
13. Lena Isaacson to Philip Katz, 1 December 1938, and Lena Isaacson to Philip Katz, 16 December 1938, both in folder 3, AR7173, LBI. Courtesy of the Leo Baeck Institute.
14. Lena Isaacson to Philip Katz, 27 December 1938, folder 3, AR7173, LBI. Courtesy of the Leo Baeck Institute.
15. It is unclear at this point which route they were taking, although this seems to imply that they would have taken an eastern route through Siberia and then proceeded down the west coast of North America. However, the Isaacsons ultimately went through the Panama Canal, prompting readers to ask how one could have a "goal" of Costa Rica and ultimately disembark in Vancouver, unless Costa Rica were a landing stop on the return route.
16. For more on immigration restriction to Canada, see Irving Abella and Harold Troper, *None Is Too Many: Canada and the Jews of Europe, 1933–1948* (Toronto: Lester & Orpen Dennys, 1982). Canada accepted eighty-two Austrian Jews between 1938 and 1945. Herbert Rosenkranz, "The Anschluss and the Tragedy of Austrian Jewry, 1938–1945," in *The Jews of Austria: Essays on their Life, History and Destruction,* ed. Josef Fraenkel (London: Vallentine Mitchell, 1967), 514.
17. Lena Isaacson to Philip Katz, 7 January 1939, folder 3, AR7173, LBI. Courtesy of the Leo Baeck Institute.
18. Lena Isaacson to Philip Katz, 11 March 1939, folder 3, AR7173, LBI. Courtesy of the Leo Baeck Institute.
19. Lena Isaacson to Philip Katz, 15 April 1939, folder 3, AR7173, LBI. Courtesy of the Leo Baeck Institute.
20. Grete Katz to Philip Katz, 11 April 1939, folder 1, AR7173, LBI. Courtesy of the Leo Baeck Institute. Translated by Kurt Heinrich.
21. Marion Kaplan, *Between Dignity and Despair* (New York, Oxford University Press, 1998), 140; and Maurer, "From Everyday Life to a State of Emergency," 357–58.
22. Grete Katz to Philip Katz, 28 January 1939, folder 1, AR7173, LBI. Courtesy of the Leo Baeck Institute.

23. Kaplan, *Between Dignity and Despair,* 57–73; and Sibylle Quack, "Everyday Life and Emigration: The Role of Women," in *An Interrupted Past: German-Speaking Refugee Historians in the United States After 1933,* ed. Hartmut Lehmann and James J. Sheehan (New York: Cambridge University Press, 1991), 102.
24. Lena Isaacson to Herr Neuron, 11 November 1938, folder 3, AR7173, LBI. Courtesy of the Leo Baeck Institute.
25. Grete Katz to Philip Katz, 3 March [1939], folder 1, AR7173, LBI. Courtesy of the Leo Baeck Institute. Translated by Kurt Heinrich.
26. Grete Katz to Philip Katz, 16 March 1939, folder 1, AR7173, LBI. Courtesy of the Leo Baeck Institute. Translated by Kurt Heinrich.
27. While many of these changes are the same for all émigrés, the ability for someone to adjust and the implications of the adjustment are different for individuals as they age. See Taylor, "Family Matters."
28. Grete Katz to Philip Katz, 30 October 1939, folder 1, AR7173, LBI. Courtesy of the Leo Baeck Institute. Translated by Kurt Heinrich.
29. An affidavit of support was needed for an American visa application if an émigré could not provide sums substantial enough to be deemed self-sufficient. The likely to become a public charge clause (LPC clause) of the Immigration Act of 1924 was often used by restrictionist American officials to deny immigration visas. An affidavit of support assured the government that the émigré would not become a public charge. However, the strength of the affidavit had to be determined by the American consular official. Grete Katz to Philip Katz, 15 January 1940, folder 1, AR7173, LBI. Courtesy of the Leo Baeck Institute. Translated by Kurt Heinrich.
30. Grete Katz to Philip Katz, 15 February 1941, folder 1, AR7173, LBI. Courtesy of the Leo Baeck Institute. Translated by Kurt Heinrich.
31. Grete Katz to Philip Katz, 24 February 1941, folder 1, AR7173, LBI. Courtesy of the Leo Baeck Institute. Translated by Kurt Heinrich.
32. Grete Katz to Philip Katz, 20 April 1941, folder 1, AR7173, LBI. Courtesy of the Leo Baeck Institute. Translated by Kurt Heinrich.
33. Department of State to Hatton Sumners, 17 July 1941; and Department of State to Hatton Sumners, 7 October 1941, both in folder 4, AR7173, LBI. Courtesy of the Leo Baeck Institute.
34. Refugee and Immigration Division of Agudath Israel Youth Council, Brooklyn, to Rudolf Isaacson, 1 December 1941; and Refugee and Immigration Division of Agudath Israel Youth Council, Brooklyn, to Rudolf Isaacson, 22 December 1941, both in folder 4, AR7173, LBI. Courtesy of the Leo Baeck Institute.
35. National Refugee Service to Lena Isaacson, 31 July 1946, folder 4, AR7173, LBI. Courtesy of the Leo Baeck Institute.
36. For the change in gender and familial roles, see Kaplan, *Between Dignity and Despair,* 57–73; Claudia Koonz, "Courage and Choice Among German-Jewish Women and Men," in *Die Juden im Nationalsozialistischen Deutschland: The Jews in Nazi Germany, 1933–1943,* ed. Arnold Paucker (Tübingen: JCB Mohr, 1986), 283–93; Maurer, "From Everyday Life to a State of Emergency," 283–90, 346–73; and Quack, "Everyday Life and Emigration,"102–8.
37. Lena Isaacson to Grete Katz, 18 March [1940], folder 2, AR7173, LBI. Courtesy of the Leo Baeck Institute.
38. Lena Isaacson to Grete Katz, 13 June 1941, folder 2, AR7173, LBI. Courtesy of the Leo Baeck Institute. By this time Lena and Rudolf had settled in New York City.
39. Lena Isaacson to Grete Katz, 17 July 1941, folder 2, AR7173, LBI. Courtesy of the Leo Baeck Institute.
40. These letters are a family dialogue, in the sense that they are replacing all forms of family communication and interaction. As readers we are not privy to understanding

the full dialogue, for we lack the knowledge of how the family interacted with each other during non-crisis situations, what role the individual personalities played, and how the individuals functioned or failed to function as a unit. Additionally, letter writers might withhold or embellish details so that the recipient might believe the sender's situation to be better than it was. See David Gerber, "Acts of Deceiving and Withholding in Immigrant Letters: Personal Identity and Self-Preservation in Personal Correspondence," *Journal of Social History* 39, no. 2 (Winter 2005): 315–30.

41. Grete Katz to Philip Katz, 18 January [1939]; Grete Katz to Philip Katz, 28 January 1939; Grete Katz to Philip Katz, 18 February 1939; all in folder 1, AR7173, LBI. Courtesy of the Leo Baeck Institute. Translated by Kurt Heinrich. These are not the only mentions of sub-renters, but just a few of the first. Information on the sub-renters is interspersed throughout 1939 and 1940. See Martin Dean, *Robbing the Jews: The Confiscation of Jewish Property in the Holocaust, 1933–1945* (New York: Cambridge University Press, 2008), 84–131.

42. Grete Katz to Philip Katz, 24 February 1939; Grete Katz to Philip Katz, 10 March [1939]; both in folder 1, AR7173, LBI. Courtesy of the Leo Baeck Institute. Translated by Kurt Heinrich.

43. Grete Katz to Lena Isaacson, 27 October 1939, folder 1, AR7173, LBI. Courtesy of the Leo Baeck Institute. Translated by Kurt Heinrich. For more on the Jewish expulsions from Vienna, see Florian Fruend and Hans Safrian, *Expulsion and Extermination: The Fate of the Austrian Jews, 1938–1945* (Vienna: Dokumentationsarchiv des österreichischen Widerstandes, 1997), 13. While Grete may very well have known what "going to Poland" meant, she certainly would not have elaborated on it in a letter for fear of censorship, at the very least. It is quite clear from the letter that she does not want to go to Poland.

44. Grete Katz to Philip Katz, 16 March 1939; Grete Katz to Philip Katz, 18 June 1939; both in folder 1, AR7173, LBI. Courtesy of the Leo Baeck Institute. Translated by Kurt Heinrich.

45. Grete Katz to Philip Katz, 27 April 1939; Grete Katz to her children, 6 July 1939; Grete Katz to Philip Katz, 12 July 1939; all in folder 1, AR7173, LBI. Courtesy of the Leo Baeck Institute. Translated by Kurt Heinrich.

46. Grete Katz to Philip Katz, 4 April 1939; Grete Katz to her children 22 July 1940; both in folder 1, AR7173, LBI. Courtesy of the Leo Baeck Institute. Translated by Kurt Heinrich.

47. Grete Katz to Philip Katz, 5 April 1940; Grete Katz to her children, 12 April 1940; both in folder 1, AR7173, LBI. Courtesy of the Leo Baeck Institute. Translated by Kurt Heinrich.

48. Lena Isaacson to Grete Katz, 18 March [1940?], folder 2, AR7173, LBI. Courtesy of the Leo Baeck Institute.

49. Grete Katz to her children, 23 April 1940, folder 1, AR7173, LBI. Courtesy of the Leo Baeck Institute. Translated by Kurt Heinrich.

50. Grete Katz to her children, 5 April 1941; Grete Katz to Philip Katz, 20 April 1941; both in folder 1, AR7173, LBI. Courtesy of the Leo Baeck Institute. Translated by Kurt Heinrich.

51. Grete Katz to her children, 31 March 1940 and 28 January 1941, both in folder 1, AR7173, LBI. Courtesy of the Leo Baeck Institute. Translated by Kurt Heinrich. In the March 1940 letter, Grete wrote that they needed to number subsequent letters in order to determine how many letters were lost. She had not heard from her children in over two months.

52. Lena Isaacson to Philip Katz, 11 March 1939, folder 3, AR7173, LBI. Courtesy of the Leo Baeck Institute.

53. Ibid.

54. Here oral histories specifically refer to those of Holocaust survivors and refugees. David Boder's 1946 oral histories of Holocaust survivors are clearly the exception. Given that oral histories of Holocaust survivors or refugees became most prevalent decades after the events (primarily beginning in the 1980s and 1990s and continuing to today), the role of memory becomes increasingly important. Naturally, memory is less of a factor in letter collections addressing contemporary events.

Bibliography

Abella, Irving, and Harold Troper. *None Is Too Many: Canada and the Jews of Europe, 1933–1948*. Toronto: Lester & Orpen Dennys, 1982.
Breitman, Richard, and Alan M. Kraut. *American Refugee Policy and European Jewry, 1939–1945*. Bloomington: Indiana University Press, 1987.
Dean, Martin. *Robbing the Jews: The Confiscation of Jewish Property in the Holocaust, 1933–1945*. New York: Cambridge University Press, 2008.
Feingold, Henry L. *The Politics of Rescue*. New Brunswick, NJ: Rutgers University Press, 1970.
Fruend, Florian, and Hans Safrian. *Expulsion and Extermination: The Fate of the Austrian Jews, 1938–1945*. Vienna: Dokumentationsarchiv des österreichischen Widerstandes, 1997.
Gerber, David. "Acts of Deceiving and Withholding in Immigrant Letters: Personal Identity and Self-Preservation in Personal Correspondence." *Journal of Social History* 39, no. 2 (Winter 2005): 315–30.
Kaplan, Marion. *Between Dignity and Despair*. New York: Oxford University Press, 1998.
Koonz, Claudia. "Courage and Choice among German-Jewish Women and Men." In *Die Juden im Nationalsozialistischen Deutschland: The Jews in Nazi Germany, 1933–1943*, edited by Arnold Paucker, 283–93. Tübingen: JCB Mohr, 1986.
Maurer, Trude. "From Everyday Life to a State of Emergency: Jews in Weimar and Nazi Germany." In *Jewish Daily Life in Germany, 1618–1945*, edited by Marion A. Kaplan, 271–373. New York: Oxford University Press, 2005.
Morse, Arthur. *While Six Million Died*. New York: Random House, 1967.
Quack, Sibylle. "Everyday Life and Emigration: The Role of Women." In *An Interrupted Past: German-Speaking Refugee Historians in the United States after 1933*, edited by Hartmut Lehmann and James J. Sheehan, 102–108. New York: Cambridge University Press, 1991.
Rosenkranz, Herbert. "The Anschluss and the Tragedy of Austrian Jewry, 1938–1945." In *The Jews of Austria: Essays on Their Life, History and Destruction*, edited by Josef Fraenkel, 479–545. London: Vallentine Mitchell, 1967.
Taylor, Melissa Jane. "Family Matters: The Emigration of Elderly Jews from Vienna to the United States, 1938–1941." *Journal of Social History* 45, no. 1 (2011), 238–60.
———. "Diplomats in Turmoil: Creating a Middle Ground in Post-Anschluss Austria." *Diplomatic History* 32, no. 5 (November 2008): 811–39.
———. "Bureaucratic Response to Human Tragedy." *Holocaust and Genocide Studies* 21, no. 2 (Fall 2007): 243–67.
Wyman, David S. *Paper Walls: America and the Refugee Crisis 1938–1941*. Amherst: University of Massachusetts Press, 1968.
Zucker, Bat-Ami. *In Search of Refuge: Jews and US Consuls in Nazi Germany 1933–1941*. London: Vallentine Mitchell, 2001.

Chapter 3

Moving Together, Moving Alone
The Story of Boys on a Transport from Auschwitz to Buchenwald

Kenneth Waltzer

On 18 January 1945, a large group of predominantly Jewish prisoners was evacuated from Auschwitz-Buna (Monowitz) and Birkenau and put on a death march to the west. Ten thousand prisoners were marched out in the frigid cold and snow for two days and nights toward Gleiwitz, a railhead and the site of several Nazi satellite camps. Prisoners unable to continue were summarily shot by SS guards along the roads. The Nazis then loaded 3,935 surviving prisoners onto open coal cars and transported them to Buchenwald, a huge Nazi concentration camp near Weimar in Germany. The weather was so cold that some prisoners used frozen corpses as benches. According to Nazi records, the transport arrived 26 January 1945, with 3,784 prisoners. Of this number, 304 youths aged sixteen or under comprised 8 percent of the human cargo.[1]

To better identify it, this transport brought Lazar (Eliezer) Wiesel from Auschwitz-Buna to Buchenwald. Wiesel, born in September 1928, was from Sighet in northern Transylvania, Romania, which was under Hungarian rule during World War II. He was deported with his family to Auschwitz-Birkenau in late May 1944. He and his father Abraham (Shlomo) were selected for work in Auschwitz-Buna, where they slaved for seven months before being moved, with thousands of others, to Germany ahead of the advancing Red Army.

At Buchenwald, the prisoners were first placed in large barracks in the *kleines Lager* (the little camp), a festering transit camp built at the bottom of the Ettersburg hill. Late in the war, Buchenwald functioned as a huge base camp and distribution center in a far-flung and expanding Nazi industrial slave empire. Prisoners were forced, under conditions of terror and privation, to work digging tunnels, building shelters, making ammunition and anti-tank weapons, and helping in brown coal operations. Wiesel entered with his father, who soon died. The boy was then moved into a children's block in the little camp, block 66. "I was transferred to the children's block, where there were six hundred of us," he wrote in a single unelaborated line in his memoir.[2]

In total, 223 prisoners (about 6 percent) were moved with Wiesel into the children's block. These included roughly half the boys sixteen and under (150, or 49 percent), plus a few score slightly older "boys" eighteen or under. Among these were some older brothers permitted to stay with younger brothers, like Alex (Sandor) Moskovic and his older brother Zoltan, from Sobrance in the former Czechoslovakia, or Israel (Sruly) Stuhl and his older brother Vilmos from Slatinsky Doly, on the Slovakian-Romanian border. Many additional brother pairs, above and below the age barrier, were in the *Kinderbarrack*. Groups of unrelated boys functioning as surrogate brothers also moved into the block.

The recent opening of the Red Cross International Tracing Service records, long held behind closed doors in Bad Arolsen, Germany, now permits scholars to examine the surviving records (e.g., transport lists, camp documents), and to conduct microstudies of groups of prisoners, prisoner society, and everyday life in the camps. So too does the rich USC Shoah Foundation archive of survivor testimonies, with testimonies completed in the 1990s by many boys, now elderly men, from this and other transports. A major idea about prisoner society that appears prominently in classic memoirs about the camps—including by Primo Levi, often restated in contemporary studies, including Wolfgang Sofsky's *The Order of Terror*—is that prisoners in the camps were radically alone or became so. They composed a coerced, seriated mass without solidarity or connection, existing amidst a deformed sociality.[3]

This literature stresses that life in Nazi camps approximated a war of all against all; prisoners were separate and apart, and social relations among them were egoistic and pathogenic. The current essay is a preliminary effort to test this proposition for youths in Auschwitz and Buchenwald late during the war, by closely studying the group of young prisoners on the same transport as Wiesel who, like him, were in block

66, or who were elsewhere, or re-transported to satellite camps. It is also an effort to fill out the larger social history behind Wiesel's account in *Night*.

These were mostly Slovakian, Hungarian, and Romanian Jewish boys who had survived terrible family losses at Birkenau in late May 1944 and who were in Birkenau or Buna under difficult conditions. A surprisingly large number of social clusters existed among them—boys with their fathers like Elie Wiesel, boys with other boys, especially brothers or cousins, and boys with relatives or friends from the same towns. As they say in their testimonies, many were acting out deep commitments to stay together and help one another. Yet, as we might expect, others were alone.

This microhistory explores how these youths at Buna and Buchenwald moved together but also alone during their tormenting experiences. It shows how a detailed focus on a distinctive group within prisoner society can show the remarkable and diverse forms of solidarity that continued to coexist in prisoner society, alongside the separateness and aloneness experienced by these largely Jewish youths. In this case, we can also discover the fates of nearly all of the boys on the transport, including those who were in block 66 like Wiesel, as well as those who were not or who were sent out to the satellite killing camps.

After Nazi Germany gained control of Hungary in March 1944, Adolf Eichmann quickly began organizing the Final Solution, commencing outside Budapest. Hundreds of thousands of Slovakian, Hungarian, and Romanian Jews in Hungarian territory were rounded up and placed in makeshift ghettos, often brick factories located near rail lines. Then, weeks later, after they had been robbed, beaten, and abused, the Jews were unknowingly brought in family groups in closed cattle cars to Auschwitz-Birkenau, where most were quickly murdered. A small portion from this forced migration were selected on the ramp under confusing conditions, told to step aside, and then shaved, disinfected, showered, and uniformed. Then, in a few days, most were tattooed and moved to Auschwitz III–Buna or other camps, where they were exploited for months.

Based on close study of the transport list, a large proportion of the boys under sixteen had entered Birkenau with their families between 22 May and 31 May and had undergone similar experiences in Buna before the terror migration to Buchenwald. Most were from cities like Ungvar, Munkacs, Nyirigyhaza, Huszt, or Slatinsky Doly and nearby towns and villages in Subcarpathian Ruthenia; or they were from Satmar and Sighet and nearby towns across the Tisa River in Maramures, in Transylvania. A small minority (7 percent) were Polish, largely from the Łódź ghetto and from towns in the Radom district. A few (6 percent) were from Germany, France, and Holland, with one youth from Italy.

These boys suffered terrible family losses at Auschwitz-Birkenau and then were inducted into a new and modern slavery. Most received tattoos on their forearms and then were brought to the IG Farben complex at Buna, where thousands worked in synthetic rubber operations making liquid fuels or doing construction, materials handling, and transportation activities. Boys sixteen and under, many of whom had lied upward about their ages, worked in labor *Kommandos* hauling heavy concrete blocks to construct fire walls in the Buna warehouses. They dug ditches and repaired buildings and roads after frequent Allied bombings, carried heavy cement sacks, stone, and wood, built shelters, and loaded and unloaded equipment and materials. Some boys, like Elie Wiesel, were in barracks with adult men, who were fathers or uncles or older brothers. Some boys were not with fathers or relatives, and several hundred were placed in barrack 44, a *Jugendblock* (youth block).

Conditions were cruel and difficult, and the plight of the young prisoners was marked by terror, starvation, and exhaustion. Many youths also recall periodic "hanging parades," where SS guards hanged young prisoners and required all others to stand at attention and watch; Elie Wiesel described one such hanging in *Night*.[4] Many boys also recall SS guards setting German shepherds to attack, or SS guards cutting off young prisoners' ears if they failed to respond to commands in German. They also remembered periodic selections where they were stripped to the waist and paraded before SS doctors, and some were returned to Birkenau to be killed.

After a time, most boys knew well that they should keep themselves looking human and fit, walk erect, hide any and all blemishes and sores, and respond quickly to all orders. The block elders and the kapos in Buna were mostly German criminals with green badges and, like the guards, treated prisoners brutally. There was also trafficking involving children, who were made into the pets of debased prisoner functionaries and compelled to share their rooms at night.

A few examples will suffice to illustrate who the boys were, whom they were with, and what work they did. Alex (Szandor) Gross, a fifteen-year-old from Palanok, near Munkacs, was with his older but younger-looking brother Sam (Samu). They were separated at Buna but met again at Gleiwitz on the march. Alex recalled carrying large industrial blocks and building firewalls in the warehouses and later digging ditches and hand-loading railroad cars. Alex and Sam were in separate blocks and saw each other infrequently, mostly at a distance. Years later, though,

Alex recalled, "It was very important to me to know that someone else in my family was still alive."[5]

Chaim (Hersz) Grossman, from Huszt, was alone and at first worked building cooling towers and carrying heavy steel I-beams. However, later he and many other boys from the *Jugendblock* entered a *Maurerschule* (brickmason school) created by a German criminal kapo named Eddie. He ended up carrying mortar and water in a brickmason *Kommando* constructing SS barracks outside the camp.[6] Alexander Berkowits (Srulik Bercovics) was fourteen, from Sighet. He was sent to a coal mine in Janinagrube, but was returned to the *Jugendblock* in Buna, where he also learned bricklaying from Eddie and a German Jewish assistant, Rudi. Srulik then worked as an apprentice bricklayer, rebuilding bombed-out buildings, and keeping makeshift shelters warm for others in his detail.[7]

Zoltan Ellenbogen, a Hassid from Nyirbator, a border town in eastern Hungary, was alone in the *Jugendblock*. Without family, Ellenbogen joined up quickly with older boys from his town, the Jakubowicz brothers, and they all looked out for each other. Ellenbogen counted nuts and bolts and was a *Laufer* (messenger).[8] Samuel Jakubowitz (no relation), a seventeen-year-old from Sighet, was also in the boys' barrack and was a friend of Elie Wiesel's. He recalls entering Buna and being taken "to a block of kids," where he joined up with a cousin.[9]

David Moskovic, a fourteen-year-old, was also in the youth block. Moskovic, who carried galvanized pipes and then trained as a bricklayer, recalled being part of a group of seven youths in the barracks. "We were like a pack of wolves. We weren't scared of no man. We stuck together."[10] Simon Neumann (Tommy Newman) from Vojnatina, Czechoslovakia, another fourteen-year-old, was also in the group. By sticking together, these youths were able to more effectively organize resources and deal on the black market.[11]

Sam Cin (Samu Cin), from Huszt, was fourteen years old and from a large family with nine children. He was with his father and cousin in Birkenau, but his father and he were soon separated. He then joined with his cousin Salomon Czen, a boy the same age from his town; both got contiguous numbers in Auschwitz I and were in the youth barrack in Buna. Cin and his cousin worked cleaning the barrack and then building a factory. They received contiguous new numbers at Buchenwald as well; they were joined together until the final two weeks before liberation.[12]

Israel (Sruly) Stuhl was a fifteen-year-old Vischnitzer Hassid from Slatinsky Doly, in the former Czechoslovakia; he, his father, and two brothers were moving together. All the Stuhl men and boys got contiguous numbers but wound up separated inside Buna: Sruly's father was in one block; his older brother Wolf (Vilmos), seventeen years old, was in another; and Sruly and his younger brother Ferencz, thirteen, were in the youth block. Sruly and Ferencz worked unloading paper from transports at Buna, and then Sruly was part of a locksmith unit, where he was the "gofer" for the group. Stuhl recalled bombings when prisoners were barred from the shelters they had built.[13]

Sigmund (Zsigismund) Weiser, sixteen years old, a Hassid from Satmar, whose father was far away in America, suffered the loss of his mother and siblings on the ramp at Birkenau. Weiser recalled the fear and confusion on entering the camp. "We were mostly women, children, and older men.... We were leaderless.... We didn't know."[14] Weiser saw prisoners shot; he saw naked women who seemed to be utterly strange and foreign "creatures." He didn't understand anything that was happening. He too was in Buna with several cousins, including Zisha, a boy his age. He worked digging ditches, filling trolleys with dirt. Later, like Hersz Grossman, he worked building houses for the SS outside Buna and lived in the youth barrack. His cousin Zisha died, leaving him alone for a time.

Ted (Tibor) Gross, sixteen years old, from Satmar, was with his father. He dug ditches for pipelines and then was in *Kommando* 90, a mechanical unit. Gross became the pet of Karlin, the alcoholic German criminal kapo; he shared the extra rations he received from Karlin and his work in the *Kommando* with his father.[15] Jakob Rozental from Comlausa, in northern Transylvania, sixteen years old, was deported with his mother and five siblings from Sevlus but now was alone in Birkenau. He recalled later with shame that he had sent his younger brother Mordcha to his mother and to the gas. In Buna, Rozental was also in *Kommando* 90 under Karlin, where he joined with a boy from his town, Sam Izsak.[16] The two youths were later paired on the march to Gleiwitz and on the transport to Buchenwald and were again together in block 66.

Even Elie Wiesel, with his father, joined up with other boys in his barrack and in the *Kommando* at Buna. In *Night*, Wiesel wrote of Tibi and Yossi, two boys from Czechoslovakia who joined up with Eliezer and his father in the electrical warehouse. These brothers "lived for each other body and soul," he observed, and "they quickly became my friends."[17] The young Zionist youths knew Hebrew songs, and the three boys spoke often about Palestine. Later, when Elie Wiesel was transferred to another barrack apart from his father, he was with Tibi and Yossi at a selection. Wiesel reported to his friends when he saw that the SS doctor failed to write their numbers; the brothers did the same for him.

Elie Wiesel was in a group of men and boys from Sighet when he was initially tattooed in Auschwitz I. Anton Meisner, another boy from Sighet, who was a year older than Elie, was in the same religious school class and studied with the same rabbi. Anton recalled that he and his father, Maximilian, were together with Elie Wiesel and Abraham (Shlomo), as well as several others from Sighet. But at Buna they were separated when placed in different barracks and given different work assignments. Anton Meisner and his father were in *Kommando* 72, which transported heavy machinery used to produce other machinery. Maximilian weakened under the harsh burden and died on the transport en route to Buchenwald.[18]

Alex (Sandor) Moskovic was thirteen years old, from Sobrance, near Ungvar, in Slovakia. His father, Josef, and his older brother Zoltan were sent to Buna, but Alex was kept with other boys in Birkenau. He was one of thousands of youths held first in barracks 11 and 13 in camp BIId, most of whom were sent to the gas; but after two months he was tattooed and shifted to camp BIIa and put on *Scheisse Kommando (garbage detail)*. Alex worked with thirteen boys from the Carpathians, who stuck together and looked out for one another. They wore harnesses and pulled a large wagon into which others dumped garbage, moving regularly among sub-camps, and picking up extra food especially from the women's camp and several kitchens. Alex caught up with his father and brother only during the evacuation. At this point, Alex abandoned his comrades—familial loyalty trumped friendship—and joined again with his father and sibling. Like Elie Wiesel's father, Alex's father, Josef, also died soon at Buchenwald, and Alex and Zoltan moved together into block 66.[19]

Three boys at Birkenau from Nagykarola, who in time were separated from family bonds, also tried to stay together. Paul Kaszovitz, later called Paul Kassy in America, along with Istvan Guttman and Imre Hirsch, schoolmates from Nagykarola, somehow took the same last name (Hirsch) in the camps. If they had the same name, they reasoned, they could stand together at roll calls. At Buna, Istvan Guttman was initially part of a *Kommando* carrying cement bags, then in a mechanical *Kommando*. Paul Hirsch, Istvan Hirsch, and Imre Hirsch were first tied with others—Paul with an uncle, Imre Hirsch with his father and brother. But they were later listed as the "Hirsch" brothers on the death march and transport. They received contiguous numbers in the Buchenwald numbering system, were in block 66, and shared the same location to the end.[20]

Finally, Lajos Weitzen and Gyula Moskovics, neighbors who attended school together in Ungvar and who were apprentice plumbers together after the school was closed, also joined up at Buna. Lajos Weitzen lost his parents and was in Buna working in *Kommando* 26 carrying cement bags, then in *Kommando* 1 in an electrical warehouse. Gyula Moskovics lost his mother and younger siblings but was with his father; however, later he was alone, cleaning pipes with a wire brush and carrying hoses. He and Lajos linked up at Buna and reaffirmed their bond during the move to Buchenwald; they remained together until after liberation.[21]

From Buna the prisoners marched five abreast in the snow, wearing thin prisoner pajamas and wooden shoes. The barrack of Alex Gross was first out. "The cruel wind howled and the snow blew in our faces, making it difficult to walk," he recalled.[22] Gross did not want to go, he feared he could not make it; but he would not give up, hoping to find his brother Sam, who was also marching. In time, Alex remembered, marching grew more difficult as ice built up on their legs and as the marchers damped down the snow, making it more slippery. Gross and most others remembered the freezing cold vividly. Sam Cin simply recalled that "people froze." "They lay down on the ground, they collapsed; they were shot."[23] Gross said the prisoners sometimes helped each other—Gross himself briefly carried another boy—but those who could not continue were shot and left where they fell.

Many boys walked with someone they knew in Buna previous to Auschwitz. Sam Cin walked with his cousin Salomon Czen, and Jakob Rozental marched with Sam Izsak. Tibor and Wilhelm Berman, brothers from Munkacs, marched together. Tibor Gross was with his father, and Lazar (Elie) Wiesel was with his father. Anton Meisner also walked with his father but then lost him in the cars. Sruly Stuhl was with his father and brothers Wolf and Ferencz. Alex Moskovic reunited with his father and brother. What seems most remarkable is that a group of boys marched together with older adults from Slatinsky Dola, eight in total, all of them named Slomovics, all with contiguous numbers. The Slomovics stayed together at Buchenwald and were in barrack 59, along with the Hirsch boys from Nagykarola. Sol Culang (Szlama Zulang), a Polish Jewish boy from Warsaw via Majdanek and Buna, marched with other boys from the *Jugendblock,* with whom he had schemed to obtain food.[24]

After Gleiwitz, the prisoners were in open coal cars exposed to the elements on trains that moved erratically to avoid Allied bombings. The prisoners made snowballs and ate them like apples. Samuel Isakovitch, another boy from Sighet, told David Boder, the American psychologist who interviewed survivors in France after the war, "Snow ... we ate the snow. We didn't have anything else to eat."[25] Sigmund Weiser recalled the fighting that broke out on these "half trains," especially when passersby in Czechoslovakia threw bread and food down from the overpasses. Srulik Bercovics also remembered the free-for-alls in the cars; he was small and knew to stay safely back in the corners.[26]

Elie Wiesel recalled the march and transport, telling of Rabbi Eliahu's son who marched ahead, abandoning his father, then of another son who stole food from his own father. God was testing his chosen people, as God had tested Abraham and Isaac earlier. The journey was also testing the bonds that tied men together as humans. Wiesel wondered if he would pass the challenge. "We received no food. We lived on snow; it took the place of bread. The days resembled the nights, and the nights left in our souls the dregs of their darkness."[27]

Samuel Isakovitch told Boder that the struggle for food on the train provoked murder, confirming the picture of a world of all against all. He recalled that a prisoner used his wooden shoe to smash another prisoner "over the head," who simply "never used to get up anymore."[28] Wiesel also wrote about men hurling themselves viciously at one another, mauling each other for crumbs of bread. "Beasts of prey, unleashed, animal hate in their eyes," he wrote.[29] But such radical Hobbesian behavior, as if the prisoners were in a pre-civilized state of nature, was at the same time matched by small-scale solidarities that continued visible and strong—men and boys under extreme conditions sticking together, seeking to help sustain a father, brother, cousin, or friend.

The prisoners arrived at Buchenwald on 26 January 1945, eight days after setting out, with scores of dead bodies in the cars. The living prisoners assembled first on the *Appelplatz* (roll call plaza) to be counted, and then a veteran prisoner announced that they would be showered, issued clothing, and sent to the blocks. After a long time, during which Srulik Bercovics was beaten for stooping to gather snow, the prisoners were shaved, doused with harsh disinfectant, and then—after further delay—showered, uniformed, registered with new numbers and badges, and finally driven down toward the *kleines Lager*.

Startlingly, many prisoners who had been moving together in the world of concentration camps managed to obtain new Buchenwald numbers alongside one another—trace elements in the prisoner documents of familial or friendship bonds—and to subsequently be placed in the same barracks. Israel (Sruly) Stuhl and his brother Vilmos received contiguous numbers and were sent to block 51; Jakob Rozental and his friend Sam Izsak received numbers together and were in block 51. Hersz (Chaim) Grossman was in block 51, so too was Samuel Isakovitch. Lazar (Elie) Wiesel was with Samuel Jakubowitz from Sighet in block 57 and was temporarily separated from his father, who was placed in block 51. Sam Cin and Salomon Czen got numbers together and were in block 58, along with Anton Meisner. The three Hirsch brothers got numbers in a row and were in block 59, as were the Moskovic brothers, Alex (Sandor) and Zoltan, along with their father.[30]

The initial placements of the prisoners from Buna were in blocks 51, 55, and 57–59, large wooden barracks with multilevel bunks lacking straw or mattresses. The prisoners crowded in, fighting for space and coveting the higher-level spots. Sigmund Weiser remarked about the sleeping arrangements: they were so tight that "if somebody wanted to turn around, everybody had to turn around."[31] Included were tough men from all over Nazi-occupied Europe—Ukrainians, Russians, and Poles—among whom many hated Jews; there were also Jews speaking many tongues from many different places. There was little solidarity among the prisoners in the aggregate, and these barracks were dangerous for youths who had to face bigger, older, rougher men. The prisoners went daily to the line in the *Kinohalle* (cinema building), where food was distributed, and then returned to their barracks. Most prisoners remained idle during quarantine, staying in their barracks or wandering nearby. Many older youths recall being put to work early in *Kommando 53*, the quarry. Later, some went to Weimar to clean up after bombings or were assigned to the wood yard.

The German Communist-led international underground at Buchenwald created block 66 not long before the arrival of the transport. Antonin Kalina, a veteran Czech Communist in the camp since September 1939, was the block leader. Kalina's deputy block elder was Gustav Schiller, a Polish Jew and Communist from Lvov, also in the camp since late 1939. Since mid-1944, Schiller had been working with Polish Jewish boys from labor camps in Poland, in a new second Jewish block created in the main camp, block 23. Now Jewish boys from Poland were moved onto one side of block 66, while Hungarian and Romanian Jewish boys were put on the other side. Veteran Czech, Hungarian, and Polish Jewish prisoners staffed the large cavernous barrack, and additional adult Polish and Czech Jewish men were recruited off new transports to serve as cadres, teachers, and mentors. From early February into mid-March 1945, Kalina and Schiller went around the barracks where the youths from Buna were initially placed and offered the opportunity to move to the *Kinderblock*, where they would have better conditions and be safer.

Sigmund Weiser recollected when these veteran prisoners appeared. "We were becoming animals," he recalled. In the large barracks, dead cadavers were piled outside daily until carted away. Death was a growing presence as the camp reached nearly eighty thousand in early 1945, while the food supply diminished under the Allied bombings. There was also danger from prisoner predators: a large Russian robbed Weiser of his food, a kapo struck him and cut a large gash on his head. Then on this day, Weiser said, all youths aged sixteen or so were told to line up and offered the choice to go to a different barrack. "We [for Weiser was again paired with another boy, Lipot Ciment, also from Satmar] were taken to a different barrack," he said. "Here there were blankets, mattresses ... ! They showered us; they cleaned us up!" Weiser recalled that the Czech Communist block elder was "a very nice man.... He guarded us like his children."[32] The Slovakian, Hungarian, and Romanian Jewish youths were less effusive about the violent Gustav, who yelled at and abused them, favoring the Jewish boys from Poland, who came to see Gustav as their father figure.

Inside *Kinderblock* 66, the youths occasionally got extra food, but everyone continued to go very hungry. The camp underground distributed a little extra food, gathering Red Cross packages from veteran political prisoners and distributing them in the block. Samuel Isakovitch told interviewer David Boder that "we had a very good man for a *blakovy* (block leader)," who worked to keep the youths alive.[33] Alex (Sandor) Moskovic said that the block elders shared information about the war regularly and that there were occasional classes and even shows and performances put on by the boys, who sang in different languages. Abraham Gottlieb (today Abraham Ahuvia) from Kozlov, near Miechow, in Galicia, who kept a Buchenwald diary, and whose older brother Chaim Meir Gottlieb was a resident teacher and chorale leader in block 66, recorded several visits to the block to watch the performances. Gottlieb observed that the presence of the youth block in Buchenwald amidst the deteriorating conditions in February and March 1945 was a remarkable phenomenon.[34]

Not all boys aged sixteen or so and not all groups of brothers from Buna went to block 66 when invited. In many cases, the choices depended on whether they could stay with those with whom they had been together in Buna or on the march. Sons with fathers had to decide whether to take advantage of the opportunity if it meant abandoning a father, who was to be sent to an outlying satellite camp. Fathers had to decide to let go of a son, or in some cases two or more sons, putting them in one another's hands. Brothers who wanted to remain together had to gauge whether this could be done better by staying in the base camp and moving to the children's block or, alternatively, taking one's chances and going again on transport. Many boys knew intuitively that Buchenwald was different and thought the children's block would be safer. Others were suspicious. In some cases, like Alex and Zoltan Moskovic from Sobrance, the boys asked if the older brother could accompany the younger one and received permission. Sam Gross was taken into block 66; Alex Gross, who looked older but was in fact younger, was not accepted at first but went there repeatedly.[35]

As best as can be determined from study of the transport list and other materials from the Red Cross ITS documents regarding the transport, there were 45 boys born 1928 or later, who were moving in forty social clusters totaling 98 persons, with fathers, brothers, cousins or, in a few cases, friends. These included 28 older men, mostly fathers, born between 1893 and 1904, and 25 young men born between 1923 and 1927, who were older brothers or, in a few cases, cousins. None of these 45 age-eligible boys went to block 66. Several sets of brothers (or cousins), marked by contiguous numbers at Buna and at Buchenwald, stayed in the adult barracks. Jeno Berger was with his older brother Moritz and father Josef in block 57. Szmul Frydrich, a Polish Jewish boy from Ostrowiec, was with his brother Hemja in block 58. The three Kaufman brothers, Bela, Josef, and Matyas, from Slatinsky Dola, stayed in block 58, as did cousins Sam Cin and Salomon Czen. The Atlasz brothers from Kassau, the Fulop brothers from Tiszanagyfalu, and the Schleger brothers from Satmar all stayed in these blocks. Two sixteen-year-olds among the Slomovits cluster of men did not go to block 66.

At the same time, several additional clusters of brothers or of fathers and sons were broken up by choice to go to the *Kinderblock*. There were an additional 41 boys born 1928 or later on the transport, who were moving together in another forty clusters involving 93 additional persons. Of these 41 boys, 33 chose to go to block 66. In most cases, older brothers did not follow or were not permitted to do so. Only Hersz Bandman, of four brothers from Kozienice, went to block 66. Samuel Slomovics was in block 66, but older brother Salomon and father Elias were not. Josef Herskovicz from Lipose left his father; Franz Steinberg from Munkacs separated from his father Moric; and Wolf Kornblum from Łódź, Poland, via Starachowice, left his father Natan and brother Moniek. Emilio Todesco from Venice, the sole Italian Jew, parted from his father Eugenio and older brother Mario.

Finally, 19 additional boys from the transport, born 1928 or after, and grouped in twelve social clusters totaling 27 additional persons, were in block 66 along with their brothers, including some older brothers. Alexander Berkowicz and his brother Elias from Ungvar were together, Jakob and Mendel Dawidowicz from Ajbriviso were together, and Mendel and Harry Fischman from Sighet were in block 66 as well.[36] The three alleged Hirsch brothers, Imre, Paul, and Istvan, were in block 66. Alex Moskovic and his older brother Zoltan, Israel (Sruly) and Vilmos Stuhl, Jakob Rozental with Samuel Izsak, and Gyula Moskovics and Lajos Weitzen were in the *Kinderblock*. Elie Wiesel bunked near Samuel Jakubowitz from Sighet, and later, after liberation, they referred to each other in interviews as youths who could vouch for one other. At the same time, there were scores of individual boys moving alone, some of whom also found refuge in block 66. Of those mentioned earlier, Hersz Grossman from Huszt and David Moskovic from Konusz were there, so too was Miklos Grüner, from Nyiregyhaza, who lost his father at Buna. Additional boys in block 66 who were alone were Andor Katz from Munkacs, Jakob Lender from Alsoviso, and Jerzy Zyskind from Łódź, who tap-danced in the block to a famous Julian Tuvim poem about a locomotive, a scene recalled by many boys years later.

The boys arrived at a moment when the Nazi satellite camps created in mid- and late 1944 in the Harz Mountains and surroundings—to host projects involving digging massive subterranean production facilities to manufacture aircraft engines, parts, and ammunition—were sharply expanding their demand for slave labor. Allied bombing necessitated the creation of hundreds of new protected underground spaces for German corporations to produce for the war effort. Of the 304 boys sixteen years old and under who arrived on 26 January 1945 and of the 154 boys not moved to block 66, some 50 or so were sent out from several of the large barracks at Buchenwald to these camps. Another 24 died in the barracks at Buchenwald during February or March, presumably too sick or weak for transport. Thus nearly half the boys sixteen and under who were not in block 66, roughly a quarter of all the youths from the transport, were sent out from Buchenwald or died in the base camp within two months.

Among the camps in the Harz Mountains was Langenstein-Zwieberge at Halberstadt, in the foothills of the Thekenbergen in Saxony-Anhalt. The Nazis called this camp Kommando BII and referred to it also as Malachyt. By February 1945, the camp was reaching five thousand prisoners. At BII-Malachyt, prisoners worked on an enormous tunnel excavation and road and railway construction project for the Junkers Aircraft Company.[37] The goal was to provide space for the Junkers Company to make jet engines and V-2 rocket parts. Workers slaved in the sandstone with primitive equipment; youths carried cement sacks weighing fifty kilograms. Survivors describe a high death rate, with prisoners in the tunnels dying on average in six weeks.[38]

Another camp in the Hils area in central Germany, west of Halberstadt in Lower Saxony, was Eschershausen, near Holzen; the Nazis referred to this as Kommando Hecht or Hecht/Stein. This was smaller than Malachyt, reaching eleven hundred prisoners. Here, too, prisoners were pushed to extraordinary lengths to drive a tunnel system into a mountain, beginning from five existing asphalt mines. Prisoners dug for Organization Todt, the German Asphalt Corporation, and for several armaments companies. The lead company was the Volkswagen Company at Wolfsburg, which sought to redistribute its manufacturing sites into newly built underground spaces to make Fi 103 (V-1) buzz bombs and engine wings for a Focke-Wolfe Ta 152 C fighter.[39] A few prisoners worked as metalworkers or mechanics in armaments production.

Finally, another outlying satellite camp, this one southwest of Buchenwald south of Gotha, was Kommando SIII, or Ohrdruf, the largest of these satellites, and the most well-known today. This camp grew through March 1945, reaching 11,700 prisoners. Here prisoners were also set to tunneling, but the focus was on building an immense communications center to serve as a redoubt for the German High Command if it had to retreat from Berlin. Prisoners dug large caverns, picked up rocks, and did other heavy work without protective equipment. Other prisoners worked in the kitchens and other camp institutions, and some worked on cadaver *Kommando,* pulling dead corpses from the tunnels and burying them in mass graves.[40]

Beginning two weeks after arrival, fifty boys from the Buna transport who remained in blocks 51 and 57–59 were sent out to these three satellite camps. On 9 February 1945, the first group, numbering about a dozen, was transported among a thousand prisoners to BII: Langenstein-Zwieberge. The boys included Max Salamonovics and his older brother Josef from Ungvar, and the Schleger brothers, David and Iszak, from Satmar. Several boys with younger brothers in block 66 were also aboard, including Martin Taub from Slatinsky Dola, who was sixteen (brother Bernat in block 66 was fifteen). Herman Stuhl, the father of Sruly, Vilmos, and Ferencz Stuhl, was also on this transport.[41]

A few days later, on 14 February, another dozen boys, mostly from block 51, were sent out in a transport of a thousand prisoners to SIII Ohrdruf.[42] These included brothers Eugen and Tomas Atlasz from Kassau and the cousins Sam Cin and Salomon Czen. At Ohrdruf, Salomon Czen weakened and later was shot in the infirmary, while Sam Cin, who worked building shelters and carrying cement bags, endured. Emil Weiss from Munkacs, another boy trained as a young brickmason earlier in Buna, slaved in a stone mine at Ohrdruf.[43]

Finally, on 17 February and 3 March, the largest group of youths sixteen and under, numbering about twenty-six, was sent to Hecht/Stein. This group also included several youths and slightly older young men listed as mechanics and metalworkers. Vilem and Salomon Slomovics from Slatinsky Dola were included with five others in their huge familial cluster; those who also went were Jeno Berger and David Nutovits from Munkacs, Szmul Frydrich from Ostrowiec, now separated from his brother Hemja at Langenstein-Zweiberge, and Zoltan Weisz from Nyiregyhaza.

One example of the youths sent out was Max Salamonovics, sixteen years old, from Uzhorod, who was with his brother Josef. "Both my brother and I were always together," Max emphasized in 1995. "We made a pact, whatever happens we will stay together."[44] At Buchenwald, they were in barrack 51. But they thought the best chance to stay together was to go out on transport, and so they soon were on the closed train heading toward Langenstein-Zwieberge. The second day, the train was attacked by Allied aircraft, and Max and Josef were each hit—Max in the hand, Josef in his leg. Even now, they hid their injuries to stay together and went on to Halberstadt, where they worked digging tunnels. This camp was the worst of all camps, where prisoners were "dying like flies." Others recalled that they worked inside tunnels, never seeing daylight, and endured beatings and frequent large explosions.[45]

Yet other boys were shifted around in Buchenwald with surprisingly positive effect, avoiding transports to the satellites. Several boys stayed in or moved to block 58 and survived under a Communist block elder named Max. These included Anton Meisner from Sighet, who was later moved to the hospital, and the three Kaufman brothers from Slatinsky Dola, Matyas, Josef, and Bela (16, 15, and 13 years old, respectively). Other boys were shifted into different blocks. One went to another children's block, block 8 in the *grosses Lager* (upper camp); eight were put in the two Jewish blocks, numbers 22 and 23, headed by the German Communists Emil Carlebach and Karl Siegmeyer; and more than a dozen were absorbed into block 49, headed by German Communist Walter Sontag. A few additional boys were in blocks 62–63, convalescent barracks. Through March 1945, traffic moved back and forth among blocks 62, 63, and 66. On the other hand, a dozen or more boys in block 66 died in March, including the young Italian Jew, Emilio Todesco.

As time wore on into early April, the youths in block 66 and elsewhere at Buchenwald grew anxious about what would happen as the Allies drew near. Would the Nazis turn over the camp intact, or would Buchenwald be evacuated like Buna, with all the prisoners again being put out on the roads? Youths who had endured the death march and transport from Buna did not wish to go out again. Then, on 4 April 1945, the loudspeaker at Buchenwald blared out a command for all Jews to report to the *Appelplatz*. Everyone knew that Buchenwald was to be evacuated, and the Jews, including Jewish youths, were to be the first sent out. In block 66, where there were now over nine hundred boys from the Buna transport and other transports, Antonin Kalina and Gustav Schiller told their charges not to report, and to stay in or near the barrack and to resist the Nazi call.

At this point, in a concerted action sanctioned by the Communist-led underground, Kalina changed the identities on all of the boys' uniforms. Red triangles with national markings identifying the boys as Polish, Hungarian, Czech, and German political prisoners were substituted for the yellow triangles they had worn below that identified them as Jews. One boy recalled, "Instead we got other letters such as F P C U B R that masked our Jewish identity. Now we were just like all the other Christian prisoners in the camp." Srulik Bercovics remarked that Kalina "made up signals [badges] for us with not any yellow in it."[46] A day or two later, when SS guards appeared down the hill outside block 66 to take Jewish children, Kalina told the guards with courage and confidence that such children were gone, and only non-Jews remained. The SS guards started to push past him into the block, but chaos in the camp above distracted them and they departed.

The Nazis led out several thousand Jews from other barracks during these first days but then started evacuating prisoners from all barracks. They left children's blocks 8 and 66 and the invalid blocks until the end. Boys in the Jewish blocks 22 and 23 were forced to hide, some going down the hill and increasing the crowding in block 66. Then, on April 10, SS guards again descended on *Kinderblock* 66 with guns and dogs, and boys were caught and led up the hill to the main gate. Some youths dropped out and fled to other barracks in the main camp, while others hid in the piles of the dead that lay all over the camp.

About mid-afternoon, most boys from the barrack were on the *Appelplatz* awaiting the gate to be opened—a couple hundred boys in an advance section had already been taken out—when Allied planes flew overhead, air-raid sirens sounded, and the SS guards fled to the shelters. At this juncture, the youths were left standing, as Wiesel describes in *Night*,[47] and Kalina then told hundreds to return to the barrack. It was too late for the Nazis to round them up that day, so they were together in the *Kinderblock* the next day, taking cover below the windows, when American forces neared and Buchenwald was liberated.

"On the 9th and 10th of April, 1944, the Nazis attempted to assemble us for evacuation," Alex Gross recalled. "We were told the camp had to be emptied by nightfall, but the sound of air-raid sirens interrupted those plans. [The SS men] ... disappeared into the air raid shelters and underground tunnels." Alex Gross and his brother Sam made it, as did Alex Moskovic, although his brother Zoltan was taken out and shot by the Nazis outside Buchenwald. Louis (Lajos) Weitzen believed that Kalina had arranged for the *Kinderblock* to be led out last, while his friend Julius (Gyula) Moskovics emphasized, "All I can say about this man [Kalina] is thank you, thank you, thank you. He was trying to help us, and console us, and say hold on [because] better days are coming."[48] Anton Meisner, Simon Neumann (Tommy Newman), and Paul Hirsch, as well as Zoltan Ellenbogen, survived in the hospital, while Imre Hirsch and Istvan Hirsch hid near the end in nearby block 67.

This microstudy of boys on a transport from Buna to Buchenwald, of their social relations in the camps and what happened in Birkenau, Buna, and Buchenwald, offers insights into the social processes and prisoner social system among these Jewish youths in the camps and also broadly accounts for most of the boys' fates. In pioneering work forty-five years ago, amidst early studies that highlighted some of the psycho-social processes of trauma and solitude in the camps, the sociologist Elmer Luchterhand emphasized the importance of prisoner relations in small groups, especially pairs. Luchterhand stressed the presence and salutary role of human groups in the struggle for survival, highlighting the role of stable pairs.[49] While massive obstacles existed to sustaining such pairs and small groups in the terror-filled Nazi universe, these stable pairs, replacement pairs, and other clusters played important life-sustaining roles. In these clusters, prisoners shared and cooperated, helped each other in need, strategized and organized, looked out for one another, and provided one another with reason and motivation to survive.

Regarding the youths at Buna and Buchenwald, we can better understand the existence of such social clusters by thinking back to the mode of their entrance into the camp system at Auschwitz-Birkenau and their experiences at Buna. They entered the concentration camp universe together with family members and fellow townspeople. Despite horrific and traumatic losses at the selections, many (but not all) were able to pair up with a father, one or more brothers, or a cousin. Even where this was impossible, it was still possible for some to find a colleague in a barrack or work group afterward, especially a friend or friends from the same hometown. At Buna too, it was possible for many fathers and sons, brothers, and others in family fragments or small clusters to live in the same barracks and work in the same *Kommandos*. Even boys moving alone in the Nazi universe or finding themselves suddenly alone after the death of a father could find others with whom to join up in the *Jugendblock* in Buna or in work groups like *Scheisse Kommando* at Birkenau.

The existence of such social clusters, involving at least 102 of the 304 Jewish youths for whom we have information from the transport, helps us understand some of the complex social dynamics of life beyond extremity in the camps—at least for late in the war, amidst the fluidity of movement affecting prisoners who were selected for work and transported between Nazi camps and satellite camps. They not only offer insights about the will to endure that many adolescent boys exhibited, but also suggest that generalizations like those made by Sofsky, about prisoner behavior and society in general during the war, may not hold precisely for the behavior and forms of solidarity of Jewish prisoners late in the war. Some were alone, and some were moving together. The existence of these social clusters may also help explain choices made along the way, such as the decision in Buchenwald to go to the protective *Kinderblock* or to avoid doing so. A barrack for youths located in a base camp automatically meant, in most cases, separation from fathers or older brothers, who were slated to be transported out. On the other hand, there was nothing rigid about the clandestine effort, and some brothers of different ages prevailed on veteran political prisoners to allow them to stay. In other cases, other prisoners thought that it was best to stay together at all costs, even by going out on transports to satellite camps.

The Israeli psychologist Shamai Davidson also wrote eloquently about human reciprocity in the camps, postulating that interpersonal bonding, reciprocity, and sharing were essential sources of strength for "adaptation" and survival. Such interpersonal support sustained the motivation to continue the struggle to live and also helped in numerous ways, such as helping people to organize and engage in the black market.[50] We see evidence of such active dyads, or two-person clusters, in this case in the documents exhibited by contiguous numberings across two camp systems, in the tattoos at Auschwitz and the badges at Buchenwald; we even sometimes see slightly larger groups together, coexisting as groups in the camp universe, alongside clear evidence of anomie and alienation. We also see that some boys remember, in testimonies many years later, that they were sworn to stick together as brothers and friends and that these mutual relationships were the primary commitments they made.

Alex Moskovic, the boy who left his work comrades to rejoin his family at Gleiwitz, a survivor who today is an educator in Florida, straightforwardly explains, "Trust was the main thing. You couldn't always stay or be together—it was just beyond your control. But having someone you could trust, where this was possible, was often a matter of life and death."[51]

As to the fates of the many boys on the transport, about half were moved with Elie Wiesel into block 66, where they found invaluable protection from a clandestine movement, whose members were committed to saving and mentoring them; about a quarter remained in the other large barracks with adult prisoners in Buchenwald, with some subsequently

Table 3.1. Boys on the Buna Transport to Buchenwald in This Microstudy

Name	Town of Origin, Country	USC Shoah Testimony	Interview
Srulik Bercovics (Alexander Berkowits)	Sighet, Romania	X	—
Samu (Sam) Cin	Huszt, Czechoslovakia	—	—
Szlama Zulang (Sol Culang)	Warsaw, Poland	X	—
Salomon Czen	Huszt, Czechoslovakia	—	—
Zoltan Ellenbogen	Nyirbator, Hungary	X	X
Berek Erlich	Warsaw, Poland	X	—
Harry Fischman	Sighet, Romania	X	—
Samu Gross (Sam Gross)	Palanok, Czechoslovakia	X	—
Szandor Gross (Alex Gross)	Palanok, Czechoslovakia	X	X
Tibor Gross (Ted Gross)	Satmar, Romania	X	—
Chaim Hersz Grossman (Henry Grossman)	Huszt, Czechoslovakia	X	—
Istvan Hirsch (Stefan Guttman)	Nagykarola, Czechoslovakia	X	
Paul Hirsch (Paul Kaszovitz, Paul Kassy)	Nagykarola, Czechoslovakia	X	X
Samuel Isakovitch	Sighet, Romania	—	Boder
Sam Izsak	Comlausa, Romania	—	—
Samuel Jakubowitz	Sighet, Romania	—	Josepher
Wolf Kornblum (William Kaye)	Łódź, Poland	—	x
David Mangarten	Starachowice, Poland	X	—
Anton Meisner (Anton Mason)	Sighet, Romania	X	—
Sandor Moskovic (Alex Moskovic)	Sobrance, Czechoslovakia	X	X
David Moskovic	Konusz, Czechoslovakia	—	—
Gyula Moskovics (Julius Moskowits)	Uzhorod, Czechoslovakia	—	—
Simon Neumann (Tommy Newman)	Vojnatina, Czechoslovakia	X	—

Jakob Rozental (Jack Rosenthal)	Comlausa, Romania	X	X
Max Salamonovics (Max Sands)	Uzhorod, Czechoslovakia	X	—
Josef Salamonovics	Uzhorod, Czechoslovakia	X	—
Israel (Sruly) Stuhl	Slatinsky Doly, Czechoslovakia	X	—
Abby Weiner	Sighet, Romania	X	X
Sigmund Weiser	Satmar, Romania	X	—
Emil Weiss	Munkacs, Czechoslovakia	X	—
Lajos Weitzen (Louis Weitzen)	Uzhorod, Czechoslovakia	—	Tzugaris
Lazar Wiesel (Elie Wiesel)	Sighet, Romania	*Night*	X
Leopold Ziment (Lipot Ciment)	Satmar, Romania	—	—
Jerzy Zyskind	Lodz, Poland	—	Widow

shifted about in the base camp strategically; and another quarter were transported to satellite camps, where they faced deadly labor assignments, or died soon after arriving at Buchenwald. Even Elie Wiesel was never completely alone in Buchenwald after his father died: although he wrote that he fell into a deep depression where "nothing mattered" anymore, he was also in a protected barrack with several other youths from his town and someone else he knew well, Samuel Jakubowitz. Even after liberation, the rebuilding of the lives and personalities of many boys, as well as their start of new lives, would also proceed based on pairs and small groups and the forging and deepening of group bonds in transitional homes in France and elsewhere.[52]

Kenneth Waltzer is professor emeritus of history at Michigan State University and a former director of MSU's Jewish Studies Program. He was also dean of James Madison College, MSU's highly reputed residential college of public affairs, and director of Integrative Studies in the Arts and Humanities in the university. He came to Michigan from Harvard University to help build James Madison College and there won numerous teaching awards during his career. In recent years, he cocreated *The American Identity Explorer: Immigration and Migration* CD ROM (McGraw-Hill) and has been researching drawing on ITS records, testimonies, and interviews on the rescue of children and youths at Buchenwald. He was historical consultant to the film *Kinderblock 66: Return to Buchenwald,* and he is the historian who found the rescuer of Israel Meir Lau in Buchenwald and also outed a Holocaust memoir fraud, *Angel at the Fence.*

Notes

Special thanks to my undergraduate assistant Justine Brunet and to researcher Bill Bilstadt for their help, and also to Bob Houbeck, director, University of Michigan–Flint Thompson Library, for arranging a feed from the USC Shoah Foundation archives via the University of Michigan. Special thanks also to Alex Moskovic, who reviewed an earlier version.

1. Transport List of New Prisoners from KL Auschwitz to Buchenwald, 26 January 1945, doc. no. 5285826#1–5285893#1 (1.1.5.1/0001-0182/0148A/0004 to 0071) (67 p.), International Tracing Services (ITS Archives).
2. Elie Wiesel, *Night* (New York: Farrar, Straus & Giroux, 2006), 113. See also Wiesel, *All Rivers Run to the Sea* (New York: Knopf, 1995); *And the Sea Is Never Full* (New York: Knopf, 1999).
3. See Primo Levi, *Survival in Auschwitz* (New York: Touchstone, 1995); Wolfgang Sofsky, *The Order of Terror: The Concentration Camp,* trans. William Templer (Princeton, NJ: Princeton University Press, 1999). See also critical essays on Sofsky in Jane Caplan and Nikolaus Wachsmann, eds., *Concentration Camps in Nazi Germany: The New Histories* (New York: Routledge, 2010).
4. Wiesel, *Night,* 61–65.
5. Alex Gross, interview 11272, Visual History Archive, USC Shoah Foundation, Atlanta, GA, 1996, See also Alex Gross, *Yankele: A Holocaust Survivor's Bittersweet Memoir* (Landham, MD: University Press of America, 2002); personal interview with Alex Gross by the author, 9 June 2005.
6. Henry Grossman (Hersz Grossman), interview 14431, Virtual History Archive, USC Shoah Foundation, New Rochelle, NY, 1996.
7. Alex Berkowits (Szrul Bercovics), interview 13792, Virtual History Archive, USC Shoah Foundation, Winnipeg, Canada, 1996.
8. Interview with Zoltan Ellenbogen by the author, 11 December 2006.
9. Interview with Samuel Jakubowitz by Brian Josepher, shared in e-mail to the author, 8 May 2009.
10. David Moskovic, interview 43392, Virtual History Archive, USC Shoah Foundation. Ottawa, Canada, 1998.
11. Thomas Newman, interview 316, Virtual History Archive, USC Shoah Foundation. Toronto Canada, 1994.
12. Sam Cin, interview 17077, Virtual History Archive, USC Shoah Foundation. Skokie, IL, 1996.
13. Sruly Stuhl, interview 43116, Virtual History Archive, USC Shoah Foundation, Denver, CO, 1998.
14. Sigmund Weiser, interview 17919, Virtual History Archive, USC Shoah Foundation, Staten Island, NY, 1996.
15. Ted Gross (Tibor Gross), interview 32863, Virtual History Archive, USC Shoah Foundation, Kingston PA, 1997.

16. Jack Rosenthal, interview 1072, Virtual History Archive, USC Shoah Foundation, Roslyn, NY, 1994. See also Interview with Jack Rosenthal by the author, 11 January 2007.
17. Wiesel, *Night,* 50–51, 71–72.
18. Anton Mason (Anton Meisner), interview 45764, Virtual History Archive, USC Shoah Foundation, Manalapan, FL, 1998. Another boy, Abby Weiner, was also in this group. Interview with Abby Weiner by the author, 14 November 2012.
19. Alex Moskovic, interview 11302, Virtual History Archive, USC Shoah Foundation, Hobe Sound, FL, 1996. See also interview with Alex Moskovic by the author, 2 June 2005; interview for Kinderblock 66, April 2010, Hotel Elephant, Weimar, Germany.
20. Phone interview with Paul Kassy (Kaszovitz) by the author, 8 May 2011; Ken Waltzer to Paul Kassy, 11 May 2011. See also Ken Waltzer to Stephan Guttman, 1 June 2011; phone interview with Stephan Guttman in Basel, Switzerland, by the author, 28 July 2011.
21. Louis Weitzen's daughter, Misty Tzugaris, provided invaluable information and leads about Lajos Weitzen. Misty Tzugaris e-mails 6 March, 3 May, 5 May 2012; Ken Waltzer to Misty Tzugaris, 3–4 March and 5–6 May 2012. Julius Moskowits, interview 4351, Virtual History Archive, USC Shoah Foundation. Toronto, Canada, 1995.
22. Alex Gross, *Yankele,* 63.
23. Sam Cin, interview 17077, Virtual History Archive, USC Shoah Foundation, Skokie, I, 1996.
24. Sol Culang (Szlama Zulang), interview 3808, Virtual History Archive, USC Shoah Foundation, Los Angeles, CA, 1995.
25. Interview with Samuel Isakovitch by David Boder, 30 July 1946, Voices of the Holocaust Archive, Illinois Institute of Technology, http://voices.iit.edu/interview?doc=isakovitchS&display=isakovitchS_en.
26. Alexander Berkowits (Srulik Bercovics), interview 13792, Virtual History Archive, USC Shoah Foundation, Winnipeg, Canada, 1996.
27. Wiesel, *Night,* 101.
28. Samuel Isakovitch with David Boder, 30 July 1946, Voices of the Holocaust Archive, Illinois Institute of Technology, http://voices.iit.edu/interview?doc=isakovitchS&display=isakovitchS_en.
29. Wiesel, *Night,* 101.
30. Block assignments are identified on List of 3935 Victims from Auschwitz in Buchenwald on 26 January 1945, record group: M.8.ITS, subsection: M.8.ITS.BD, file no.: BU 17; original file no.: GCC 2/181 I B / 9, ITS Archive.
31. Sigmund Weiser, interview 17919, Virtual History Archive. USC Shoah Foundation, Staten Island, NY, 1996.
32. Sigmund Weiser, interview 17919, Virtual History Archive, USC Shoah Foundation, Staten Island, NY, 1996.
33. Weiser, interview 17919, USC Shoah Foundation; Samuel Isakovitch with David Boder, 30 July 1946, Voices of the Holocaust Archive, http://voices.iit.edu/interview?doc=isakovitchS&display=isakovitchS_en.
34. Kenneth Waltzer, "Abraham Gottlieb's Buchenwald Diary" (paper presented at the 44th Association of Jewish Studies Conference, Chicago, 18 December 2012). Gottlieb's unpublished diary, "A Human Being at Buchenwald," is an important eyewitness document on the final months in Buchenwald and on the *Kinderblock*.
35. Alex Gross says he could not find a permanent place in the block but went there repeatedly.
36. Harry Fischman, interview 39977, Virtual History Archive, USC Shoah Foundation, Los Angeles, CA, 1998.

37. See entry for "Halberstadt-Langenstein-Zwieberge" ("Malachit," "BII") in *U.S. Holocaust Memorial Museum Encyclopedia of Camps and Ghettos, 1933–1945*, ed. Geoffrey Megargee (Bloomington: Indiana University Press, 2009), 1:357–60.
38. Ibid., 358.
39. See entry for "Eschershausen" ("Stein") and also for "Holzen" ("Hecht") by Therkel Straede, in *U.S. Holocaust Memorial Museum Encyclopedia of Camps and Ghettos, 1933–1945*, ed. Geoffrey Megargee (Bloomington: Indiana University Press, 2009), 1:339–41. See also Catalogue of the Permanent Exhibition, Place of Remembrance of Forced Labor in the Volkswagen Factory, which opened in 1999 on the site of the Wolfsburg plant.
40. See entry for "Ohrdruf" ("SIII") by Christin Schmidt van der Zenden, in *U.S. Holocaust Memorial Museum Encyclopedia of Camps and Ghettos, 1933–1945*, ed. Geoffrey Megargee (Bloomington: Indiana University Press, 2009), 1:402–4.
41. Transport List of Prisoners to Aussenkommando Halberstadt ("Malachyt") 9 February 1945, doc. no. 5318265#1–5318269#1 (0183-0356/0300/00063@1.1.5.1 to 0183-0356/0300/00068@1.1.5.1), ITS Archives.
42. Transport List of Prisoners to Aussenkommando Ohrdruf ("Slll"), 14 February 1945, doc. no. 5320505#1–5320509#2 (/0183-0356/0312/0191@1.1.5.1 to 0183-0356/0312/0194@1.1.5.1, ITS Archives.
43. Sam Cin, interview 17077, Virtual History Archive, USC Shoah Foundation, Skokie, IL, 1996; Emil Weiss, interview 46612, Virtual History Archive, USC Shoah Foundation, Encino, CA, 1998.
44. Max Sands (Max Salamonovics), interview 849, Virtual History Archive, USC Shoah Foundation, Westwood, CA, 1995.
45. Max Sands, interview 849. David Fiszl described Langenstein-Zwieberge as "a death trap" and said, "We worked inside a tunnel, never seeing daylight." Paul Gottesman from Uzhurod recalled moving equipment and carrying heavy materials. See David Fiszl, interview 8003, Virtual History Archive, USC Shoah Foundation, Des Moines, IA, 1995, and Paul Gottesman, intervciew 43171, Virtual History Archive, USC Shoah Foundation, N. Hollywood, CA, 1998.
46. Letter from Victor (Zeev) Borger, 26 May 2011 to Dr. Irena Steinfeld, Director, Department of the Righteous, Yad Vashem (copy to the author); Alexander Berkowits (Srulik Bercovics), interview 13792, Virtual History Archive, USC Shoah Foundation, 1996.
47. Wiesel, *Night*, 114–115.
48. Julius Moskowitz (Gyula Moskovics), interview 4351, Virtual History Archive, USC Shoah Foundation, Toronto, Canada, 1995.
49. Elmer Luchterhand, "Prisoner Behavior and Social System in the Nazi Camp," *International Journal of Psychiatry* 13 (1967): 245–64.
50. Shamai Davidson, "Human Reciprocity among the Jewish Prisoners in the Nazi Concentration Camps," in *The Nazi Concentration Camps* (Jerusalem: Yad Vashem, 1984), 555–72; also Shamai Davidson, "Group Formation and Human Reciprocity in the Nazi Concentration Camps," in *Holding on to Humanity—The Message of Holocaust Survivors: The Shamai Davidson Papers,* ed. Israel Charney (New York: New York University Press, 1992), 121–42.
51. Alex Moskovic, conversation with the author, October 2012.
52. See Wiesel, *Night*, 113; see Eva Fogelman, "The Role of Group Experiences in the Healing Process of Massive Childhood Holocaust Trauma," *Journal of Applied Psychoanalytic Studies* 4, no. 1 (January 2002): 31–47. "We became like brothers," Sigmund Weiser recalled of his days at Ambloy and Taverny with the OSE in France. Weiser, interview 17919, Virtual History Archive, USC Shoah Foundation, Staten Island, NY, 1996.

Bibliography

Caplan, Jane, and Nikolaus Wachsmann, eds. *Concentration Camps in Nazi Germany: The New Histories*. New York: Routledge, 2010.
Davidson, Shamai. "Group Formation and Human Reciprocity in the Nazi Concentration Camps." In *Holding on to Humanity—The Message of Holocaust Survivors: The Shamai Davidson Papers*, ed. Israel Charney, 121–42. New York: New York University Press, 1992.
———. "Human Reciprocity among the Jewish Prisoners in the Nazi Concentration Camps." In *The Nazi Concentration Camps* (Jerusalem: Yad Vashem, 1984), 555–72.
Fogelman, Eva. "The Role of Group Experiences in the Healing Process of Massive Childhood Holocaust Trauma." *Journal of Applied Psychoanalytic Studies* 4, no. 1 (January 2002): 31–47.
Gross, Alex. *Yankele: A Holocaust Survivor's Bittersweet Memoir*. Landham, MD: University Press of America, 2002.
"Halberstadt-Langenstein-Zwieberge" ("Malachit," "BII"). In *U.S. Holocaust Memorial Museum Encyclopedia of Camps and Ghettos, 1933–1945*, ed. Geoffrey Megargee, 1:357–60. Bloomington: Indiana University Press, 2009.
Levi, Primo. *Survival in Auschwitz*. New York: Touchstone, 1995.
Luchterhand, Elmer. "Prisoner Behavior and Social System in the Nazi Camp." *International Journal of Psychiatry* 13 (1967): 245–64.
Schmidt van der Zenden, Christin. "Ohrdruf" ("SIII"). In *U.S. Holocaust Memorial Museum Encyclopedia of Camps and Ghettos, 1933–1945*, ed. Geoffrey Megargee, 1:402–4. Bloomington: Indiana University Press, 2009.
Sofsky, Wolfgang. *The Order of Terror: The Concentration Camp*. Translated by William Templer. Princeton, NJ: Princeton University Press, 1999.
Straede, Therkel. "Eschershausen" ("Stein"). In *U.S. Holocaust Memorial Museum Encyclopedia of Camps and Ghettos, 1933–1945*, ed. Geoffrey Megargee, 1:339–40. Bloomington: Indiana University Press, 2009.
Straede, Therkel. "Holzen" ("Hecht"). In *U.S. Holocaust Memorial Museum Encyclopedia of Camps and Ghettos, 1933-1945*, ed. Geoffrey Megargee, 1: 340-41. Bloomington: Indiana University Press, 2009.
Waltzer, Kenneth. "Abraham Gottlieb's Buchenwald Diary." Paper presented at the 44th Association of Jewish Studies Conference, Chicago, December 18, 2012.
Wiesel, Elie. *Night*. New York: Farrar, Straus & Giroux, 2006.
———. *And the Sea Is Never Full*. New York: Knopf, 1999.
———. *All Rivers Run to the Sea*. New York: Knopf, 1995.

Chapter 4

Dehumanizing the Dead
The Destruction of Thessaloniki's Jewish Cemetery

Leon Saltiel

In December 1942, three months before the deportations of the Jews of Thessaloniki began, a rare event in the history of Nazi-occupied Europe took place: the destruction of the vast and ancient Jewish cemetery of Thessaloniki. The Nazis lacked a consistent policy regarding Jewish cemeteries, and as Carla Hesse and Thomas W. Laqueur point out, "In general, the Nazis did not systematically direct their fury against bones and monuments. All of Europe's major Jewish cemeteries—except for that of Thessaloniki—survived the Holocaust more or less intact. This includes those in the very heart of National Socialism."[1] The same can be said for all other Jewish cemeteries in Greece that survived the war.

The old Jewish cemetery of Thessaloniki was probably the largest Jewish necropolis in Europe, numbering nearly 500,000 graves and covering an area of 350,000 square meters (86.5 acres)—a powerful symbol of the centuries-old Jewish presence in the city. Initially outside of the city walls, the cemetery became a central area as the city expanded eastward. Its vast area gradually inhibited local transportation, and residents would complain that it attracted illegal and immoral activities in the late hours.

Beginning in 1919, various city plans aimed to transform the area into a park and, later, into the main campus of Aristotle University of Thessaloniki, by relocating the cemetery outside the city boundaries. This issue was a cause of friction between the Greek authorities and the 50,000-strong Jewish community in this city of 250,000 residents. Using religious and political arguments, the Jews managed to delay this discussion.

In 1937, a law was adopted that gave part of the cemetery land to the university, while the rest of the area would be turned into a park, with the existing tombs remaining untouched.[2] Burials in the old cemetery would be prohibited after one year. Although a part was indeed given to the university, burials on the remaining land continued, and a park was never created.

This essay will show how the destruction of the cemetery—not directly linked to the Nazi "Final Solution"—nevertheless set the stage for the events that were put in motion a few weeks later. It is not a coincidence that writing a few months after the destruction of the cemetery, Yomtov Yacoel, legal counsel for the Jewish community and one of its leaders at the time, called it "the harbinger" of the community's general destruction.[3]

Call for Slave Labor

The first major anti-Semitic measure after the German army occupied Thessaloniki in April 1941 was the compulsory assembly of all Jewish males in Liberty Square on Saturday, 11 July 1942, to mobilize for forced labor. The "Black Sabbath," as it came to be known, saw approximately eighty-five hundred Jewish men aged eighteen to forty-five go through humiliating gymnastics under a blistering sun. German soldiers beat those unlucky Jews who arrived late, smoked, or dared to sit down.[4] The purpose for forcibly drafting such a labor force was mainly for construction work, overseen by the Todt organization.

This measure was an initiative on the part of German military headquarters based in Thessaloniki "at the suggestion of the Department of Administration and Economy"[5] and "originat[ed] neither from Berlin nor from the Eichmann Referat [Department]."[6] The focus on the Jews may have been triggered by Colonel Athanassios Chrysochoou, an important and well-connected senior member of the Greek regional administration, who complained to the Germans that "the Jews—in contrast to the large part of the population—are not obliged to carry out labor work or provide contributions in kind."[7]

In the following weeks and until the end of August 1942, some thirty-five hundred Jewish men were drafted and sent to different parts of Greece to build roads, railways, and airports and to work in mines. Most of them had never been employed in heavy construction and were far from qualified. Many suffered under a harsh regime of hard labor and limited food and hygiene, and when the first bodies were returned to Thessaloniki, there was outrage in the Jewish community.[8]

The hardships increased as winter approached. The community's legal counsel, Yomtov Yacoel, visited different sites on 1 October and saw firsthand the miserable conditions of the laborers. Approximately one hundred Jews may have died by then.[9] Upon conclusion of Yacoel's visit, Ioannis Miller, the Greek German civilian contractor in charge of most of the work projects, proposed replacing Jewish forced laborers with qualified Greek Christian ones, whose salaries would be paid by the Jewish community.

On 13 October, a first meeting took place in the basement of Matanoth Laevionim, the community's soup kitchen, between the community elders and Dr. Maximilian Merten, the 31-year-old German officer in charge of civilian affairs. The amount Merten proposed for the replacement of the Jewish workers with other laborers was three to five billion drachmas. The only hitch in the plan was the great sum of money requested, to be paid in such a short amount of time.

At the second meeting with the community leadership, on 15 October, Merten approved a deal of 2 billion in cash, but added a new stipulation: the destruction of Thessaloniki's old Jewish cemetery, whose land he valued at 1.5 billion drachmas.[10]

Negotiations over the Cemetery

Merten's new demand caught the community leaders off guard and left them with little room for maneuver. The demand for the cemetery in addition to the ransom for the release of the Jewish laborers further complicated the discussions. Although he had been in Thessaloniki for just a few months, Merten quickly realized that the cemetery was a "wedge issue" between the Greek authorities and the Jewish community. Merten must have been informed from his briefings with the Greek authorities that according to Jewish tradition, a cemetery can never be destroyed. Nevertheless, he showed no signs of compromise, and the Jewish leaders were left with no choice.

On 17 October 1942, a protocol was signed between the community and Merten. "Dr. Merten left after he bid farewell to each of the members of the central committee with a handshake."[11] At eight o'clock the next morning, Yacoel and community officials went to work preparing the lists of community members and the amounts each should pay to raise the two billion needed.[12] A letter sent from the German military administration summarized the agreement:

> For the rest of the 1.5 billion drachmas, the religious [Jewish] community of Saloniki has put at our disposal the Jewish cemetery located in Saloniki itself, which in the past had obstructed the organic development of Saloniki, and which at any rate would have to disappear in the interest of public order and safety in Saloniki. This measure resolves a problem that has preoccupied Greek public opinion for many years.[13]

A few days later, a letter was sent from the governor general of Macedonia to the Jewish community:

> [The document] called the Jewish community to, on the one hand, collaborate with the municipality for the relocation of the Jewish cemeteries and, on the other, to cooperate for the organization of two new Jewish cemeteries. ... Moreover, it specified a very brief deadline for the implementation of the orders, under the threat of demolition of the [old] cemeteries by the municipality, and removal of the materials from [funerary] monuments. At the same time, burials in the old cemeteries were immediately forbidden.[14]

The community rushed to implement these decisions—collection of the two billion drachmas and relocation of the cemetery—while coordinating the release of the slave laborers. At the end of November, the community set up a committee to oversee the issue of the cemetery, chaired by Chief Rabbi Zvi Koretz.

The German military authorities transmitted their orders to the Greek governor Vassilios Simonidis, making him responsible for the demolition of the old cemetery and the preparation of the two new sites. In a follow-up letter dated 28 November 1942, Merten instructed Simonidis: "A proposal for the establishment of a second substitute cemetery has to be handed in within a week. ... We have to begin immediately with the flattening of the old cemetery." Merten concluded his letter with a strong warning to Simonidis: "The immediate execution of this order is an obligation. Delays in the work will be punished by the occupying power."[15]

In order to implement all these orders on the practical level, a first meeting took place at city hall, to be followed by another the next day, on 3 December 1942. The meeting, chaired by German commissioner of civilian affairs Bohlke, brought together senior officials from the office of the governor general of Macedonia, the municipality of Thessaloniki, and the Jewish community to discuss the implementation of the issued orders.

> Dr. Koretz raised objections ... and requested that, if possible, the graves of the old [existing] cemetery remain intact, according to the understanding up until now. If this is not possible, the deadline should be extended so that the Jewish community or its members could transfer the remains and memorial stones to the new cemeteries. However, Commissioner Bohlke clearly stressed that the orders of the military administration explicitly command the flattening of the old Jewish cemetery, and no one is in the position to bring about the slightest modification.[16]

The exchange of letters and the official minutes of the meetings clearly show that the German officers were directing the whole project. The Greek authorities proposed no modifications and were tasked with the implementation of the decisions. The only voice against the plans came from Chief Rabbi Koretz, who tried to buy more time but was quickly dismissed. Yacoel provides us with an insight into what probably took place at the 3 December meeting, which the official minutes did not record:

> Wasn't the senior technical employee of the governor general heard saying, even in the presence of German officers, that the chief rabbi's request—for a delay of a few months in the demolition work on account of winter—should be rebutted, for its aim was to gain time until the British came to the assistance of the Jews?[17]

Yacoel was not present at the meeting, but a community participant communicated this information to him. His account of the engineer's hostile stance and hateful words showed how much it resonated with the Jewish leaders. The engineer, Athanassios Broikos, played a central role in the issue during the following months. His background and ideological leanings will be discussed in detail later on.

Destruction of the Cemetery

The destruction process of the vast Jewish necropolis began on 6 December 1942, marked by a meeting of Merten, Simonidis, Koretz, and others on the cemetery grounds.[18] Rabbi Michael Molho, who had studied the ancient cemetery, was an eyewitness and wrote an account of what took place.[19]

Molho identified several tombs of significant historical value. Mihail Almeidas, the general secretary of the Greek governor, argued for a complete expropriation of the land, while representatives of the Jewish community pleaded to safeguard as much of the ancient cemetery as possible. Listening to both sides, Merten decided to expropriate the part of the old cemetery adjacent to the university and populated areas and to leave the rest intact. Even if Merten's new position seemed to be a compromise, in reality it was just an effort to temporarily appease the Jewish community, while ultimately maintaining his previous firm stance. As Merten was entering his car, the Greek authorities gave the order to demolish everything, even the historic and recent graves.

Five hundred workers were reportedly hired for the task, with the municipality spending around 100 million drachmas for the destruction of the graves and the gathering of the materials in piles.[20] Both Yacoel and Molho noted the remarkable speed and zeal the workers showed in their task. "It is obvious from the haste and excessive enthusiasm shown by the Greek authorities that it was not just beautification of the city that motivated the authorities to quickly demolish the Jewish monuments."[21] Greek archaeologists were present to catalogue the few tombstones with Greek or Latin inscriptions.

In just a couple of weeks, wrote Molho, "the vast necropolis, scattered with fragments of stone and rubble, resembled a city that had been bombed or destroyed by a volcanic eruption."[22] As the workers destroyed the cemetery, local Jews ran to save the remains of their loved ones.[23]

On 23 December 1942, the Thessaloniki municipal council, sitting in a special session, adopted decision 507, which rubber-stamped the decisions of the 3 December meeting and formally handed over two plots of municipal land to the Jewish community to serve as future burial grounds. What followed this decision is a revealing discussion among the city council members on the ownership of the land and materials.[24]

Some council members opposed the municipality's provision of the two new parcels of land, since the area of the old cemetery would become state rather than city property. The main council member behind this opposition was Periklis Garofallou, the brother-in-law of Sotirios Gotzamanis, the high-profile finance minister of the collaborationist government in Athens at the time.[25] Garofallou argued, "We must think what we are going to ask in exchange. I am of the opinion that we have to ask for part of the plot that is liberated by the demolition of the old Jewish cemeteries." Mayor Konstantinos Merkouriou agreed and proposed that either the state reimburse the municipality or the municipality become owner of the land from the old Jewish cemetery. City engineer Georgios Malakis responded that it was the municipality's responsibility to provide its citizens with burial grounds. At the end of the meeting, the city council members deputized the city's legal counsel to examine, "posthaste," whether the municipality could lay claim to the old cemetery land and, if not, what it should receive from the state in exchange for the loss of the two new parcels.[26]

In his response on 18 May 1943, legal counsel Petros Iatropoulos argued that the municipality had neither legal title over the Jewish cemetery land nor the right to reclaim the site. The holiness of the site should not be compromised because, according to Jewish law, the removal of remains is prohibited. Last but not least, he argued that Jewish communities were responsible for their cemeteries, not municipalities.[27] The efforts by the city for expropriation of the land in exchange for the two new locations were eventually put on hold on 11 June 1943, following the opinion of legal counsel and the fact that "almost all the Jews [have] departed from our city."[28]

A few weeks after the destruction of the cemetery, the Jews of Thessaloniki were forced into ghettos, from which they were transported to the Nazi death camp in Auschwitz, Poland. The cemetery grounds became in effect a huge quarry. The Germans, the church, the city, associations, and theaters used the marble stones and bricks as construction materials. On 14 October 1943, the grounds of the old cemetery were formally registered as a public domain, and the land came into the possession of the Greek state.[29] However, due to its vast size and the number of graves, as well as limited means, destruction of the cemetery was not completed during the war, but continued after the liberation. Aristotle University of Thessaloniki, which is built on this land, thus became "owner of an exceptional plot, for its future use."[30]

Tombstones as Building Materials

As the cemetery was being demolished, its marble stones and bricks became a commodity that was much in demand, serving to build and repair many public and private buildings, including churches, and even serving for the needs of the German military cemetery. A modern visitor to Thessaloniki can still see stones with Hebrew inscriptions in parks and churchyards. Molho describes what happened to the materials:

> The memorial stones remain piled up, mixed up, in the old necropolis. They are at the disposal of the first passerby. The marble merchants enrich their stock, delete the inscriptions and use the marble in various ways. Churches pave their courtyards with them. They are used to adorn and repair nearby houses. Some schools pave their courtyards, without even caring to erase the visible signs that betray the origin. The Nazis take them to construct a swimming pool. The whole city is full of them, and the price of marble has fallen

on the market.... [After the war,] the plunder continues, and the venerable cemetery is transformed into a big marble quarry, supplying all buildings.[31]

The authority that was initially in charge of the materials was the office of the governor general of Macedonia, particularly the public works division. Its work was supervised by the German military headquarters, which often had the last word and which eventually took over in June 1944.[32] The municipality, the church, and other agencies would play the role of intermediary.

In early March 1943, the office of the governor general approved the municipality's request for one hundred thousand bricks from the demolished Jewish cemetery "for the needs of the municipality."[33]

The children's soup kitchens of the Ioannidis School and the sailing club also requested building materials from the old Jewish cemetery. The Ioannidis School received fifty thousand bricks and one hundred square meters of marble "destined for the construction of toilets for the use of the children using the soup kitchen."[34]

The sailing club wrote to the city council, informing it of the creation in February 1942 of a soup kitchen to feed 250 poor children:

> For the better operation of the soup kitchen, a pavilion is required to house the small children using the soup kitchen, because it is not possible to house them in a closed space and because both in winter and summer the food is distributed outdoors, and the danger of catching cold in the winter and sunstroke in summer is obvious.

They had already received thirty thousand bricks from the Jewish cemetery for the said pavilion and were asking for more materials.[35]

When the State Theater of Thessaloniki was established in August 1943, "the director of the theater addressed the German administration, which responded willingly, and after a few days Theatre Square was laid with marble originating from the Jewish cemetery."[36] On 6 November 1943, a tender was held "for the processing and paving of the sidewalk in front of the National Theater [utilizing] 250 square meters of plaques measuring fifty by fifty centimeters from marble from the ex-Jewish cemeteries."[37]

The nearby Christian cemetery of Agia Fotini also used materials from the destroyed Jewish cemetery. On 15 May 1943, the municipality decided to build a small chapel, parts of which were constructed "with marble from the old Jewish cemeteries being demolished."[38] In early 1944, it requested marble, stones, and bricks "necessary for the continuing work on this cemetery (fence, buildings, courtyards, etc.)." This arrangement was beneficial for the municipality, since "the cemeteries service believes that the municipality is going to profit severalfold from the value of these useful and necessary materials, charged only with the transport and processing of the marble and other materials."

Similar requests also came from churches. Ritzaleos counted seventeen such requests from churches in Thessaloniki between 16 January 1943—two months before the start of the deportations—and 18 October 1943. Church councils would either make requests for the materials directly to the public works division of the governor general of Macedonia or through the bishop, who would forward the request a few days after receipt, with the aforementioned division approving it a few weeks later. The reasons offered varied from the "need to expand the church" to "future paving."[39]

Some churches may have made their demands directly to the German city authorities. That seems to be the case with the Church of Kimisseos Theotokou (Dormition of Mary) in the Saranta Ekklision Quarter, which bordered the cemetery area. The office of Thessaloniki's German mayor, Dr. Blessing, approved the head of the church council's request—dated 20 September 1943 and asking for six hundred square meters of marble for the floor of the church[40]—on 1 October 1943.[41]

Detailed examination of the fate of the tombstones demonstrates a cold, indifferent approach by the local Greek Christian population, without regard for the holiness and symbolism of the location. It should be noted that the destruction of sacred space has a long tradition in that region and that the cemetery had come to symbolize certain problematic relations between Christians and Jews, with the Christians aiming to "Hellenize" the city[42] and often identifying the Jews with the former Ottoman rulers. Yet the seemingly organized and legal manner in which the plundering of the cemetery materials was conducted is comparable to the plundering and distribution of Jewish property during the same period. The stones became an object of both necessity and greed, coupled with elements of convenience and anti-Semitism. The Jewish community, even as it was undergoing ghettoization and deportation, was present at the beginning of this process and able to witness the fate of its ancestors.

Many actors were involved in the plunder of the cemetery—the state, the municipality, the church, local associations, and businessmen—with complex relations and competing roles, all aided by the lack of a clear hierarchy. The Germans kept overall control, while the office of the governor general would designate, on behalf of the Greek state, the agency responsible for the land of the former Jewish cemetery and its materials. The responsible government agency changed several times during the occupation.[43] The municipality would execute some of the ensuing orders, such as designating funds for the transfer of the tombstones, regulating their allocation, and paying the guards for the site. Other institutions would appeal to these actors to get a share of the materials, depending on their access or influence.

Moral considerations are nowhere to be found during this act. On the contrary, its destruction continued even after the war. In July 1946, a Jewish delegation to Thessaloniki, which included Dr. Cecil Roth, reader of Jewish studies at Oxford University, "saw carts in the cemetery removing Hebrew tombstones, on the instructions of the Director of Antiquities for the province,"[44] and visited the church of Saint Demetrius to witness repair work done using the said tombstones. They contacted Stylianos Pelekanidis, the curator of Byzantine antiquities for northern Greece, and the main person responsible for the church's restoration. He saw only the holy and positive sides of his actions: use of the marble "for such holy work as the reconstruction of St. Demetrius Church" was even a positive action, considering that "stones from the Jewish cemetery had been ... used for all sorts of purposes, even for pavements and toilets." He also blamed the Jews for not indicating to his service the tombstones of historical value prior to the deportations and offered additional legalistic excuses, arguing that the Jewish community had no property deeds.[45] According to another report, Pelekanidis "expressed amazement at Jewish protests against the use of the stones in a church. He claimed that some of the stones, those with Greek and Roman inscriptions, had originally been stolen from Christian graves,"[46] although these constituted a very small percentage compared to the total number of tombstones.

The Main Actors

Yacoel writes that "satisfaction of a long-standing demand on the part of Christian public opinion led to the Germans becoming involved in this non-military, purely political issue."[47] Indeed, "the rapidity and purposefulness with which the vast 350,000-square-meter Jewish cemetery was destroyed, the fact that its bones were left in the ground, and that all traces of its existence are lost to contemporary memory,"[48] as well as the fate of its tombstones, all point in one direction. There were also no official reactions to this act of sacrilege, similar to the silence during the Liberty Square events.

Senior Greek leaders at the time of the German occupation openly stated that the people's wish was to move the cemetery to another location. Colonel Chrysochoou, testifying as a defense witness at Merten's trial in 1959, said, "It was a general request of the Christians of Thessaloniki for the cemetery to leave the city center and go further away, because it was now next to houses."[49] Governor general of Macedonia Vassilios Simonidis described the destruction of the cemetery as a "big beautification project, which will by and large have a beneficial influence on the development of the city."[50]

Merten told the assembled Jewish community elders during their second meeting in the soup kitchen basement, "Many here are your enemies and repeatedly lobby the German military administration for the destruction of the cemeteries and for the implementation of anti-Semitic measures."[51]

Chrysochoou went further and testified during Merten's trial that "the destruction of the cemetery was celebrated as a huge benefit," prompting the reporting journalist to add that this phrase stirred "emotions among the audience."[52] Yacoel provided similar information. "Besides, it became known that Christian representatives visited the German military commander to thank him on behalf of the city's Greek population for the definitive solution of this issue."[53] Furthermore, in reply to the presiding judge's question, "Could you now tell us who dug it up and sold its marbles?" Chrysochoou stated, "It was said that what we wanted to do, we did through Merten."[54]

When pushed by the prosecutor, Merten stated in a "coarse manner" that "the cemetery was destroyed by the Greeks for two reasons: to get rid of it, because it was next to their houses, and to take the [gold] teeth of the dead."[55]

The person in the Greek administration who was in charge of the cemetery's destruction was chief engineer Athanassios Broikos, working under Macedonia's governor general. Molho pointed to "city engineer P. [meaning B.]" as the "main instigator of this vandalism."[56] He added:

> An architect—one who apparently was not very concerned by his official duties, sought new endeavors, and often visited the offices of *Befehlshaber* [Commander] Baelke,[57] Abteilung Militärverwaltung Saloniki-Aegae [Military Administration, Department of Salonika-Aegean]—was the most active protagonist of the definitive destruction of the big Jewish necropolis.[58]

In his chronicle of the city's history, Kostas Tomanas squarely names Broikos as the main actor: "On 6 December [1942], following a proposal by engineer Athanassios Broikos, the destruction of the Jewish cemeteries commenced, which extended to the whole area where the university installations are today."[59]

In referring to the engineer, Molho used an erroneous first initial, while Yacoel provided no name at all. It could be that neither of them remembered his name at the time of writing or that they were both cautious not to provide it, due to a fear of a lawsuit or possible intimidation. Under normal circumstances, such a position is plainly bureaucratic, and very few people can name such an official. However, Broikos was not a random person; indeed he was very well connected with the city leadership.

Born around 1900, Broikos studied civil engineering in Switzerland and did his Ph.D. at the University of Thessaloniki. He continued his studies in Mussolini's Italy in 1939, a year before the Greek-Italian war. He returned to Thessaloniki where, between 1940 and 1945, he served as a public works engineer with the governor general of Macedonia, in charge of, inter alia, "17 excavators."[60]

We have already discussed Yacoel's description of the attitude of the engineer, who was most probably Broikos, while attending the city hall meeting of 3 December chaired by Bohlke. It was Broikos who openly opposed Koretz's request for a postponement of the cemetery demolition due to winter. The Jewish participant who related the discussion to Yacoel conveyed Broikos's hostile stance and anti-British attitude.[61] We can also glean hints from this about his ideological leanings.

An example of Broikos's standing in the Thessaloniki society of the time is his participation on the board of the State Theater of Thessaloniki. In the first months of 1943, amid fears that the Bulgarians were trying to bring a theatrical group to Thessaloniki for propaganda reasons, Bishop Gennadios and Governor General Simonidis took the initiative to establish a Greek theater. The first board of the theater consisted of Broikos, together with Stilpon Kyriakidis, Alexandros Letsas, Giannis Vasdravelis, and Dimitrios Panou.[62] Most of them were the founding leaders of the Society for Macedonian Studies[63] and part of the city's Greek elite.[64]

Broikos was accountable to Governor General Simonidis, the most senior Greek official in the region, whose role is quite controversial given that he was a key facilitator of German commands. Hesse and Laqueur conclude:

> The story of the destruction of the Jewish cemetery from the landscape of modern Thessaloniki lies ... in the temporal convergence of three narratives: that of the Holocaust; that of modernization and a shift in the places of the dead away from the living; and finally that of Greek national integration. Nowhere else, in no other great city, did the imperatives of modernity and of nation-building telescope so decisively with the crisis of occupation and genocide.[65]

The timing of the destruction of the Jewish cemetery of Thessaloniki, three months before the deportations, serves as a unique case study to examine the status of the Jewish community at this crucial historical juncture. The main initiators against the local Jews were the local Germans, acting without any instructions or involvement from Berlin, and with the contribution of local Greek Christians. Consequently, and although unrelated to the "Final Solution," the deliberations on the fate of the cemetery served as a bridge between these two periods and helped prepare the ground for what was to come next.

As the anti-Semitic measures were multiplying and intensifying, the Jews felt like a separate element in the city, more isolated than ever before, whose plight did not concern the Greek Christian majority.[66] The destruction of the cemetery made them realize that they had few friends to side with them. Yacoel must have understood this when he concluded his diary for 1942 with the following sentence: "[It is in] ... the above atmosphere of anxiety and fear for the future [that] the end of the year 1942 and the beginning of 1943 finds the Jewry of Thessaloniki."[67]

The presence of the Germans accelerated developments that had been in motion for decades, but hidden just below the surface. They were the enablers and catalysts who were responding to a local demand and willing to accommodate certain wishes of the local Greek Christian population and its leaders. They had the main role in all of the events, issuing the orders, chairing the meetings, and even regulating the allocation of tombstones.

During this time, there were no official reactions from the Greek authorities or the Christian population for either the Liberty Square events, the forced labor, or the destruction of the cemetery. In a certain way, the extensive use of the tombstones from the destroyed cemetery by all sectors of Thessaloniki's society, including the church, gave this action a sense of legality and invited every ordinary citizen to participate. Parts of the cemetery were already in ruins when the plunder of Jewish property started days before the deportations began. The role of the city's Greek Christian elite during this period is crucial: in their *realpolitik* view of the situation, they realized that the Germans were their best bet to safeguard and promote what they considered their priorities at the time. Helping the Jews was not at the top of the list.

Yacoel and Molho were aware of this reality, hinting at it in their books, yet they stopped short of pointing fingers. Yacoel, writing from a safe house in 1943, and Molho, from Buenos Aires in the 1950s, both refrained from naming the people who did not help the community in its time of need or who even exploited it in its distress. Why did they decide not to record these names?

Two months before Eichmann's men, Dieter Wisliceny and Alois Brunner, arrived in Thessaloniki to execute the Nazi Final Solution, the city's Jews saw their historic cemetery destroyed by an alignment of interests, ideology, and a disoriented moral compass. The Jews lost their connections to their roots just as they themselves were about to be uprooted. They were met with neglect, indifference, and—worse— hostility by the authorities, the same people who should have protected them during those difficult times. And as we now know, their fate had already been sealed.

Leon Saltiel is a Ph.D. candidate of contemporary Greek history at the University of Macedonia, in Thessaloniki, Greece, with a focus on the Holocaust of the Jews of Thessaloniki. Leon was a Fulbright Scholar at Georgetown University, earning a master's degree in foreign service. He has received fellowships, among others, from the German Marshall Fund, Yad Vashem, and the Institute for the Study of Diplomacy. During 2013–14, he curated the exhibit entitled "Salonika: Epicenter of the Destruction of the Jews of Greece" at the Paris Mémorial de la Shoah.

Notes

A fuller version of this essay was published in *Yad Vashem Studies* 42, no. 1 (2014): 11–46. I want to thank the journal's anonymous reviewers and editors as well as this volume's referees and editors for their comments and edits, which significantly improved the content of the article. This article contains some new information since its first publication. If not otherwise indicated, translations are by the author.

1. Carla Hesse and Thomas W. Laqueur, "Visible and Invisible Bodies: The Erasure of the Jewish Cemetery from the Life of Modern Thessaloniki," in *The Production of the Social Body* [in Greek], ed. Martha Mihailidou and Alexandra Halkia (Athens: Katarti, 2005), 45. Several other smaller Jewish cemeteries in Europe were desecrated or destroyed by the Nazis, specifically in German-occupied Poland, where this practice was more common, such as Plaszow in Krakow.
2. Law 890 of 11 October 1937 (*Government Gazette,* no. 394, issue A, 13 October 1937).
3. Yomtov Yacoel, *Memoirs 1941–1943* [in Greek] (Thessaloniki: Paratiritis, 1993), 88.
4. Ibid., 58.
5. Report of 30 October 1942, Bundesarchiv/Militararchiv RW 29/109.
6. Hans Safrian, *Eichmann's Men* (Cambridge: Cambridge University Press in association with USHMM, 2010), 153.
7. Hagen Fleischer, *Crown and Swastika: Greece during the Occupation and the Resistance 1941–1944* [in Greek] (Athens: Papazisis, 1995), 303–4. However, I have not been able to cross-reference it or find the original source.
8. Yacoel, *Memoirs,* 63.
9. Ibid., 71.
10. For comparison, in December 1942, the daily salary of an ordinary worker was 3,000 drachmas and that of an artisan 5,000. The municipality paid Jews in forced labor in its road cleaning department 1,000 drachmas a day. So two billion drachmas amounted to around seven hundred thousand daily salaries for an ordinary worker. Thessaloniki History Center, General Records of the City of Thessaloniki, 1943, f. 6, sub. 2, Division of Technical Services.

11. Yacoel, *Memoirs*, 76.
12. The narration so far is based on Yacoel, *Memoirs*, 61–83.
13. Pramann to several, 18 October 1942, Testimony of Max Merten at the Eichmann Trial, Israel State Archives, 40-14-2-10.
14. Yacoel, *Memoirs*, 84.
15. Merten to Simonidis, 28 November 1942, Testimony of Max Merten at the Eichmann Trial, Israel State Archives, 40-14-3-10.
16. *Minutes of the Municipal Council*, 23 December 1942, 40:847–50.
17. Yacoel, *Memoirs*, 87.
18. "Present: Dr. Merten, the governor general [Simonidis] and his general secretary [Almeidas], city engineer P., the main instigator of this vandalism which is about to be confirmed, Chief Rabbi Koretz, engineer Eli Modiano, and the author of the present record [Molho], who was invited as an expert." Michael Molho and Joseph Nehama, *In Memoriam: Dedication to the Memory of the Jewish Victims of Nazism in Greece* [in Greek] (Thessaloniki: Jewish Community of Thessaloniki, 1974), 414. Brackets are mine.
19. Ibid., 414–15. The description that follows is based on these pages.
20. Report of the Division of Technical Services to the Mayor of Thessaloniki, 15785/1436 of 3 July 1944, in *Minutes of the Municipal Council*, July 1944, 753–56.
21. Yacoel, *Memoirs*, 87.
22. Molho and Nehama, *In Memoriam*, 415.
23. Ibid.
24. Merkouriou was appointed mayor in 1937, and the Germans kept him in that position until February 1943.
25. Garofallou together with Gotzamanis tried unsuccessfully to establish a National-Socialist Party in Thessaloniki in early 1943.
26. *Minutes of the Municipal Council*, 23 December 1942, 40:847–50.
27. Iatropoulos to Mayor, 18 May 1943, Thessaloniki History Center (THC), 1943, f. 14, sub. 4a.
28. *Minutes of the Municipal Council*, 11 June 1943, THC, 1943, f. 14, sub. 4a.
29. Greek Ministry of Finance, explanatory report for the draft law "Combating tax evasion, staffing of auditing services and other provisions under the purview of the ministry of finance," 22 February 2011, article 45, para. 10.
30. Vassilios Kyriazopoulos, "Aristotle University of Thessaloniki," in *Thessaloniki 1912–1962* [in Greek], ed. Alexandros Letsas (Thessaloniki: Ministry of Northern Greece, 1963), 243.
31. Molho and Nehama, *In Memoriam*, 417.
32. Simonidis to Municipality of Thessaloniki, protocol number 51745/2745, 27 June 1944, Agency for the Custody of Jewish Property, Jewish Museum of Greece, box 2.
33. Decision 216, 13 April 1943, THC, 1943, f. 13, sub. 3a.
34. Decision 315, 29 May 1943, THC, 1943, f. 13, sub. 2.
35. Decision 384, 9 July 1943, THC, 1943, f. 13, sub. 2.
36. Katerina Kostiou, "State Theater of Thessaloniki," *Epta Meres Kathimerinis* [in Greek], 21 September 1997, 10.
37. Decision 171, 30 November 1943, THC, f. 17, sub. 2.
38. Decision 297, 15 May 1943, THC, 1943, f. 12, sub. 1.
39. Based on Vassilis Ritzaleos, "The Greek Orthodox Church of Thessaloniki and the Holocaust," in *The Holocaust in the Balkans* [in Greek], ed. Giorgos Antoniou, Stratos Dordanas, Nikos Zaikos, and Nikos Marantzidis (Thessaloniki: Epikentro, 2011), 323–26.
40. A German mayor of the city was appointed on 2 August 1943, following the creation of the German administrative region of Macedonia in July 1943.

41. Document in Archive of Giannis Megas. These stones can still be seen at the entrance of the church to this day.
42. It is telling that Mark Mazower, in his seminal work *Salonica City of Ghosts: Christians, Muslims and Jews, 1430–1950* (New York: Alfred A. Knopf, 2005), entitled the third part of his book dealing with the period 1912–45 as "Making the City Greek."
43. Report of the Division of Technical Services to the Mayor of Thessaloniki, 15785/1436 of 3 July 1944, in *Minutes of the Municipal Council*, July 1944, 753–56.
44. Cecil Roth, "The Last Days of Jewish Salonica," *Commentary* 10 (1950): 55.
45. Maria Vassilikou, "The Jewish Cemetery of Salonika in the Crossroads of Urban Modernization and Anti-Semitism," *European Judaism* 33, no. 1 (Spring 2000): 128.
46. "Greek Authorities Defend Use of Ancient Jewish Tombstones to Reconstruct Church," *Jewish Telegraphic Agency*, 18 October 1946, www.jta.org/1946/10/18/archive/greek-authorities-defend-use-of-ancient-jewish-tombstones-to-reconstruct-church.
47. Yacoel, *Memoirs*, 87.
48. Hesse and Laqueur, "Visible and Invisible Bodies," 49.
49. *Makedonia*, 18 February 1959, 3.
50. Simonidis to Municipality of Thessaloniki, protocol number 51745/2745, 27 June 1944, Agency for the Custody of Jewish Property, Jewish Museum of Greece, box 2.
51. Yacoel, *Memoirs*, 74.
52. *Eleftheria*, 18 February 1959, 5.
53. Yacoel, *Memoirs*, 87.
54. *Makedonia*, 18 February 1959, 3.
55. *Makedonia*, 1 March 1959.
56. Molho and Nehama, *In Memoriam*, 414.
57. Most probably referring to Commissioner Bohlke.
58. Molho and Nehama, *In Memoriam*, 413.
59. Kostas Tomanas, *The Chronicle of Thessaloniki* [in Greek] (Thessaloniki: Nisides, 1992), 2:229.
60. Athanassios Broikos, curriculum vitae, Thessaloniki, May 1955, Historical Archive of the Polytechnic School, Aristotle University of Thessaloniki.
61. Yacoel, *Memoirs*, 87.
62. Ekaterini Kilesopoulou, "The Beaux Arts in Thessaloniki during the Period 1912–1967" [in Greek] (Ph.D. diss., Aristotle University of Thessaloniki, 2006), 206.
63. The Society for Macedonian Studies was established in Thessaloniki in 1939 "from select members of Thessaloniki society who belonged to the intellectual and commercial worlds of the country." Its primary goal was "the defense and the promotion of Greek Macedonia." During the German occupation, many of the leaders of Thessaloniki served on its board.
64. Kyriakidis was the dean of the university, Letsas the president of the Traders Association, Vasdravelis a senior executive at the port, while Panou was a senior bank official and liaison between Simonidis and the Germans.
65. Hesse and Laqueur, "Visible and Invisible Bodies," 55.
66. See Varon Odette, "A 'Silence' of the Written Sources" [in Greek], *Sychrona Themata* 52–53 (July–December 1994): 81.
67. Yacoel, *Memoirs*, 99.

Bibliography

Fleischer, Hagen. *Crown and Swastika: Greece during the Occupation and the Resistance 1941–1944* [in Greek]. Athens: Papazisis, 1995.

Hesse, Carla, and Thomas W. Laqueur. "Visible and Invisible Bodies: The Erasure of the Jewish Cemetery from the Life of Modern Thessaloniki." In *The Production of the Social Body* [in Greek], edited by Martha Mihailidou and Alexandra Halkia. Athens: Katarti, 2005.

Kilesopoulou, Ekaterini. "The Beaux Arts in Thessaloniki during the Period 1912–1967" [in Greek]. Ph.D. diss., Aristotle University of Thessaloniki, 2006.

Kostiou, Katerina. "State Theater of Thessaloniki." *Epta Meres Kathimerinis* [in Greek], 21 September 1997.

Kyriazopoulos, Vassilios. "Aristotle University of Thessaloniki." In *Thessaloniki 1912–1962* [in Greek], edited by Alexandros Letsas. Thessaloniki: Ministry of Northern Greece, 1963.

Mazower, Mark. *Salonica City of Ghosts: Christians, Muslims and Jews, 1430–1950*. New York: Knopf, 2005.

Molho, Michael, and Joseph Nehama. *In Memoriam: Dedication to the Memory of the Jewish Victims of Nazism in Greece* [in Greek]. Thessaloniki: Jewish Community of Thessaloniki, 1974.

Odette, Varon. "A 'Silence' of the Written Sources." *Sychrona Themata* 52–53 [in Greek]. (July–December 1994).

Ritzaleos, Vassilis. "The Greek Orthodox Church of Thessaloniki and the Holocaust." In *The Holocaust in the Balkans* [in Greek], edited by Giorgos Antoniou, Stratos Dordanas, Nikos Zaikos, and Nikos Marantzidis. Thessaloniki: Epikentro, 2011.

Roth, Cecil. "The Last Days of Jewish Salonica." *Commentary* 10 (1950).

Safrian, Hans. *Eichmann's Men*. Cambridge: Cambridge University Press in association with USHMM, 2010.

Saltiel, Leon. "Dehumanizing the Dead: The Destruction of Thessaloniki's Jewish Cemetery in the Light of New Sources." *Yad Vashem Studies* 42, no. 1 (2014).

Tomanas, Kostas. *The Chronicle of Thessaloniki* [in Greek], vol. 2. Thessaloniki: Nisides, 1992.

Vassilikou, Maria. "The Jewish Cemetery of Salonika in the Crossroads of Urban Modernization and Anti-Semitism." *European Judaism* 33, no. 1 (Spring 2000).

Yacoel, Yomtov. *Memoirs 1941–1943* [in Greek]. Thessaloniki: Paratiritis, 1993.

CHAPTER 5

RECONSTRUCTING TRAJECTORIES OF PERSECUTION
REFLECTIONS ON A PROSOPOGRAPHY OF HOLOCAUST VICTIMS

Nicolas Mariot and Claire Zalc

Comparing the number of Holocaust victims against estimates of the prewar Jewish population has allowed historians to calculate deportation rates in Western Europe with reasonable accuracy, with figures of 25 percent for France, 40 percent for Belgium, and even 73 percent for the Netherlands. Numerous studies have proposed stimulating hypotheses to account for these disparities, typically proceeding on a macrosociological level by focusing on factors such as relations between Nazis and local officials, the role of Jewish community representatives, the extent of relationships among different ethnic communities, as well as the effects of religion and the amount of assistance and rescue support available.[1]

Sometimes priority has been given to a more individual approach, particularly when focusing on the choices and options available to victims. Firsthand accounts by survivors, which were initially studied for memorial purposes, have more recently contributed to a broader understanding of the genocides.[2] Yet as Michael Pollak's work has forcefully demonstrated, these accounts—which are often haunted by the question of "How and why did I survive?"—reveal and reflect upon the methods and characteristics of survival.[3] The insights provided by this approach have stark implications for historians. Firstly, since researchers know how the story ends, such accounts may lead to arguments that explain persecution trajectories by way of a regressive logic. Historians may be tempted to mirror the polarized thinking of survivor accounts, which embrace binaries such as "good" or "bad" choices, or individuals who are naïve or lucid, "fortunate" or "unfortunate."

It is on this individual scale of analysis that we seek to proceed, although we reject the notion that decisions—whether to register as a "Jew" with the authorities, whether to leave or stay—can solely be explained by way of individual choices supposedly made with full awareness. The following methodological principles that we used stem from this position:

- Instead of basing our analysis on survivor testimony, we propose using archival documents that were for the most part contemporary with the persecution, in an attempt to reconstruct the world of possibilities surrounding these trajectories, while freeing ourselves from our knowledge about how these stories end.
- Instead of focusing on a limited set of carefully selected cases, we attempt to define and assess actual trajectories within a relatively large group in order to make statistically verifiable comparisons. Quantitative analysis helps avoid an approach focusing on individual cases and provides a certain detachment that is particularly helpful with controversial subjects and matters involving collective memory. A case study method would have risked focusing on "exemplary" or "non-normative" cases, those involving the most powerful or compelling evidence, or on cases that are familiar through privileged access to descendants or private archives. This makes it possible to compare individual and family trajectories that would otherwise remain apart in their solitary singularity.
- Rather than a corpus of unrelated individuals, we have chosen a well-defined community with preexisting bonds of acquaintance and reputation, whose members were faced with the same situations. By following a cohort of people over the five-year war period, we have attempted to transcend psychological judgments about the choices made by individuals. We do not believe that these actors made moral decisions with a supposed full awareness of their possible outcomes or consequences, nor have we evaluated their choices through the prism of the preestablished categories of researchers

or readers. Instead, we have resituated their decisions within the familial, economic, and local environments in which they were made. This study is therefore predicated on the assumption that the individual or family decisions made by victims, whether voluntary or imposed, inevitably had a social dimension. They therefore have meaning only within the restricted limits of a particular life or lives, in which relationships between people and the resources at their disposal are accounted for and analyzed by restoring the original social "thickness" to an individual persecution itinerary.

We believe that a monographic approach is essential for putting these methodological principles to the test. It provides the only way of anchoring analysis of behaviors within the social spaces in which they take on concrete form and meaning. The present study is based on a cohort of approximately one thousand Jews residing before the war in the Lens area, a city in the Pas-de-Calais department in northern France.[4] We chose this location firstly because of the wealth of sources, which makes it possible to document on a local level the process of stigmatizing and persecuting groups. In addition to standard sources, including both national (Aryanization and naturalization dossiers) and international (ITS Archives and Swiss government files), local departmental archives have, in a rare occurrence, notably conserved all of the self-declarations of Jewishness mailed from Lens to prefecture authorities.

It is important to note at the outset that the local situation in Lens was highly particular and distinguished it from the persecution of Jews in the rest of France. Firstly, the town's Jewish community, which in the 1930s represented 3 percent of the population of thirty-three thousand, was particularly devastated by these policies, as nearly half of the Jews in Lens were deported, as opposed to a quarter for France as a whole. Secondly, Lens was part of the "forbidden zone" encompassing the "Nord" and "Pas-de-Calais" departments, which was annexed to Belgium by the Germans after the Armistice. The local chronology differs relatively little from the more familiar chronology of the larger "occupied zone." In the fall of 1940, the first statute targeting Jews came into effect, and the first census of Jews in the northern zone—required but based on self-declaration—was conducted. The first expulsions from professions also occurred during this period, as did the Aryanization of businesses and the internment of some foreign Jews. In June and July 1941, the second statute on Jews took effect, the program of professional quotas and expulsions was expanded, while a second census was conducted. Curfews were imposed in the spring and summer of 1942, as well as the law requiring Jews to wear the Star of David. French authorities also conducted frequent roundups of Jews, whom they then turned over to the Germans, while mass arrests and deportations also continued from the summer of 1942 through 1944. The incorporation of Pas-de-Calais into the German wartime administration of Belgium had harsh consequences for the local Jewish population; in the case of Lens, the French Jews who remained there became like any other foreigner, and Jewish families no longer had the protection of French nationality during local roundups in the summer of 1942.

In this respect Lens is not at all representative of France, a circumstance often referred to in microhistory as a "normal exception." Our priority was not to select a representative area, but to write the story from the bottom up in order to understand precisely why Lens is non-representative and why the persecution inflicted on Jews there was so severe. What's more, it is not Lens that proves this history correct; the research could have focused on many other locations, although it had to be situated "somewhere," in a setting that could be identified as social space, a well-defined terrain of observation where it becomes possible to reconstitute—between choice and imperative—the social factors that shaped the decisions made by the individuals concerned.

The essay unfolds in four parts. We begin by introducing sources, based on a household monograph, pertaining to anti-Semitic persecution against a particular group of Jews who resided in the Lens area in 1939. This first section attempts a step-by-step reconstruction of certain aspects of the lives of Jews, in order to shed light on the actual experiences of those facing persecution. Next, we pursue our effort to construct a prosopographic approach by exploring different ways of treating the data that we uncovered. We will then discuss the problems associated with applying different quantification and modeling methods to this specific case, which involves discrimination, persecution, and extermination. We will conclude by presenting potential complementary projects to engage in both a microhistorical and sequential approach for this singular context.

Selecting Sources: Different Persecution Trajectories in the Same Household

Joseph Dawidowicz and His Close Relatives

In October 1944, after four years spent evading German and French authorities, Joseph Dawidowicz finally returned to Béthune only to learn that his lease had been canceled on 13 May 1942, allowing the city government to purchase his apartment building. A neighbor housed him while he appealed to have the lease reinstated, and he sent the following letter to the prefect of Pas-de-Calais after his appeal was denied:

> I would ask you very respectfully, *Monsieur le Préfet,* to be kind enough to contact *Monsieur le Maire* and to allow him to authorize me to live in my home, which is unoccupied, so that I may house my family, which comprises eight members, four of whom are minors, who need to rest because of the constant travel that they have been forced to endure for the past four years. *Monsieur le Préfet,* please accept my assurances of the deepest respect.[5]

This was not the first time that Joseph had addressed the prefect. He had sent a handwritten letter four years earlier in response to a census of the Jewish population that began on 13 December 1940. His letter stated that he was born in 1886 in a village near the Polish city of Łódź, which at the time was under Russian rule, and that he had settled in Béthune as a "purveyor of clothing and furs" with his wife Chana, and their children Jean (aged nineteen), Jenny (fourteen), Fanny (eleven), and Simon (ten).[6]

On 16 December 1940, three days after Joseph drafted his letter, the Germans decided to expel Jews from Boulogne-sur-Mer and Béthune as part of their effort to "protect" the coastal zone, which was at risk of a British invasion. Learning from a friend on the police force that he was on the list, Joseph and his family fled in the middle of the night, the first stage in an extended odyssey that would eventually take them to Pau, Lyon, Nice, and Uriage.

The Dawidowicz family had first left Béthune in mid-May 1940 during a mass exodus in advance of German troops. They climbed into the family Peugeot sedan "with a trunk in the back," followed by a Ford truck borrowed from a mechanic friend carrying household items such as "bedding, packages, suitcases of clothing and linens, and medication."[7] The first halt on their trip was at Noisy-le-Grand with the Jablon family, who owned a distillery: "We thought we would stay a little while in Noisy; with a bit of patience, once the Germans were defeated, we would then return to Béthune." The Germans were steadily advancing, however, and Joseph, who had already spent several years as a German POW in the previous war, quickly decided to take to the road.

They would never again see the Jablons, who disappeared after their deportation. The family next halted in Angoulême, where they met a cousin who had fled from Metz, but who was unable to take them in. They again departed, traveling first to Cognac and later to Bordeaux, where Joseph searched in vain for a boat to Africa. Soon enough, the Germans arrived there as well. "We were unable to escape," wrote Jean, the eldest son, explaining their decision to turn around and return to

Béthune. While his mother, brothers, and sisters returned home by train, he and his father transported the family's luggage and personal effects, crossing the Somme River at a tiny village, Pont-Rémy, where a German guard briefly detained them. The Dawidowicz family eventually found their way home to Béthune, with no plans to leave again.

For Joseph, leaving had always been a possibility. Until he settled in the North of France, his itinerary was like that of thousands of other Jews who emigrated for economic reasons from Central Europe at the turn of the century. Some of his cousins left for England, but he traveled to Germany sometime in 1901 or 1902 and found work as a cabin boy on a coaster plying the waters between Hamburg and coastal ports in the Netherlands, Denmark, and Great Britain. In 1914, he was imprisoned as a "Russian emigrant" and conscripted to work at a meat-curing plant. After he was liberated in 1918, he returned to his native village in Poland and married, before quickly leaving again in 1921, this time for France. Chana and Joseph first traveled to Nancy and later to the Meuse region, where their oldest son Jean was born in 1921. They then moved to the area in the North around Douai in 1924. Rumors were circulating that in the wake of mass migrations of Polish miners to the coal-mining region in northern France, there was a market for Jewish immigrants who could speak Polish and who were familiar with the tastes of this potential market. Joseph first opened a small shop in Douai that sold *Salaisons douaisiennes* (Douai cured meats), before moving to Béthune and establishing himself in a well-located boutique on the town's main square as a purveyor of women's clothes, under the appealing name "À la Femme Chic" (The Chic Woman's Shop).

This may indicate that the family was relatively comfortable financially by this time, and at some point in the interwar period, Joseph and Chana requested and were granted French nationality. Joseph socialized with other members of the Jewish community in Lens, most of whom had arrived in the area in the 1920s and '30s, like he and Chana. Yet he simultaneously cultivated professional and personal contacts beyond this circle of fellow immigrants, particularly in an association for fellow former German POWs. The family may also have served as a type of model for friends and relatives who later moved to the region. For example, in 1928, Joseph's youngest brother, Abraham, moved to Avion (near Lens), where he worked as a shoemaker. Abraham was married and had three children, two born in Berlin in the late 1920s, and the youngest, Liliane, born in Avion in 1941. Another relative, Moïse Dawidowicz, lived in the nearby coal-mining town of Sallaumines with his wife and two children, who were born there in 1932 and 1937. One of Chana's sisters, Sara Glicksman, lived in Douai with her husband and their five children.

Like Joseph and his immediate family, all three related families officially registered themselves as "Jews" in December 1940 in accordance with the 18 November 1940 regulations "relative to the measures against the Jews." Article 3 of the regulations stated that "any Jewish person will be required to present themselves without delay to the sub-prefect of the district of their residence to be registered in a special ledger. The declaration of the head of household will be valid for the entire family."[8]

However, unlike other families, they remained in the town, submitting to three censuses and enduring the Aryanization of their businesses and homes (in Sallaumines, a neighbor residing in the same street made an offer on Moïse's house[9]); they were eventually arrested on 11 September 1942 during a wave of mass arrests among the remaining vestiges of the Jewish community of Lens.[10] The 10 September "daily report" to the mayor from the Sallaumines police commissioner reported two events that day under the heading "interesting events public order"—the "arrival of five new guardians of the peace," and the "arrests of the Jewish Katz, Klajnberg, and Dawidowicz families by German authorities. Their animals and fowl were donated to the *Secours national*"—before concluding that there were "no major events."[11] After first being transferred to Malines in Belgium, all three families were deported by Convoy X to Auschwitz on 15 September 1942. When they arrived, Moïse was registered and assigned to forced labor under the registration number 42,828. He survived less than three months, dying on December 3. The other members of the household were gassed immediately on 17 October after descending from the train.

Approximately one thousand Jews lived in the coal-mining basin surrounding Lens in early 1940. Following the exodus of about half of this number beginning in May 1940, the December 1940 census recorded 482 "Israelites." The census of 1 October 1942, less than two years later, noted a total of thirteen survivors.

How to Interpret the Dawidowicz Family Itineraries

This recursive narrative of the itineraries of the Dawidowicz household provides the basis for a family monograph, like those written by Daniel Mendelsohn and Götz Aly.[12] In methodological terms, the history of Joseph's immediate family and close relatives is remarkable in that it spanned the entire period that began with their exodus in May 1940 and ended with their return as refugees and survivors in late 1944 and early 1945. This family's history demonstrates the importance we have given to chronology in analyzing individual, familial, and collective itineraries. Establishing the precise timing of their initial departures also offers information on the means and methods of itineraries, as well as their determining factors. This is particularly useful in explaining certain points in the family members' itineraries that remained murky, such as their return in late 1944. Even at the time, local authorities experienced considerable difficulty relinquishing the old reflexes from the era of "Jewish affairs" (*affaires juives*) under the Vichy regime.

Joseph's narrative is also unusual because his was one of the few family trajectories that can be traced through practically every layer of intersecting documentation that we unearthed for the study. This enabled us to construct a portrait of the family's history based on a wide array of original resources, varying both with regard to where and by whom they were produced. The sources include the testimony of one of Joseph's daughters, Fanny (which was collected and preserved by the Yad Vashem Institute in memory of the non-surviving members of her family), as well as individual refugee and displaced person search-service files created by the International Red Cross (and consulted online on the USHMM website in Washington), Aryanization files in the French National Archives, documents located at the Center for Contemporary Jewish Documentation (particularly deportation lists), and a major trove of administrative and police documents stored in departmental archives (including inventories of people and property, surveillance and pillaging reports, commercial ledgers, distribution documents concerning yellow stars, arrest lists, and return documents). Only two other sources are missing in the case of the Dawidowicz family—the naturalization requests filed by Joseph and Chana (because the dossier is inexplicably missing), and Swiss refugee dossiers, which are stored in Bern (because none of the Dawidowiczes pursued this route). These documents represent potentially fertile additional sources, since the firsthand narratives they contain date from before and during the family's persecution.

The dispersed geographic locations of the archives used in this study, although not unusual, were further complicated by the fact that the four related families in the study resided in four municipalities—Béthune, Sallaumines, Avion, and Douai. The first three of these municipalities are in two different districts (Béthune and Arras) of the department of Pas-de-Calais, while Douai is located in the neighboring department, the Nord. The families' records are consequently stored in three different sub-prefectures, a distribution of sources that illustrates the principle we used to shape our choice of population: instead of dividing the population sample according to basic administrative divisions (a history of the Jews of the city of Lens, for example, or "from the Béthune district" would have constituted a more convenient sample), we have focused on the group's boundaries as the group members themselves defined them, notably by using the list engraved in the room that once served as a synagogue; this list includes all local victims of deportations, whether they were arrested in the immediate region or elsewhere in France and whether they were residents of Lens itself or of neighboring towns.

With respect to the origins of the documents, the itineraries of Joseph and his family members are corroborated by direct testimony from the study subjects themselves. Some accounts were collected by officials at the time—as seen earlier, this includes an unusual collection of handwritten self-declarations that offer a privileged look at the different approaches adopted by the Jews of Lens in their written declarations. Additional narratives were collected in the course of our investigation, including an oral interview with Jean Dawidowicz, and two short memoirs of his recollections, one typed and the other handwritten. The close correlation between sources indeed indicates an astonishing degree of reliability. Clearly, if we possessed only Jean's testimony, we would have had no information about the declarations of Jewish identity submitted to the authorities by the three heads of household. Nor would we have been aware of the conflict between the Béthune town hall and Jean's father after he returned (because Jean's father did not allude to the declaration), and we obviously would have remained ignorant about the experience of the family members who remained behind (because Jean was not present). And finally, without Jean's firsthand account, we would have lacked basic but critical details concerning the family's exodus, their decisions en route, and the various people they met along the way.

The startling depth of these sources allowed us to conduct the intensive and strictly localized study that we argued was needed to answer our initial research questions. Our recourse to the monographic genre is not justified solely for this reason, but also because the local setting makes it possible to closely contextualize individual trajectories by giving them back their social depth.

A series of questions arises from this perspective: Should one report oneself as a Jew? If so, when? Should one simply continue with one's business? Should one flee? If so, how? Should families remain together or travel separately? What should be done with property and assets, and who could be trusted?

Additional related questions also arise. What factors influenced individual answers to these questions and, more broadly, the future of the Dawidowicz household? What was the effect of such factors as nationality, the family's relative wealth, their length of residence in the area, or the diversity of their local and broader social networks? The answers to these questions often draw on individual consciousness and then translate to the register of choice, sense of responsibility, or even moral judgment, contrasting the "naiveté" of some against the "lucidity" of others, or "consent" with "resistance." It is precisely because such questions involve the inner world of individual consciousness that they arguably cannot be adequately addressed in a historical study. They are supposed to be private, personal decisions that cannot be evaluated or judged, yet too often this is how reconstruction of the possible range of options available to individuals is conceived, even and especially when this range is limited not to discussion of what they supposedly had in mind, but more simply to retrace the order of the thinkable and the possible at a given point in time.

Intensive analysis of the sources on the ground level implies resituating the unusual trajectory of the Dawidowicz family in its material and social context, partly by comparing it with the trajectories of other families who did not declare themselves or who either did not leave or left under different circumstances (as a group, at another time). The goal of giving observable itineraries and decisions their social depth or of establishing links between individual behaviors and personal characteristics makes quantitative analysis necessary.

A Household within a Community: Was the Dawidowicz Family's Trajectory Representative?

Quantitative analysis does not merely imply counting how many people were dispossessed, hidden, and deported, but instead knowing who they where and how they were different (or where not) from those who did not suffer the same fate. The first step was to create a detailed chart, with the names of individual family members in the left-hand column and, in the corresponding columns to the right, as many personal and family variables as the data allow, including age, nationality, date of entry in France, family composition, and profession. These data were then compiled into a single database that allowed basic statistical analysis to establish the relationships between individual fates and personal variables. Significantly, this also made it possible to compare characteristics and itineraries among individuals and family groups according to whether they had declared themselves as Jews, whether they departed or remained in Lens, and whether they were placed under house arrest, interned, or "departed with no forwarding address" during the course of the occupation. Without quantitative analysis, in other words, it would have been difficult to accurately compare the Dawidowicz family's departures to other Lens residents.

Let us begin by returning to the December 1940 census. The four Dawidowicz households all chose to officially declare themselves as "Jews." Each member of the four families was registered on the first set of lists created by the prefecture. The decision to register, which may have been jointly agreed to during an extended family meal, can be compared to that of other members of the Jewish population of Lens. Based on their letters of declaration preserved in the archives, we are able to describe their reactions to the official self-declaration requirement.

The declaration letters represent an exceptional archival resource that is in many ways the product of a historical accident. In Paris and most other cities, Jews declared themselves in person directly to the authorities, encounters that left no detailed trace. Lens, however, was so remote from prefectural headquarters that direct registration was considered impractical, and many declarations were therefore submitted in writing. The resulting documents provide a privileged glimpse of the act of self-declaration and the way in which the declarant experienced and represented this act to the authorities.[13]

In one letter, for example, a father declares himself to be Jewish—"as a nationality"—but describes his daughter as "French" because "she was born in France." At approximately the same time, a woman wrote to the sub-prefect in Béthune to explain her reluctance to respond. Acknowledging that she was of "Jewish origin," she also argued that she was born a French citizen and was the child of French parents. She also noted that her father had volunteered for military service in 1870, followed by her husband, who had volunteered in 1914, and her son in 1939. "I therefore come to you to ask, Monsieur le Sous-Préfet, if, with all these French qualities, I should be classified among the Jews who are currently being investigated." Her reasoning demonstrates the extent to which prewar "Israélites" had internalized the dichotomy between citizens and foreigners, which is central to French jurisprudence. Her case also reflects a sociological distinction between, on the one hand, long-standing French citizens of Jewish faith or culture, who were endowed with "French qualities," and on the other, *Ostjuden*, who were immigrants seeking employment or refugees fleeing official anti-Semitism in their native countries—the "Jews who are currently being investigated" referred to by the author of the letter. This distinction offers a significant clue into how French Jews positioned themselves.

The official reply that arrived a few days later pursued a rather different interpretation of what it meant to be a Jew, by asserting that "[because you were] born, as you yourself declare, to parents of Jewish origin, you belong to the Jewish race." The petitioner was compelled to declare herself at the Lens town hall, demonstrating that the bureaucracy of the time was entirely indifferent to logic or even legality. Indeed, the variety of ways in which individuals declared their Jewish identity differed markedly from how the resulting data were treated at the time and subsequently interpreted by historians and others.

We have attempted to answer two simple but hitherto largely neglected questions concerning these letters of self-declaration:

1. What concrete steps were taken to identify and list Jews in France during World War II?
2. Who was in charge of this operation, and what criteria and methods did they use?

Our findings show that three-fourths of the Jewish population in and around Lens elected to self-declare, contradicting the widely held view that most Jews were identified by being detected by the Vichy government and were therefore to be treated as foreigners according to Third Republic policy. The self-declaration initiative was not widely contested, despite taking place on a massive scale, with 90 percent of the Jews in the department of the Seine, for example, ostensibly self-declaring (although the source of this estimate is unknown).[14] Declaration letters also revealed the gray area between self-identification as Jewish by religion and Jewishness construed as "nationality," "origin," or "race."

Self-declaration varied across categories and locations. Younger and single people, as well as those who were spatially isolated, were born in France, or had entered the country more recently, were least likely to declare themselves (see table 5.1). Socio-professional status, however, was not closely related to whether individuals or families self-declared,

Table 5.1. Characteristics of Self-declared and Non-declared Jews

	Non-declared	Self-declared	
Type of household (chi-sq. ***)			
Single	44%	56%	100% (34)
Couples	22%	78%	100% (54)
Families of 3 to 4 members	21%	79%	100% (310)
Large families	31%	69%	100% (192)
Total	26%	74%	100% (590)
Age (chi-sq. ***)			
0–16	32%	68%	100% (181)
16–30	28%	72%	100% (107)

31–45	20%	80%	100% (197)
46 and over	17%	83%	100% (96)
Total	25%	75%	100% (581)
Entry into France (chi-sq. ***)			
Born in France	31%	69%	100% (177)
Prior to 1928	20%	80%	100% (97)
Between 1928 and 1930	13%	87%	100% (132)
Between 1931 and 1934	16%	84%	100% (55)
1935 and subsequently	27%	73%	100% (62)
Total	22%	78%	100% (523)
Number of households per street (chi-sq. **)			
One household	37%	63%	100% (86)
2 to 4 households	26%	74%	100% (118)
5 to 9 households	19%	81%	100% (160)
More than 10 households	24%	76%	100% (221)
Total	25%	75%	100% (585)
Socio-professional status (chi-sq. *)			
Student	30%	70%	100% (64)
Minor	33%	67%	100% (135)
Self-employed	20%	80%	100% (143)
Employee	22%	78%	100% (63)
No profession	21%	79%	100% (155)
Overall total	24%	76%	100% (560)
Real estate ownership (chi-sq. **) (total households for which information is available)			
No	12%	88%	100% (57)
Yes	29%	71%	100% (35)
Total	18%	82%	100% (92)

The chi-square test of significance assesses the difference between an observed situation and the theoretical independence of variables, making it possible to measure the extent to which two variables are related to each other. By convention, the symbol *** is used to indicate that the value of the chi-square test is significant to the level of 1%. The interpretive risk in minimal, because there is only one chance in one hundred that the gap observed with respect to the situation of independence is due to chance (i.e., the situation in which self-declaration or non-self-declaration was unrelated to family status, age, date of entry into France, or professional status). The symbol ** indicates that the chi-square value is significant to 5%, and the symbol * to indicate that it is significant to 10%; NS indicates no significance.

as self-employed workers, employees, and the unemployed were equally likely to register. The influence of age was enormous, which explains the over-representation of bachelors and individuals "born on French soil" among those who chose not to self-declare. The non-declared group included a relatively higher proportion of young adults, who were evidently less likely to comply with the declaration requirement. It also included more children, whom heads of household tried to protect by not declaring. If we change scale, it is also possible to observe dynamics of social contagion, as non-declared Jews were highly concentrated in two streets in Lens, rue Flament, where three out of five households did not declare, and rue Félix Faure, where eight out of thirteen heads of household decided not to declare their families to the authorities. Elsewhere, declarations were made en masse: all eleven families residing in rue Gauthier, ten out of the twelve Jewish households in rue Pasteur, and eight of the Jewish households in rue Camille Beugnet officially registered themselves as Jewish.

This micro-local approach helps better understand the factors determining the act of declaration. Let us examine rue Félix Faure. Of the sixteen Jewish families residing in the street, three left Lens at the time of the initial exodus in 1940 (living at numbers 14, 16, and 39), and eight did not declare themselves. These latter lived at numbers 14, 14bis, and 15. However, five families chose to declare, those residing at numbers 12, 14bis, 15bis, 16, and 39. Considering the proximity of the addresses of the non-declared households and the range of responses within the same street, it is difficult to argue that ignorance or isolation were factors in explaining non-declaration. This is particularly true given that the same address, number 14, housed both the household of Jechezkiel Himmelbarb, president of the Israelite Community of Lens, and the headquarters for the Association of the Jewish Faith. The decision of whether to obey the order to register was probably a topic of discussion among neighbors. Did these discussions juxtapose legalism with the sense of a perceived threat? We do not know the precise nature of such discussions, as they have left no traces.

A second indicator nevertheless makes it possible to determine the relative level of local integration of non-declaring households. Over 25 percent of property-owning households (ten out of thirty-five) did not respond to the declaration requirement (as compared to 12 percent of non-property-owning households). Should we conclude that it was precisely the lesser degree of social fragility and the higher visibility of property-owning Jewish households that encouraged them not to declare (particularly since non-declaration did not prevent them from being identified beginning in December 1940)?

From the perspective of those who did self-declare, the various Dawidowicz couples are highly consistent with the choices of their neighbors in Lens. These similarities within extended families and with respect to other Jews in the area tend to mask the highly exceptional nature of the itinerary of Joseph Dawidowicz's household during the war. Quantitative analysis can again provide revelatory information. Examining the relationship between household size and family ties outside of the Lens area reveals that Joseph's family actually had a high statistical probability of not leaving because, as tables 5.2 and 5.3 illustrate, higher numbers of children per family as well as more local family ties increased the probability of being arrested.

Table 5.2. Those Who Left and Those Who Remained: Household Size

Household type (chi-sq. ***)	Departed	Remained	Total
Single-member households	73%	27%	100% (70)
Couples	73%	27%	100% (110)
Families of 3 to 4 persons	65%	35%	100% (508)
Large families	51%	49%	100% (298)
Total	62%	38%	100% (986)

Table 5.3. Kinship Network and Arrests of Departed (compared to total number of households)

Ties to other Lens households (chi-sq. ***)	Not arrested	Arrested	Total
No family ties acknowledged with other households	78%	22%	100% (125)
One family tie with other households	73%	27%	100% (44)
From 2 to 4 ties with other households	51%	49%	100% (39)
Total	72%	28%	100% (208)

How can the differences between the itineraries of the various Dawidowicz family members be explained?

First, it is worth recalling that Joseph and his family were forced to flee within a few days of having filed their self-declaration, meaning that, unlike other families, their choice was not independent of the circumstances. Jean's testimony also informs us of the person who notified the family that they were on the arrest list and how they organized their "furtive departure," to use language typical of police records. On the evening of 15 December 1940, Jean learned of their imminent arrest from a brigadier from local police headquarters, which was immediately across the street from the family business, where the German occupying force's *Kommandantur* (local headquarters) was also located. The statistical relationship between time of departure and individual destinies also shows that the family's forced departure took place at exactly the "right" moment. Their incentive to remain discreet, if not completely hidden, along with the certainty that any eventual return would be in the distant future, was far clearer than at the time of their first departure in May 1940; however, the ability of Jews to flee or circulate and reach the unoccupied zone was better than in the summer of 1942 (see tables 5.4 and 5.5).

Table 5.4. Destination as a Function of Time of Departure

(chi-sq. ***)	Destination unknown	Unoccupied zone	Occupied zone	Switzerland	Total
Departure prior to December 1940	47%	27%	17%	9%	100% (388)
Departure in 1941	40%	41%	11%	8%	100% (98)
Departure in 1942	52%	14%	24%	10%	100% (124)
Total	48%	26%	17%	9%	100% (610)

Table 5.5. The Effect of Departure Time on Arrest Rates

(chi-sq. ***)	Arrested	Not arrested	Total
Final departure before December 1940	34%	66%	100% (388)
Final departure between December 1940 and December 1941	17%	83%	100% (98)
Final departure between January and September 1942	20%	80%	100% (124)
Total	28%	72%	100% (610)

Joseph's networks—local, in Paris, and elsewhere—significantly improved the conditions under which the family departed, as well as their eventual chances of surviving. Beginning on the morning of December 16, the aid network for lost British soldiers to which Joseph and Jean both belonged was mobilized to help organize their departure. Fanny and Simon, aged ten and eleven, left first, blending in with other children at the town hall in the care of Monsieur Delestrez, the same person Joseph consulted regarding his letter to the prefect in October 1944. Joseph remained in the shop until he met his wife and oldest daughter, Jenny, who was fourteen, in a café. They were then driven to Noeux-les-Mines and temporarily hidden by a laborer family. Jean was assisted by a merchant from Lens who had a stall in the Béthune town market. These connections also made it possible for Joseph to use the truck and identity card of an Italian (who could circulate freely because Italy was allied with the Germans) in order to reach Albert Goldberg's apartment on the rue de la Paix in Lens. He eventually arrived at the nearest railway station and boarded a train to Paris.

The family then separated, and the oldest child, Jean, left for Paris, while Joseph, his wife, and their oldest daughter, Jenny, found refuge at the Caine's home in Noeux-les-Mines thanks to the assistance of a Red Cross worker. The two youngest children, Fanny (eleven) and Simon (ten) were entrusted to Monsieur Delestrez at the Béthune town hall. Their parents and Jenny were able to reach the capital several weeks later, where they joined Jean, who then returned north to retrieve Fanny and Simon. The entire family was finally reunited in Paris before departing for Grenoble, where they remained in hiding until the end of the war.[15]

The destiny of this family is without question highly exceptional. The Dawidowiczes were only able to leave in separate groups because they enjoyed a series of networks and trusted friends, as well as acquaintances who consented to hiding their children. The home of the Delestrez family, who were municipal employees, was on the top floor of the Béthune town hall, directly opposite German police headquarters on the town square. The Dawidowicz family was additionally able to find shelter with cousins in Paris. Support networks and relatives outside of Lens—more specifically in the southern zone—clearly facilitated departures in a significant way, because there were no guarantees, even after the occupied/unoccupied line had been crossed (see table 5.6).

Table 5.6. Arrest as a Function of Final Destination

(chi-sq. ***)	Arrested	Not arrested	Overall	As %
Occupied zone	62%	38%	100% (107)	17%
Unoccupied zone	25%	75%	100% (165)	27%
Switzerland	0%	100%	100% (54)	9%
Unknown destination	14%	86%	100% (290)	47%
Total	24%	76%	100% (616)	100%

Individual testimonials also demonstrate the crucial importance of the material resources available to Joseph during the latter stages of the family's forced exodus. In January 1941, they were able to arrange for the family to be reunited in late February 1941 and to stage their crossing into the "free zone": they used a Parisian apartment in the rue Notre Dame de Nazareth belonging to suppliers of their clothing shop, as well as a hotel where "they usually stayed." They also benefited from the involvement of the Béthune support network, including a neighbor who was a *charcutier* (a purveyor of cured meats) and a "devoted" salesclerk, who helped remove and sell the remaining merchandise from the clothing shop. It was Jean who clandestinely returned to Béthune via Lens and the rue de la Paix to recover the proceeds from this sale along with the younger children. Later, each phase of their wanderings appears to have been chosen based on the location of friends or acquaintances. In Pau, they stayed with other "refugees from Lens," in particular "the insurance agent and friend" Léon Baron. This socialist activist was close to the local *député* (congressman), the former president of the association of the internees at Gurs, who is buried in the Jewish cemetery of Eleu-dit-Leauwette) on the outskirts of Lens.

Jean related another significant episode that took place while they were in Pau. Jean's parents heard about the first mass arrests of foreign Jews in the occupied zone and decided to send Jean north one last time in April 1941 to persuade the other branches of the family to join them. He thus returned a second time to Lens, again staying with the Goldbergs. Neither friends nor family members heeded his pleas, however: "They answered that they had done everything they could, and that they were working and earning an honest living. And that if we, the Dawidowiczes, had been harassed ... it was because we had engaged in reprehensible activities." Their refusal to leave is a testament to the influence of peer pressure on decision-making. Unlike Joseph, who was isolated in Béthune and maintained contacts with non-Jews, the other Dawidowicz households, particularly those in Douai and Sallaumines, lived in streets in which five to nine other Jewish families resided. Yet judging from table 5.7, living in a street shared by other members of the same faith seems to have made it harder to decide to leave, perhaps because these households felt protected by this proximity to one another.

The Chronology of Persecutions and the Changing Effects of Variables

The statistical approach used in the previous sections provides several interesting findings, particularly concerning the reasons for departure,

Table 5.7. Departing versus Remaining in Lens: Street Addresses and Proximity

Number of Jewish households in street (chi-sq. ***)	Departed	Remained	Total
Isolated household	35%	65%	100% (114)
2 to 4 households	62%	38%	100% (186)
5 to 9 households	72%	28%	100% (272)
More than 10 households	62%	38%	100% (370)
Overall	62%	38%	100% (942)

while revealing powerful differences for several of the variables at work. On the other hand, our quantitative methodology is not effective in reflecting relationships of causality between variables that change over time. Nor would more sophisticated statistical procedures such as logistical regression have provided more nuanced information about evolving relationships between variables. Indeed, on several occasions we observed that the negative and positive effects of certain variables evolved over time as the geographic and chronological situations of individuals changed. Something that was a handicap in Lens could become an advantage in another setting or vice versa. What follows is a description of several important examples of this chronological phenomenon that reveals the fundamental patterns underlying persecution, including a tendency toward increasing arbitrariness in which searching for causative factors loses its meaning amid the reality that every Jew was eventually a target for repression.

In introducing these findings, we would like to call particular attention to the systematic results of the chi-square tests of significance/non-significance that were used in this study. As we know, the test makes it possible to determine the significance or non-significance of the results obtained. We also wish to underscore the fact that a finding of statistical non-significance can in fact provide important insights. For example, the relationship between self-declaration (or not) and deportation (or not) is quite revealing. As a general rule, with regard to the probable uses of the census data, it is conceivable that the act of self-declaration indicates a certain level of naïveté or even blindness on the part of the families. But this viewpoint fails to consider the time frame—declaring oneself Jewish in 1940 was not necessarily perceived as suggesting a tragic future outcome. More specifically, whether one self-declared or not did not change the risk of being arrested, as noted previously. As table 5.8 illustrates, the same proportion of declared and non-declared households were deported to the East two years later.

Table 5.8. Family Declaration in December 1940 and Deportation

(chi-sq. NS)	Not deported	Deported	Total
Not declared—identified by authorities	43%	57%	100% (37)
Self-declared	46%	54%	100% (150)
Total	45%	55%	100% (187)

Having demonstrated a probable statistical independence between declaring oneself Jewish (or not) and subsequently being deported (or not) is very important. It allows us to avoid value judgments concerning the alleged "quality" of the "choice" made by the individual families.[16] In this sense, the creation of a database is also an argument for a depersonalized and collective analysis of what could be called extreme situations.

The role of nationality illustrates how the effects of a particular variable can change over time. Nationality played a relatively minor role in the decision to remain in Lens or to leave. There is a slight disparity, however, between French and Polish citizens, who represented the majority of those who left, and other nationalities, who were more likely to remain. It is very likely that French and Polish citizens, who represented the majority of the local Jewish population, had more local acquaintances, both in the region and throughout occupied France, and thus confronted fewer obstacles to departing and/or going into hiding (in some cases even by remaining near the Lens area) (see table 5.9).

Table 5.9. Nationality and Departure between 1940 and 1942

Nationality (chi-sq. **)	Departed	Remained	Total
French	62%	38%	100% (218)
Polish	59%	41%	100% (491)
Other	47%	53%	100% (142)
Total	46%	54%	100% (851)

Nationality was a predictor of arrest, however. In theory at least, French citizens in the forbidden zone that included Lens were considered foreigners just like everyone else, since the region, as mentioned, came under German command and was annexed to Belgium (see table 5.10). Yet there were disparities in arrest rates depending on nationality. "Only" 36 percent of Jews in the Lens area who had French nationality were arrested, compared with 59 percent for Polish citizens and 63 percent for other nationalities (e.g., Romanians, Czechs, Russians). This result stems from the fact that the table does not take displacement or chronology into account. Jews who left the Lens area—which once again was administratively attached to Belgium—and entered the "French" zones regained the prevailing "national" criterion used for managing arrests. They therefore once again became "nationals," whereas the Polish remained just as foreign as they had been in the "forbidden zone."

Table 5.10. Nationality and Arrest

Nationality (chi-sq. ***)	Not arrested	Arrested	Total
French	64%	36%	100% (218)
Polish	41%	59%	100% (491)
Other	37%	63%	100% (142)
Total	46%	54%	100% (851)

Leaving Lens and entering occupied France guaranteed nothing, for the French or for anyone else. In fact, when they crossed the border between these two sectors, Jews from Lens who had acquired French nationality after 1927 were no longer necessarily protected by it. The law of 22 July 1940 stipulated that citizens naturalized after that date would have their cases reexamined and risked being stripped of naturalized French citizenship. Indeed, over fifteen thousand individuals lost their French nationality in this way between 1940 and 1944, including approximately ten Jews from Lens.

Finally, the "nationality" variable shows a strong positive correlation with the date of departure from Lens. On average, 20 percent of Jews from Lens left in 1942, but this number comprised 41 percent of the French, as opposed to only 19 percent of Poles and 8 percent of other nationalities (see table 5.11). As we had hypothesized, the sense of being protected by their nationality influenced the decision of French citizens to leave.

Table 5.11. Nationality and Date of Departure

Nationality (ch-sq. ***)	Final departure before December 1940	Final departure between December 1940 and December 1941	Final departure between January and September 1942	
French	39%	21%	40%	100% (135)
Polish	65%	16%	19%	100% (284)
Other	79%	13%	8%	100 % (191)
Total	64%	16%	20%	100% (610)

The effects of socioeconomic status represent a mix of the two previously discussed variables. Indeed, although it was relatively strongly related to the likelihood of departure, the relationship between socioeconomic status and being arrested and eventually deported disappears completely. The binary opposition between "staying in Lens" and "leaving Lens" serves as an example of this distinction. There is a marked effect for socioeconomic status, although it appears to be less significant than variables such as age and especially household size; on average, 56 percent of the Jews living in or near Lens left, but the rate was 62 percent for independent workers and 53 percent for salaried employees (see table 5.12).[17]

Table 5.12. Socioeconomic Status of Jews Who Left Lens between 1940 and 1942

Employment status (over 16 years of age) (chi-sq. **)	Departed	Remained	Total
Independent workers	62%	38%	100% (229)
Salaried employees	53%	47%	100% (88)
No profession	49%	51%	100% (201)
Overall	56%	44%	100% (518)

Factors correlated with being arrested or not suggest a non-significant relationship with socioeconomic status: similar percentages of independent workers, salaried employees, and those with no profession avoided arrest (roughly 45%); this was also true of individuals who self-declared (see table 5.13).

This can easily be explained, as Aryanization files and professional declarations from the different occupation censuses make it possible to verify the socioeconomic status of Jews residing in Lens in the fall of 1939. Auschwitz entry questionnaires also provide evidence that some individuals continued to occupy their professions even until entering the camps—at least those who were not immediately gassed on arrival. The confiscation of Jewish property as early as the latter half of 1940, coupled with being banned from practicing their professions, however, renders any attempt to establish the socioeconomic classification of Jews meaningless. The population's socioeconomic categories therefore evolved over time, making this an unstable statistical criterion. In fact, it was impossible for Jews to convert currency under the Vichy regime, because as early as the fall of 1940, there was a concerted effort in the occupied zone to despoil them and to confiscate their assets and property. This was accompanied by the loss of any legitimate means of earning a living, which forced Jews to survive without work for several years, sometimes in a new location (this was also true in the southern zone for individuals who lacked community connections). This also helps to explain why, for some individuals and in some cases over the long term, forced participation in a Groupement de Travailleurs Etrangers (GTE; Foreign Workers' Group of the Vichy regime) offered a credible solution to the profound hardships suffered by Jews who fled after May 1940.

Table 5.13. Socioeconomic Status and Arrest

Employment status of individuals over 16 years of age (chi-sq. NS)	Not arrested	Arrested	Total
Self-employed	48%	52%	100% (229)
Salaried employees	45%	55%	100% (88)
No profession	42%	58%	100% (201)
Total	45%	55%	100% (518)

Indeed, our search for causal factors rapidly encountered the arbitrariness that characterized the application of persecution policies and, to some extent, the lack of evidence for a relationship between socioeconomic status and whether an individual was arrested or not.

Discussion and Conclusions

These examples of the interplay of variables show that answering the question haunting the contemporary historian as he or she narrates (or as the reader reads about) the fate of 991 Jews from Lens during World War II—"Why did some people survive while others did not?"—is difficult using an approach favoring "linear causality." The research conducted on the Jews of Lens facing persecution suggests the importance of abandoning the fiction of monolithic determining factors and accepting that the variables have different meanings.[18] More broadly, this involves rethinking both how variables are constructed and how they are used.

Yet in the same field of operation, variables can vary over time, with differing methods and effects. Our selected area of Lens directly confronted us with this fact: the context speeds up time, often from one day to the next, and the factors characterizing individuals evolve.

We readily acknowledge that the statistical approach that we used in this study has failed to a certain extent, because it proved unable to offer a plausible explanation for the chronological variability in the destinies of the roughly one thousand Jewish subjects of our study. For a particular variable "to be explained" (for example, leaving Lens, regardless of time of departure), some variables are determinant, such as household size, whereas others have been shown to be non-determinant (such as gender) or only slightly determinant (such as socioeconomic status or nationality). There are nevertheless difficulties, as revealed even by our book's table of contents (*Face à la persécution. 991 Juifs dans la guerre*). Indeed, the relevance of "spaces of possibilities" (to borrow terminology used by microhistorical studies) diminishes significantly as individual itineraries move forward in time from one period—the early days of the persecution (between the summer of 1940 and spring 1942)—to a later one (summer 1942, when circumstances worsened significantly). In the process of attempting to make sense of the causative factors for actions revealed by our data and to present and interpret our findings in writing, we have increasingly been struck by the apparently random nature of persecution, a gloomy sensation that became increasingly powerful as our project advanced. The population's room to maneuver shrank gradually but steeply, and the categories of victims seem to have become increasingly blurred. The logic behind the various methods of persecuting the population varied from place to place and from one official to another, ultimately evolving into the steamroller that carried a significant portion of the Jewish population of Lens inexorably toward death. As researchers, we are left with the sense of having failed to decipher any overall causal pattern, despite our best efforts to make sense of a rich collection of data on this specific, well-defined population.

We also confronted another pitfall, in that the implementation of a causal explanation clashes with the arbitrariness specific to the policy of persecution; in a certain sense, the lack of a relation between socioeconomic status and arrest that we presented already indicates the presence of this arbitrary element. Is there any sense in parsing variables in the summer of 1942? Were there improbable situations whose possibility can nevertheless be examined? The lives of the Jews living in Lens appear to have often hung by a thread, like that of young William Scharfman, arrested with his mother on 11 September 1942, but saved by a railway worker on the station platform.[19] A fleeting, apparently random incident thus determined the boy's survival, but how can such apparent randomness be accounted for empirically?

In the face of the difficulties presented by quantitative analysis, a doubt can arise—should one quite simply give up? The difficulties encountered are not specific to the period or the subject studied—as numerous colleagues continue to believe by arguing that the radical singularity of the genocidal war context dooms any attempt at modeling to failure—but rather to a way of conceiving the social. For this reason, we anticipate reorienting the investigation by adhering to other ways of reading the data and formulating the thinking, as well as modeling the data. As we became aware that the deck of cards was reshuffled at every phase of the persecution, we realized that we needed a way to analyze trajectories that could also account for particular "turning points" and "bifurcations" in individual itineraries. It is unclear, in fact, whether concepts such as "career" or "sequence" are even relevant to the fates of this population or to the ebb and flow of their itineraries during different phases of persecution. This suggests that studies should be based on shorter-term strategies and on a direct approach to the methodological question of how to accommodate unpredictable or missing data, all the more important as the individuals escaped persecution. These are promising subjects that future research should address.[20]

As is clear, a microhistorical approach and quantitative analysis are not contradictory, and the shifting scale of analysis does not necessarily require a monographic or linear narrative. On the contrary, the example of the Jews from Lens offers a reminder that monographic endeavors are not part of the Labroussian model of puzzle pieces that one attempts to put together.[21] To conclude, one of the results of this text is to promote, in spite of the methodological challenges, a new approach to studying the Holocaust process, using all of the traditional methods in the historian's toolbox. We remain convinced that social science research methods can be applied to research subjects that, due to their exceptional character, are also subjects of debate and contention. There is no reason why the history of this period should be written using tools that are different from those of other historians and social scientists.

Translated from the French by John Angell and Arby Gharibian.

Nicolas Mariot is Research Professor at the National Center for Scientific Research (CNRS, France). Among his publications are *Face à la persécution. 991 Juifs dans la guerre* published with Claire Zalc (Odile Jacob, 2010); "Does Acclamation Equal Agreement? Rethinking Collective Effervescence through the Case of the Presidential *Tour de France* during the 20th Century," *Theory & Society* 40, no. 2 (March 2012): 191–221; and *Tous unis dans la tranchée? 1914–1918, les intellectuels rencontrent le people* (Seuil, 2013). His website is http://www.jourdan.ens.fr/~mariot/.

Claire Zalc is Research Professor (directrice de recherche) in history at the Institut d'histoire moderne et contemporaine, (CNRS-ENS), and at the EHESS. Her publications include *Face à la persécution: 991 Juifs dans la guerre* (2010), *Pour une microhistoire de la Shoah* (2012), and "L'histoire de la Shoah face à ses sources," a special issue of *Vingtième siècle. Revue d'histoire* (2018). She specializes in the history of immigration in twentieth-century France and the history of French Jews during World War II. She was awarded the CNRS Bronze Medal in 2013.

Notes

1. Pim Griffioen and Ron Zeller, "La persécution des Juifs en Belgique et aux Pays-Bas pendant la Seconde Guerre mondiale. Une analyse comparative," *Cahiers d'Histoire du Temps Présent*, CGTP-BEL 5 (1998): 73–132. For discussions based on statistical analyses of municipal data, see Marnix Croes, "Anti-Jewish Policy and Organization of the Deportations in France and the Netherlands, 1940–1944: A Comparative Study" and "The Holocaust in the Netherlands and the Rate of Jewish Survival," *Holocaust and Genocide Studies* 20, no. 3 (Winter 2006): 437–73 and 474–99; also see Peter Tammes, "Jewish Immigrants in the Netherlands during the Nazi Occupation," *Journal of Interdisciplinary History* 37, no. 4 (Spring 2007): 543–62. For the debate regarding survival rates in France, see Jacques Semelin, *Persécutions et entraides dans la France occupée. Comment 75% des Juifs en France ont échappé à la mort* (Paris: Les Arènes-Éd. du Seuil, 2013), as well as the controversy surrounding this book, particularly Robert O. Paxton, "Comment Vichy aggrava le sort des juifs en France," *Le Débat* 183 (2015): 173–81.
2. Annette Wieviorka, *The Era of the Witness* (Ithaca, NY: Cornell University Press, 2006). For examples of studies, see Christopher Browning, *Remembering Survival: Inside a Nazi Slave Labor Camp* (Chicago: WW Norton, 2010); Götz Aly, *Into the Tunnel: The Brief Life of Marion Samuel, 1931–1943* (New York: Metropolitan Books, 2007); Jürgen Matthäus and Mark Roseman, *Jewish Responses to Persecution*, vol. 1, *1933–1938*, Documenting Life and Destruction: Holocaust Sources in Context (Lanham, MD: AltaMira Press, 2010).
3. Michael Pollak, *L'expérience concentrationnaire. Essai sur le maintien de l'identité sociale* (Paris : Métailié, 1990).
4. Nicolas Mariot and Claire Zalc, *Face à la persécution. 991 Juifs dans la guerre* (Paris: Odile Jacob, 2010).
5. Departmental Archives (AD), Pas-de-Calais, 1Z499.
6. AD Pas-de-Calais, 1Z500 bis.
7. Jean Dawidowicz Archives, untitled two-part memoir, part handwritten and part typed, "1939–1941" and "1941–1945," undated, but after 1990, partially published in *"Un jeune couple dans la guerre. Témoignage de Jean et Charlotte Dawidowicz"* [A young couple in the war: The testimonials of Jean and Charlotte Dawidowicz], *Tsafon, revue d'études juives du Nord* 47 (2004): 41–60.
8. Journal Officiel (*Verkündungsblatt des Oberfeldkommandanten*) containing the orders of the Military Governor of the Departments of the Nord and Pas-de-Calais, no. 7, 6/12/1940, pp. 129–30, ADPC 1Z497.
9. Archives Nationales (AN), AJ38/4932 dossier 8874.

10. Two of Joseph Dawidowicz's nephews, Léon and Paul Glicksman (aged twenty and twenty-six), were arrested and "recruited" to work on the Todt organization's fortifications on the Anglo-Norman islands. They were deported on Convoy No. 55, which left Drancy for Auschwitz on 23 June 1943.
11. Daily report from the police commissioner to the mayor, dated 10/9/1942, Municipal Archives of Sallaumines.
12. Daniel Mendelsohn, *The Lost: A Search for Six of Six Million* (New York: HarperCollins, 2006); Aly, *Into the Tunnel*. More generally, see Matthäus and Roseman, *Jewish Responses to Persecution*, vol.1, *1933–1938*.
13. Nicolas Mariot and Claire Zalc, "Identifier, s'identifier: recensement, auto-déclarations et persécution des Juifs lensois (1940–1945)," *Revue d'Histoire Moderne et Contemporaine* 54, no. 3 (July–September 2007): 91–117.
14. Jean-Jacques Becker and Annette Wieviorka, eds., *Les Juifs de France de la révolution française à nos jours* (Paris: Liana Levi, 1998), 200.
15. "Témoignage de Mme Fanny Fleinman, née Dawidowicz," collected by Danielle Delmaire, *Tsafon, revue d'études juives du Nord* 9–10 (Summer–Fall 1992) : 6–11.
16. Mariot and Zalc, "Identifier, s'identifier."
17. The study considered only individuals over sixteen years of age.
18. Andrew Abbott, *Time Matters: On Theory and Method* (Chicago: University of Chicago Press, 2001).
19. Interview with William Scharfman, Lille, January 2011.
20. Pierre Mercklé and Claire Zalc, "Trajectories of the Persecuted during the Second World War: Contribution to a Microhistory of the Holocaust," in *Advances in Sequence Analysis: Theory, Method, Applications,* ed. Philippe Blanchard, Felix Bühlmann, and Jacques-Antoine Gauthier (New York, London: Springer, 2014), 171–90.
21. Peter Bruke, *The French Historical Revolution: The Annales School 1929–1989,* Key Contemporary Thinkers (Palo Alto, CA: Stanford University Press, 1990).

Bibliography

Abbott, Andrew. *Time Matters: On Theory and Method.* Chicago: University of Chicago Press, 2001.
Aly, Götz. *Into the Tunnel: The Brief Life of Marion Samuel, 1931–1943.* New York; Metropolitan Books, 2007.
Becker, Jean-Jacques, and Annette Wieviorka, eds. *Les Juifs de France de la révolution française à nos jours.* Paris: Liana Levi, 1998.
Browning, Christopher. *Remembering Survival: Inside a Nazi Slave Labor Camp.* Chicago: WW Norton, 2010.
Bruke, Peter. *The French Historical Revolution: The Annales School 1929–1989.* Key Contemporary Thinkers. Palo Alto, CA; Stanford University Press, 1990.
Croes, Marnix. "Anti-Jewish Policy and Organization of the Deportations in France and the Netherlands, 1940–1944: A Comparative Study." *Holocaust and Genocide Studies* 20, no. 3 (Winter 2006): 437–73.
———. "The Holocaust in the Netherlands and the Rate of Jewish Survival." *Holocaust and Genocide Studies* 20, no. 3 (Winter 2006): 474–99.
Griffioen, Pim, and Ron Zeller. "La persécution des Juifs en Belgique et aux Pays-Bas pendant la Seconde Guerre mondiale. Une analyse comparative." *Cahiers d'Histoire du Temps Présent, CGTP-BEL* 5 (1998): 73–132.
Mariot, Nicolas, and Claire Zalc. *Face à la persécution. 991 Juifs dans la guerre.* Paris : Odile Jacob, 2010.

———. "Identifier, s'identifier: recensement, auto-déclarations et persécution des Juifs lensois (1940–1945)." *Revue d'Histoire Moderne et Contemporaine* 54, no. 3 (July–September 2007), 91–117.

Matthäus, Jürgen, and Mark Roseman. *Jewish Responses to Persecution*. Vol. 1, *1933–1938. Documenting Life and Destruction: Holocaust Sources in Context*. Lanham, MD: AltaMira Press, 2010.

Mendelsohn, Daniel. *The Lost: A Search for Six of Six Million*. New York: HarperCollins, 2006.

Mercklé, Pierre, and Claire Zalc. "Trajectories of the Persecuted during the Second World War: Contribution to a Microhistory of the Holocaust." In *Advances in Sequence Analysis: Theory, Method, Applications*, edited by Philippe Blanchard, Felix Bühlmann, and Jacques-Antoine Gauthier, 171–90. New York, London: Springer, 2014.

Paxton Robert O. "Comment Vichy aggrava le sort des juifs en France." *Le Débat* 183 (2015): 173–81.

Pollak, Michael. *L'expérience concentrationnaire. Essai sur le maintien de l'identité sociale*. Paris : Métailié, 1990.

Semelin, Jacques. *Persécutions et entraides dans la France occupée. Comment 75% des Juifs en France ont échappé à la mort*. Paris: Les Arènes-Éd. du Seuil, 2013.

Tammes, Peter. "Jewish Immigrants in the Netherlands during the Nazi Occupation." *Journal of Interdisciplinary History* 37, no. 4 (Spring 2007): 543–62.

"Témoignage de Mme Fanny Fleinman, née Dawidowicz." Collected by Danielle Delmaire. *Tsafon, revue d'études juives du Nord* 9–10 (Summer–Fall 1992): 6–11.

"Un jeune couple dans la guerre. Témoignage de Jean et Charlotte Dawidowicz" [A young couple in the war: The testimonials of Jean and Charlotte Dawidowicz]. *Tsafon, revue d'études juives du Nord* 47 (2004): 41–60.

Wieviorka, Annette. *The Era of the Witness*. Ithaca, NY: Cornell University Press, 2006.

Chapter 6

Microhistories, Microgeographies
Budapest, 1944, and Scales of Analysis

Tim Cole and Alberto Giordano

Explaining her decision to write about Martin Guerre, Natalie Zemon Davis argued that its being "an unusual case serves me well, for a remarkable dispute can sometimes uncover motivations and values that are lost in the welter of the everyday." Like other microhistorians, Zemon Davis made no claims to the representability of her study.[1] However, in examining the "exceptional normal,"[2] "microhistorians are actually trying to discover very big things with their microscope and magnifying lenses."[3]

While, by his own admission, Mark Roseman's study of Marianne Ellenbogen's life in hiding in wartime Berlin seemed "too singular to offer more than peripheral insights into the nightmare from which she had so unusually managed to escape," Roseman discovered that "although the drama of Marianne's survival was unique, its backdrop was so well illuminated and its cast of players so large that her story sheds light on the whole theatre in which it took place."[4] Tim had a similar experience telling what geographer Hayden Lorimer dubbed "small stories" about particular people and places in Hungary in 1944, ones that suggested far bigger stories of the gendering of the Holocaust, the complex and multiple roles played by ordinary Hungarians, and the centrality of asset stripping to the concentration and deportation process.[5]

There is an attraction in telling "small stories" given that, in John Roth's words, "sound Holocaust teaching and research must concentrate on the particularity of the Holocaust, for the evil—and the good—exists in the details."[6] But more significantly, perhaps, "small stories" also have the potential to nuance and challenge bigger stories,[7] revealing greater complexity[8] and pointing to power lying not just at the center.[9] However, in that process of reframing, we do well to remember that microhistories—given their focus on exceptions—are best seen as "experiments rather than examples."[10] It is in that spirit that we reflect on writing microhistories and microgeographies of an exceptional ghetto that was both highly dispersed and ultimately liberated rather than liquidated.[11] While ghettoization is generally imagined as an act of concentration and segregation, the microhistory/microgeography of Budapest suggests a need to rethink these assumptions, particularly as we move from the scale of the city to that of the apartment building or the individual apartment. As we do, we are not suggesting that concentration and segregation were not part of the story of the ghettoization in this city—they clearly were. However, adopting a microhistorical/microgeographic approach that delves inside one of the apartment buildings that made up the dispersed ghetto in Budapest reframes our understanding of ghettoization as segregation. In particular, it suggests that the dispersed ghetto in this city separated Jews from other Jews (and not just Jews from non-Jews). Moreover, because of the scale at which ghettoization was enacted (in practice the microscale of the individual apartment), social networks between Jews and non-Jews assumed heightened significance within "ghetto" houses that were sites of Jewish and non-Jewish exchange. Taken together, microhistories and microgeographies of ghettoization in this city challenge the usual macrostory that ghettoization was a simple act of spatial segregation.

Ghettoization as Concentration?

Through the summer and fall of 1944, the approximately two hundred thousand Jews living in Budapest were confined to 1,948 apartment buildings—marked with a yellow star—spread throughout the city.[12] Although this degree of dispersion appears unusual, it reflected a wide degree of flexibility in the shape of ghettos created in Hungary. According to the ghettoization decree published on 28 April, ghettos could be created at the macroscale of the city *or* the intermediate scale of the street *or* the microscale of the individual apartment building or house, and it is clear that all these options were implemented across the country.[13] This flexibility appears to have been driven by a concern to impact non-Jewish home owners as little as possible by adopting the most pragmatic and low cost of solutions, overlaid in Budapest with an argument that dispersed ghettoization could act as a human shield of sorts offering protection for the entire city, whereas a single closed ghetto would leave the remainder of the city vulnerable to enemy bombers. The narrative that linked Jews, ghettoization, and Allied bombing was complex and shifting. At its core lay a perception of Jews as outsiders—quite literally a fifth column with links that were assumed to be closer to the Allied bombers than to "Christian Hungarians."[14] However, as Tim has explored elsewhere, this discourse was highly flexible. While in the spring of 1944 the anti-Semitic press was drawing links between Allied bombing, the Jews, and the dispersed shape of the ghetto—seeing strategic placing of Jews in the city as a means of saving the city—by midsummer they were suggesting that the Jews needed to be punished, through deportation rather than ghettoization, for the Allied bombing that had taken place.[15]

While restricting Jews to 1,948 houses was a highly dispersed form of ghettoization compared to other major cities, the first set of plans issued were even more dispersed—listing 2,639 buildings across the city. In earlier work Tim emphasized the differences between these two lists of ghetto addresses issued in quick succession on 16 June and 22 June 1944. He had read all the petitions sent by Jews and non-Jews in this chaotic week in mid-June that he could find in the Budapest archives and assumed from this mass of paperwork (perhaps on reflection being seduced by the sheer mass of paperwork in the archive) that things had changed dramatically during what he assumed to be a pivotal period. In some ways they had. The number of designated houses fell by just under a quarter. The ghetto did become more concentrated, in particular with a marked shift from the periphery to the center and from Buda to Pest. However, in his own earlier mapping of this, he had simply placed points on the map to mark individual ghetto houses in one district.[16] Engaging in more critically interdisciplinary fieldwork—working with a geographic information science (GIS) scholar Alberto Giordano—we quickly became aware that marking these houses with equal-sized dots on the map did not do justice to the material architecture of interwar Budapest, which ranged from large multistory apartment buildings in the city center to small single-story family homes in the suburban outskirts.

In order to rectify this, we reconstructed the entire city, block by block, in a digital map drawing on census returns to weight properties. Applying a number of GIS analytical methods (mean center analysis, directional distribution, standard distance, and kernel density)[17] to this mapping was for us a eureka moment. It suggested that while ghettoization did become somewhat more concentrated, the center of gravity of ghettoization shifted hardly at all between 16 and 22 June (nor indeed did it change that much between the utopian plans of early May 1944 through the ultimate implementation of two ghettos in the winter of 1944–45).[18] In short, taking the materiality of the ghetto houses seriously suggested that there were greater continuities in ghettoization in Budapest through 1944 that drew upon (and hardened) a longer history of Jewish demographic patterns. Jews had historically resided in much greater numbers and higher proportions in the central districts than in the rest of the city. The increased concentration of Jewish residences in central Pest was a change in the degree, but not in the kind, of residential patterns that had prevailed for many years. The dominant idea that remained constant throughout the process of ghettoization in Budapest was taking the ghetto to the Jew, rather than taking the Jew to the ghetto.[19] While ideology is a part of this story—a notion of the Jew's place in the city—bringing the ghetto to the Jew signaled the persuasiveness of pragmatic concerns that ghettoization avoid displacing non-Jews.

This signals the importance of considering the ways in which ghettoization was not simply a story of moving—or rather not moving—Jews, but also a story of moving—or rather not moving—non-Jews. The reshaping of cities that ghettoization entailed did not simply involve Jews (and fears of *Ostjuden*). As Gordon Horwitz has shown in the case of Łódź, ghettoization also centrally involved Poles and Germans within a radical reimagining of the city.[20] While anti-Semitic discourses were central to the restructuring of urban space into German, Polish, and Jewish quarters, ghettoization was about more than simply anti-Semitism.[21] Social and economic issues and pragmatism appear to have played their part. The pragmatic was particularly important in the context of Budapest, where ghettoization was implemented simultaneously with the deportation of Jews from towns and cities outside the capital.[22] In many ways, local officials in Budapest opted for a low-cost (for non-Jews) solution to ghettoization, which meant that the ghetto was dispersed throughout the city. However, thinking about the ways that sensitivities to non-Jewish opinion played out in 1944 led us to think about what appeared to be an even more significant act of pragmatism on the part of the local authorities. Here, writing microgeographies of ghettoization in Budapest resulted in rethinking how segregation operated as the ghetto was finally implemented on the ground.

Ghettoization as Segregation?

Three days after the second definitive list of 1,948 ghetto houses was issued, the city authorities issued a long list of regulations that marked the formal closing of this dispersed ghetto. Although easy to skip over in a quick reading of this bureaucratic document, the eighth rule was particularly significant and represented a major compromise on the part of the authorities, with important implications for both non-Jews and Jews. Forbidding non-Jews from allowing Jews to enter "for no matter how brief a period into either Christian houses or the Christian-tenanted portions of Jewish houses," this rule signaled that non-Jewish neighbors would be allowed to continue living in their apartments inside buildings marked with a yellow star, which indicated that the building in question was part of the ghetto.[23] It seems that large numbers of non-Jews decided to stay put.[24] The journalist Jenö Lévai's postwar claim that twelve thousand non-Jews lived in ghetto houses is hard to substantiate, but it may well be not far from the mark, given that in the area of the city that later became the site of the closed Pest ghetto in the winter of 1944, 144 of the 162 ghetto houses were inhabited by non-Jews as well as Jews throughout the summer and fall.[25] If we can extrapolate from these figures, then it would seem that the vast majority of the 1,948 ghetto houses identified on 22 June were in reality "mixed houses," where Jews and non-Jews lived alongside on other.

What this coexistence of Jews and non-Jews within individual ghetto houses meant in practice on the ground can be seen by looking at the experience of one Jewish family living in Budapest in 1944. The Brody family, according to Judit, who was eleven in 1944, "were lucky" given that their apartment building was included within the final list of 1,948 houses. This meant not only that the family continued to live in their own apartment with their own furniture, but more critically that they stayed within a social space that entailed continuing access to "connections" and "contacts." Outside of the apartment building, it meant that Judit's mother could get hold of scarce foodstuffs through her network of good relationships with stallholders at the nearby market hall. Inside the apartment building, it meant that Judit's family could draw on the help of their non-Jewish neighbor and the caretaker and his family, in what was, like so many other ghetto buildings, in reality a mixed house. Given the increasingly difficult conditions during the summer of 1944, Judit's parents decided it would be safer if she went into hiding outside of Budapest rather than stay with them. They turned to their non-Jewish next door neighbor, who "helped find somebody who was willing, for payment of course, to take me away." Judit assumed a new persona complete with forged papers, that of Edit, the caretakers' daughter who had been evacuated to the countryside to avoid the bombing. While in hiding, the next-door neighbor served as the main point of contact between Judit and her parents, receiving letters sent from her to her "godfather" and sending news from her parents back to her in a prearranged code. He was a pivotal figure in facilitating her hiding, as apparently was the building caretaker. The caretaker and his wife continued to play an important role in the family's story of survival. After Judit returned to Budapest in the late summer and early fall, it was the caretaker's wife who warned the Brody family that an Arrow Cross gang (members of the native fascist Nyilas Party) had raided the building and were being kept occupied by her husband. She also found them a hiding place.[26]

As the example of the Brody family illustrates, social networks between Jews and non-Jews within mixed houses were vitally important during the summer and fall of 1944.[27] We believe this calls for a reimagining of ghettoization in Budapest as an act of segregation. The initial paperwork that carved the city up into Jewish—and by oppositional definition—non-Jewish houses seemed to indicate that ghettoization at the scale of the city was an act of dispersed segregation. However, as we have suggested, even within the municipal paperwork, there is at least a hint that the situation on the ground was more complex, given that non-Jews were permitted to stay in Jewish houses. When we look inside one of those buildings, as the Brody family's story allows us to do, the nature and significance of interactions between Jews and non-Jews becomes clear. The enacting of ghettoization in Budapest at the scale of the individual apartment meant that the so-called Aryan side in Budapest was *within* many ghetto buildings, being found just down the corridor or up the stairs. On paper, non-Jewish apartments within what were in practice mixed houses were out of bounds to Jews.[28] However, the public spaces within apartment buildings—staircases, corridors, and courtyards—were sites of potential exchange between Jews and non-Jews. Moreover, the policing of the internal world of what were in effect mini-ghettos, where the apartment wall was the ghetto wall, was effectively an internal matter depending in large part on the role played by the caretaker (the Hungarian term is *házmester*, literally "house master") and those non-Jewish neighbors who had decided to remain in their apartments. This is part of a broader story of the growing importance of apartment building caretakers in particular, noted by Máté Rigó, who has indicated how, after June 1944, "social networks within the segregated residential community and its relations with the superintendent acquired more significance than ever before."[29] However, what Rigó fails to recognize is that ghetto walls were in reality being lived at the scale of the apartment, and not the apartment building. This simply meant that caretakers were not effectively the enthusiastic or reluctant organ of the state within homogenous segregated Jewish houses, but were at the heart of policing relationships within these more complex "mixed" houses where Jews and non-Jews continued living next door to each other. Technically speaking, the front door of the Brody family apartment, as well as the wall separating it from their non-Jewish neighbor's apartment, functioned as a ghetto boundary during the summer and into the fall of 1944. However, tens of thousands of mini-boundaries like these were impossible to police.[30] Moreover, with the caretaker on their side, Judit's family was able to take advantage of the presence of a non-sympathetic non-Jewish next-door neighbor, just on the other side of what was in reality a highly porous ghetto wall.

However, that wall, while porous, did mark the boundary between two radically different realities in the summer and fall of 1944. While Judit's widower neighbor continued living in his apartment on his own, her family's story was rather different. They were, as Judit was well aware, fortunate to be able to continue living in their prewar home, yet their living conditions changed markedly as a result of the ghetto order. Their four-room apartment was now shared with two other families and their grandmother. Given that it was their home, they got to choose who those families were, and so Judit's parents invited family friends to move in. This nevertheless meant a radical shake-up of the domestic space. One family moved into the bedroom of Judit's parents, and another into the dining room. Sharing a bathroom and kitchen could be, and often was, a source of conflict.[31] Across the city, ghettoization meant that Jewish families were living one family to a room; ghettoization meant overcrowding, worsened in reality by the continued presence of non-Jewish residents living in the already inadequate number of designated buildings.

The experience of overcrowding was heightened by the fact that Jews were confined to their apartment buildings for most of the day and all of the night. Initially a curfew was set, which meant Jews could leave their buildings for only three hours a day in order to shop or obtain medical assistance. Later this window was widened a little.[32] Judit recalled:

> Because we could not leave the building in the evening, after dark we dragged chairs out onto the corridor that ran the length of the building. Parents sat on the third floor discussing the day's events, the state of the war, and other important issues, children sat on the second floor watching the occasional smoldering ash from their cigarettes and cigars flit through the air from above.[33]

What was happening in Judit's apartment building was mirrored across the city, as courtyards, stairways, internal balconies, and even the rooftop became crowded communal meeting places.[34] Enclosed within the apartment building, public spaces were being negotiated between adults and children in search of places to play.[35] This restricted space was not always remembered in an entirely negative light. In the memories of those who were children at the time, for example, it was often remembered as a time of readily available playmates close at hand.[36] However, in the oral history interviews and memoir literature, it is striking how the recollection of lives shrunk to the confines of the apartment building have a claustrophobic quality to them.

Imagining the lived experience of ghettoization in Budapest in terms of just under two thousand distinct, crowded, and claustrophobic microworlds is reinforced by shifting the scale of analysis back to that of the city as a whole and then mapping the dispersed ghetto in terms of distance. Using the street network that formed one layer within the GIS that we constructed made it possible to imagine multiple "invisible walls" within this dispersed ghetto that separated Jews from other Jews, as well as from vital resources like food, health care, and paperwork.[37] Visualizing Budapest in terms of the time it would take to walk to and from a range of key points reveals how this ghetto—due to the decision to designate apartment buildings across the city, stretching from the outskirts of Buda to the outskirts of Pest—can be conceptualized as a divided space. It was physically impossible to walk across the entire city (and back again) within the three-hour window initially allowed for a round-trip journey. Naomi Gur, who was fourteen in 1944, remembered running on her way back from the hospital in Buda, where she had taken kosher food to her mother, in order to get back home to her yellow-star house in central Pest before 5:00 PM.[38] As she was well aware, distance mattered. Given the degree of dispersion and the temporal limits placed on Jewish access to the public space of the city, Jews were limited in how far they could go, and therefore where they could go and whom they could get to. This meant that Jews were in effect separated from other Jews within this highly dispersed ghetto.

The Importance of Two Gates?

Moving between a variety of scales—from the city to the apartment building down to the individual apartment—we are struck by the significance of two gates or doors that functioned within this highly dispersed ghetto. Focusing initially on the gate into the apartment building marked with a yellow star points to the lived experience of concentration. As Jews were initially confined to their apartment buildings for twenty-one hours a day and spatiotemporally limited in where they could go when permitted to leave the building, in addition to being fearful of being exposed to abuse on the streets,[39] there was a turn inward as well as a shrinking of lived space for Jewish families in Budapest such as the Brodys.[40] The individual apartment building—itself in effect a "microghetto"—increasingly became the operational scale at which day-to-day life was lived. This shrinking down of life to an apartment shared with other families within an apartment building, where public space became both playground and meeting room, reveals a particular experience of claustrophobic concentration within this unusually dispersed ghetto. At first glance, what is striking about Budapest is the adoption of a highly dispersed form of ghettoization in comparison to what is often seen as the norm of a single, enclosed ghetto area. The highly dispersed nature of the ghetto at the scale of the city, combined with the introduction of a curfew for Jews, meant that Jews were isolated, including from each other. This was a city where the ghetto separated Jews from other Jews.

Turning to look at another door, it is clear that this Budapest was also a city where the ghetto in some senses brought Jews and non-Jews closer together. As the Brody family story illustrates, there is a need to move within the closed gate of the apartment building and to walk the corridors, where Judit recalled "gentiles could stay put if they so wished and put a printed notice on their front door."[41] The ghetto wall was in reality located not solely at the main gate of the apartment building, but also at the front door of individual apartments. Within what was both a patchy and dispersed ghetto, Jews could be—and were—physically closer to non-Jews than to other Jews. Consequently, the importance of relations between Jews and non-Jews within the social space of apartment buildings became heightened. In this context, staying put to maintain long-term relationships with non-Jewish neighbors and building caretakers was of supreme importance. The Brody's non-Jewish neighbor was a critical contact who could breach the "invisible walls" created by dispersed ghettoization, as he was not subject to the curfew that limited where Jews could and could not go.

The ongoing presence of the Brody's non-Jewish next-door neighbor in the ghetto building demonstrates the need of shifting the scale for Budapest to the level of the individual apartment if we are to understand the lived experience of ghettoization. The end result is a need for microhistories (and geographies) of individual apartment buildings, ones that examine the prewar and wartime lives of those living and working there in order to better understand everyday life in a ghetto that, through the summer and fall of 1944, was made up of just under two thousand isolated but not yet entirely segregated social worlds. This is not to focus on the particular for its own sake. As we suggested at the outset, microhistory uses microscopes to uncover big things. We hope in this essay that we have been able to do a little bit of that shifting from the micro to the macro. Looking at ghettoization at the scale of one corridor within an apartment building in Budapest calls for a more radical rethinking of the assumption that ghettoization was, by definition, about the segregation of Jews and non-Jews. As this microhistory and microgeography suggest, ghettoization played out on the ground in rather complex and unexpected ways.

Tim Cole is professor of social history at the University of Bristol and also the director of the Brigstow Institute, which brings academics and nonacademic partners together to reimagine self and society. Tim's research interests range around Holocaust studies, landscape histories, digital humanities, and environmental histories. He is the author of *Images of the Holocaust/Selling the Holocaust* (1999), *Holocaust City* (2003), *Traces of the Holocaust* (2011), and *Holocaust Landscapes* (2016) and a coeditor of *Militarized Landscapes* (2010) and *Geographies of the Holocaust* (2014).

Alberto Giordano is professor and chair in the Department of Geography at Texas State University. His research focus is on the geography of genocide and the Holocaust, Historical GIS, and spatial forensics. He is the co-author of *Il Controllo di Qualità nei Sistemi Informativi Territoriali* (1994) and a coeditor of *Geographies of the Holocaust* (2014).

Notes

This material is based in part on work supported by the National Science Foundation under grant nos. 0820487 and 0820501. Any opinions, findings, conclusions, or recommendations expressed in this material are those of the author(s) and do not necessarily reflect the views of the National Science Foundation.
1. Natalie Zemon Davis, *The Return of Martin Guerre* (Cambridge, MA: Harvard University Press, 1983), 4.
2. Carlo Ginzburg, *The Cheese and the Worms: The Cosmos of a Sixteenth-Century Miller* (Baltimore: John Hopkins University Press, 1997). See here the ethical attraction of microhistory to the historian of the Holocaust, insofar as it seeks to write "a prosopography from below" of "the lost peoples of Europe." See Carlo Ginzburg and Carlo Poni, "The Name and the Game: Unequal Exchange and the Historiographic Marketplace," in *Microhistory and the Lost Peoples of Europe*, ed. E. Muir and G.

Ruggiero (Baltimore: Johns Hopkins University Press, 1991), 7. There is an ethical attraction to writing prosopographies of the Holocaust from below, given that, as Ruth Wisse suggests, "individualizing the Holocaust undoes the levelling work of the Nazi regime." See Ruth Wisse, introduction to *Holocaust Chronicles: Individualizing the Holocaust through Diaries and Other Contemporaneous Personal Accounts*, ed. R. Shapiro (Hoboken, NJ: Ktav, 1999), xviii.

3. Matti Peltonen, "Clues, Margins, and Monads: The Micro-Macro Link in Historical Research," *History and Theory* 40 (2001): 348, 356–57. See also Jürgen Schlumbohm, ed., *Mikrogeschichte, Makrogeschichte: komplementär oder inkommensurabel?* (Göttingen: Wallstein Verlag, 1998); and Giovanni Levi, "On Microhistory," in *New Perspectives on Historical Writing*, ed. P. Burke (Cambridge: Polity Press, 1991).
4. Peltonen, "Clues, Margins, and Monads," 350.
5. Mark Roseman, *A Past in Hiding: Memory and Survival in Nazi Germany* (New York: Henry Holt, 2000), 11. Roseman describes the correspondence between Marianne and her fiancé Ernst as "unique," 13 (emphasis mine).
6. Tim Cole, *Traces of the Holocaust: Journeying in and out of the Ghettos* (London: Continuum, 2011); Hayden Lorimer, "Telling Small Stories: Spaces of Knowledge and the Practice of Geography," *Transactions of the Institute of British Geographers* 28, no. 2 (2003): 197–217.
7. John K. Roth, "Equality, Neutrality, Particularity: Perspectives on Women and the Holocaust," in *Experience and Expression: Women, the Nazis, and the Holocaust*, ed. E. Baer and M. Goldenberg (Detroit: Wayne State University Press, 2003), 14. "Having taught about the Holocaust for many years," Roth reflected, "I have discovered that the best learning strategies often involve concentrating on small details, on events that are utterly particular but charged with intensity. As one explores how these details developed, how those events took place, they lead outward in spiralling concentric circles to wider historical perspectives."
8. Dan Stone, *Constructing the Holocaust* (London: Vallentine Mitchell, 1973), 212, 224, calls for historians to generate "new narratives" given "the obviously chaotic nature" of an event that "questions that very reliance on coherence, traditionally the *obbligato* of narrative."
9. Barry Reay, *Microhistories: Demography, Society and Culture in Rural England, 1800–1930* (Cambridge: Cambridge University Press, 1996), 258, writes that "the advantage of placing a small community under the microscope is that it becomes possible to see and explore the complexity of social interaction and social and economic processes." Dave Rollison suggests that microhistories of early modern England have revealed a past that is "more anarchic, various and eccentric than authorized styles and versions have had us believe"; D. Rollison, "Microhistory and Epic History," conference paper given at the University of East Anglia (24 April 2002), cited in Judith Spicksley, "Conference Report: The Social and Cultural History of Early Modern England: New Approaches and Interpretations. University of East Anglia, 24 April 2002," *Social History* 28, no. 1 (2003): 84.
10. Giovanni Levi, "The Origins of the Modern State and the Microhistorical Perspective," in *Mikrogeschichte, Makrogeschichte: komplementär oder inkommensurabel?*, ed. J. Schlumbohm (Göttingen: Wallstein Verlag, 1998), 61–62.
11. Peltonen, "Clues, Margins, and Monads," 349, who suggests, "The unifying principle of all microhistorical research is the belief that microscopic observation will reveal factors previously unobserved.... Phenomena previously considered to be sufficiently described and understood assume completely new meanings by altering the scale of observation. It is then possible to use these results to draw far wider generalizations although the initial observations were made within relatively narrow dimensions and as experiments rather than examples."

12. These ideas emerge from my own earlier work on Budapest: see Tim Cole, *Holocaust City: The Making of a Jewish Ghetto* (New York: Routledge, 2003), as well as more recent collaborative work with geographic information scientist Alberto Giordano as part of a wider research project into Holocaust geographies. On the wider work, see Waitman Beorn et al., "Geographical Record: Geographies of the Holocaust," *Geographical Review* 99, no. 4 (2009): 563–74. On the specific focus on Budapest, see Giordano and Cole, "On Place and Space: Calculating Social and Spatial Networks in the Budapest Ghetto," *Transactions in GIS* 15, no. S1 (2011): 143–70; Cole and Giordano, "Rethinking Segregation in the Ghetto: Invisible Walls and Social Networks in the Dispersed Ghetto in Budapest, 1944," in *Lessons and Legacies*, vol. 11, *Expanding Perspectives on the Holocaust in a Changing World,* ed. H. Earl and Karl A. Schleunes, 265–91 (Evanston: Northwestern University Press, 2014); Cole and Giordano, "Bringing the Ghetto to the Jew: Spatialities of Ghettoization in Budapest," in *Geographies of the Holocaust*, ed. Anne Kelly Knowles, Tim Cole, and Alberto Giordano, 120–57 (Bloomington: Indiana University Press, 2014).
13. Decree no. 1.610/1944. M.E. (Prime Minister's Office) (28 April 1944), *Budapesti Közlöny* 95 (April 28, 1944) (emphasis mine). Three weeks earlier, the secret ghetto order issued by Baky had specified that Jews living in towns or large villages were to be housed in "Jewish buildings or ghettos." See Randolph L. Braham, *The Politics of Genocide. The Holocaust in Hungary* (New York: Columbia University Press, 1994) 574; Cole, *Traces of the Holocaust*, ch. 4.
14. On the centrality of the notion of "Christian Hungary," see Paul A. Hanebrink, *In Defense of Christian Hungary: Religion, Nationalism and Anti-Semitism, 1890–1944* (Ithaca: Cornell University Press, 2006).
15. Cole, *Holocaust City,* esp. ch. 6, where I argue that this discourse needs to be read historically as one that shifted across 1944. See also Tim Cole, *Traces of the Holocaust,* esp. ch. 3; Cole, "Contesting and Compromising Ghettoization, Hungary 1944," in *Lessons and Legacies,* vol. 9, *Memory, History and Responsibility: Reassessments of the Holocaust, Implications for the Future,* ed. John Roth, Lynn Rapaport, and Jonathan Petroulous (Evanston: Northwestern University Press, 2010), 152–66.
16. Cole, *Holocaust City,* see esp. chs 5 and 6.
17. Mean center analysis identifies the geographic center of a distribution, shown as a solid circle on the map. Directional distribution finds the overall directional pattern of the data. Standard distance measures the degree of concentration; the larger the circle, the more dispersed the locational pattern. Unlike the mean center, standard distance, and deviational ellipse, which return a single value, kernel analysis calculates a density surface around points or areas, returning a set of continuous values. The result is a more detailed representation of the phenomenon under study.
18. For more on those other plans, see Cole, *Holocaust City,* esp. chs 4 and 8. For more on this mapping, see Cole and Giordano, "Bringing the Ghetto to the Jew."
19. Cole, "Contesting and Compromising Ghettoization."
20. Gordon Horwitz, Ghettostadt. *Łódź and the Making of a Nazi City.* Cambridge, Mass.: The Belknap Press of Harvard University Press, 2008. See also Tim Cole, "Ghettos and the Remaking of Urban Space: A Comparative Study of Budapest and Warsaw," in *Cities into Battlefields: Metropolitan Scenarios, Experiences and Commemorations of Total War,* ed. S. Goebel and D. Keene, 133–149 (London: Ashgate 2011).
21. Dan Michman, *The Emergence of Jewish Ghettos during the Holocaust* (New York: Cambridge University Press, 2011).
22. However, I would be cautious of drawing too close a line between the two, and it seems in particular that actors at a local level were operating with different assumptions and timescales than actors at a national level. On this see Cole, *Holocaust City,* 77–80, 95–100.

23. Braham, *Politics of Genocide*, 737–38.
24. *Esti Ujság* (13 July 1944); *Esti Ujság* (21 July 1944).
25. Jenö Lévai, *Fekete Könyv a Magyar Zsidóság Szenvedéseirol* (Budapest: Officina, 1946), 156; Braham, *Politics of Genocide*, 735; New Hungarian Central Archives [ÚMKL] XXXIII–5–c–1, XI.23.
26. Interview with Judit Brody (Oxford, 26 November 2009); Judit Brody, unpublished memoir; Judit Brody (Edit), letter to her "Godfather" (11 July 1944, 14 July 1944).
27. Braham, *Politics of Genocide*, 853. On the importance of Jewish/non-Jewish social networks in Warsaw, see G. S. Paulsson, *Secret City* (New Haven: Yale University Press, 2002), esp. 26–7.
28. Braham, *Politics of Genocide*, 737–38.
29. Maté Rigó, "Ordinary Women and Men: Superintendents and Jews in the Budapest Yellow-star Houses in 1944–1945," *Urban History* 40, no. 1 (2013): 71–91. See also Istvan P. Adam, *Budapest Building Managers and the Holocaust in Hungary*. Houndmills: Palgrave Macmillan, 2016.
30. My sense is that ghetto boundaries elsewhere were more porous than we often imagine. See my discussion of this in Tim Cole, "Building and Breaching the Ghetto Boundary: A Brief History of the Ghetto Fence in Körmend, Hungary, 1944," *Holocaust and Genocide Studies* 23, no. 1 (2009): 54–75.
31. Interview with Judit Brody; Brody, unpublished memoir.
32. M. kir. Rendőrség budapesti főkapitánya 7200/fk.eln.1944 sz., reproduced in Ilona Benoschofsky and Elek Karsai, *Vádirat a Nácizmus Ellen. Dokumentumok a Magyarországi Zsidóüldözés Történetéhez*, vol. 2 (Budapest: A Magyar Izraeliták Országos Képviselete Kiadása, 1960), between 304–5. For a translation, see Braham, *Politics of Genocide*, 855–56. This three-hour window was extended later on. In early July, Jews were permitted to leave their homes for six hours each day, from 11:00 AM on weekdays and from 9:00 AM on Sundays. See Braham, *Politics of Genocide*, 856; Ernő Munkácsi, "Hogy történt? XXXI A Budapesti Zsidóság Összeköltöztetése," *Új Élet* 2, no. 32 (8 August 1946), cited in Benoschofsky and Karsai, *Vádirat a Nácizmus Ellen*, 2:348; *Esti Ujság* (8 July 1944); *Függetlenség* (9 July 1944), *Összetartás* (3 August 1944); RWPA, F2C 21/535, Alfred Schomberger; *Függetlenség* (1 September 1944); *Esti Ujság* (22 September 1944).
33. Brody, unpublished memoir.
34. Raoul Wallenberg Project Archive, University Library Uppsala (hereafter RWPA) F2C 16/339, Zsuzsa Gordon; RWPA F2C 11/340 Erzsébet Rosenberg; RWPA F2C 17/343, István Bélai; RWPA, F2C 19/503; Ernő Szép, *The Smell of Humans* (Budapest: Central European University Press, 1994), 28; interview with TK and JK (London, 19 November 2010).
35. See, e.g., RWPA, F2C 20/518, Dr Paul Milch.
36. A particularly striking example is found in Zsuzsanna Ozsváth, *When the Danube Ran Red* (Syracuse, NY: Syracuse University Press, 2010).
37. Giordano and Cole, "On Place and Space"; Cole and Giordano, "Rethinking Segregation"; Cole and Giordano, "Bringing the Ghetto to the Jew."
38. RWPA, F2C 3/118, Naomi Gur.
39. Erika Gottlieb, *Becoming My Mother's Daughter. A Story of Survival and Renewal* (Waterloo: Wilfrid Laurier University Press, 2008), 62; Laura Palosuo, *Yellow Stars and Trouser Inspections: Jewish Testimonies from Hungary, 1920–1945* (Uppsala: Uppsala Universitet, 2008), 151–53; RWPA F2C 7/307 Miklósné Kellner; RWPA F2C 18/349, Erwin Forester; RWPA F2C 19/503 Peter Tarjan; Szép, *The Smell of Humans*, 19–20.
40. Szép, *The Smell of Humans*, 10–32.
41. Brody, unpublished memoir.

Bibliography

Adam, Istvan P. *Budapest Building Managers and the Holocaust in Hungary.* Houndmills: Palgrave Macmillan, 2016
Benoschofsky, Ilona, and Elek Karsai. *Vádirat a Nácizmus Ellen. Dokumentumok a Magyarországi Zsidóüldözés Történetéhez.* Vol. 2. Budapest: A Magyar Izraeliták Országos Képviselete Kiadása, 1960.
Beorn, Waitman, et al. "Geographical Record: Geographies of the Holocaust." *Geographical Review* 99, no. 4 (2009): 563–74.
Braham, Randolph L. *The Politics of Genocide. The Holocaust in Hungary.* New York: Columbia University Press, 1994.
Cole, Tim. "Ghettos and the Remaking of Urban Space: A Comparative Study of Budapest and Warsaw." In *Cities into Battlefields. Metropolitan Scenarios, Experiences and Commemorations of Total War,* ed. S. Goebel and D. Keene, 133–49. London: Ashgate 2011.
———. *Traces of the Holocaust: Journeying in and out of the Ghettos.* London: Continuum, 2011.
———. "Contesting and Compromising Ghettoization, Hungary 1944." In *Lessons and Legacies,* vol. 9, *Memory, History and Responsibility: Reassessments of the Holocaust, Implications for the Future,* ed. John Roth, Lynn Rapaport, and Jonathan Petroulous, 152–66. Evanston, IL: Northwestern University Press, 2010.
———. "Building and Breaching the Ghetto Boundary: A Brief History of the Ghetto Fence in Körmend, Hungary, 1944." *Holocaust and Genocide Studies* 23, no. 1 (2009): 54–75.
———. *Holocaust City: The Making of a Jewish Ghetto.* New York: Routledge, 2003.
Cole, Tim, and Giordano, Alberto. "Rethinking Segregation in the Ghetto: Invisible Walls and Social Networks in the Dispersed Ghetto in Budapest, 1944." In *Lessons and Legacies,* vol. 11, *Expanding Perspectives on the Holocaust in a Changing World,* ed. H. Earl and Karl A. Schleunes, 265–91. Evanston, IL: Northwestern University Press, 2014.
———. "Bringing the Ghetto to the Jew: Spatialities of Ghettoization in Budapest." In *Geographies of the Holocaust,* ed. Anne Kelly Knowles, Tim Cole, and Alberto Giordano, 120–57. Bloomington: Indiana University Press, 2014.
Ginzburg, Carlo. *The Cheese and the Worms: The Cosmos of a Sixteenth-century Miller.* Baltimore: John Hopkins University Press, 1997.
Ginzburg, Carlo, and Carlo Poni. "The Name and the Game: Unequal Exchange and the Historiographic Marketplace." In *Microhistory and the Lost Peoples of Europe,* ed. E. Muir and G. Ruggiero. Baltimore: Johns Hopkins University Press, 1991.
Giordano, Alberto, and Tim Cole. "On Place and Space: Calculating Social and Spatial Networks in the Budapest Ghetto." *Transactions in GIS* 15, no. S1 (2011): 143–70.
Gottlieb, Erika. *Becoming My Mother's Daughter. A Story of Survival and Renewal.* Waterloo: Wilfrid Laurier University Press, 2008.
Hanebrink, Paul A. *In Defense of Christian Hungary: Religion, Nationalism and Anti-Semitism, 1890–1944.* Ithaca, NY: Cornell University Press, 2006.
Horowitz, Gordon J. *Ghettostadt. Łódź and the Making of a Nazi City.* Cambridge, Mass.: The Belknap Press of Harvard University Press, 2008.
Levi, Giovanni. "The Origins of the Modern State and the Microhistorical Perspective." In *Mikrogeschichte, Makrogeschichte: komplementär oder inkommensurabel?,* ed. J. Schlumbohm. Göttingen: Wallstein Verlag, 1998, 53–82.
———. "On Microhistory." In *New Perspectives on Historical Writing,* ed. P. Burke. Cambridge: Polity Press, 1991, 93–113.

Lorimer, Hayden. "Telling Small Stories: Spaces of Knowledge and the Practice of Geography." *Transactions of the Institute of British Geographers* 28, no. 2 (2003): 197–217.
Michman, Dan. *The Emergence of Jewish Ghettos during the Holocaust.* New York: Cambridge University Press, 2011.
Ozsváth, Zsuzsanna. *When the Danube Ran Red.* Syracuse, NY: Syracuse University Press, 2010.
Palosuo, Laura. *Yellow Stars and Trouser Inspections: Jewish Testimonies from Hungary, 1920–1945.* Uppsala: Uppsala Universitet, 2008.
Peltonen, Matti. "Clues, Margins, and Monads: The Micro-Macro Link in Historical Research." *History and Theory* 40 (2001): 348, 356–57.
Reay, Barry. *Microhistories: Demography, Society and Culture in Rural England, 1800–1930.* Cambridge: Cambridge University Press, 1996.
Rigó, Maté. "Ordinary Women and Men: Superintendents and Jews in the Budapest Yellow-Star Houses in 1944–1945." *Urban History* 40, no. 1 (2013): 71–91.
Roseman, Mark. *A Past in Hiding: Memory and Survival in Nazi Germany.* New York: Henry Holt, 2000.
Roth, John K. "Equality, Neutrality, Particularity: Perspectives on Women and the Holocaust." In *Experience and Expression: Women, the Nazis, and the Holocaust*, ed. E. Baer and M. Goldenberg. Detroit: Wayne State University Press, 2003, 5–22.
Schlumbohm, Jürgen, ed. *Mikrogeschichte, Makrogeschichte: komplementär oder inkommensurabel?* Göttingen: Wallstein Verlag, 1998.
Spicksley, Judith. "Conference Report: The Social and Cultural History of Early Modern England: New Approaches and Interpretations. University of East Anglia, 24 April 2002." *Social History* 28, no. 1 (2003), 83–87.
Stone, Dan. *Constructing the Holocaust.* London: Vallentine Mitchell, 1973.
Wisse, Ruth. Introduction to *Holocaust Chronicles: Individualizing the Holocaust through Diaries and Other Contemporaneous Personal Accounts*, ed. R. Shapiro. Hoboken, NJ: Ktav, 1999, xiii–xviii
Zemon Davis, Natalie. *The Return of Martin Guerre.* Cambridge, MA: Harvard University Press, 1983.

Part II

FACE-TO-FACE
VICTIMS AND PERPETRATORS

Chapter 7

Microhistory of the Holocaust in Poland
New Sources, New Trails

Jan Grabowski

> *Everything that happened, happened because someone, an individual, made a decision ... the Holocaust is so big, the scale of it is so gigantic, so enormous, that it becomes easy to think of it as something mechanical. Anonymous. But everything that happened, happened because someone made a decision. To pull a trigger, to flip a switch, to close a cattle car door, to hide, to betray. It was this consideration in mind—which to the record of historical facts ... adds the invisible dimension of morality.*
> —Daniel Mendelsohn, *The Lost: A Search for Six of Six Million*

Microhistorical Approach: History and Challenges

Microhistory of the Shoah began as soon as people started searching for their close relations, tracking the odd bits of information that, assembled together, became stories of individual families' struggle for survival. With the passing years and decades, this search—conducted now with more resources and patience by amateur genealogists—found itself at the root of many extraordinary books, such as the novel by Daniel Mendelsohn cited above. On another level, microhistory of the

Shoah became the domain of *Landsmannschaften* [Associations of Jews from a given shtetl or city] which, with the help of books of memory (*Izkor*), tried to capture as much as humanly possible from the vanished world of the former shtetls. Although produced without academic rigor, these studies, filled with the testimonies of survivors, are often the only source enabling our search for answers into the destruction of Jewish communities. Finally, on an academic and scholarly level, study of the Holocaust initially developed along different lines, devoting considerable attention to the history of institutions. These top-down studies, focusing on what may be called "the elegance of the decision-making processes," are part of the *Tätervorschung*, or study of perpetrators. It is in this context that Saul Friedländer commented:

> The Germans were bent on exterminating the Jews as individuals.... The "history of the Holocaust" cannot be limited only to recounting of German policies, decisions, and measures that led to this most systematic and sustained of genocides, it must include the reactions (and at times the initiatives) of the surrounding world and the attitudes of the victims, for the fundamental reason that the events we call the Holocaust represent a totality defined by this convergence of distinct elements.[1]

Microhistory should not be equated with local history, although microhistory can, at times, also be local history. Descending to the level of individual experience, a historian follows the personal trajectories of people fighting for survival or, conversely, the trajectories of those who made their survival so desperately unlikely. Historians using the tools of the microhistorical trade will thus often become familiar with the local history; however, the mobility of their subjects requires constant shifts in geographic focus and seamless transitions from local to more general history.

Whether one is looking at the Jews of Lens[2] or those hiding in the Prefecture d'Isère,[3] in distant Łuków or at the house of horrors known as village Gniewczyna,[4] one is following the people rather than the buildings, streets, towns, and counties they left behind in their search for a safe heaven. Research into the microhistory of the Holocaust can be based on various and often neglected or overlooked primary sources—in short, on all documents that shed light on the fate of survivors, as well as the much more numerous group of those who perished. But writing the microhistory of the Shoah can also take on the novel form of exploring the role of "third party" institutions, seen not so much through the prism of their institutional mission, but rather through the decisions of people who had to act one way or another. Laurent Joly, in his recent study of the Parisian police, conducted a detailed inquiry into one particular office, Office 91 (to be even more specific, an office located on the third floor of the west wing of Parisian police headquarters), to demonstrate the impact that individual choices made by particular employees in this office had in determining the fate of Parisian Jews.[5] Incidentally, Benjamin Frommer, who conducted an inquiry very similar to Joly's, has confirmed the promise that such "microhistorical" research exploring the actions of employees of non-German institutions has for the study of the Shoah. Frommer, who turned his attention to several policemen working within the heart of the *Judenreferat* [Jewish Section] in the Czech criminal police in Prague, was able to convincingly demonstrate the extent to which the decisions of these few individual Czech bureaucrats and officers destroyed the lives of the Jews of Bohemia.[6] And this is only the beginning of a long process that has called into question the whole concept of an impartial "bystander" as a useful and historically justified concept in the study of the Shoah.

New Sources for the Study of the Holocaust

During the last few years, a very significant amount of previously unknown sources from the archives of the former Soviet Bloc countries has entered the public domain. In the case of Poland, these new sources not only can make a marked contribution to our knowledge of the period, but can also change our understanding of some of the most important related issues. One can start with the thousands of Jewish testimonies recorded shortly after the war and preserved in the Jewish Historical Institute in Warsaw. These testimonies, written in Polish or Yiddish, until recently remained largely unknown to researchers. As far as Western historiography of the Holocaust is concerned, they still remain a rarely used source. While the testimonies of survivors tell us an important part of the story, they do not tell us most of the story. And here the new sources from the Polish archives can make a difference. Most importantly, the new historical evidence allows us to hear the voices of those who perished. The Holocaust was, above all, the experience of death, and not one of survival. In Poland, home to the largest Jewish population in prewar Europe, the chances of survival for Jews were on the order of 1.5 to 2 percent.[7] Given these numbers, one has to wonder to what extent our understanding of the Holocaust can depend on the testimony of such an exceptional few. In order to hear the voices of those whose struggle for survival proved ultimately unsuccessful, we should first turn to the files of wartime German and Polish courts. Soon after the conquest of Poland, the Germans reorganized the institutional structures of the occupied land. While many institutions of the former Polish state were suppressed, the courts had already been reopened before the end of 1939. In the so-called General Government, the occupier established a dual structure made up of German and Polish courts. While the former catered to Germans and the Volksdeutsche (ethnic Germans), they were also given jurisdiction over all violations of the new German Order and could act whenever the "vital interests of the German People" were threatened. At the same time, the Polish courts (Sądy Grodzkie, municipal or lower courts, and Sądy Okręgowe, regional or higher ones) retained jurisdiction in "regular" matters involving non-Germans (i.e., all matters that the occupation authorities found of no interest to themselves). In both cases, the Jews were frequent "clients" of tribunals. As German regulations grew more restrictive, Jewish poverty and misery became more dramatic, and increasing numbers of Jews turned to the courts. In all cases, witness depositions and interrogations of the accused allow us to hear the voices of people who, in the vast majority of cases, would not survive the rapidly approaching "Final Solution."

The more serious cases involving Jews were transferred under the authority of German *Sondergericht* (special courts) or *deutsches Gericht*. [German court] These included Jews who left the ghetto without proper authorization or the required *"Zionistenstern"* armband (as it was described in arrest protocols), engaged in black-market activities, were found with false ID or doctored ration cards, or openly expressed their displeasure with the German Order. Once again, thousands of preserved interrogations and depositions constitute an extraordinary source of information given by those who, for the most part, perished in the Holocaust. In addition to the Jewish voices, the wartime court files provide us with the observations made by Polish police officers (who were in charge of initial investigations for both the Polish and the German courts) and more importantly by gentiles involved in various ways in the "Jewish" cases. Their statements are quite likely to change our understanding of the term "bystander" as used in the Holocaust literature.

Even more revealing and valuable from a historian's standpoint are the postwar investigations into wartime collaboration with the enemy. These trials (known in Poland as the "August trials") were conducted on the basis of the 31 August 1944 decree "concerning the punishment of Fascist-Nazi criminals, guilty of murders and mistreatment of civilians and prisoners of war and traitors of the Polish Nation." Similar proceedings were conducted in other countries of Eastern Europe and the Soviet Union. In our case, we shall pay particular attention to these "traitors of the Polish Nation," because it is among them that we find individuals who denounced, mistreated, or simply murdered their fellow Jewish citizens. According to the contemporary interpretation of the law, all actions undertaken by Poles that helped the Germans exterminate Jews constituted a form of collaboration with the enemy. Between 1945 and 1946, the August trials were heard by Special Criminal Courts (*Specjalny Sąd Karny*), but already by late 1946 regular courts had taken over. The cases followed a normal judicial process, starting with the local district courts, then the appellate courts, and sometimes appealed all the way to the Supreme Court. More importantly, there is no evidence that the "Jewish" trials were tampered with by the ruling communists. Quite the contrary, in the aftermath of the Kielce pogrom, the authorities seem to have been reluctant to pursue these cases (possibly for fear of an international backlash); the sentences were light, and suspects were quickly released from prisons. A typical "August" file numbers two hundred to five hundred pages and includes records of the investigation (e.g., witness depositions, interrogations of suspects, denunciations), transcripts of court hearings, sentences, appeals to the Supreme Court, requests for pardon, and collectively signed petitions in favor of the accused or the convicts. The August files cover the entire territory of occupied Poland, and "Jewish" cases—those involving the murders and denunciation of Jews—run into the thousands. The court records provide us not only with the names of thousands of Jewish victims, but also with the circumstances of their deaths. The August files also allow looking at the "Polish" (or Ukrainian, Slovak, Lithuanian, or Czech, depending on the case) side of the equation, through the prism of thousands of witness depositions and interrogations of the accused. All in all, historians are faced here with the largest, and quite possibly the last, unknown repository of information on the Holocaust of such size.

Microhistory: Following the Trajectories of Survivors and Those Who Perished from Dąbrowa Tarnowska, Kraków District, General Government

The new sources from the archives, combined with Jewish testimonies, allow us to better "triangulate" the historical evidence, in order to descend to the level of the individual experience of Jews fighting for survival. In this case, the triangulation will test the limits of the historical records, enabling us to follow the fates of nine people who tried, with varying degrees of success, to survive in county Dąbrowa Tarnowska, a rural area located some ten miles north of Tarnów and forty miles northeast of Kraków in southeastern Poland.

In the summer of 1942, at the time of the liquidation of a small ghetto in Dąbrowa Tarnowska, Melania Weissenberg (illustration 7.1) was an

Illustration 7.1. Melania Weissenberg (middle) with her mother, Sara, and brother Zygmunt (Zyga), Kraków, 1936(?). Photo from the Weissenberg family archive.

impressionable, precocious, 12-year-old girl, enamored with her much older best friend, Sabina Goldman (illustration 7.2). Chaja Rosenblatt (illustration 7.3), 21 years old, had just been married and had to care for her aging and sick parents. Rivka Shenker, the same age as Chaja, arrived in the Dąbrowa ghetto just days before its liquidation. Sisters Salomea and Hela Süss hailed from a small village close to Dąbrowa; they were, respectively, 17 and 19 years old. Estera Metzger was a 35-year-old mother of two. Her daughter's name was Tolka, and the name of her 12-year-old son remains unknown. Before mid-July 1942, all of them found themselves, together with some thirty-five hundred other Jews, behind the wood and barbed wire fence that separated them from the Aryan side of the city. In July 1942, when this account begins, all of them had already heard about the impending liquidation of their ghetto.

Different Ways to Flee the Liquidation of a Ghetto

The main "liquidation action" in Dąbrowa took place on 17 July 1942, when nearly two thousand Jews were deported to Bełżec, and one hundred others were executed in the streets. The first description of this *Aktion* comes from Chaja Rosenblatt, who, having learned from a well-informed Pole about the imminent "resettlement," chose to gather her family and flee in the night. Shortly after dawn, marching through the woods near the main road toward Tarnów, she suddenly heard "a horrible, terrifying, noise. We turn our eyes on the road, and we see a long column [of cars] rolling toward Dąbrowa. In the column we could see army lorries, cars, and armored cars. The column was nearly a kilometer long. It was obvious that the deportation commission was on its way to Dąbrowa to exterminate the Jews."[8] Many inhabitants of Dąbrowa Tarnowska, who, unlike Chaja, had no foresight, resources, or will to flee the ghetto before the imminent *Aktion,* hid instead in hideouts they had previously prepared inside their houses. One of them was Rivka Shenker, who saw from the attic of her house the arrival of the "deportation column" that had been seen a few moments earlier by Chaja Rosenblatt:

> At 4:00 AM, as I watched through a little hole in the wall of the hideout, I saw many cars arrive, we heard the shouts: *"Aufmachen!"* but Sala left the front door open. They went into the house, started to shout hysterically that everyone had to leave the house and that if they found anyone in hiding, they would shoot them right away. I cannot even find the right words to describe my feelings back then. I was certain that our last moment had arrived; Daddy

Illustration 7.2. Sabina Golman, Dąbrowa Tarnowska ghetto, 1941.

hugged me and started to kiss me. We all remained as if paralyzed. They climbed into the attic, where we were hidden, they started to knock on the walls and probe them with bayonets. At one point I heard the shouts, and one German said: "I think I heard something, there is someone hidden here!" They broke down the planks and took our neighbors. Their screams were horrible. We had no idea that our neighbors had built their hideout so close to ours. I saw them being tied up and marched to the square.[9]

In early October, Rivka Shenker decided to flee:

> There was a fellow, his name was Lasota, and this Lasota knew quite well how to reach the Dulcza forest. He even had friends among the policemen. It must have cost a lot of money to get us over, each of us had to pay fifty zlotys, and there were five of us—two women and three men. I will never forget that day, it was 5 October [1942], it kept raining, it was pitch black, very windy, and very dangerous, but Janek made up his mind and decided that we had to leave at 4:00 AM. We were ready, we crossed the electric fence and all went well. Lasota waited on the other side with a strong rope, which we had to hold onto, so that we wouldn't get lost on the way. We ran so fast that I can hardly believe one can be so strong.... At 6:30 AM we reached Dulcza forest, and we were so glad that we could finally rest.

Unlike Rivka Shenker, who ended up hiding in bunkers in the forest some fifteen miles east of Dąbrowa, twelve-year-old Melania Weissenberg and her older cousin Helena went into hiding at a peasant's farm on the outskirts of Dąbrowa. While in hiding, Melania managed to keep a diary, in which she noted important events that marked her everyday existence.[10] On Thursday, 10 September 1942, she noted:

> I am now at one peasant woman's place, where I went hiding with my family in order to flee the storm, which has to pass over the city. Oh, how much I fear about my love [author's friend, Sabina Goldman], who stayed behind in this awful city [Dąbrowa Tarnowska]! Now, I have all the time I want, so I keep thinking a lot. And I shiver at the thought that Binieczka might not leave the town in time!

Indeed, Melania's fears were soon to be confirmed. In her last letter, written on 11 September 1942, Sabina Goldman wrote from Dąbrowa to her young friend:

> My beloved child! I really have nothing to say because anything I will write will be empty and stupid, but I know you will accept even so little. What can one write at a time like this? We have already been in dire straits many times, but never before in such a situation as we are now. And we are completely powerless. Whether we hide or flee, will it change anything?? No, never! We have to accept the thought that our lives are nearly over. We can say to our-

selves that we are already seventy years old and that we leave this world to other people. Unfortunately, we are not leaving this world to make room for our children or our grandchildren! But what can we do? The N. say that if one encounters a Jew after the war, they will have to salute him from afar. I hope that the N. are wrong. But let's not think about it. These are perhaps the last hours of our lives, so why should we poison them? I have no idea, perhaps some of us will survive? Perhaps someone will live through all of this? Be well and pray to the Lord that we see each other once again, yourloving Sabina.[11]

A few days later, on 18 September 1942, the final *Aktion* struck the ghetto. Sabina Goldman was hauled out from her hideout, arrested by the Polish "blue" police, and later delivered to the Germans. It is uncertain whether she was shot by the gendarmes or sent on to the death train destined for Bełżec. The news of her friend's death reached Melania on 28 September 1942. She wrote in her diary:

> So all my fears, unfortunately, were proved right! I wish this day never came, when I learned from my father's letter that my dearest, most beloved creature had been deported to a certain death! And after they kill her with electricity they will suck off her fat for soap! Oh, it's horrible, incomprehensible! To cut down this beautiful flower! If I survive, horrible will be my vengeance! It's for that vengeance that I lead this horrible life. This is the only thing that keeps me alive. When can I settle the score?

Chaja Rosenblatt hailed from the small town of Radomyśl, located east of Dąbrowa, in neighboring Mielec county. In the early summer of 1942, just before the destruction of Radomyśl, "people who had money or other goods could stay with friendly farmers whom they knew in the area," Chaja noted in her memoir. Unfortunately, as soon as the deportations began, the peasants, terrified of their own neighbors and the Germans, threw "their" Jews out, regardless of previous payments, promises, and arrangements. Chaja and her husband and parents began a long journey through the woods to the liquidated ghetto in Dąbrowa, and she later sought refuge in the large Tarnów ghetto. Fleeing another liquidation in January 1943, she left Tarnów and returned to the village of Small Dulcza, close to her native Radomyśl. After several unsuccessful attempts at hiding among the peasants or in the Mielec-area work camps for Jews,[12] Chaja and her husband found refuge in bunkers in the Dulcza forest.

While Chaja and Rivka dug bunkers in the Dulcza forest, Melania and Helena remained hidden at the farm of their original rescuer, very close to Dąbrowa, some twelve miles west of Dulcza. In the winter of 1943, their host moved them from the original hideout in the attic over the barn quite literally underground. In her diary Melania noted:

Illustration 7.3. Chaja Rosenblatt (Garn) second from the left, with her parents and sisters, Radomyśl Wielki, 1935(?). Photograph from the Rosenblatt family archive.

25 January 1943. A great change in my life! We have changed our "apartment." From our hideout in the barn, we moved to a box placed underground. There is, one has to say, an opening through which light and air can enter, but we cannot even sit up. It is terrible to lie and do nothing the whole day. Only at night can we exit to the stinking stables; cold and dark and shiver whenever the dog barks. In any case, this is [pure] delight because having lain still the whole day we can't feel our bones anymore. But how long can you stand in this stink, cold, and darkness? Already after two hours, both of us very cold and tired, we crawl back to our hole, in which we have a cover and a pillow. At 6:00 AM we leave the hole for a moment, to wash up and relieve ourselves. Later, until the evening, we stay [in the box]. In the evening we leave the hole once again, and so on. My Kitten [Helena, the author's cousin] is the sweetest in the whole world. True? All of this is interrupted often with scares and with unpleasant messages from our "uncle," for instance: "Again, they found a Jewish family somewhere, and shot all of them!" So we have to consider ourselves lucky. And we have to thank God a hundred times a day that it's not worse.

Trying to Survive in a Home Village

While Chaja Rosenblatt and Rivka Shenker were digging bunkers in the forest east of Dąbrowa, and while Melania Weissenberg and her cousin Helena were shivering in the cold hole dug into the earth floor of a barn, sisters Salomea and Hela Süss decided to flee Dąbrowa and go back to Gorzyce, a nearby village where they were born and raised, and where they hoped to find assistance. This pattern of returns to more familiar areas seems to have been as appealing as it was deadly to Jews on the run. Initially, however, their strategy for survival had been sound, since they managed to stay hidden at various peasants' farms for several months. Their luck run out in late spring of 1943. From the testimonies of local peasants and their wives, and according to interrogations of Polish blue policemen, we also learn that the girls found shelter in at least three households. In the beginning they paid their hosts for shelter, and once their money ran out, they started to pay in kind, working in the households of their hosts. Finally, they had to pay with their bodies and were then denounced to the Polish police by one of their treacherous rescuers. Jan Stachowicz, a Polish blue policeman, was ordered to march Salomea and Hela Süss away from the village. "I saw these young Jewesses," he testified after the war. "I remember how they begged us to set them free. They told us that the Germans would kill them, but the commanding officer refused to even listen to them."[13] The girls were wrong; the Germans would not kill them and were not even in the area. The execution was decided on and carried out by the Polish police officers. Jan Szewczyk, another officer of the Polish blue police from the local detachment, described the last moments of two girls in the following words:

> Commander [of our detachment] Lewandowicz said to me, and to the young Officer Stachowicz, "Since you have done nothing yet, now you have to fix them," which meant that I and Stachowicz had to kill the Jewesses. I told him that since I hadn't shot anyone yet, I didn't want to shoot the Jewesses now. So then he told me that I was an arse and not a policeman. Then he turned to the Jewesses and ordered them to get off the road and to go to the bushes nearby. So at this point the young policeman Stachowicz fired off one round from his carbine. One of the girls fell to the ground, and the other cried out and rushed toward the lying Jewess. At this point I fired a shot, and this second Jewess shouted even louder and fell next to the other Jewess, who had been wounded before. Seeing this, Commander Lewandowicz said with irony, "What are you screwing around!?" It meant, why we hadn't finished the Jewesses off right away. So the commander approached the lying Jewesses, took out his pistol, and shot them twice, and they were still.

Szewczyk completed his testimony by saying that "I would also like to add that before the shooting, the commander told Dulka, one of the peasants, to dig a grave for the Jewesses."[14]

Illustration 7.4. Exhumation of the remains of Hela and Salomea Süss, Dąbrowa Tarnowska, December 1945.

1944: Hiding in the Forest

At the time of Salomea and Hela's death, Chaja Rosenblatt and her husband drew on their dwindling financial resources to buy occasional shelter among the peasants in the Dulcza-area villages and then moved to the bunkers in the forest. Before the war was over, Chaja Rosenblatt managed to have a child (which she had left at the doorstep of a peasant couple in Dulcza) and saw the death of her husband, killed during a manhunt by German soldiers. She later wrote in her account: "On 11 November 1944 there was another manhunt. This time the Poles alerted the Germans and led them to our bunker. Close to the large bunker we had prepared small foxholes, precisely to save us in situations like this one."[15] Unfortunately, the tracks on the freshly fallen snow were a dead giveaway, and the foxholes were discovered one by one by the hunters. Some of the Jews (among them Chaja's husband) were shot immediately, while others were transferred into the custody of the Tarnów Gestapo. Chaja went on to survive the tortures in the Tarnów Gestapo prison, lasted through the beatings in the notorious Montelupich prison in Kraków, survived the Płaszów concentration camp, lived through the "death marches" of the winter of 1945, and finally, in the spring of 1945, saw the liberation in Bergen-Belsen.

On that fateful day of 11 November 1944, Rivka Shenker found herself in the same group as Chaja Rosenblatt, and the Germans also captured her. She noted in her memoir:

> Suddenly we heard horrible shouts in German, and we quickly went back to the hideout. I was barely able to cover our tracks when the shooting started. My heart started to race; we looked at one another and kept quiet. We heard the terrifying cry: "Either you leave your bunker, or we will throw in the grenades!" We were as if paralyzed, and we stared at each other. Then they started to shoot in the air, to scare us. I immediately opened the doors, which were so beautifully masked. The Germans said: "Hands up!" and told us to surrender all weapons. We all crawled out and were as pale as if we were dead. I felt so miserable—I was hiding in the forest for such a long time, and now they managed to catch me. It was in [November] 1944.[16]

At the Same Time, in Hiding under the Peasant's Barn

Incidentally, the news of Chaja's and Rivka's capture reached Melania, who (together with her cousin Helena) was finishing her second year in hiding in a dugout under the barn of their Polish host (now affectionately and diminutively referred to as "Ciuruniu"). In November 1944, she made a short note in her diary: "Ciuruniu [the Polish rescuer] has changed completely. As if he were a different man; he changed in a terrible way. That's the reason why we suffer greatly. November was full of suffering. November 11 they brought a score of Jews to Dąbrowa."

With each month, with each denunciation, murder, and manhunt, the number of Jews surviving in hiding dwindled. Not surprisingly, Melania and Helena's situation in their dugout grew increasingly desperate. Ciuruniu, their host, knew well that hiding the Jews put him in mortal danger. The main threat were not even the Germans, who had little knowledge of village realities and who ventured rarely into the farms, but the neighbors and the Polish blue police, who both had an excellent and intimate knowledge of the people and the area. Sometime in mid-1943, Helena and Ciuruniu became lovers. A few months later, Melania also started having sex with her Polish rescuer.

> He came to us on 26 [January] but Kitten had her period, so he came again on 3 February. The cold is horrible, and we have nothing to warm us up, but we don't want to complain. To make matters worse, we get no food and winter is all around us. On 3 July [1944], the bastard came to me, on 5 [July] he came to Kitten, on 10 [July] again to me, and on 12 July Kitten got angry and said that she had to have it. All the time Ciuruniu is in a good mood, because of the assassination attempt [on Hitler] and on account of the front drawing near us. Two days ago he brought us four apples and today—six. On 30 July Ciuruniu brought us a bouquet of flowers. Absolutely incredible!!! Thursday, 3 August [1944]: During the last few days the front moved much closer and is right next to Rzeszów. Although August started well, it soon got much worse. First of all, we have learned that in town [Dąbrowa Tarnowska] everything has gone back to normal. The worst is that the police are back. To make it even worse, the front stopped moving and got stuck close to Radomyśl, barely fifteen kilometers from here. Ciuruniu lost his good spirits and walks around in a foul mood.[17]

Analysis of this passage offers more challenges than this historian is able to overcome. The Polish peasant, with time, became (in the eyes of these two women) not only their savior and only link to the "real" world, but also a godlike figure who manipulated them and who, in a way, could be manipulated. It is not entirely surprising, therefore, that several decades later Melania requested that Yad Vashem bestow upon "Ciuruniu" the medal of Righteous among the Nations. And Yad Vashem, having heard a much sanitized and changed story, granted Melania's request.

Death in the Forest: The Fate of the Metzger Family

Unlike Chaja, Rivka, Melania, Sabina, and Helena, 35-year-old Estera Metzger refused to move to the Dąbrowa ghetto from her native village of Brnik. She took her two children and decided to take her chances in a bunker in the nearby woods, hoping for assistance from their "Aryan" friends and neighbors. Brnik is just a few miles from Dąbrowa Tarnowska. The area, densely populated, was not good for hiding, and the nearest police station was also too close for comfort. To make matters worse, the woods in which Estera and her children sought shelter are rather small and cannot even be compared with the large Dulcza forest situated east of Radgoszcz, where Chaja Rosenblatt and Rivka Shenker went into hiding. Despite these odds, Estera and her two children (along with a few other anonymous Jews who joined them during the fall) managed to survive a whole year in the bunkers. Their luck ran out in early July 1943, when local peasants tracked them down. Władysław Rzepka from Brnik was able not only to recall the events in question, but also to place them precisely in chronological sequence: "On 7 July 1943 I married Weronika Moździeż from Szarwark commune," he testified in 1948.[18] One evening, a few days before the wedding, Rzepka went to Szarwark, to visit his fiancée. On his way through the woods, the same woods that had been home to the Metzgers since the previous summer, Rzepka stumbled on several corpses of dead Jews.

> At the edge of the forest I met Feliks Węgrzyn, who, when asked, told me that the Germans had been shooting the Jews. At this point I saw Adam Kmieć, who emerged from the rye field, marching two Jewesses in front of him. When I came back home around noon, I learned from my mother that the gendarmes had been in the village and shot two Jewesses.

Józef Grabka, another citizen of Brnik, provided some more details. While Rzepka left to visit his fiancée in Szarwark, Grabka was on his way back home and saw a whole crowd in front of Franciszek Owsiak's house.[19]

> I saw a few members of the commune night watch. I was curious, so I went inside. In Franciszek Owsiak's apartment I saw two Jewish women sitting on the bench, next to the oven. In the same room I saw Franciszek Owsiak himself, Adam Kmieć, and Feliks Węgrzyn, although the latter two went out into the corridor, and there they stood. When I asked the older Jewess [what was happening] she replied, "What did I do to Franciszek Owsiak? Why did they bring me here?"

These are the last recorded words of Estera Metzger, who, with her daughter Tolka, waited for the executioners to arrive. Stanisław Bartosz, the village elder, added that "the old mother told me to take them to the ghetto, while the younger one was shaking with fear."[20]

Unfortunately, "taking them to the ghetto" was no longer possible: by then the Dąbrowa ghetto had long been liquidated, and the last Jews of Tarnów were being taken away to the Bełżec extermination camp or to the concentration camp at Płaszów. Grabka soon "felt uncomfortable" and went back home, while the village night watch took over the guard duties.[21] The next morning the notorious *Jagdkommando,* made up of German gendarmes and Polish blue policemen, arrived in Brnik, took Estera and Tolka Metzger from Owsiak's house, and shot them in the woods nearby. After the execution, the village elder instructed brothers Wojciech and Józef Grabka and Piotr Skrzyniarz to bury the women at the same spot. According to one of the witnesses, the gravediggers had to stop when one more Metzger, a young lad, showed up above the ditch and told the peasants that he wanted to be buried together with his sister and mother. Skrzyniarz and the Grabka brothers obliged and sent for an officer, who shot the boy and ordered him buried along with his mother and sister.[22] This highly unlikely scenario falls apart, however, when confronted with the recollections of other local people. Rozalia Kowalczyk, still today living in Szarwark, recalled that there was only one Jewish survivor of the initial manhunt, a fourteen-year-old boy, probably the young Metzger.[23] He too did not last long and was soon caught by the locals and delivered into the hands of the Germans. Józef Pabian, from Dąbrowa, recalled in 2011 that one local peasant named Starzec had caught young Metzger:

> I remember it as vividly as if it happened yesterday. Starzec took the Jew, tied his hands behind his back, and forced him to sit on the ground in his field. I don't know who went to get the Gestapo, but after a while a German arrived from Dąbrowa on a horse. The German placed one foot on the young lad's shoulder ... and the Jew kept saying, *"Tarnów giet, Tarnów giet,"* because the Jews knew that they were supposed to report to the Tarnów ghetto.[24]

These, by the way, are the last recorded words of Estera Metzger's fourteen-year-old son. The German placed the gun on the back of his head and squeezed the trigger. I can still see, as if it happened yesterday, how [the Jew's] teeth fell out and how he fell dead to the ground.

The gravediggers' problems were not over, however. At one point they found out that Tolka Metzger, although badly wounded, was not quite dead. They buried her alive.[25]

Chaja Metzger and her children were caught in July 1943 by Polish peasants during a manhunt and later delivered to the Germans for execution. Their bodies were never exhumed, and they probably still lie in the Brnik forest, where they were buried. Melania Weissenberg and Helena survived the war and left Poland before the end of 1945. Chaja Rosenblatt found her way to Paris, France. She passed away in 2013 at ninety-one, surrounded by her son, daughter, grandchildren, and great-grandchildren. Rivka Shenker survived too, and she made her way to Canada. Today she lives in Toronto, not far from Melania, although the two ladies have never met. The officers of the Polish blue police killed Salomea and Hela Süss in the commune of Gorzyce in 1943. Their bodies were exhumed by distant relatives in the winter of 1945/46 and later transferred to the Jewish cemetery in Dąbrowa, although I was unable to locate the grave.

So what is the point of such a microhistory? One can surmise that in order to understand the genocide, we need to reconstruct the events from the bottom up: from the local level, from the level of single murders, all the way to the planners of the *Endlösung*. An analysis of the situation in one chosen area, such as a single county or a small part of it, can bring us closer to the stated goal. But this objective, however praiseworthy and methodologically sound, cannot be the only justification of this endeavor. At this point it is appropriate to go back and once again quote from Daniel Mendelsohn's *The Lost*:

> A notorious problem of translation arises in the Cain and Abel story. What the Hebrew text actually says at one point is "the voice/sound of your brother's bloods are crying to me from the ground...." The strange Hebrew of the [biblical] text suggests, quite vividly, that even after it is shed, screams of innocent victims do not cease to issue from the earth where their blood was spilled.[26]

Jan Grabowski is a professor of history at the University of Ottawa and a founding member of the Polish Center for Holocaust Research in the Polish Academy of Sciences. Professor Grabowski has taught at University of Ottawa since 1993, and his teaching focuses on the history of the Holocaust. He has been an invited professor at universities in France, Israel, Poland, and the United States. In 2011 Dr. Grabowski was appointed the Baron Friedrich Carl von Oppenheim Chair for the Study of Racism, Antisemitism, and the Holocaust at Yad Vashem, Jerusalem, Israel. He has authored and edited fourteen books and published more than sixty articles in English, French, Polish, German, and Hebrew. His most recent book, *Hunt for the Jews : Betrayal and Murder in German-Occupied Poland* (2013), was awarded the Yad Vashem International Book Prize for 2014.

Notes

1. Saul Friedländer, *The Years of Extermination: Nazi Germany and the Jews, 1939–1945* (New York: HarperCollins, 2008), 14–15.
2. Nicolas Mariot and Claire Zalc, *Face à la persécution. 991 Juifs dans la guerre* (Paris: Odile Jacob, Fondation pour la mémoire de la Shoah, 2010), 302.
3. Tal Bruttmann, *Aryanisation économique et spoliations en Isère, 1940–1944* (Grenoble: Presses universitaires de Grenoble, 2010).
4. Alina Skibińska and Tadeusz Markiel, *Zagłada domu Trynczerów* (Warsaw: Stowarzyszenie Centrum Badań nad Zagładą Żydów, 2011), 315. *The Holocaust in the Polish Countryside: A Witness Testimony and Historical Account* (Berghahn Books, forthcoming, March 2017); Tal Bruttmann, *Aryanisation économique*; Nicolas Mariot and Claire Zalc, *Face à la persecution*.
5. Laurent Joly, *L'antisémitisme de bureau* (Paris: Grasset, 2011), 444.
6. Benjamin Frommer, "Verfolgung durch die Presse: Wie Prager Büroberater und die tschechische Polizei die Juden des Protektorats Böhmen und Mähren isolieren halfen," in *Leben und Sterben im Schatten der Deportation: Der Alltag der jüdischen Bevölkerung im Großdeutschen Reich 1941–1945*, ed. Doris Bergen, Andrea Löw and Anna Hájková (Munich: Oldenbourg, 2013), 137–50.
7. Excluding, of course, those who fled the Nazis and survived the war in the Soviet Union.
8. Archive of the Jewish Historical Institute in Warsaw (AŻIH), 302/318, testimony of Chaja Rosenblatt.
9. Memoir of Rivka Shenker (née Regina Goldfinger), from Radomyśl Wielki. I am indebted to Leila Férault for making a copy of this document available to me.
10. I am deeply grateful to Melania W. for making her diary available to me.
11. Sabina Goldman's letter has been preserved and made available to me by Melania W.
12. In German documents, camps of this type were referred to as *JULAG*, or *Judenlager* (camp for Jews).
13. National Archive in Krakow (APK), Collection of the Krakow Appellate Court (SAKr), dossier 1055, IVK/344/50, 38.
14. APK, SAKr, 1055 IV K 344/50. The Süss sisters managed to survive almost a year in hiding. More information about their life and fate can be found in APK, SAKr 1034/IV K/204/50.
15. Visual History Archive (VHA), testimony of Hela Levi (Rosenblatt), born in 1921, index no. 9617.
16. Memoir of Rivka Shenker, 72–73.
17. Diary of Melania W.
18. APK, SAKr 967, p. 153/49, 72, deposition of witness Władysław Rzepka, 24 January 1949.
19. APK, SAKr 967, p. 153/49, 73, deposition of witness Grabka, 24 January 1949.
20. APK, SAKr 967, k. 153/49, 37, questioning of Elder Stanisław Bartosz.
21. APK, SAKr 967, k. 153/49, 18, questioning of Adam Kmieć, 18 October 1948. "The elder told us to take these Jewesses to Franciszek Owsiak's house and to watch them until the morning. So we obeyed his order, took the Jewesses to Owsiak's house, and guarded them the whole night."
22. APK, SAKr 967, k. 153/49, 77–79, testimony of Piotr Skrzyniarz, 24 January 1949.
23. In February 2011, I shared my research with journalists working for the Polish TV station TVN24. They followed up on the archival evidence presented here and conducted a series of interviews in the area. The quotes above are from a program produced by Marek Osiecimski, which aired on TVN24 on 24 February 2011.

24. At the time, the *Restghetto* (secondary ghetto) still existed in Tarnów, although its inhabitants were successively executed or removed to the Płaszów concentration camp.
25. APK, SAKr 967, k. 153/49, 41, testimony of Stanisław Bartosz, 15 October 1948.
26. Mendelsohn, *The Lost*, 135.

Bibliography

Bruttmann, Tal. *Aryanisation économique et spoliations en Isère, 1940–1944*. Grenoble: Presses universitaires de Grenoble, 2010.
Friedländer, Saul. *The Years of Extermination: Nazi Germany and the Jews, 1939–1945*. New York: HarperCollins, 2008.
Frommer, Benjamin. "Verfolgung durch die Presse: Wie Prager Büroberater und die tschechische Polizei die Juden des Protektorats Böhmen und Mähren isolieren halfen." In *Leben und Sterben im Schatten der Deportation: Der Alltag der jüdischen Bevölkerung im Großdeutschen Reich 1941–1945*, edited by Doris Bergen, Andrea Löw and Anna Hájková. Munich: Oldenbourg, 2013.
Joly, Laurent. *L'antisémitisme de bureau*. Paris: Grasset, 2011.
Mariot, Nicolas, and Claire Zalc. *Face à la persécution. 991 Juifs dans la guerre*: Paris, Odile Jacob, Fondation pour la mémoire de la Shoah, 2010.
Mendelsohn, Daniel. *The Lost: A Search for Six of Six Million*. New York: HarperCollins, 2006.
Skibińska, Alina, and Tadeusz Markiel. *Zagłada domu Trynczerów*. Warsaw: Stowarzyszenie Centrum Badań nad Zagładą Żydów, 2011. (Forthcoming in English: *The Holocaust in the Polish Countryside: A Witness Testimony and Historical Account* [Berghahn Books, 2017]).

CHAPTER 8

JEWISH SLAVE WORKERS IN THE GERMAN AVIATION INDUSTRY

Daniel Uziel

Sidney Birnbaum was born in 1925 in Moraczow, in eastern Poland. The Germans arrested him in Kraków in 1941 and sent him to work in a logging camp. In early 1942 he was transferred to the Mielec camp, where he was briefly trained before serving as a riveter in the nearby Heinkel aircraft factory. In mid-1944, he was evacuated with other inmates to Wieliczka, where Heinkel had built an underground factory. As the Germans abandoned this project due to technical difficulties, the inmates were transferred to Flossenbürg in Germany. Oddly, although aircraft producer Messerschmitt had operated several workshops in this camp since late 1943 (with around 5,200 inmates in October 1944), Birnbaum and other Mielec veterans were allocated to a ditch-digging detachment. At the end of 1944 Birnbaum and others were moved to Dachau, and from there to an underground factory near Leonberg that produced wings for jet fighters, where he once again worked as a riveter.[1]

Birnbaum's story is a microstory that provides valuable information about an important macro element of the Holocaust: slave labor in the German aviation industry, which became a major employer of Jewish slave labor in 1944.

This phenomenon—the employment of slave labor in one of Nazi Germany's largest and most modern industrial sectors—has until now been the subject of scholarly research only within the context of general studies of the German aviation industry[2] or that of specific aviation-related firms and sites.[3] Although a quick search of survivor testimony databases reveals that many of them worked in an aviation-related production facility at one time or another, there is no comprehensive study dealing with the story from their perspective. This perspective is vital because it provides us with information not only about the fate of individuals as slave workers, but also about their employers and the working environment. The aim of this chapter is therefore to examine several of the key issues associated with slave labor in the aviation industry and to demonstrate how survivor testimonies can be used as a source for researching a topic that is largely unknown in studies of the Holocaust.

Using Slave Labor in the German Aviation Industry

In many respects, the aviation industry was the equivalent of the today's high-tech industry. During the twelve years of the Third Reich, it produced highly sophisticated, world-class products. Its workers enjoyed generous contracts, a modern social welfare system and working environment, as well as high esteem. When the Nazis came to power in 1933, Germany's aviation industry was a marginal industrial branch, but with rearmament between 1933 and 1939, it became the fastest expanding industrial branch in Germany. While in 1933 only 36 aircraft were produced in Germany and the entire branch employed only 3,988 men and women,[4] in 1939 its output reached 8,295 aircraft,[5] and by October 1938 the number of people employed in the aircraft and aero-engine industry jumped to 293,000.[6]

This massive expansion continued after the outbreak of World War II but was obstructed by several factors. Besides mismanagement, most important among them was the increasing difficulty in finding skilled workers in Germany. Already in the summer of 1940, the Reich's Air Ministry (Reichsluftministerium—RLM) started recruiting foreigners and POWs and offering them to different firms. However, this solution failed to solve the problem in the long term, mainly because most foreigners declined to renew their contracts after one year.[7] Since the summer of 1941, the RLM had discussed the possibility of using concentration camp inmates in selected production programs, but the only documented use in that year resulted from the local initiative of the Austrian Steyr-Daimler-Poch aero-engine producer and the Mauthausen concentration camp.[8] In early 1942, following Germany's failure in the East and the transition of World War II into a global conflict, Erhard

Milch, state secretary of the RLM, turned to Himmler and asked for help. Himmler responded positively, and thus the SS started allocating concentration camp inmates to specific firms and factories. Prominent among these early partners in the slave labor scheme was bomber producer Heinkel, which employed inmates in several plants. These included three factories in the General Government, collectively known as the "Budzyn Block" factories. The largest among them was Mielec, established in 1939 in the existing facilities of a Polish aircraft factory. Beginning in the early summer of 1942, Jews from local ghettos formed a meaningful portion of the workforce in these factories. Ernst Heinkel, the general director and owner of the firm, confirmed the usefulness of the new workers to Milch and declared his firm's intention to expand their employment.[9] In parallel, Heinkel started to employ inmates from the Sachsenhausen concentration camp in its large factory in Oranienburg, north of Berlin. Daimler-Benz, a key aero-engine manufacturer, also used Jews from the ghettos in its General Government operations.[10] Although the number of Jewish slave workers increased in these eastern plants, Jews generally formed a marginal proportion of the increasing number of slave workers employed by the aviation industry. Beginning in late 1942, the employment of slave workers was accelerated, and cooperation between the SS, the RLM, and individual firms flourished. In 1943, as the SS fully realized the profit potential of aviation production, it began converting its stone-cutting and quarry businesses in the concentration camps of Mauthausen and Flossenbürg into aviation-related production. Well-established concentration camps, like Dachau, Buchenwald, and Sachsenhausen, also became closely associated with the aviation industry in 1943.[11]

In early 1944, Himmler reported to Göring that the total number of inmates working in the aviation industry was around thirty-six thousand—most of them obviously non-Jewish—and declared his intention to expand the number to ninety thousand.[12] By that time most leading aviation firms, including BMW, Messerschmitt, Volkswagen,[13] and Junkers employed varying numbers of slave workers.

The largest influx of Jewish slave workers came after massive Allied air raids (popularly known as "Big Week") heavily damaged twenty-six key factories of the aviation industry in February 1944. Consequently, the Reich's leadership established an emergency inter-ministerial commission, the Jägerstab (Fighter Staff), in order to restore and increase aircraft production. The establishment of the Jägerstab was a dramatic move initiated by Milch and Speer to save aircraft production.[14] Chaired by Karl Otto Saur, head of the technical department in the Reich's Armaments Ministry, the staff possessed almost unrestricted authority to mobilize manpower and resources from different state and Nazi Party authorities. SS-Gruppenführer Hans Kammler, the powerful head of *Amtsgruppe C* (construction matters) within the Main Economic and Administration Office of the SS, was a permanent member of the staff. He not only was responsible for the underground relocation of several key factories—a task entrusted to him after he proved himself in managing the construction of the Mittelwerk underground missile factory in 1943—but also liaised between the SS and the staff. After initial survey of the damage caused by the Big Week raids, the staff estimated the number of additional workers required to accomplish its tasks at one hundred thousand.[15] The immediate and long-term tasks were indeed enormous: repairing the twenty-six damaged main factories, transferring existing production programs into hundreds of new factories, and transferring several key programs to underground locations, including six massive bunker factories. Responding to these requirements, Hitler ordered the SS, during the first week of April 1944, to allocate 100,000 Jews to the Jägerstab.[16] The timing was perfect because Hitler's order came just as the Germans were preparing to round up Hungary's large Jewish community. Although the Germans planned the deportation of the Hungarian Jews long before the February crisis, their deportation not only became a crucial part of the "Final Solution," but also formed part of the solution to the Jägerstab's manpower problem. As approximately 400,000 Hungarian Jews were deported during the spring and early summer of 1944 to Auschwitz, those considered fit for work were taken aside to form the main core of inmates allocated to the Jägerstab. Jews from other countries were also selected. The historian Edith Reim has estimated that between 130,000 and 160,000 inmates were allocated to the aviation industry in 1944, most of them Jewish.[17]

Business History of the Aviation Industry

In order to analyze the microhistory of slave labor in the aviation industry, it is necessary to examine the business history of this industry. Business history helps explain why the aviation industry was one of the first German industrial branches to initiate the use of slave labor in its factories and is particularly helpful in explaining why specific firms were more eager than others to enter this field, as well as the timing of their entry. The Heinkel AG firm is a prime example of the usefulness of this historical approach. Ernst Heinkel made no secret of his aspirations to become Germany's largest aircraft producer, aspirations that formed the general background for Heinkel's massive prewar and wartime expansion. The firm's business strategy sought to create as much extra production capacity as possible by constructing multiple new factories in the eastern provinces of the Reich and Austria. The firm's business strategy, and especially its expansion in the General Government, is therefore crucial to explaining its early association with slave labor. The main motivation behind this expansion was the need to solve the chronic and worsening workforce shortage at the firm's traditional centers. This shortage threatened to obstruct the largest production program in the firm's history: mass production of the He 177 heavy bomber. Moreover, the trouble-prone He 177 project is crucial for understanding the firm's particularly massive need for manpower in early and mid-1942—right at the time the RLM initiated its cooperation with the SS. The RLM approved the purchase of eight hundred He 177s in late 1939, even before the first flight of the prototype. Both the RLM and Heinkel entered this program with high expectations, which were however repeatedly frustrated by endless technical difficulties encountered during the development and testing of the aircraft. By the end of 1941, it was thought that these problems were largely solved, and Heinkel prepared to initiate series production.[18] The factories in the East were supposed to enable the firm to continue some of its older bomber production and general maintenance operations, while it retooled its established factories in northern Germany for the production of the new bomber. Both intakes of slave workers to Heinkel's factories in 1942 (in Oranienburg and in the General Government) were thus closely related to the evolution of the He 177 program. Heinkel's twin-pronged initiative was crucial to the employment of slave labor in the aviation industry. The experiments, first in the East and then in Oranienburg, proved the feasibility of producing high-tech products with poorly trained and unmotivated manpower. While the firm's successful General Government enterprises proved the general soundness of the slave labor scheme within the firm and to the RLM, the successful employment of inmates from Sachsenhausen in the Oranienburg-Germendorf plant also caught outside attention. Unlike in the General Government, at this location Heinkel sought, beginning in the summer of 1942, to use inmates in the production of its most modern and complicated product, the He 177. Throughout the summer and spring of 1942, the plant lost an increasing number of mostly skilled German workers, mainly due to drafting into the Wehrmacht.[19] Increased use of slave workers therefore represented for Heinkel the only plausible solution to the problem of carrying out a massive and urgent production program with dwindling German manpower. Other firms and organizations involved in high-tech military production also faced the same difficulty at this time. In April 1943, a high-ranking delegation from the army's Peenemünde missile development center visited the Oranienburg plant. The positive impression of using inmates in the production of a large and complicated bomber convinced the heads of the V-2 ballistic missile program to employ inmates in its upcoming production.[20] The effectiveness of the Oranienburg plant became fully evident, albeit only later. While in 1941–42 Oranienburg-Germendorf produced, under license, a monthly average of twenty-five wing sets for the Ju 88 light bomber, in mid-1944 it reached a monthly output of forty wing sets for the much larger He 177. Within approximately this same time frame, inmates formed more than 48 percent of the entire workforce of the Oranienburg complex.[21] Taking into account that most inmates were employed in tasks directly related to production, their share on the production lines was evidently even higher.

Another important aircraft producer, Messerschmitt, started cooperating with the SS in late 1942, after it failed in its initiative to overcome the manpower shortage through increased recruitment of German women. Since 1938 (and practically until the war's end), the firm had produced the Luftwaffe's main single engine fighter, the Me 109, but unlike Heinkel, Messerschmitt concentrated most of its wartime operations in a specific region, Bavaria. It sought to boost its productivity through the expansion of existing factories and the introduction of modern production methods and machinery. By 1942 it operated large factories in Regensburg and Augsburg, although it failed to obtain the manpower needed for its expanded production lines. The firm first sought the support of the SS in October 1942, and by July 1943 it employed 2,299 inmates in its Augsburg factory.[22] At the same time, Messerschmitt formed a partnership with DEST, the SS stone-cutting and quarrying enterprise. This resulted in the construction of workshops for parts production in several concentration camps in southeastern Germany.[23] The Erla engineering firm, which produced the Me 109 under license in Leipzig, cooperated closely with the Buchenwald concentration camp. In March 1943, a sub-camp of Buchenwald code-named "Emil" was constructed in Leipzig, and in April its inmates started working in Erla's three factories in and around Leipzig. More sub-camps were later constructed next to these factories to accommodate the increasing number of inmates arriving from Buchenwald.[24]

Germany's other important fighter producer, Focke-Wulf, as well as other firms, at first sought to increase capacity by outsourcing some of their production to firms in the occupied countries. Focke-Wulf concentrated its outsourcing efforts mainly in France, where it contracted several firms to produce parts and even complete aircraft. The German firm even outsourced some development projects to French firms, including a couple of civilian airliner projects intended for the postwar era.[25] In 1941 Messerschmitt also outsourced production of its liaison plane to the French firm SNCAN in Les Mureaux, in order to free its German capacity for the production of fighters.[26] Other German firms cooperated with firms in Czechoslovakia, Holland, and Italy. Most of these cooperation projects largely failed, as a result of different difficulties with the partner firms. Production in France proved especially troublesome because of the poor efficiency of partner firms and the low motivation of their workers. Ultimately, the contribution of foreign firms to the total output of German aviation production was marginal and was composed mainly of second-line aircraft. Focke-Wulf thus turned to slave labor only after its disappointing experience with the aviation industry of occupied France.

Toward the end of World War II, slave labor became so widespread and obvious in the German aviation industry that the production plan of Germany's last-resort jet fighter, the He 162, included massive allocation of inmates right from prototype manufacture and the preproduction run. Massive use of slave labor was thus part of the initial production plans of this aircraft, and all of the factories allocated to its series production employed large number of inmates even before they started its production.[27]

Microhistory of Slave Labor in the Aviation Industry

The microhistory discussed here is the story of inmates' daily life in the different factories, on construction sites, and in their associated camps. Personal accounts represent the main source basis of this microhistory, because official records related to the aviation industry usually say little about the daily life of the workforce, and particularly about slave workers. Testimonies should be treated with caution though, as there are several problems with testimonies in general, particularly those related to slave labor in the aviation industry. Firstly, many testimonies suffer from meaningful gaps, caused by failing memory, repression of traumatic memories and over-expression of positive ones, retrospective reconstruction of memories, lack of knowledgeable guiding questions, or a combination of reasons. Due to these and other reasons, some witnesses confuse places, persons, events, and times.

Secondly, the lack of technical knowledge makes it difficult to rely on this source when dealing with technical aspects. Many former inmates, for instance, were unable to explain what they produced or what the end product of their factory was.

Nevertheless, despite the need for caution when working with testimonies, when writing microhistory their shortcomings as a historical source are less critical. Exact dates, reliable personal identities, and other details requiring a high degree of accuracy are less relevant here. The general information about daily life, provided by most witnesses through small vignettes and anecdotes that stuck in their memory, makes this source indispensable for certain studies. Naturally, as with other sources, cross-referencing is important, for it helps to overcome the inherent problems associated with testimonies and can neatly complement them (or vice versa). For instance, some witnesses were not fully aware of what they were producing, who their employer was, and who supervised them. Normally, it is easy to complete these details by using other sources. Cross-referencing with other testimonies also helps to complete and confirm information, especially in the narratives of witnesses who worked in the same place.

The value of these accounts even goes beyond telling the story of slave labor, for although survivors possessed little or no technical knowledge, their stories can help reconstruct the general story of the German aviation industry in World War II. The inmates' perspective provides glimpses into many factors, such as the working environment, nutrition, working regime, danger of air raids, extreme conditions inside underground production facilities, and so on. All of these factors also affected the German workforce. We also learn through such testimonies about the relations between the inmates and German workers and foremen. Despite early intentions to almost completely separate inmates from German workers,[28] we learn from the testimonies that in most places Germans and slave workers worked closely together and interacted. Therefore, inmates were able to observe the work and behavior of the German workforce, particularly in the late phases of World War II.

The daily life of inmates and the different aspects of their forced labor are nevertheless the focus of this chapter. Testimonies confirm that in many places, firms sought to give inmates some basic technical training in order to perform their work, thus viewing them as at least a medium-term workforce worth investing in. Heinkel introduced this praxis in 1942, and other firms followed suit.[29] Volkswagen, for instance, sent one of its engineers to Auschwitz in late May 1944 to locate skilled workers for the highly secret V-1 flying bomb production. He interviewed inmates who responded to a call for skilled metalworkers and asked them to perform different technical tasks in order to assess their skills. According to the results of the interview, he divided those who passed into two groups. The first, with around three hundred of the most successful interviewees, was sent in June to the huge Fallersleben plant, where its members received additional training. They were then transported to the new underground factory in Tiercelet, where they formed the initial cadre of slave workers. The others were sent directly to Tiercelet, where the first group integrated them into the work.[30] Evidently, the training process in most cases was less elaborate. Junkers personnel taught Jewish women brought to the Markkleeberg labor camp how to take accurate measures, and only after they learned this skill they were put to work in the adjacent aero-engine factory.[31]

Selection for forced labor in an aviation industry factory in 1944 saved the life of these inmates and also meant improved jail conditions for many them. Agnes Geva came to a small camp near Calw in late 1944, where she and other Hungarian Jewish women learned how to manufacture propeller parts. She recalled that "the training camp was quite pleasant, although it was well guarded." Quite remarkably, she liked her work and tried to find a similar job after immigrating to Israel after the war.[32] Her odd description of the camp as "pleasant" makes sense considering that she was previously detained in the Auschwitz and Plaszow camps. This type of comparative remark appears repeatedly in survivor testimonies in a more or less explicit way. Such remarks surely cannot be viewed as an objective yardstick of the brutal treatment or jail conditions, but they point to a subjective feeling of improvement compared to the earlier or later jail conditions experienced by the witness. This feeling was based of course on real facts that appear repeatedly in the testimonies: better accommodations, better treatment, less exhausting work, improved food supply, and the ability to interact regularly with human beings outside the bubble of the camp system.

The narratives of many survivors nevertheless describe frequent and somewhat chaotic transfers between factories and camps, especially in the late war period. These transfers, along with the general war situation, had an effect on the inmates' condition. Sidney Birnbaum was not the only slave worker to become skilled and then be shifted around by chaotic SS allocation policies, thus wasting his skill precisely when the Germans were desperately looking for skilled slave workers. Moreover, his jail conditions once he was transferred to Flossenbürg evidently deteriorated meaningfully.[33] However, once allocated and trained, it seems that Jews performed almost every possible production task in factories, in some rare cases even quality control of finished components. Peter Erben, a young Jew from Czechoslovakia, became a quality controller in the "Bergkristall" underground factory, where he inspected and certified completed fuselages of the highly modern Me 262 jet fighter.[34]

Jewish slave workers became part of a huge army of foreigners and slave workers employed in the German war industry in 1944. Their testimonies reflect the "Tower of Babylon" nature of most factories and camps during this period. Eva Bohcher, a Slovak Jew, described the workforce she encountered when she arrived at the Arado aircraft factory in Freiberg: "There were around 3,000 foreign workers there at that time, among others from Belgium, Italy, France, and Russia. The Russians were POWs recruited by the Germans. There were 1,000 Jewish women: 500 from Hungary and 500 from Slovakia."[35] Miriam Givon encountered a similar manpower composition at the Jumo aero-engine factory in Zittau, where she was sent from Auschwitz. She and other women from the same transport shared a large camp with French and Soviet POWs.[36]

As mentioned before, most survivors were able to tell very little about the work they performed or the end product of their factories. While lack of a technical background played a role in this ignorance, it also reflected the modern mechanized production system that was broadly introduced into aviation production in Germany beginning in 1942. This system, based on established mass-production methods from the automobile industry, replaced the static workbench system, which relied on well-trained production workers. The conveyor-belt-based assembly line was a key factor in enabling the large-scale use of inmates in the production of complicated aircraft and aero-engines. It divided the production process into smaller segments, where workers performed specific manufacturing tasks requiring only limited training or no training at all.[37] This system explains, for instance, the striking incompatibility of the technical modernity of jet engines that entered series production in the summer of 1944 and the unskilled Jewish housewives and girls allocated to their factories. Rachel Zolf, who worked along with other Jewish women and girls from Hungary on the production line of the Jumo 004 jet engine in Markkleeberg, described her work:

> There was a line of machines, and I worked on the first one. It was called *Drehbank* [lathe]. I received a large piece of iron, maybe more than one meter long, and put it in the machine. I was supposed to cut it into pieces, take off the black iron from the top, and drill a round hole in the middle with different knives [the cutting tools of the lathe] ... then they passed it on to the second machine behind me. So it went like a conveyor belt and each woman made a part [sic].[38]

Such work required only basic and task-specific training that was normally completed within a couple of hours. The new production system therefore opened the main bottleneck of aviation production, namely manpower. It enabled the mass employment of unskilled and undermotivated workers that was needed to operate idle production equipment and populate empty production facilities. This system and the slave workers it involved thus stood at the core of German aviation's so-called Production Miracle, which managed an output of almost 40,000 aircraft in 1944 compared to only 25,527 in 1943.[39] The massive use of slave labor in the aviation industry beginning in 1943 thus fully supports Rainer Fröbe's argument that, at least in 1944–45, the National Socialist policy of extermination of certain human groups according to racial ideology became more pragmatic and less central in light of wartime necessities. Accordingly, the Germans tried to preserve a large proportion of the workforce available to them in the concentration camp reservoir and to fully exploit it in the interests of their wartime economy.[40]

The fair treatment and reasonable jailing conditions described by many survivors reflect this effort to preserve slave workers and motivate them to work not only through terror, but also by more positive means. Here, again, testimonies usually provide evidence, by way of comparison with previous experiences in the Nazi persecution system. Upon arrival at the Jumo aero-engine factory in Zittau from Auschwitz in early summer 1944, Miriam Givon found significantly improved living conditions:

> We were billeted in a three-story building and it was a paradise in comparison to Auschwitz. Each inmate got his own bed with a straw mattress and a pillow. We got food and they told us: "Kinder, you are now in the hands of civilians, so have no fear. We will take care of you and everything will be all right. You are going to work and in the evenings you will return here and get enough food." There were baths and a WC with running water. We got dishes and spoons with our numbers (which was not tattooed on us).[41]

The situation in Zittau deteriorated in late 1944, and living conditions became difficult, yet most Jews allocated to this factory survived. Mordechai Lustig and a group of inmates also came from Auschwitz to a small Philips aviation electronics and instrument factory in Horenburg. They were housed in rooms with heating and a bed for each inmate. There were showers and toilets in their building.[42]

Despite the harsh regime and brutal discipline in labor camps and numerous worksites, many former inmates also reported relatively reasonable treatment by the foremen and German coworkers in the factories. Such fair treatment did not necessarily reflect a declared factory policy, but rather an atmosphere of general mobilization of resources and production capacity, as well as the presence of a civilian environment inside factories. The bare fact that inmates were now mostly supervised by civilians rather than by trained and indoctrinated SS guards also played a role in this generally improved treatment. Josef Pinsker told a Junkers representative who came to Buchenwald in autumn 1944 that he knew how to operate a lathe. On the first day at the Junkers factory in Niederorschel, a German engineer came to him, gave him a technical sketch, and ordered him to produce the item, which he was unable to do. An elderly German worker came and asked him, "Why are you crying?" Pinsker told him that "now they are going to kill me because I don't know how to do the work." The German then explained to him how to make the part, and two hours later the engineer returned and said, "Bravo!" after looking at the part he had manufactured. He became highly skilled and was allocated to more complex jobs.[43] Tzipora Shwiatowitz's foreman also treated her well after he saw the quality of her welding. He regularly brought her a sandwich and protected her from SS guards.[44]

Inmates sometimes received small rewards for their work. Miriam Frank once worked four consecutive night shifts in a parts factory near Görlitz. She was dead tired, but surprisingly she got two days off on the weekend and could sleep thirty-six hours.[45] In some places, inmates performing what was considered extra-hard labor received additional food rations, a common practice with German workers. Miriam Alter, who operated a mechanical drill at an aircraft parts factory in Raguhn, received extra soup on top of the standard daily ration of soup and two slices of bread.[46] Zehava Fruchter reported that the inmates at the Junkers aero-engine factory in Markkleeberg were even allowed to eat at the employee cafeteria.[47]

Oddly, in 1943 Heinkel encouraged inmates at the Oranienburg factory to submit suggestions for improvement to the factory management. The firm agreed with the SS that if a suggestion by an inmate were found useful, he would be rewarded with extra rations. In March 1944, Himmler boasted that two hundred suggestions by inmates had already been received and implemented in Oranienburg and that the concerned inmates were rewarded.[48] However, there are no indications that similar schemes were used in other factories where Jewish inmates were employed in large numbers.

Even though the short-term chances for survival of inmates allocated to an aviation factory increased meaningfully, that does not mean that they were not brutalized and maltreated. Jail and working conditions deteriorated meaningfully throughout the winter of 1944–45, although brutality and violence were an integral part of the slave labor system in the aviation industry from the beginning. Brutal treatment was the general practice in Heinkel's early enterprises in the General Government, especially at the Mielec camp, where Ukrainian auxiliaries were used as guards.[49] Regardless of jail and working conditions, inmates were severely punished for every act of real or perceived sabotage, resistance, or other offenses. Itzchak Pankowski was beaten twenty-five times at the factory construction site for the BMW Allach aero-engine after being caught with a potato.[50] The SS officer in charge of the labor camp next to Arado's Freiberg factory used to publicly beat inmates in the main production hall for the slightest offense.[51] Inmates at Heinkel's Barth factory were also punished for the slightest disciplinary offense by beating or deprivation of food rations. Conditions in the camp were also harsh, with inmates repeatedly suffering from lice and some dying of typhus.[52]

An inmate at the Heinkel Heidefeld factory near Vienna reported daily maltreatment by the *Kommandoführer* and the kapos, who were usually veteran Polish or Russian inmates. Each evening brought the daily "payback," usually in the form of twenty-five whiplashes.[53] Incidentally, a boy working at Heidefeld's mother factory at the Vienna-Schwachet airport reported fair treatment there.[54] Most witnesses reported that the guards and kapos usually practiced maltreatment, although once in a while they encountered cruel factory personnel.

Executions were rather rare, usually following alleged sabotage, and generally took place away from the workplace, either in the camps or in prison.

Fear of sabotage was not just paranoia, and here survivor testimonies provide another important insight. Sabotage became a chronic problem in the aviation industry in 1943–45, as the increased use of under-motivated foreigners and inmates resulted in a steady deterioration in production standards and quality. The Germans were familiar with this problem, which caused much concern because of its grave consequences for aircraft and their crews.[55] Former Luftwaffe pilot Adolf Dilg commented, after experiencing a forced landing due to sabotage-induced damage, "Every time we had such an incident the Gestapo would make a lot of fuss, but although they would take the odd scapegoat the problem of sabotage was one we had to live with."[56]

Milch repeatedly demanded severe punishment for any foreigner, POW, or inmate caught sabotaging or refusing to work. As he put it in 1944, "If he [a worker of the above categories] preformed an act of sabotage or refused to work, let him be hanged right where he works. I am convinced that this will not miss its effect."[57] Fear of sabotage was one of the reasons slave workers were evacuated with the rest of the factory's personnel to air-raid shelters during bombing raids.[58]

As some former inmates reported, sabotage was normally performed by damaging products and not adhering to manufacturing standards. Mark Stern, a young Polish Jew who worked in aircraft factories in Mielec and Flossenbürg, described how he and other inmates sabotaged products:

> The only way that we knew of how to fight back was by sabotage. I was part of it. I remember being told by somebody that the proper way to sabotage is to weaken the wings of the planes that we were building. So, we riveted; we drilled out rivets and replaced them with other ones; replaced them with weaker rivets. I am sure that some of it worked. We didn't know exactly how to sabotage but we tried our best.[59]

This chapter has so far examined the inmates used to produce different aviation-related products, yet it should also be noted that large numbers of inmates were allocated in the spring of 1944 to the construction sites for new factories. These construction projects were part of the general dispersal scheme of aviation production, while some factories were transferred to underground facilities. All testimonies used in this research suggest that inmates allocated to construction sites generally fared much worse than those employed in production. At most of these sites SS guards supervised the inmates nonstop and thus brutalized them not only in the camps but also at work. Furthermore, the SS managed a large portion of the underground dispersal scheme, which was based largely on the model of the notorious Mittelwerk project of 1943.[60] Josef Weiss briefly described the typical conditions prevailing in an underground construction site near the Gusen camp complex: "Conditions were very harsh: three men shared a single bench, meager food rations, many night shifts, beatings by the SS and the kapos, and hard physical labor."[61]

It is thus no wonder that in 1944 the death rate of inmates employed on construction sites in the Mauthausen camp complex—most of them related to the aviation industry—was over 30 percent.[62] Therefore, unlike existing factories, construction sites can be viewed as part of the "normal" camp system, with its extreme living and working regimen.

As we have seen, good treatment at the hands of civilian managers and workers explains, among other things, what appears to be a relatively high survival rate for inmates allocated to aviation-related factories. Even when the Germans started evacuating factories into the heart of the Reich in late 1944, in many cases they sought to preserve a large portion of this workforce by bringing it along. While some of the evacuations turned into massacres and death marches,[63] it seems that most factory evacuations were performed with the intention of leaving the workforce intact for use in the new location. One of the most visible features of this effort was the orderly transportation of workers by trains or trucks, sometimes with production tooling. When Daimler-Benz evacuated its plant in Rzeszów in the late summer of 1944, it moved all of its Jewish workers to a new underground factory near Wesserling-Urbès in Alsace. The firm put experienced Jewish workers to work again on the production lines, so their expertise was not wasted.

The inmates who were still working on the construction of this factory under SS supervision even complained that the Jews received better treatment from their Daimler-Benz supervisors, who obviously appreciated their value.[64] When Volkswagen evacuated its Tiercelet V-1 underground factory in Lorraine in late 1944, most of its workers, who had been selected earlier in Auschwitz specifically for this location, were evacuated along with the plant's machinery to the "Rebstock" factory, located in a tunnel near Dernau in western Germany. After working for a short time in the new factory, they were evacuated again with the same machinery to the V-1 factory in Mittelwerk, where the U.S. Army liberated them.[65] In many cases, inmates were liberated after being left to their own devices in an idle factory.

It is obvious though that in the chaotic situation prevailing at the time, transports sometimes got lost or turned into death marches. Eva Bohrer was evacuated with other inmates from Arado's Freiberg factory in mid-April 1945. It is not clear what the original destination of the transport was, but their train traveled for two weeks through Germany and Czechoslovakia before finally arriving at Mauthausen.[66]

The last part of Sidney Birnbaum's story demonstrates rather well the fate of many inmates who worked in the German aviation industry. In the early spring of 1945, the Germans evacuated the Leonberg factory, where he worked as a riveter. Sidney and his fellow inmates were marched to another Messerschmitt factory in Augsburg and shortly after were taken on trucks to Mühldorf, to one of the camps associated with the "Ringeltaube" bunker factories project. As this ambitious project was never completed, they never actually worked there, although Sidney was injured from a bomb splinter during an Allied air attack. He and other inmates were soon evacuated again, this time in a train to Sternberg, in Czechoslovakia. On the way they experienced firsthand the Allied aerial campaign against transportation targets, as their train was attacked from the air, causing its German escort personnel to flee. They were liberated shortly afterward by the U.S. Army.[67]

Microhistory is a useful research approach when writing the history of the German aviation industry in World War II. By looking at specific places, firms, and experiences, we can gain insights into the works and functions of this large industrial branch. Two different historical approaches have appeared in this chapter. The first was business history, based mostly on "traditional" primary documentary sources and used to gain an overview of the firms employing forced labor. The other approach was microhistory, based primarily on the study of personal accounts, in order to highlight certain aspects of slave labor—aspects that hardly appear in official records. In many respects, survivor accounts represent a modern-day version of storytelling, the oldest form of historical narrative. Like storytelling, testimonies suffer from several shortcomings as a historical source. However, using them carefully and critically—and perhaps most importantly, only when they are relevant—can offer historians meaningful advantages. As Guido Ruggiero, one of the leading advocates of the use of personal accounts and storytelling in microhistories has written:

> Rather than retelling their tales, I have attempted to use the techniques of microhistory to craft their truths, half-truths, and evident lies into stories that reveal the underlying complexities of late-sixteenth century culture and values, shared (and at many times not shared) from which their tales sprang and drew meaning.[68]

Microhistory reveals the underlying complexities of Nazi Germany's large aviation industry on different levels. Understanding these complexities is crucial to grasping how this industry became one of the largest employers of slave labor. Besides helping to reconstruct the collective story of the slave workers, microhistory offers important glimpses into broader issues related to German aviation production in World War II. Perhaps most importantly, it provides a grassroots perspective into the massive social change that the manpower composition of this industry underwent during the war. The shift from an elite branch of highly trained professionals to a haphazard collection of POWs, foreigners, and inmates from all over Europe was a dramatic change, with many consequences. This change brought with it, among others, the gradual degradation of the working environment, as well as different production planning and models of employment. Microhistory also sheds light on the decline of production standards beginning in 1943—a degradation that affected the fighting power of the already weakened Luftwaffe. Since the aviation industry, through its massive allocation of Jewish inmates, became part of the Nazi persecution system, this microhistory also offers us valuable insights into the history of the Holocaust.

Daniel Uziel studied history and international relations at the Hebrew University and pursued his Ph.D. studies in Freiburg, Germany; his Ph.D. dissertation is entitled "Army, War, Society and Propaganda: The Propaganda Troops of the Wehrmacht and the German Public 1938–1998." His postdoctoral research at the National Air & Space Museum in Washington, DC, sponsored by the Smithsonian Institution, is entitled "The German Aviation Industry, 1943–45." He currently works in the Yad Vashem archives and International School of Holocaust Studies and teaches modern history and military history at the Haifa and Ben-Gurion Universiies. His areas of interest include modern German history, military history, history and technology, and culinary history. His books include *Arming the Luftwaffe: The German Aviation Industry in World War II* (2011) and *The Propaganda Warriors: The Wehrmacht and the Consolidation of the German Home Front* (2008).

Notes

1. Yad Vashem Archives (YVA), O.3/6463, Testimony by Sidney Birnbaum.
2. See especially Ralf Schabel, *Die Illusion der Wunderwaffen: Die Rolle der Düsenflugzeuge und Flugabwehrraketen in der Rüstungspolitik des Dritten Reiches* (Munich, 1994); Lutz Budrass, *Flugzeugindustrie und Luftrüstung in Deutschland 1918–1945* (Düsseldorf, 1998).
3. See, for example, Neil Gregor, *Daimler-Benz in the Third Reich* (New Haven, 1998); Hans Mommsen and Manfred Grieger, *Das Volkswagenwerk und seine Arbeiter im Dritten Reich* (Düsseldorf, 1996); Edith Raim, *Die Dachauer KZ-Außenkommandos Kaufering und Mühldorf: Rüstungsbauten und Zwangsarbeit im letzten Kriegsjahr 1944/1945* (Landsberg a. Lech, 1992); Jan-Christian Wagner, *Produktion des Todes: Das KZ Mittelbau-Dora* (Göttingen, 2004); Constanze Werner, *Kriegswirtschaft und Zwangsarbeit bei BMW* (Munich, 2006).
4. Edward M. Homze, *Arming the Luftwaffe: The Reich Air Ministry and the German Aircraft Industry 1919–1939* (Lincoln, 1976), 93.
5. U.S. National Archives (NARA), RG243/6/Box158, USSBS, Over-all Report (European War), 30 September 1945, 11.
6. Homze, *Arming*, 84–85.
7. See, for example, NARA, T177/34/3723696, Vierteljahresbericht für den Aufsichtsrat der Junkers Flugzeug- und Motorenwerke AG, April–Juni 1941.
8. Bertrand Perz, "Politisches Management im Wirtschaftskonzern. Georg Meindl und die Rolle des Staatskonzerns Steyr-Daimler-Puch bei der Verwirklichung der NS-Wirtschaftsziele in Österreich," in *Konzentrationslager und deutsche Wirtschaft 1939–1945*, ed. Hermann Kaienburg (Opladen 1996), 101–5; Perz, "Der Arbeitseinsatz im KZ Mauthausen," in *Die nationalsozialistischen Konzentrationslager—Entwicklung und Struktur*, ed. Ulrich Herbert, Karin Orth, and Christoph Dieckmann (Göttingen, 1998), 2:535–39.
9. Archiv des Deutschen Museums (DM), FA001/260, Heinkel an Milch: Verlagerung, 18 Juni 1942, 6.
10. Birgit Weitz, "Der Einsatz von KZ-Häftlinge und jüdischen Zwangsarbeitern bei der Daimler-Benz AG (1941–1945). Ein Überblick," in *Konzentrationslager und deutsche Wirtschaft 1939–1945*, ed. Hermann Kaienburg (Opladen, 1996), 171.
11. Hermann Kaienburg, *Die Wirtschaft der SS* (Berlin, 2003), 618–19; Hans Brenner, "Der 'Arbeitseinsatz' in den Außenlagern des KZs Flossenbürg," in Herbert, Orth, and Dieckmann, *Die nationalsozialistischen Konzentrationslager*, 1:686–88.
12. NARA, M888/6/544–547, Himmler an Göring, Einsatz von Häftlingen in der Luftfahrtindustrie, 9 März 1944.
13. Volkswagen became an aviation producer following the collapse of its "KdF Car" scheme with the outbreak of World War II. Mommsen and Grieger, *Das Volkswagenwerk*, 677–82.

14. Bundesarchiv-Berlin (BA-B), R50II/46a, Anordnung des Reichsministers für Rüstung und Kriegsproduktion vom 1 März 1944 über die Errichtung des Jägerstabes.
15. NARA, M888/6/662–663, Stenographischer Bericht über die Jägerstab Besprechung am Freitag 17 März 1944, 13–14.
16. NARA, RG243/6/Box224, Punkte aus den Besprechungen beim Führer am 6 und 7 April 1944, 6.
17. Raim, *Die Dachauer*, 36.
18. National Air & Space Museum (NASM), 3237/560, Kommando der Erprobungsstellen an R.d.L u. Ob.d.L./GL üb., 17 August 1942.
19. DM, FA001/866, Heinkel an von Pfistermeister, 19 Oktober 1942.
20. Bundesarchiv-Militärarchiv (BA-MA), RH8/1210, Heeresanstalt Peenemünde: Besichtigung des Häftlings-Einsatzes bei den Heinkel-Werken, Oranienburg, am 12 April 1943. It should be emphasized here that the V-2 was an army project and therefore was developed and produced by firms outside the aviation industry.
21. Budrass, *Flugzeugindustrie*, 778–80.
22. Ibid., 798.
23. Kaienburg, *Die Wirtschaft*, 618–19.
24. Klaus Hesse, *1933–1945 Rüstungsindustrie in Leipzig*, Vol. II (Leipzig, 2000), 86.
25. Daniel Uziel, *Arming the Luftwaffe: The German Aviation Industry in WWII* (Jefferson, 2011), 176–77. Amazingly, Focke Wulf continued this cooperation even after D-day.
26. Peter Schmoll, *Nest of Eagles: Messerschmitt Production and Flight Testing at Regensburg 1936–1945* (Hersham, 2010), 34–35.
27. Daniel Uziel, "Volksjäger: Rationalisierung und Rationalität hinter Deutschlands letztem Jäger im Zweiten Weltkrieg," in *Rüstung, Kriegswirtschaft und Zwangsarbeit im Dritten Reich*, ed. Andreas Heusler, Mark Spoerer, and Helmut Trischler (Munich: BMW Perspektiven, 2009), 3:77–81.
28. See for instance Budrass, *Flugzeugindustrie*, 779.
29. BA-MA, RH8/1210, Heeresanstalt Peenemünde: Besichtigung des Häftlings-Einsatzes bei den Heinkel-Werken, Oranienburg, am 12 April 1943.
30. Mommsen and Grieger, *Das Volkswagenwerk*, 821–23. A description of the procedure from the inmate perspective in: YVA, O.3/10384, Testimony by David Mitler, 3.
31. YVA, O.3/3676, Testimony by Rachel Zolf.
32. YVA, O.3/6277, Testimony by Agnes Geva.
33. See, for example, YVA, O.3/7643, Testimony by Itzhak Baldinger.
34. YVA, O.3/7250, Testimony by Peter Erben.
35. YVA, O.17/30, Testimony by Eva Bohcher.
36. YVA, O.3/4745, Testimony by Miriam Givon.
37. Daniel Uziel, "Between Industrial Revolution and Slavery Mass Production in the German Aviation Industry in World War II," *History & Technology* 22, no. 3 (2006): 277–300.
38. YVA, O.3/3676, Testimony by Rachel Zolf.
39. The United States Strategic Bombing Survey (USSBS), *Aircraft Division Industry Report*, 2nd edn, (n.p., 1947), figure VI-I. On the specific role of slave labor in the aviation "Production Miracle," see Ralf Schabel, *Die Illusion der Wunderwaffen: Die Rolle der Düsenflugzeuge und Flugabwehrraketen in der Rüstungspolitik des Dritten Reiches* (Munich, 1994), 226. On the "Production Miracle" in general, see Werner Abelshauser, "Germany: Guns, Butter and Economic Miracles," in *The Economics of World War II: Six Great Powers in International Comparison*, ed. Mark Harrison (Cambridge, 1998), 151–76.
40. Rainer Fröbe, "KZ-Häftlinge als Reserve qualifizierter Arbeitskraft. Eine späte Entdeckung der deutschen Industrie und ihre Folgen," in Herbert, Orth, and Dieckmann, *Die nationalsozialistischen Konzentrationslager*, 2:637.

41. YVA, O.3/4745, Testimony by Miriam Givon.
42. YVA, O.3/5348, Testimony by Mordechai Lustig.
43. YVA, O.3/6906, Testimony by Josef Pinsker.
44. YVA, O.3/8099, Testimony by Tzipora Shwiatowitz.
45. YVA, O.3/7936, Testimony by Miriam Frank.
46. YVA, O.3/7379, Testimony by Miriam Alter.
47. YVA, O.3/6617, Testimony by Zehava Fruchter.
48. Lutz Budrass, "Der Schritt über die Schwelle. Ernst Heinkel, das Werk Oranienburg und der Einstieg in der Beschäftigung von KZ-Häftlinge," in *Zwangsarbeit während der NS-Zeit in Berlin und Brandenburg,* ed. Winfried Meyer (Potsdam, 2001), 158.
49. See, for example, YVA, O.3/7643, Testimony by Itzhak Baldinger.
50. YVA, O.3/7202, Testimony by Itzchak Pankowski.
51. YVA, O.3/6447, Testimony by Hanna Sternlicht.
52. YVA, O.15E/1404, Testimony by Eva Gruenfeld.
53. YVA, O.15E/1424, Testimony by Samuel Krainer.
54. YVA, O.15E/1380, Testimony by Sámuel Abrahamovics.
55. NARA, RG243/31/Box1, USSBS: Interview no. 36. Interrogation of Officers of the *Luftwaffe,* 21 June 1945, 6.
56. Alfred Price, *The Last Year of the Luftwaffe: May 1944 to May 1945* (Stillwater, MN: Motorbooks International, 1991), 15.
57. NARA, M888/6/331, Stenographischer Bericht über die Besprechung mit den Flotteningenieuren und Oberquartiermeistern unter dem Vorsitz von Generalfeldmarschall Milch am Sonnabend, 25 März 1944, 19.
58. NARA T83/14/3357768, Der Betriebleiter, Bad Eilsen: Mitteilung. Tagesalarm, 21 Dezember 1943.
59. YVA, O.69/310, Testimony by Mark Stern.
60. On this project, its continuation in 1944, and the working conditions there, see Wagner, *Produktion des Todes.*
61. YVA, O.3/8028, Testimony by Josef Weiss.
62. Perz, "Der Arbeitseinsatz," 543, 548. Another large-scale underground project involving massive allocation of slave labor was "Ringeltaube." See Raim, *Die Dachauer.*
63. For instance, the evacuation of the Heinkel factories around Vienna. Geoffrey Megargee, ed., *The United States Memorial Museum Encyclopedia of Camps and Ghettos, 1933–1945,* vol. 1, part B (Bloomington, 2009), 960; YVA, O.15E/1424, Testimony by Samuel Krainer.
64. Fröbe, "KZ-Häftlinge," 646.
65. Mommsen and Grieger, *Das Volkswagenwerk,* 822.
66. YVA, O.17/30, Testimony by Eva Bohrer, 4–5.
67. YVA, O.3/6463, Testimony by Sidney Birnbaum.
68. Guido Ruggiero, *Binding Passions: Tales of Magic, Marriage, and Power at the End of the Renaissance* (Oxford 1993), 19.

Bibliography

Abelshauser, Werner. "Germany: Guns, Butter and Economic Miracles", in *The Economics of World War II: Six Great Powers in International Comparison,* ed. Mark Harrison, Cambridge: Cambridge University Press, 1998, 151–76.
Brenner, Hans. "Der 'Arbeitseinsatz' in den Außenlagern des KZs Flossenbürg." In *Die nationalsozialistischen Konzentrationslager—Entwicklung und Struktur,* ed. Ulrich Herbert, Karin Orth, and Christoph Dieckmann, Göttingen: Wallstein, 1998, 1:686–88.

Budrass, Lutz. "Der Schritt über die Schwelle. Ernst Heinkel, das Werk Oranienburg und der Einstieg in der Beschäftigung von KZ-Häftlinge", in *Zwangsarbeit während der NS-Zeit in Berlin und Brandenburg,* ed. Winfried Meyer, Potsdam: Berliner Wissenschafts-Verlag, 2001, 129–162.

———. *Flugzeugindustrie und Luftrüstung in Deutschland 1918–1945.* Düsseldorf: Droste, 1998.

Fröbe, Rainer. "KZ-Häftlinge als Reserve qualifizierter Arbeitskraft. Eine späte Entdeckung der deutschen Industrie und ihre Folgen", in *Die nationalsozialistischen Konzentrationslager—Entwicklung und Struktur,* ed. Ulrich Herbert, Karin Orth, and Christoph Dieckmann, vol. 2., Göttingen: Wallstein, 1998, 636–681.

Gregor, Neil. *Daimler-Benz in the Third Reich.* New Haven, CT: Yale University Press, 1998.

Hesse, Klaus. *1933–1945 Rüstungsindustrie in Leipzig.* Vol. II. Leipzig: Slebstverlag, 2000.

Homze, Edward M. *Arming the Luftwaffe: The Reich Air Ministry and the German Aircraft Industry 1919–1939.* Lincoln: University of Nebraska Press, 1976.

Kaienburg, Hermann. *Die Wirtschaft der SS.* Berlin: Metropol, 2003.

Megargee, Geoffrey, ed. *The United States Memorial Museum Encyclopedia of Camps and Ghettos, 1933–1945.* Bloomington: Indiana University Press, 2009.

Mommsen, Hans, and Manfred Grieger. *Das Volkswagenwerk und seine Arbeiter im Dritten Reich.* Düsseldorf: Econ, 1996.

Perz, Bertrand. "Der Arbeitseinsatz im KZ Mauthausen." In *Die nationalsozialistischen Konzentrationslager—Entwicklung und Struktur,* ed. Ulrich Herbert, Karin Orth, and Christoph Dieckmann, Göttingen: Wallstein, 1998, 535–39.

———. "Politisches Management im Wirtschaftskonzern. Georg Meindl und die Rolle des Staatskonzerns Steyr-Daimler-Puch bei der Verwirklichung der NS-Wirtschaftsziele in Österreich", in *Konzentrationslager und deutsche Wirtschaft 1939–1945,* ed. Hermann Kaienburg, Oplanden: Springer, 1996, 101–5.

Price, Alfred. *The Last Year of the Luftwaffe: May 1944 to May 1945.* Stillwater, MN: Motorbooks International, 1991.

Raim, Edith. *Die Dachauer KZ-Außenkommandos Kaufering und Mühldorf: Rüstungsbauten und Zwangsarbeit im letzten Kriegsjahr 1944–1945.* Landsberg a. Lech: Landsberger Verlaganstalt, 1992.

Ruggiero, Guido. *Binding Passions: Tales of Magic, Marriage, and Power at the End of the Renaissance.* Oxford: Oxford University Press, 1993.

Schabel, Ralf. *Die Illusion der Wunderwaffen: Die Rolle der Düsenflugzeuge und Flugabwehrraketen in der Rüstungspolitik des Dritten Reiches.* Munich: Oldenbourg, 1994.

Schmoll, Peter. *Nest of Eagles: Messerschmitt Production and Flight Testing at Regensburg 1936–1945.* Hersham: Classic Publications, 2010.

Wagner, Jan-Christian. *Produktion des Todes: Das KZ Mittelbau-Dora.* Göttingen: Wallstein, 2004.

Weitz, Birgit. "Der Einsatz von KZ-Häftlinge und jüdischen Zwangsarbeitern bei der Daimler-Benz AG (1941–1945). Ein Überblick", in *Konzentrationslager und deutsche Wirtschaft 1939–1945,* ed. Hermann Kaienburg. Oplanden: Springer, 1996, 169–195.

Werner, Constanze. *Kriegswirtschaft und Zwangsarbeit bei BMW.* Munich: Oldenbourg, 2006.

Uziel, Daniel. *Arming the Luftwaffe: The German Aviation Industry in WWII.* Jefferson: McFarland, 2011.

———. "Volksjäger: Rationalisierung und Rationalität hinter Deutschlands letztem Jäger im Zweiten Weltkrieg." In *Rüstung, Kriegswirtschaft und Zwangsarbeit im Dritten Reich,* ed. Andreas Heusler, Mark Spoerer and Helmut Trischler, Munich: BMW Perspektiven, 2009, 77–81.

———. "Between Industrial Revolution and Slavery: Mass Production in the German Aviation Industry in World War II", *History & Technology* 22, no. 3 (2006), 277–300.

CHAPTER 9

THE DEVIL IN MICROHISTORY
THE "HUNT FOR JEWS" AS A SOCIAL PROCESS, 1942–1945

Tomasz Frydel

*Evil is unspectacular and always human,
And shares our bed and eats at our own table.*
—WH Auden, "Herman Melville"

An Integrated Microhistory

One of the most influential dictums of historians of the Holocaust has been Saul Friedländer's call for an "integrated history" aimed at combining elements of the Hilbergian machinery of destruction—the perpetrator perspective—with the experience of its various victim groups and individuals.[1] Historians, including Friedländer himself, have in their own ways sought to follow this narrative and interpretive framework.[2] In the case of Eastern Europe and the Soviet Union, where thousands of ghettos and camps were established under Nazi German rule, microhistory has understandably emerged as the preferred method of historical reconstruction.[3] This essay asks what it means to write an integrated *micro*history of the Holocaust. Its goal is to reconstruct elements of a local history as an integrated history that foregrounds German violence against one victim group (Poles) as a conditioning factor in its relations with the primary victim group (Jews) of the Holocaust.

In the case of genocide in occupied Poland, one important benefit of an integrated microhistory is that it can serve as an antidote to a polarized historiography. The Rzeszów (or Subcarpathian) region under consideration is perhaps most emblematic of this polarized landscape. On the one hand, it is the site of the most commemorated family of Polish rescuers of Jews – the Ulma family in the village of Markowa (Łańcut county). On 24 March 1944, Józef Ulma, his pregnant wife Wiktoria and six children were executed by German gendarmes along with the eight Jews of the Szall and Goldman families, whom they had sheltered since 1942.[4] In 1995, the Ulma couple was posthumously given the titles of Righteous among Nations by Yad Vashem. Since then, they have occupied center stage in the Polish pantheon of national heroes as a kind of Holy Family of the Holocaust. On 17 March 2016, the site of their murder saw to the opening of a long-awaited museum, unambiguously named "The Ulma Family Museum of Poles Saving Jews in World War II," which enjoyed the presence of Poland's president, Andrzej Duda.[5] On the other side of this well-maintained narrative wall, though garnering much less public attention, just thirty kilometers northeast of Markowa, lie the bodies of eighteen Jews in the village of Jagiełła-Niechciałka (Przeworsk county). These Jews were from the neighboring villages of Gniewczyna Tryniecka and Gniewczyna Łęczycka, who were robbed, tortured, and raped by members of the fire brigade prior to their being handed over to the German police for execution.[6]

Forms of help and harm by ethnic Poles toward Jews form a spectrum of behavior and both have their place in the history of occupied Poland. The danger for scholarship and public memory, however, lies in treating these respective narratives in isolation so that they come to represent separate academic "fields" and ways of remembering the past. Yet not only were the above phenomena part of the same social continuum, they were at times causally connected in important ways. Here, one cannot study the mechanisms of rescue without simultaneously linking these to the mechanisms of destruction. While historical inquiry must, understandably, often proceed according to a division of labor among historians, such a division runs the risk of being reified or essentialized into separate subfields, or genres, of scholarship. One analytical danger of such a dichotomy lies in falsely suggesting that entirely different social groups (such as the "criminal margins") and individuals (or moral agents) were involved in ways of protecting Jews and ways of harming them.[7]

This chapter will sketch out important features of a microhistory of the Holocaust in rural Poland that complicate the above historiographical trends and ought to inform the basis of a social history of this period. Its primary geographical focus is southeastern Poland, with some examples drawn from other regions of the General Government (GG) – the name given to the main zone of German occupation formed from the Second Polish Republic. The thematic focus is the German "hunt for Jews" (*Judenjagd*), the final stage of Operation Reinhard, as it manifested itself in this region from 1942-45.[8]

Genocide from Above

On 13 March 1943, the head of the SS and German police in District Warsaw sent out a secret memo to the heads of the civil administration concerning the "arrest and liquidation of Jews who remain in hiding." The head of the SS and police outlined the strategy along four axes:

> I order immediate and most energetic action to apprehend the Jews, who have to be transferred to the gendarmerie for liquidation. More specifically, we are dealing here with Jews who roam the cities and countryside without an armband, who were able to flee the earlier deportation actions. In order to succeed, one has to involve the *Sonderdienst, the Polish Police, and informers* [*V-Männer*]. *It is also necessary to involve broad masses of Polish society....* Persons who have helped to apprehend the Jews can receive up to one-third of the seized property [emphasis mine].[9]

These parameters formed the outline of the "hunt for Jews" in what could be described as a top-down, Nazi policy-directed "genocide from above." The system of German control over the countryside was based on two pillars of rural authority: village heads and local Polish police forces. The village head (*sołtys*) functioned as a crucial link in the system of rules and regulations imposed by the occupation authorities. His main responsibilities consisted of the following: (1) to collect food quotas from each family for the German army, (2) to collect, in cooperation with the Labor Office (*Arbeitsamt*), "human quotas" of young Polish men and women to be sent as forced laborers (often by force) to the German Reich, and (3), following the launch of Operation Barbarossa on 22 June 1941, to ensure that the village under his jurisdiction was not harboring anyone without proper identification (*Kennkarte*), such as fugitive Jews, Soviet prisoners of war (POWs), partisans, and any outsiders. If a member of any of these groups was discovered, it was the responsibility of the village head to apprehend them and notify the Polish Police or gendarmerie or, barring that, take the initiative in delivering the suspect to the police station. Village heads were equipped with the manpower necessary to carry out these tasks in the form of village guards (*Ortschutz* or *Ortschutzwache*), often directly adapted from existing fire brigades. Stepping down from the position of village head (most were elected prior to war) was regarded as a form of sabotage of the German war effort. When the *Judenjagd* was mobilized after the liquidation of ghettos in the summer and fall of 1942, these local structures – village heads, village guards, fire brigade units, messengers, foresters, and gamekeepers – formed the security net around villages. This system of surveillance represented the lowest reaches of German authority in village society.

Local Polish police forces represented the second pillar of German control over the countryside. On 17 December 1939, General Hans Frank formally declared the creation of the Polish Police, which was partly reconstituted as the Polnische Polizei (PP), and made subordinate to the German Order Police (Ordnungspolizei), which in rural regions meant the gendarmerie.[10] The policemen continued to wear their prewar uniforms with the emblems of the Polish Second Republic removed (the eagle on the cap was replaced with the city or commune coat of arms). The PP was the only armed and uniformed Polish formation under German occupation in the GG. In December 1942, PP forces counted twelve thousand policemen.[11]

However, the PP was modified in important ways. Many of the policemen did not return from hiding. Those who did return to service did so under the threat of incarceration in a concentration camp. Following Polish defeat after the dual German and Soviet attack, a large percentage of policemen found themselves in Soviet POW camps. The Ostaszków camp contained the largest number of policemen—sixty-five hundred police and security forces from all strata—who were then executed by the People's Commissariat for Internal Affairs (NKVD) in the nearby village of Miednoje.[12] This local police vacuum required finding new recruits. Many were drawn from the Polish population deported to the GG following the annexation of the Warthegau into the German Reich (many new recruits came from Silesia and the Poznań area). A three-month course in a police academy in Nowy Sącz was created to train recruits without prior experience. In general, each commune (*Sammelgemeinde*) contained a PP station, which usually included six to eight policemen. Gendarme posts were mostly restricted to larger towns and cities, except in the case of large ethnic German (*Volksdeutsche*) villages. The PP therefore had a degree of limited autonomy that was kept in check by a system of rotating gendarmes (usually of ethnic German background) as commandants of the PP posts to provide oversight and to build group morale by fraternizing with its members.[13]

The main responsibilities of the PP included maintaining law and order, enforcing the system of exploitation imposed on village society, and combatting the growing rise of banditry in the countryside. This meant fining or arresting farmers for a variety of infractions, such as failing to tag pigs and cattle (in an attempt to avoid their seizure during quota collections), shirking forced labor in Germany, and participating in the black market. During the so-called liquidation stage of ghettos, the PP was drawn deeper into the process of guarding ghettos and participating in the capture and killing of fugitive Jews. At the same time, as the underground movement increased its anti-German struggle, the Polish Police was drawn into the anti-partisan struggle.

Genocide from Below

The *Judenjagd,* understood in terms of the axes outlined in the memo, was essentially a project to make segments of occupied society complicit in genocide. Involving "broad masses of Polish society" meant hammering segments of the local population into the desired shape, in order to radically transform social norms and behavior. It is impossible to write a history of this process without discussing the social anxieties unleashed by these new conditions. Naturally, it took on different forms depending on the region. For example, in the summer of 1942, German authorities organized a meeting in the village of Antoniów (Tarnobrzeg county). Stanisław Rydzewski, the village messenger, was told to call out all the inhabitants. The German army then surrounded the inhabitants as the following lesson was conducted:

> A German spoke in Polish at this meeting and told us not to attempt to help the Jews, not to hide them. As an example, so that people would not try to maintain any contacts with Jews, they took a Jew and beat him with a stick. In the course of beating the Jew, one of the German officers turned to the people, saying that every good Pole should treat Jews in the same way.[14]

It is not clear how extensive these methods were, but such public spectacles undoubtedly had an impact on villagers like Rydzewski, who was accused after the war of directing the gendarmerie to the whereabouts of various Poles, a Soviet POW, and a twelve-year-old Jewish girl. Top-down directives often ricocheted in unpredictable and surprising ways on the local level. "Genocide from above" gave rise to existential dilemmas in village society that came to form the bottom-up push of denunciation and killing, or "genocide from below." Local violence is thus seen here as a product of the dynamic that emerged between these two force fields. This section will discuss in outline some of the manifestations of the system of pressures generated from below.

In this social landscape, one prominent pattern of peasant aggression toward Jews centered around instances of extreme violence toward Poles for sheltering Jews—particularly in connection with "pacification actions" (*Pazifizierungsaktionen*). The pattern of expelling, capturing, and killing Jews accelerated most dramatically in the immediate aftermath of these acts. State terrorism in the form of pacification actions could thus function to provide a climate conducive for searching out Jews, as the presence of fugitive Jews became increasingly associated with communal survival. For example, on 23 April 1943, two trucks filled with German soldiers and gendarmes with police dogs arrived in the village of Podborze (Mielec county). They had received information that the Dudek family was sheltering Jews and ordered Michał Pająk, the village head, to take them to their house. However, when they arrived on the scene, there was no sign of either the Polish or the Jewish family.[15] The Germans then threatened locals with execution and proceeded to set fire to the village, beginning with the Dudek household. A total of twenty-three properties were burned to the ground. Although no one in the village was killed, a close reconstruction of events shows that the pacification action resulted in the capture and death—with the help of locals—of a total of approximately 25–30 Jews across three communes in the immediate weeks following the event. If viewed on a map, subsequent peasant violence toward Jews formed a ring around the site of repression.[16] To ethnic Polish communities, it was likely that anything was preferable to inviting the unpredictable violence of the German police.

The outline of this structure of violence brings us back to the murder of the Ulma family in the village of Markowa on 23 March 1944, mentioned at the outset. According to Yehuda Erlich, who survived in hiding in the nearby village of Sietesz, the brutal murder of the Ulmas and the Jews they were sheltering had a galvanizing effect: "Polish peasants who were hiding Jews fell into a terrible state of panic. The next day, twenty-four Jewish bodies were found in nearby fields. They were Jews murdered by these peasants, who had been sheltering them for the previous twenty months."[17] This testimony suggests that the killing proceeded along a similar arc. Further, the region around Markowa was subjected to a series of German repressions from 1942 to 1945. From 6 to 8 March 1943, repressions (mostly targeted at the underground movement) swept across local villages: Łopuszka Wielka (19 people), Rączyna (18), Pantalowice (17), Rokietnica (45), Kaszyce (121), and Czelatyce (15).[18] Approximately 235 people were killed in these actions. Of course not all pacification actions were a result of locals sheltering Jews, but they were steeped in a climate of ongoing repressions. Sietesz itself was "pacified" twice in connection with locals sheltering Jews and Soviet POWs.[19] Under similar allegations, Pantalowice was targeted previously in 1942. In the nearby village of Pawłosiów, the Czerwonek family was shot by the German police for the same "crime" in July of 1943. Added to this was the fact that the precise reasons for repressions in neighboring villages were not always clear, which probably caused fear of German terror to be very common in the minds of the local population.

The dynamic of fear appears to have been much more widespread. To take another example, in the Tarnów region, the very act of posting a notice by the *Kreishauptmann* (county chief) on 9 September 1942 was sufficient cause for a dramatic change in behavior:

> The Poles were basically afraid of helping the Jews, because the *Kreishauptmann* had made it known to local Poles, through the use of posters, that every person who hides a Jew will be killed.... As a result of such notices, even decent Poles drove Jews out of their homes, who subsequently fell into the hands of the Gestapo.[20]

In another part of the General Government, the direct effect of German terror was to cut off the food supply to Jews in hiding, such as Józef Goldfinger: "After the pacification in Kaszów and Liszki, people who until the pacification had willingly given him shelter and food began to refuse, fearing the consequences of German regulations."[21] As a further consequence, the shortage of food, combined with an increasingly hostile population, compelled many Jews to turn themselves in. The pattern examined here may also be applicable beyond the General Government. For example, in the small Lithuanian town of Butrimonys, Lithuanian policemen hunted down Jews following an *Aktion* in 1942. After the head of the Golembowski family was arrested and shot for sheltering Jews, many other Jews were subsequently turned out by their protectors.[22]

A second core component of this pattern was the belief that the preemptive capture or killing of fugitive Jews by local villagers and police forces would save a family or village in the event that a captured Jew denounced their former protectors. The death penalty against Poles for sheltering Jews introduced a new teleology of violence. The likelihood of denunciation certainly increased when sheltering Jews had developed into a small-scale economy of "rescue for money," where desperate fugitives were left vulnerable to financial exploitation and robbery.[23] If we return to the case of Podborze, Polish policemen Jan Pielach and Michał Strząpka were called to the nearby village of Dąbie in the summer of 1943. They arrived to a scene where a crowd of villagers had surrounded a Jewish man and woman. The policemen followed protocol, placed the Jews on a wagon to turn them over to the gendarmerie and began making their way toward Mielec, but the Jewish man allegedly "uttered some threats against the people of Dąbie, [stating] that he will teach them a lesson, and complained that they took twelve dollars from him." Peasants ran alongside the wagon begging the policemen not to hand the Jews over, as the village could face repression as a consequence. Pielach, the commandant, then "came to the conviction that delivering these Jews to Mielec, with the possibility of their providing testimony, could end unpleasantly for the population of Dąbie."[24] The policemen stopped the wagon and shot the siblings in a nearby field. In the village of Zimna Woda (Jasło county), a Jew by the name of Tolek was captured by the village guard when he caused panic by appearing in the village in broad daylight. According to Franciszek Wojnar, Tolek allegedly "made threats to the entire community, saying that 'half the village will go down with me.'"[25] When the police arrived, Tolek was shot on the spot.

This line of defense should be approached with a dose of skepticism, as it was undoubtedly exploited by the accused for exculpatory purposes and, in the case of policemen, to give their actions a veneer of "patriotism." Such cases should be examined by the historian on a case-by-case basis. Yet it is impossible to entirely dismiss the claims, as this form of reasoning became anchored in an occupational logic of survival that is echoed throughout real-time sources. Along these lines, an underground report issued by the Home Army (AK) on 12 March 1943 stated:

> There has not been a single incident in which a captured Jew did not denounce everyone who offered them help. In many cases, they maliciously give surnames [of those] who are completely uninvolved. All are shot on the spot. We have borne many losses because of this. Therefore, I forbid any contact with and help to fleeing Jews.[26]

Similar fears are echoed in the chronicle kept by Franciszek Kotula in the city of Rzeszów during the war. On 16 December 1942, he wrote:

> News is arriving from all directions that the Germans are murdering entire Polish families when they discover that they are sheltering Jews. Whoever is still sheltering someone expels him, and when the Germans catch that person, he most often reveals where he was and who fed him. After all, he knows that he's going to die anyway. Panic has erupted among those who once sheltered Jews, and they are running off into the woods. Even if a Jew manages to escape the ghetto, he will no longer be able to find shelter in the countryside, not even a corner, not for a moment.[27]

The practice of interrogating Jews about who gave them food and shelter was not systematic, but it was made sufficiently routine to cause panic among peasants. If we freeze the narrative frame in this moment, we see various reactions. In the village of Gamratka (Mińsk Mazowiecki county) in July 1943, the gendarmerie arrived at the home of Zofia Kur, who was sheltering Jews in a bunker. The policemen threw a grenade into their bunker and ordered locals to pull the Jews out. Three young men, covered in blood and with limbs blown off, were pulled out of the bunker. In the words of the village head:

> We laid the three Jews on the ground, and the German gendarmes brought all of the men and women of Gamratka around the Jews and asked them [the Jews] whether they knew us. The Jews replied that they didn't know us. One of them knew me from having seen me before, but he told the gendarmes that he didn't know me.[28]

Yet in a number of cases, the threat of death often bore fruit. Around the same time, in the vicinity of the village of Malinie (Mielec county), the German police had captured a Jewish woman, who was marched through local villages and beaten into admitting who had given her help, before being shot.[29] Her seventeen-year-old daughter was captured shortly after and allowed to be kept alive if she helped denounce local Poles who offered her help. She was executed in the village of Grochowe after leaving behind a trail of fourteen dead people whom she had denounced.[30] According to Jan Fereński, who was both a former Polish policeman and a member of the Home Army, the Czajka family of six in the village of Libusza (Gorlice county) was shot by the Germans for sheltering Jews: "Morgenstern hid with them. When they realized that they were being observed, they moved Morgenstern to Czermno, where he was captured by the Germans and betrayed the names of those who had sheltered him."[31]

In other instances, promises made by German policemen appeared to have been effective. For example, in Wólka Ogryzkowa (Przeworsk county), Nathan Haske was shot by German police during a hunt for Jews in a nearby forest. One of the policemen "gave him water to drink and promised him that if he tells them everything that they ask, they will send him to a hospital and then to Germany, where he would live." Haske allegedly supplied the police with the names of members of the Peasant Battalions in nearby villages. Another German policeman noted everything down. When his information was exhausted, "Gestapoman Zajder told him to get up, as he would be taken to a hospital," and then shot Haske in the forehead.[32] The archival record has preserved two such interrogation reports given by Izek Zylberberg after his capture in November of 1942 near the town of Iłża (Radom county). Zylberberg had taken shelter with a group of partisans consisting mostly of fugitive Jews and was the only one taken alive after the Germans had attacked their forest bunkers. In the last report, the interrogating policeman noted that "this Jew had not yet been shot, so as to allow him to provide further testimony."[33] However, it must be emphasized that the dynamic around the fear of denunciation was certainly not specific to Jews, but was inherent to hiding any fugitives, though they were the largest fugitive group. For example, an underground newspaper bemoaned a practice among Soviet POWs of betraying their former protectors in the hope of "extend[ing] their life by a few days" when faced with "the inevitable bullet."[34] There is no doubt that the will to survive and the prospect of even a few more days of life was a powerful force for those fleeing certain death.

The use of torture in such cases was not uncommon. In January of 1943, the Augustyn family was denounced for sheltering three Jews in the village of Ołpiny (Jasło county). The Polish police arrived from the Szerzyny station and transported them to the gendarmerie in Jasło. The file suggests that the Augustyns may have denounced the Jews themselves, but in order to protect the Augustyns, policeman Mikołaj Leszega and his colleagues falsified their report to state that the Jews had just arrived on their farm. Nevertheless, three weeks later, a member of the Jasło Gestapo, Karl Hauch, arrived in the village and shot Józef Augustyn, because during interrogation the captured Jews had revealed that they were sheltered for three months.[35] Further, both those receiving and providing shelter faced the prospect of torture. In the village of Brzeziany (Dębica county), Andrzej Andreasik brought food to Jews hidden in a forest bunker. Several policemen from the PP station in Wielopole Skrzyńskie, headed by gendarme Wilhelm Jaki, arrived at his home.

> Jaki took me out into the field and began to ask me where the Jews are. I told him that I don't know anything. He told me to lie on the ground and started to beat me with a stick. After hitting me several times, he told me to get up again and continued to ask me about the Jews. I continued to say that I don't know, and he hit me two more times in the face with the stick, but I did not reveal anything.

Andreasik was then taken to the police station, where, kept without food or water, he continued to be beaten every one and a half hours for three days, in an unsuccessful attempt to have him reveal the whereabouts of the Jews. The lesson he drew from the experience was that Poles who sheltered Jews simply broke down too easily under physical pressure: "I criticized the actions of the local population, who sheltered Jews but then betrayed them as a result of torture applied by the Germans.... If I was beaten by the Germans, I would not break down so easily."[36]

A third layer of the hunt for Jews was informed by the presence of numerous informers, or *V-Männer* [*Vertrauensperson* or "trusted person"], dispatched by German authorities to entrap peasants and report on activities deemed illegal. This was a broad strategy usually coordinated by the local Gestapo to apprehend sheltered Jews, escaped Soviet POWs, and members of the underground. In a striking case, in 1948 Stanisław Bajorek stood accused of collaboration with the German occupation authorities for handing over a Soviet POW in Rzepiennik Strzyżewski (Tarnów county) and was sentenced to five and a half years in prison. In a dramatic overturn of the verdict by the District Court of Jasło, Bajorek was acquitted when additional evidence revealed that the alleged Soviet POW was in fact an informer, known for wandering through villages to compile lists of peasants who opened their doors and gave him shelter. The gendarmerie would then return to these homes and arrest and execute the peasants.[37]

In a number of instances, Jews themselves were used to entrap peasants hiding Jews. In the spring of 1943, Edward Sypko and his father had given a certain "Rubin" shelter several times in the village of Brzóza (Brzuza, Węgrów county). On 3 March 1943, Rubin had returned with the Gestapo and arrested Edward Sypko and his father, along with six others, who had also given help to Rubin. The operation, coordinated by the Gestapo of Ostrów Mazowiecka, resulted in the arrest of twenty people from Brzoza. Among the arrested Poles were two Russian POWs and a teenage Jewish boy. The next day, seven of the prisoners were executed in the woods of Szynkarzyzna, the younger Sypko's father among them. On 5 March 1943, Edward Sypko and the remaining prisoners were sent to Treblinka.[38] Word of this wave of "provocations" in Węgrów county and the area near Treblinka was reported by underground publications, such as the weekly *Wieś* (The Village), issued in Warsaw and circulated throughout the General Government. It decried the actions of this Jewish informer, allegedly a former "member of a Bolshevik band," who was behind the "enormous wave of German terror" targeted at "village families for helping Soviet POWS and Jews who had escaped from ghettos."[39]

Similarly, in the spring of 1943, Bogdan Protter, a fugitive Jew hiding in the village of Chrząstów (Mielec county), met a well-dressed and clean-shaven stranger walking around the village:

I saw the individual and recognized him as a Jew, whom I didn't know. We immediately began to speak Yiddish and I learned from him that he was from the Tarnobrzeg region. This really surprised me, because it would have been more natural for him to hide in his own region. I didn't like this Jew based on his behavior. He began to ask how many Jews were hiding in the region, and where. He showed no sign of fear or anxiety. When I told him that a few more Jews were hiding in the nearby forest of Malinie, he suggested that we go there together. Here I would like to add that I had already heard that some Jew by the name of Kapłan was a German informer, and informed the Germans about Jews hiding in the region, employing several people in the process.[40]

As a result of the encounter, another fellow Jew, Herschek, and his son, were persuaded by the stranger to enter a labor camp near Mielec, where Herschek and his son were later shot. The informer had also learned of the whereabouts of the barn in nearby Złotniki where Protter and his brother were hiding. On that very same day, the barn was surrounded by gendarmes and searched without success, as Porter and his brother avoided returning to it after this encounter. Kapłan himself and some of the other members of this network were themselves former members of the Mielec and Pustków camp Jewish Councils (Judenräte). Their gradual transformation into informers exemplifies the narrowing of the range of choices and the emergence of a new survival strategy that adapted itself to the needs of the *Judenjagd*. Yet knowledge of such operations likely became more widespread, and the perception came to form a reality. We see it recorded by Kotula some sixty kilometers away, who noted the following anecdote on 15 July 1942:

> Some Jews are trying to escape the ghetto one way or another. The Gestapo is surely aware of this, and is trying to figure out how to capture and exterminate these people. And they have sophisticated ways of doing this. They tell the following tale:
>> A Jew comes to the home of a peasant, who lives close to the woods in Babice, and asks to hide him for three months. The peasant is indignant and doesn't want to hear of it. The Jew pulls out money, a lot of money, and thrusts it before the peasant. But the peasant threatens the Jew to leave right away. The alleged Jew then changes into a Gestapo man, praises the peasant, and gives him a few packs of tobacco and 200 zł in reward.
>
> Such a story spreads at lightning speed. It is certain that the Gestapo put the story into circulation by means of its agents in order to evoke suspicion and fear.[41]

Rumors in a time of war, with limited access to reliable information, are known to have particular staying power, as their importance was often tied to survival. The toxic mix of real incidents and rumors, like the one above, were likely in high circulation during the occupation and informed the popular imagination of peasants vis-à-vis fugitive Jews.

At other times, fear of informers overlapped with fear of pacification actions. After the war, the deputy village head of Straszęcin (Dębica county), Jan Skowroń, along with members of the village night guard, were accused of capturing two Dutch POWs, who had allegedly escaped from the nearby Pustków camp, and of handing them over to the Polish Police in the summer of 1943. The two men had previously been sheltered by Stanisław Wojko. The pacification of the nearby village of Bobrowa on 9 July 1943, where more than twenty inhabitants were killed and their property burned down, played a crucial role in the future course of events. One of the accused night guards stated the following:

> Sometime in the summer of 1943, already after the pacification of Bobrowa, Skowroń came to my house and told me to come with him to capture people, who were dangerous to the village—some sort of spies, who some said were Dutchmen. I said that maybe we could get by without doing this, but he replied that they were dangerous, that things could end tragically the way they did in Bobrowa. In Bobrowa, a stranger had spent the night in the home of Mordyńska, and then the Germans shot several people in her home and those of others and burned down two homes.[42]

Another of the accused night guards, Ludwik Adamowicz, testified:

> I was called by Skowroń and Kolbusz, who were standing in front of the home of Wojko, and told me that there were German spies in his home. Skowroń gave me a chain and told me to go and tie them up. I told him that perhaps they were Poles, Jews, or Russians, who were hiding from the Germans. Skowroń replied: here I am refusing to tie them up, while they could be spies, who could very well be spying on me, and that half the village could be shot because of me, just as in Bobrowa. So I took the chain and went to the home of Wojko.[43]

Taken together, the congruence of fears surrounding pacification actions, the potential of betrayal by those who were given help, the temptation to rob and denounce Jews, and the existence of undercover agents gave the *Judenjagd* deadly momentum, especially as it was connected to a larger hunt for Soviet POWs, partisans, German deserters, and other fugitives.[44] These elements formed the matrix of pressures from below that shaped the behavior of all victim groups on the local level. What is striking here in terms of those who found themselves on both sides of the help and harm spectrum is that rescuing and killing were not infrequently carried out by the same people. Many village guards who had to participate in hunts for Jews or Soviet POWs often sheltered such fugitives themselves. Some policemen killed one group of Jews while sheltering others. For example, policeman Michał Strząpka, who participated in the killing of over a dozen Jews following the Podborze *Pazifizierungsaktion,* had since 1940 been active, along with his wife and daughter, in coordinating the rescue of the Berl family from Kraków, without any material reward in exchange.[45]

The Devil in the Details

"Unweaving" the Holocaust into discrete parts to be studied in "cross-sections" can be analytically useful in bridging certain of its aspects (as well as connecting the Holocaust to other genocides). For example, historian Daniel Blatman's findings on the "death marches" bear some similarity to the "hunt for Jews."[46] Blatman found that anti-Semitism was not central: all marching victim groups received the same brutal treatment. In the death marches, killing was not immediate, as in a death camp or a mass execution over a death pit; deportations created a drawn-out process of gradual killing. A large number of the perpetrators were ordinary Germans who had no prior experience in killing. Many of them crossed the boundary from passive observers to participants. There was no centralized bureaucracy or authority controlling this process.

A fundamental goal of history is to seek explanations of past events by recourse to patterns and processes that are not always evident to its subjects. It is also to make the world of its subjects—and the actions emanating from it—more comprehensible. I have tried to cull from the sources a matrix of local pressures that gave shape to the unfolding of genocide following the major "liquidation actions" of ghettos in the General Government. The call "to involve broad masses of Polish society" contained within it a whole social world that unfolded for approximately three years. Today it represents a rich but as yet unwritten social history, with its own social dynamics and mechanisms of local violence, which a microhistory is ideally suited to reconstruct. A macrohistorical view of local murder as a form of ethnic cleansing motivated primarily by anti-Semitism or extreme nationalism disintegrates under the microscope of a local history. The *Judenjagd* occurred in the midst of a radical transformation of social relations conditioned by a brutal occupation and itself functioned as a powerful driver of this process. Within the parameters set out here, this period likely witnessed a transformation in the nature of anti-Semitism, no doubt facilitated by the deepening of ethnic thinking and categories, which affected everyone under occupation.

The danger inherent to a historical reconstruction based on trial material is to assume the narrative of the accused, who were no doubt trying to present their actions in the best possible light before investigators and judges. In the subject examined here, it can also run the risk of blaming the victim. The challenge for the historian is to retain the grain of truth in the claims of those who were complicit, in order to uncover the social mechanisms of violence that shaped local relations and perceptions. Yet the strength of a microhistorical approach is to shed light on the slow unfolding of violence accompanied by an entangled victimhood of Poles and Jews. By restoring a sense of individual agency and ordinary human motivation, it can serve as a lens for examining the "intimacy of violence" in the colonial space that was the General Government. A microhistory thus allows us to view genocide stripped down to its homicidal proportions, while an integrated history shows how local attitudes and violence against Jews was connected with—and conditioned by—violence against Poles for sheltering Jews.

Franciszek Kotula noted that "Jews know very well that to ask for help from someone and expose him to death is inhuman."[47] In the morally inverted universe created by the occupation authorities, the decision of its most condemned to seek survival meant bringing into orbit the lives of others. The relationship between the helper and the helped could transform over time into a two-way street between the denouncer and the denounced, the perpetrator and the victim. These are findings that will not satisfy those who expect a black-and-white story of perpetrators and victims, heroes and villains. The Polish philosopher Leszek Kołakowski often spoke of the presence of "the devil in history" in the twentieth century,[48] while the American scholar Lawrence Langer coined the term "choiceless choices" to describe the situations of conflict and the moral circumstances that Jews found themselves in during the Holocaust. The devil in a microhistory of the Holocaust shows the uncomfortable truth that even in the most hopeless of situations every human being has a choice and that the narrower the margin of choices tied to survival, the greater the potential for evil.

Tomasz Frydel is a Ph.D. candidate in the Department of History and the Anne Tanenbaum Centre for Jewish Studies at the University of Toronto.

Notes

1. Saul Friedländer, "An Integrated History of the Holocaust: Possibilities and Challenges," in *Years of Persecution, Years of Extermination: Saul Friedländer and the Future of Holocaust Studies,* ed. Christian Wiese and Paul Betts (London: Continuum, 2010), 21–29.

2. Saul Friedländer, *Nazi Germany and the Jews*, vols 1–2 (New York: HarperCollins, 1998–2008). For a discussion of the possibilities of different "axes of integration," see Donald Bloxham, "Europe, the Final Solution and the Dynamics of Intent," *Patterns of Prejudice* 44, no. 4 (2010): 317–35.
3. Both the intentionalist and functionalist trends in Holocaust historiography were not sensitive to local complexities. See Thomas Kühne and Tom Lawson, eds, *The Holocaust and Local History: Proceedings of the First International Graduate Students' Conference on Holocaust and Genocide Studies* (London: Vallentine Mitchell, 2011), introduction, 1–12. For a theoretical overview of microhistory, see Sigurður G. Magnússon and István Szíjártó, *What Is Microhistory? Theory and Practice* (London: Routledge, 2013).
4. Józef Ulma, also helped another Jewish family construct a bunker in a nearby forest and supplied them with food, although they, too, were later killed. See Mateusz Szpytma, *The Risk of Survival: The Rescue of the Jews by the Poles and the Tragic Consequences for the Ulma Family from Markowa* (Warsaw: IPN, 2009).
5. The official museum website: http://muzeumulmow.pl/en/ (accessed 20 July 2016).
6. See Tadeusz Markiel and Alina Skibińska, *"Jakie to ma znaczenie, czy zrobili to z chciwości?" zagłada domu Trynczerów* (Warsaw: Association of the Polish Center for Holocaust Research, 2011). A counterpoint to these events is offered by Piotr Chmielowiec, "Sprawa Józefa Laska. Z dziejów ludności żydowskiej w Gniewczynie Łańcuckiej," *Glaukopis* 23–24 (2011–12): 10–45.
7. The most insightful road map for further research that breaks this dichotomy can be found in Havi Dreifuss (Ben-Sasson), *Changing Perspectives on Polish-Jewish Relations during the Holocaust* (Jerusalem: Yad Vashem, 2012).
8. For a discussion of the *Judenjagd*, see Christopher R. Browning, "'Judenjagd'. Die Schlußphase der 'Endlösung' in Polen," in *Deutsche, Juden, Völkermord: der Holocaust als Geschichte und Gegenwart*, ed. Jürgen Matthäus and Klaus-Michael Mallmann (Darmstadt: Wissenschaftliche Buchgesellschaft, 2006), 177–189. For a full monograph on the subject, see Jan Grabowski, *Hunt for the Jews: Betrayal and Murder in German-Occupied Poland* (Bloomington: Indiana Univ. Press, 2013).
9. Bundesarchiv in Ludwigsburg (BAL), collection B 162, file 19161, 45–46, investigation into the representatives of Kreishauptmannschaft Bilgoraj.
10. Marek Getter, "Policja Polska w Generalnym Gubernatorstwie 1939–1945," *Przegląd Policyjny*, Wydawnictwo Wyższej Szkoły Policji w Szczytnie 1–2 (1996): 1–2. For the only monograph on the Polish Police, see Adam Hempel, *Pogrobowcy klęski: rzecz o policji "granatowej" w Generalnym Gubernatorstwie, 1939–1945* (Warsaw: Państwowe Wydawn. Nauk., 1990).
11. Getter, "Policja Polska w Generalnym Gubernatorstwie 1939–1945," 9. According to Getter, it is difficult to determine a definite number of policemen beyond this date, as the German authorities began to count Polish and Ukrainian police forces together as the "German Police" from 1943 to 1944 (under this rubric, the PP counted 13,437 in January 1943 and approximately 17,000 in May 1944).
12. Mielec county lost twenty-five prewar state policemen held in the Ostaszków camp. See "Lista oficerów Wojska Polskiego i funkcjonariuszy Policji Państwowej zamordowanych przez NKWD—Synów Ziemi Mieleckiej pomordowanych przez NKWD wiosną 1940 roku," *Rocznik mielecki* 2 (1999): 186–188.
13. BAL B 162/7478, 73–74, prosecutor's case against the German administration of Kreis Debica.
14. Archives of the Institute of National Remembrance in Rzeszów (AIPN Rz), file 353/277, testimony of Stanisław Rydzewski, 1950, 7–8.
15. Jan Ziobroń, *Dzieje Gminy Żydowskiej w Radomyślu Wielkim* (Radomyśl Wielki,

2009), 87–92. The Dudeks were sheltering members of the Siegfried family from the same village.
16. For a close study of the effects of German repression on anti-Jewish violence in the Mielec region, see Tomasz Frydel, "The *Pazifizierungsaktion* as a Catalyst of Anti-Jewish Violence: A Study in the Social Dynamics of Fear," in *The Holocaust and European Societies: Social Processes and Dynamics*, ed. Andrea Löw and Frank Bajohr (Palgrave Macmillan UK, 2017) (forthcoming).
17. Yad Vashem Archive (YVA), Department of the Righteous, file no. 2340.
18. AIPN Rz 353/113, 114–17, statement by the legal defense. Trial of Teofil Ryzner and others accused of helping to capture Jews in the woods near the village of Sietesz (1949–50).
19. AIPN Rz 353/114, 211–16, testimony of witnesses. Trial of Augustyn Wiglusz and others accused of handing over several Jews to the Germans in the village of Sietesz in August 1942. According to witnesses, one of the so-called pacifications of Sietesz consisted of German policemen rounding up one thousand of its inhabitants in the nearby school. The policemen demanded that locals hand over any Jews and Soviet POWs being hidden in the village.
20. BAL B 162/2166, testimony of Izaak I., 6631. I am grateful to Dr. Melanie Hembera for sharing this document.
21. National Archives of Krakow (ANK), collection 1042, file IV K, 252/50, testimony of witness Franciszek Gołecki, 33.
22. Martin Dean and Geoffrey P. Megargee, eds., *Encyclopedia of Camps and Ghettos, 1933–1945*, vol. 2, pt B (Bloomington: Indiana University Press, 2012), 1045–47. I am grateful to Martin Dean for bringing this case to my attention.
23. See Jan Grabowski, *Rescue for Money: Paid Helpers in Poland, 1939–1945* (Jerusalem: Yad Vashem, 2008).
24. AIPN Rz 34/61, vol. 2, testimony of witness Jan Pielach, trial of Michał Strzępka, 1965–75, 24–31. Pielach offered the same reasons in his own trial in 1949–50 (AIPN Rz 32/1, 95), in which he was sentenced to fifteen years in prison.
25. AIPN Rz 353/98, testimony of the accused Franciszek Wojnar, 29–30.
26. AIPN Rz 105/7, Order No. 3, Point 21 of instructions issued by the commander of District AK Rzeszów-South, Col. Józef Maciołek ("Żuraw"), 120.
27. Franciszek Kotula, *Losy Żydów rzeszowskich 1939–1944. Kronika tamtych dni* (Rzeszów: Społeczny Komitet Wydania Dzieł Franciszka Kotuli, 1999), 147.
28. BAL B 162/6842, testimony of Zbigniew Grędziński, 1972, 54–58. The eighteen-year-old son of Zofia Kur, Aleksander Kur, was shot and buried along with the three Jewish men. Grędziński, as village head, was threatened with execution for failing to report that Zofia Kur sheltered Jews, 44–48.
29. AIPN Rz 358/48, testimony of Stefan Hejnas, 25–25v; testimony of Władysław Witek, 4–4v, 96–97.
30. AIPN Rz, OKŚZpNP, II Ds. 28/70, testimony of Michał Ochalik, 23; AIPN Rz, OKŚZpNP, S 91/09/Zn vol. 1, testimony of Władysław Pieróg, 163; AIPN Rz 373/9, testimony of Władysław Witek, 83–85v.
31. Archiwum Diecezjalne w Tarnowie (ADT), collection ARz 221/1, file 39, testimony of Jan Fereński ("Sęp"), 3.
32. AIPN Rz 359/21, testimony of the accused village head, Jan Janas, 16–17.
33. Bundesarchiv in Berlin-Lichterfelde (BAB), R 19/462, Ordnungspolizei Hauptamt, interrogation of Izek Zylberberg on 30 November 1942, 119, and 2 December 1942, 123–25, by Maj. Schwieger, commander of the First Motorized Gendarmerie Battalion stationed in Iłża.
34. "Ivans and Vasyls," *Wieści* (News), no. 6, 6 July 1944, 3–4.

35. AIPN Rz 354/73, testimony of the accused Mikołaj Leszega, 35–37.
36. AIPN Rz 275/4, testimony of Andrzej Andreasik, 4–7.
37. AIPN Rz 354/26, verdict by the District Court of Jasło on 13 May 1948, 119–23. Evidence about the informer was provided by Franciszek Pękala, the chief of the PP in Rzepiennik Strzyżewski. Pękala stated that this informer was later dispatched to Silesia after his cover was blown following numerous arrests of locals who gave him shelter.
38. BAL B 162/3835, testimony of Edward Sypko, 4733–34.
39. "Kronika cierpienia wsi" [A chronicle of the suffering of villages], Wieś, no. 8, 13 March 1943, 3–4. This issue speaks of "approximately a hundred peasants" murdered as a result of the provocations. Reporting on developments in District Radom, the same issue railed against peasant "gullibility" in opening their doors to gendarmes, Polish policemen and informers posing as partisans, who then arrest those same peasants; "Prowokacja, Łatwowierność i Nieszczęścia" [Provocations, gullibility, and tragedy], 2–3.
40. AIPN Rz 353/61, testimony of Bogdan Protter, 256–61.
41. Kotula, Losy Żydów rzeszowskich, 119.
42. AIPN Rz 358/59, testimony of Stanisław Kolbusz during the main proceedings, 280–310.
43. Ibid., testimony of Ludwik Adamowicz. According to the testimony of Stanisław Golemo, Wojko's wife had "complained to Skowroń with tears in her eyes that she was afraid that the Germans would kill them [the Wojkos] or burn them down, because they were in her house, and she begged him to take them away from her."
44. For a discussion of peasant hunts for Soviet POWs and other targeted groups, see Tomasz Frydel, "*Judenjagd*: Reassessing the Role of Ordinary Poles as Perpetrators in the Holocaust," in *Perpetrators: Dynamics, Motivations and Concepts for Participating in Mass Violence*, ed. Timothy Williams and Susanne Buckley-Zistel (University of Pennsylvania Press) (forthcoming).
45. AIPN Rz 34/61, vol. I, trial of PP Michał Strząpka, testimony of witness Wiktoria Wolińska (Berl), 183–88. The rescued family members included Wiktoria Wolińska, Salomon Berl, and Adela Berl.
46. Daniel Blatman, *The Death Marches the Final Phase of Nazi Genocide* (Cambridge, MA: Belknap Press of Harvard University Press, 2011).
47. Kotula, *Losy Żydów rzeszowskich*, entry on 2 October 1942, 139.
48. Leszek Kołakowski and George Urban, "The Devil in History: A Conversation with Leszek Kołakowski," *Encounter* (January 1981): 9–26; see also Vladimir Tismaneanu, *The Devil in History: Communism, Fascism, and Some Lessons of the Twentieth Century* (Berkeley: University of California Press, 2012).

Bibliography

Blatman, Daniel. *The Death Marches: The Final Phase of Nazi Genocide.* Cambridge, MA: Belknap Press of Harvard University Press, 2011.
Bloxham, Donald. "Europe, the Final Solution and the Dynamics of Intent," *Patterns of Prejudice* 44, no. 4 (2010): 317–35.
Browning, Christopher R. "'Judenjagd'. Die Schlußphase der 'Endlösung' in Polen", in *Deutsche, Juden, Völkermord. Der Holocaust als Geschichte und Gegenwart*, edited by Jürgen Matthäus and Klaus-Michael Mallmann. Darmstadt: Wissenschaftliche Buchgesellschaft, 2006, 177–189.

Chmielowiec, Piotr. "Sprawa Józefa Laska. Z dziejów ludności żydowskiej w Gniewczynie Łańcuckiej." *Glaukopis* 23-24 (2011-12), 10–45.
Dean, Martin, and Geoffrey P. Megargee, eds. *Encyclopedia of Camps and Ghettos, 1933–1945*. Vol. 2. Bloomington: Indiana University Press, 2012.
Dreifuss, Havi. *Changing Perspectives on Polish-Jewish Relations during the Holocaust*. Jerusalem: Yad Vashem, 2012.
Friedländer, Saul. "An Integrated History of the Holocaust: Possibilities and Challenges", in *Years of Persecution, Years of Extermination: Saul Friedländer and the Future of Holocaust Studies*, edited by Christian Wiese and Paul Betts, London: Continuum, 2010, 21–29.
———. *Nazi Germany and the Jews*. Vols 1–2. New York: HarperCollins, 1998–2008.
Frydel, Tomasz. "The *Pazifizierungsaktion* as a Catalyst of Anti-Jewish Violence: A Study in the Social Dynamics of Fear", in *The Holocaust and European Societies: Social Processes and Dynamics,* edited by Andrea Löw and Frank Bajohr. Palgrave Macmillan UK, 2017. (forthcoming).
Getter, Marek. "Policja Polska w Generalnym Gubernatorstwie 1939–1945" [Polish Police in the General Government 1939–1945]. *Przegląd Policyjny* [Police Review], Wydawnictwo Wyższej Szkoły Policji w Szczytnie, 1–2, 1996.
Grabowski, Jan. *Hunt for the Jews: Betrayal and Murder in German-Occupied Poland*. Bloomington, Indiana: Indiana Univ. Press, 2013.
———. *Rescue for Money: Paid Helpers in Poland, 1939–1945*. Jerusalem: Yad Vashem, 2008.
Hempel, Adam. *Pogrobowcy klęski. Rzecz o policji "granatowej" w Generalnym Gubernatorstwie, 1939–1945* [The inheritors of defeat: The "blue" police in the General Government, 1939–1945]. Warsaw: Państwowe Wydawn. Nauk., 1990.
Kołakowski, Leszek, and George Urban. "The Devil in History: A Conversation with Leszek Kołakowski." *Encounter,* January 1981, 9–26.
Kotula, Franciszek. *Losy Żydów rzeszowskich 1939–1944. Kronika tamtych dni* [The fate of the Jews of Rzeszów 1939–1944: A chronicle of those days]. Rzeszów: Społeczny Komitet Wydania Dzieł Franciszka Kotuli, 1999.
Kühne, Thomas, and Tom Lawson, eds. *The Holocaust and Local History: Proceedings of the First International Graduate Students' Conference on Holocaust and Genocide Studies (Strassler Family Center for Holocaust and Genocide Studies, Clark University, 23–26 April, 2009)*. London: Vallentine Mitchell, 2011.
Magnússon, Sigurður G., and István Szíjártó. *What Is Microhistory? Theory and Practice*. London: Routledge, 2013.
Markiel, Tadeusz, and Alina Skibińska. *"Jakie to ma znaczenie, czy zrobili to z chciwości?" Zagłada domu Trynczerów* ["What does it matter if they did it out of greed?" The destruction of the house of Trynczer]. Warsaw: Association of the Polish Center for Holocaust Research, 2011.
Szpytma, Mateusz. *The Risk of Survival: The Rescue of the Jews by the Poles and the Tragic Consequences for the Ulma Family from Markowa*. Warsaw: IPN, 2009.
Tismaneanu, Vladimir. *The Devil in History: Communism, Fascism, and Some Lessons of the Twentieth Century*. Berkeley: University of California Press, 2012.
Ziobroń, Jan. *Dzieje Gminy Żydowskiej w Radomyślu Wielkim* [The history of the Jewish community in Radomyśl Wielki]. Radomyśl Wielki, 2009.

CHAPTER 10

ON THE PERSISTENCE OF MORAL JUDGMENT
LOCAL PERPETRATORS IN TRANSNISTRIA AS SEEN BY SURVIVORS AND THEIR CHRISTIAN NEIGHBORS

Vladimir Solonari

The study of collaboration and perpetration of crimes against humanity by the local residents in Nazi-occupied Europe has made substantial progress in the past few years. Taking leads from the older historiography of Nazi perpetrators and also making productive use of previously classified communist-era archival documents, scholars have elucidated social backgrounds, ideological convictions, life experiences, as well as a host of other factors in the quest to explain how, in the matter of weeks or months, former Soviet citizens were transformed into perpetrators of the most horrible crimes.[1] The study of perpetrators' motivations, as this subfield has come to be known, has seemingly led to the emergence of a broad consensus among scholars. According to Claus-Christian W. Szejnmann, who summarized the findings of other scholars, the list of motives that conditioned perpetrators' participation in the Holocaust includes vengefulness (that is, the desire to avenge those who suffered at the hands of the Soviets), careerism/conformism, attempts to expiate service to the Soviets by exaggerated loyalty to the new masters, ideological anti-Semitism, sadism, and "lust for power."[2] Scholars usually argue that while the list is rather long and can also include banal envy of victims' belongings, "a combination of several of these motivations played a role within each individual."[3]

Scholars also distinguish between "ideal types" of perpetrators. For example, for Christopher Browning, who conducted exemplary, multi-year research on German and (mostly) Ukrainian killers from the Soviet territories, perpetrators can be seen as belonging to three categories: eager, ideologically motivated killers, who volunteered for murderous assignments; conformists, who "undertook whatever task they were assigned"; and "evaders," who shirked the "duty" to kill, usually by pretending they were "too weak" to do so rather than by invoking moral arguments. Browning believes that both the first and second groups were minorities, while conformists composed a clear majority.[4] As he put it, "A core of eager and committed men, aided by an even larger block of men who complied with the policy of the regime ... [without any] overt ideological conviction, was sufficient to commit genocide."[5] In a brilliant article devoted to the study of the Ukrainian police in Generalbezirk Kiew, Alexander Prusin offered a slightly different taxonomy: "political activists," driven by ideological convictions and vengefulness against the Soviets; "ambitious conformists," who served in the middle and lower levels of the Soviet administration and who were eagerly expatiating their "guilt" under the Germans by demonstrating their loyalty to the new masters by zealously carrying out whatever assignments they received; and "ordinary executioners," who unflinchingly performed their duties simply because they knew no better. The first group was the smallest, the last the biggest; Prusin refrained from evaluating the importance of each group in the killing operations.[6] In studying the psychological types of perpetrators, I came to conclusions close to those of these scholars, while emphasizing the role of anti-Semitic ideology, as well as resentment of the Soviets that was channeled by the occupiers against the Jews as supposed "bearers of communism."[7]

In spite of this consensus among microhistorians of the Holocaust, one renowned historian recently questioned the very usefulness of such research, arguing that local helpers of Nazis and their allies had very little choice in whether to participate in crimes against humanity. Their behavior was, as he put it, "just as predictable as obedience to the authority," and as such requires "less (not more) explanation."[8] In a broad sweep, and without engaging in a substantive discussion of the existing historiography of Holocaust microhistory, Timothy Snyder denied local perpetrators any agency, transforming them into voiceless instruments of the occupier's will, thus rendering meaningless any investigation of their role in the Holocaust. Since all decisions were made at the level far above their horizons and without consulting them in the least, only the policy of the occupier and its supreme leaders can explain the purposes, dynamics, and outcome of the murderous persecution of Jews. This kind of "colonial history," as Jan Gross aptly called Snyder's book, suggests that local Christians must be absolved of any responsibility for the fate of their Jewish neighbors. Partially to counter this approach, I propose to more closely investigate how survivors and local Christians perceived perpetrators. Did they see them as an undifferentiated gray mass, as voiceless and powerless extensions of the occupier's machine of oppression, or did they see them as human individuals, fully accountable for their actions? Did they differentiate between them? Did they measure their cruelty? Did they judge them in moral terms, or were all moral categories extinguished in the face of absolute evil? If humans are moral beings, then the very survival of moral judgment, if its traces are gleaned from the sources, would decisively rehumanize the stories of local massacres, all of them performed by concrete people on their defenseless victims.

In his exemplary research on the perception of Jewish survivors from the Starachowice labor camp, Browning suggested that they quite clearly remembered, decades after the events, the psychological traits of most Ukrainian guards. Browning suggested that this was the case because their very survival depended on their ability to "read" their tormentors' psyche, in order to know what they could expect from whom. As a result, they learned to distinguish between those who were "crazed killers and sadists," those who could "turn their back," allowing them to leave the camps in search of income and food, and among this latter category, those who were "lenient and approachable, and others at least corruptible."[9]

In the following essay, I will show how newly available sources can be used to outline moral evaluations of local killers by Jewish survivors and their Christian neighbors. My research focuses on a region in southwestern Ukraine—located between the Dniester and Southern Buh rivers, with its center in Odessa—that was occupied between 1941 and 1944 by Romania. During that time, this region, then known as Transnistria, served as a dumping ground for Romania's ethnic undesirables, Jews and Roma. In 1941–42, they deported around 150,000 Jews and 20,000 Gypsies there, whom they interned in ghettos and concentration camps together with local Jews. As a result of atrocious treatment, hunger, epidemics, and mass executions, between 105,000 and 120,000 deported Romanian Jews, 115,000 to 180,000 indigenous Jews, and about 10,000

Roma perished by the early spring of 1944, when the Red Army liberated the area.[10] In carrying out executions of Jews—including the gigantic massacres in the villages of Bogdanovka (50,000 to 70,000 victims) and Domanevka (around 20,000 victims) in Golta county in eastern Transnistria, as well as smaller butcheries at various sites in Berezovka county to the north of Golta—Romanians relied heavily on local helpers who were members of the so-called local police, sometimes referred to as the Ukrainian police, as well as on members of the militia of ethnic German residents, the Selbstschutz.[11] Massacres were carried out in broad daylight, and although the places were cordoned off, many local residents who were not members of the police observed the events from a distance or from nearby. In Bogdanovka, 120 Jewish internees survived the massacres as members of the so-called work brigade or work teams.[12] It was on depositions from these survivors and eyewitnesses—as well as from the perpetrators themselves, which they made after having broken down during confrontations with survivors and each other—that Soviet postwar prosecutors heavily relied while investigating war crimes.

Most of the materials I used for this essay come from Soviet and Romanian investigative files.[13] The use of such communist-era sources raises a number of methodological questions, the most important of which is their reliability. Since I have recently expounded my views on this issue at some length elsewhere, I will refrain from doing so again here and will limit myself to a brief presentation of my views without developing and substantiating them.[14] First and foremost, I believe that in the great majority of cases, this essay focuses on Soviet and Romanian investigators who were honestly trying to establish the guilt of their defendants and to reconstruct, to the best of their abilities, the true story of their crimes. This assertion might appear counterintuitive, given what we know about the highly politicized nature of the judiciary in Communist countries and the long record of manipulation of the judicial process by Communist authorities. However, the perpetrators this essay focuses on were low-ranking collaborators, and Communist authorities had zero interest in the fate of each particular accused. Consequently, investigators were not micromanaged by their superiors in order to steer the findings of individual cases in preconceived directions. They interrogated survivors and other eyewitnesses, confronted defendants with them and with one another, reconstructed crime scenes, and reenacted crimes on the spot. As Diana Dumitru demonstrated, in the neighboring region of Bessarabia, findings of postwar Soviet trials are usually confirmed, excepting insignificant details, by the eyewitness interviews conducted decades after the trials.[15] According to Soviet investigative practice (less so the Romanian one), detailed records of interrogations were kept in the files, with questions followed by answers. It is in these records that one can find stories about conversations and attitudes regarding the butchers' actions, along with evaluations of their personalities.

Black, White, and Shades of Gray

From late December 1941 to April 1942, about one hundred policemen—including about seventy local policemen from Golta county under the command of Afanasii Andrusin, and members of the Selbstschutz from the Neue-Amerika village hamlet (*hutor*) under the command of SS-Obersturmführer Rudolf Hartung and local ethnic German Ivan (Johannes?) Bihler (Bichler?)—shot more than fifty thousand Jews.[16] Executions took place at the edge of a ravine, where victims were brought by policemen or the Jews from the work brigade. They were shot from a short distance using rifles, usually five to six shooters "working" while their colleagues waited to replace them. At the bottom of the ravine was a flaming pyre, into which members of the work brigade threw the dead bodies of their kin, friends, and other co-sufferers. Substantial numbers of survivors from the work brigade, as well as eyewitnesses among local residents, allow us to reconstruct the actions of individual perpetrators better than in many other circumstances.

The primitive way in which an enormous number of people were shot at a short distance could not help but put a heavy psychological burden on the executioners. Later on, when under investigation, many of them claimed that they agreed to this "job" only under duress, due to pressure and threats from their superiors. For example, Vladimir Gipner claimed that when ordered to join an execution squad, he initially tried to refuse, but Bihler told him that if he did so, he and his family would be executed, and so he had to submit.[17] However, prosecutors understandably saw such claims as suspect and self-serving and routinely dismissed them unless confirmed by a third party. Such confirmations were forthcoming only very rarely. In one such case, a local policeman whose last name Jewish survivors recalled alternatively as Samoliuka/Samoil/Samoilenko (they could not remember his first name) threw his rifle down and refused to kill. Two Soviet citizens, along with Jewish survivors and one Romanian recalled this episode, with a time span between their depositions of more than twenty years.[18] This very fact testifies to the veracity of the episode, however incredible it might seem. As to why this policeman waited until the last moment to air his refusal to murder, the answer might be found in the deposition of another policeman, who claimed that Andrusin failed to disclose the purpose of their trip to Bogdanovka until well after the crew had left Golta.[19] It is worth noting that these survivors were not asked about those policemen and ethnic German militiamen who *refused* to murder, simply because prosecutors were interested in perpetrators, not righteous policemen, and the fact that they still mentioned this episode means that in their eyes it possessed a moral value far beyond its practical—and negligible—effect: for them it served as proof of the survival of *minima moralia* under the most improbable of circumstances.

On the opposite pole was Anna Roginskaia (or Rolinskaia), known at the execution site as "Vera," who was a hospital attendant (*sanitarka*) from the Golta police department, and the only woman among the butchers.[20] Jewish survivors unanimously remembered her as one of the worst and most sadistic individuals, overtly enjoying her "job," and never tiring of humiliating her victims in their last moments. They also described her as a greedy, hateful, and bloodthirsty anti-Semite. To their horror, she was sentimental while killing, shedding "crocodile tears" and asking for "understanding" from her victims. To cite just a few examples, Efim Gitgaru recalled how Vera plundered the best clothes left from Jews. Her booty was so voluminous that she had to leave it for safekeeping with the director of the Bogdanovka state farm and to return with a horse-drawn cart she had to hire to carry them away. When Jews were brought to the execution site, she addressed them "in the Jewish language," saying, "That's enough, you have had it quite good for twenty-three years. Now put down your little heads." "If she saw good clothing on a Jew, she would bring him to those who were undressing them [that is, Jews from the work brigade] and say, 'It would be a pity if his clothes burned with him.'"[21] Iakov Iusim, who was thirteen at the time, and called her "auntie Vera," as is customary in Russian in reference to an elder woman, recounted how she cried out when she saw him attempting to flee, "Where are you going, Stalin's falcon? Go back to the pit." Later on, in 1942, after the end of the executions, she would come to visit the survivors from the work brigade who still lived in the camp, bewailing her fate and seeking consolation from them. She forced kisses and hugs on them and explained her recent cruelty by saying, "So, what could I do, babies? They just forced me to."[22]

Most perpetrators likely did not belong to these two poles but populated the axis between the two. While their own confessions as to their supposed moral qualms can be dismissed as self-serving, depositions of eyewitnesses are more reliable, sometimes portraying psychologically complex personalities. One such eyewitness, an ethnic German from Neue-Amerika hamlet named Peter Akkerman, gave detailed and nuanced evaluations of his co-villagers who served in the Selbstschutz. His trustworthiness is supported by the fact that he managed to shirk service in the Selbstschutz, except for a very short time at the beginning of the occupation, and did not take part in executions. This was either because he was married to a Ukrainian and therefore considered unreliable by Selbstschutz commanders or for some other unknown cause. According to another ethnic German eyewitness, Peter Akkerman's own reluctance to serve had also played a role.[23] Akkerman seemed to have divided Selbstschutz members into three broad categories (not his own taxonomy). The first included commanders and other committed killers, whom he saw as being moved by "hatred of everything Soviet." These people were moved by a strong desire to avenge the suffering of family members murdered or repressed by the Soviets, and some of them seem to have derived pleasure from inflicting suffering on other people. Another group included those perpetrators whom Akkerman saw as dim-witted and lacking judgment. They unflinchingly and thoughtlessly followed orders from their superiors belonging to the first category. Finally, the third category consisted of youngsters, in fact teenagers, who could not be held fully accountable for their criminal actions (Soviet judges spared the lives of this last category of perpetrators, while condemning all other killers to death by firing squad, even if they claimed they had acted under duress).[24] Joseph Scheel, an ethnic German eyewitness who did not serve in the Selbstschutz, probably due to his old age, and the perpetrator Gregor Anton, who was executed by a firing squad, gave evaluations of Selbstschutz killers that were remarkably similar to Akkerman's.[25]

Gender Roles?

The fact that survivors so persistently remembered Roginskaia and identified her as particularly brutal can hardly be attributed solely to her character traits. After all, almost all male executioners were described by them as brutal, cynical, greedy, and depraved. It is likely that Vera stood out among other perpetrators due to her sex. According to the precepts of traditional culture, women were expected to alleviate the suffering of others, to caress and intercede on their behalf before their superiors, and Vera defied this stereotype in the most provocative and terrifying manner. Significantly, when women do appear in recollections by survivors and eyewitnesses, they often do so as the ones who tried to help Jews, and sometimes scolded, shamed, or otherwise sought to stop the brutal behavior of their spouses, sons, brothers, or male acquaintances. Again, from the great quantity of available cases, I will cite just a few, which I consider to be the most eloquent ones.

Eyewitness Liubov' Doiuch from the village of Raidolino, from Veselinovo district in Berezovka county, testified that she and other Ukrainian women used to bring food to the Jews interned in a local concentration camp, but policeman Alexei Sergeev forbade them from doing it and beat them. He asked them, "Why are you bringing food to them? Let them kick off from famine."[26] In the village of Vradievka, in the district of the same name in Golta county, according to the witness Anna Bordiuzha some villagers adopted Jewish children whom their parents had abandoned en route to the camps, in the hope that local Christians would raise them as their own. Later, however, police would seize and carry the Jewish kids away, with their further fate unknown. In October 1941, Bordiuzha also found a homeless child on the street called Alla, whose parents had been shot by the Romanians. Bordiuzha adopted Alla as her own child, and Alla started to call her mama, but in April 1942 the authorities demanded that she register Alla as a Jewish girl. Bordiuzha argued in vain that "her baby" was Russian and that she wore a cross, but they would not even listen to her. In early May 1942, policeman Nikolai Ermolaev showed up at her doorstep and requested that she hand the child over to him. The first time she seems to have persuaded Ermolaev to leave them alone, but then he showed up again and this time was unresponsive to her pleas. Bordiuzha remembered crying when he told her, "Why are you crying for Yids? Bring her to the gendarmerie office." And so Bordiuzha did, although Alla escaped and came back. She was rearrested (Bordiuzha failed to clarify under what circumstances), carried away, and eventually shot "as all other Jewish children were," concluded Bordiuzha in her heartrending story.[27] In a similar story from the village of Bolgarka located close to Bogdanovka, two Ukrainian women related how they tried to hide Jewish children, but when threatened by policeman Ivan Studzinskii that they would share the same fate as the Jews, they eventually surrendered them. One of these two, Vera Shetun, testified that she tried to hide a Jewish boy, first in her house and then in the cattle shed, but later yielded to threats and revealed the boy's hideout. When Studzinskii put him on the horse cart, her children brought him a bottle of milk, but Studzinskii smashed it in a fit of rage.[28] Shetun, a poor Ukrainian mother of six, invoked this scene during her second interrogation without being prompted by the prosecutor, thus indicating that for her, Studzinskii's wanton destruction of the precious commodity of milk was full of terrifying symbolism.

Decades after the war, many Jewish survivors from Transnistria still remembered Ukrainian women displaying compassion and offering them help. For example, Roza Giventer, native of Bessarabia but deported to Transnistria, testified, "I remember how Ukrainian women wept looking at us, [how they] brought apples to the columns of people, milk for the kids, but the occupiers drove them away."[29] Getsl' Postel'nik, originally from the Bessarabian city of Hotin, was first driven from his home to the concentration camp at Sochireni in the same province and later was deported across the Dniester river into Transnistria. In his deposition, he contrasted the behavior of "local nationalists" in Bessarabia, who "beat us up, plundered all our possessions," with the behavior of "Ukrainian women" in Transnistria, who "helped us children as best they could."[30] Roza Fel'dman, recalling their suffering and survival in Transnistria, singled out the "kind, humane attitude of Ukrainian women," for which she was still deeply grateful.[31] Instances like these are too numerous to be dismissed as rhetorical formulas that reflect cultural conventions rather than actual reality; they most probably reveal an important truth regarding a gender-specific attitude in local Christian communities toward the persecution of Jews. Survivors never seem to have pondered why females were more sympathetic to their plight or more willing to help them than males, possibly considering these differences "natural" attributes of respective sexes. However, it may be more productive to think of them as males and females conforming to the norms and expectations conditioned by traditional peasant culture, which prescribed "hardness" as an attribute of masculinity, and "softness" and intercession for the weak and suffering as an attribute of femininity.

This perspective may enrich our understanding of numerous depositions concerning tensions in perpetrators' families over their service in the police, particularly over participation in killing operations. Female spouses might have been under the pressure of contradictory norms in traditional culture, which prescribed, on the one hand, taking pride in the important and male-specific functions their husbands performed in the public sphere and, on the other, serving as guardians of moral norms of communities. In the first instance, wives were expected to publicly display such pride and to privately comfort their husbands, while in the second they might have been torn by doubts as to the morality of their actions. There is indeed plenty of evidence in the sources of such tensions, which often came to the fore over the issue of using the killers' loot, such as victims' clothing. This should not be a surprise, since Soviet law considered personal use of a victim's belongings an aggravating circumstance, and prosecutors were persistent in their search for the evidence of such behavior.

Transcripts of interrogations testify to the enormous variety of reactions perpetrators' wives displayed when their husbands brought home clothes from their victims after killing operations. It should be noted that in the province's war-torn economy, where any and all consumer goods of non-agricultural provenance were exceedingly difficult to come by, clothes were precious objects; they could be worn by perpetrators and their spouses or sold on the black market to generate considerable revenue. Such loot was routinely distributed to killers, and leaders of execution squads saw to it that the most zealous and efficient ones got the best portion. This, in its own turn, created competition among killers. Judging from the transcripts, getting such trophy objects more often than not did not generate any tension in a killer's family, as the spouses of perpetrators washed, patched, line-dried, ironed, and then wore them in public or gave them to family members to wear. For example, according to the convicted perpetrator Alexander Orgiianov from Neue-Amerika hamlet, who took part in the killing operations in Bogdanovka and elsewhere, when Selbstschutz men brought home the clothes of killed Jews, the wife of another perpetrator, Vladimir Gipner, would hang them on a clothesline. Peter Akkerman, who was mentioned earlier, confessed that Selbstschutz members and their wives and children had a lot of good clothes.[32] These clothes would sometimes become objects of envy and boasting. For example, according to the deposition of eyewitness Akulina Kozlova from the village of Domanevka, she once overheard the wife of policeman Iosif Vuich publicly scolding him for bringing home clothes from a recent shooting expedition in Bogdanovka that were good for nothing (*barahlo*), unlike those brought by another policeman, which were of much higher quality. She threatened that the next time he brought such rags, she would not iron them.[33] Thus, she encouraged her husband to kill more in order to earn better remuneration. According to a Ukrainian woman named Niura Andriiasova—who was married during the war to an ethnic German from Neue-Amerika hamlet, whom she later divorced—the wives of Selbstschutz men would "show off" (*shchegoliali*) new gowns after massacres.[34]

On the other hand, some perpetrators testified that although they did receive clothes of Jewish victims, they were afraid to bring them home, lest their wives scold them. For example, Hristian Shvab (Christian Schwab?) related that when he brought home looted Jewish belongings for the first time (this was before the massacres, when policemen and Selbstschutz men were "just" robbing camp inmates of their possessions), he decided to take some home but temporarily leave the rest at Retler's (Rötler's) home, because he was afraid that his wife would curse him out. Later, however, he learned that his fear was unjustified, since she in fact accepted this plunder, fitting it for their son and herself. He summarized her attitude thusly: "she would scold me, but would accept the things."³⁵ This was also the dynamic in Alexender Jonus's family, whose wife, as he confessed, scolded him severely and repeatedly for killing people but accepted and later wore the looted belongings when he brought her "something" from his victims.³⁶ In other families, however, wives were determined not to accept any "gifts" of that nature. Florian Koch, another perpetrator from Neue-Amerika, confessed that when he brought home things from Jews who had been shot, his wife lashed out at him and refused to accept them, so much so that he had to transport them to Odessa and sell them there.³⁷ Only in one case did such reproaches result in a perpetrator mending his ways. This happened with Joseph Rötler, who, according to his own deposition, was yelled at so severely and persistently by his wife that he eventually requested release from service in the Selbstschutz (he claimed that he had his own qualms, too). He managed to obtain one, in spite of his boss's initial reluctance (Rötler claimed poor health).³⁸

Sometimes, the very fact that a spouse took part in a shooting operation produced arguments in the families of perpetrators. One of the most notorious killers from Neue-Amerika, Johannes Gertner, asserted that while he could not remember Selbstschutz members discussing the reasons for the executions of Jews (probably a mendacious statement), "at home, women were naturally indignant at us for shooting those innocent people."³⁹ In addition to spouses, mothers also were sometimes said to have admonished their sons to not take part in executions. For example, Rafael Seifert, who at the time of the massacres was only seventeen and later invoked his young age as an attenuating circumstance, also remembered how his "late old mother" advised him to quit the police because, as she used to say, "the time would come sooner or later when they [the other killers] would have to account for their deeds."⁴⁰

Women outside of the immediate families of perpetrators were also remembered as attempting to shame them for their crimes. For example, Liudmila Gild (maiden name Zerr) recounted how she used to admonish Jakob Gertner for taking part in the murder of Jews. Gertner responded by denying it and insisted that he was "only" conveying them to the site of execution.⁴¹ In early 1942, the ethnic German Ekaterina Vezner (Wessner?)—who worked as a teacher in the local school of the Ukrainian village of Stepanovka since before the war—heard screams from the Jews she was sheltering in the school. She ran from her rented room in the school building and saw Selbstschutz member Peter Scheel, whom she had known for some time, plundering their possessions. Vezner verbally assailed him for this villainy, although apparently to no avail, for not only did Scheel continue robbing Jewish victims, but he also later took part in many executions.⁴² According to the eyewitness

Efrosin'ia Cherniavskaia, in the village of Vradievka, where Romanian gendarmes carried out mass executions of Jews in the fall of 1941, local women yelled and verbally abused Romanian gendarme private first class Constantin Munteanu for tormenting Jews. Cherniavskaia herself screamed that if his mother knew what he was doing in Transnistria, she would not let him back in Romania, to which Munteanu answered that they had not killed enough of them yet.[43]

The fact that women were able to summon courage and display outrage at the shooting of Jews in an outward manner may be explained by the age-old tradition of females taking the lead in public protests against the authorities for actions that ran against their community's established norms. As researchers of Russian and Soviet peasantry have long noted, authorities were less willing to use brute force against women, at least in public; knowing this, women would sometimes appear as ringleaders of local protests that would have been punished much more severely if initiated by men.[44] This observation raises the possibility that the feelings of local men about the executions of Jews might have been closer to those expressed by local women, except that they were more reluctant to show them publicly. Indeed, some male eyewitnesses testified to their angst at seeing the execution of Jews. One Khristofor Samuliak, from the village of Podoleanka in Berezovka county, where in January 1942 the Selbstschutz shot approximately three hundred Jews, recounted how on the day of the shooting the local mayor ordered him to bring straw in his oxen-driven cart to the place of the massacre. However, when Samuliak approached the site and realized what was going on, he categorically refused to go any further. "You might as well shoot me, too," he said, then burst into tears and protested the killing, asking the policemen why they were killing Jews who were not guilty of any crime. The policemen did not respond and instead took his cart and ordered him off the site.[45] Survivors also remembered some local men being overwhelmed by grief and horror at the sight of so many innocent people being massacred. Ida Shul'man, whose family was spared execution because the mayor of Bogdanovka village selected them as craftsmen necessary for the local community (they were shoemakers), recounted how a Ukrainian man named Fedorenko, in whose hut they were staying at the time of the massacre, expressed his feelings regarding the butchery: "Those skunks, they shot a whole lot of people!" (*Skol'kih liudei postreliali, gady!*).[46] Safran Cholovskii, an eyewitness from Bogdanovka, recalled that another local resident, Ivan Granchak, who happened to see the scene of execution, had the following to say: "What a disaster, a horrible sight" (*Beda, strashno smotret'*).[47] This generalized "disaster" may imply the view that the event was an incomprehensible catastrophe, akin to the blind play of natural forces, which can neither be understood nor averted. However, it can also suggest that Granchak saw it as an omen presaging even worse things to come, possibly as divine punishment for the inhabitants of this land who allowed such crimes to take place.

Perpetrators were moral beings, not in the sense that what they did was somehow "moral," but in the sense that their actions and personalities were liable to moral judgment. Although killing defenseless and pitiful civilians—including women, children, and the elderly—at close distance from a position of absolute safety was as horrendous as evil could be, each perpetrator was an individual conscious of his (and very rarely her) actions, possessing individual character traits. Each of them dealt with their new "jobs" in their own individual ways and were observed and assessed on the basis of their own actions, words, and emotions as conveyed through their body language.

The Holocaust in the occupied Soviet Union could not be normalized by virtue of its taking place "out there" at a great distance, or by mechanized means of murder, as Zygmunt Bauman suggested; nor could it be banished from the conscience as a routine bureaucratic activity, for which the little cogs ultimately bore no responsibility, as Hannah Arendt conceived it.[48] Yet perpetrators and local Christians sympathetic to them could and did find justification for their crimes in anti-Semitism and the notion of Judeo-Communism, reinforced by German and Romanian propaganda. Conformism and a perceived necessity to obey authority provided another excuse. Traditional morality was at loggerheads with these forms of self-justification, the latter diminishing but never eliminating the constraints of the former.

The spouses and family members of perpetrators were exposed to contradictory pressures of traditional cultural norms, which demanded that they support and comfort their kin, as well as maintain the ethical standards of the community. The same was ultimately true of other locals. Interactions between perpetrators and other local Christians, both intimate and more remote, were dramatic to the utmost: anxiety, thirst for approval, fear of censure, angst, and anger were present on the part of perpetrators; and for locals, there was endorsement, whether tacit or verbalized, indifference, horror, shame, greed, grief, and revulsion, all against the background of the mass murder in their midst. With its fundamentally human character relentlessly exposed, moral judgment was inescapable. It stands as an irrefutable proof of perpetrators' culpability as moral beings conscious of their own agency.

Vladimir Solonari is associate professor at the Department of History, University of Central Florida. He received his Ph.D. in history from Moscow State University in 1986. Since 2003, he has been teaching Russian and Soviet history at the University of Central Florida. He is the author of *Purifying the Nation: Population Exchange and Ethnic Cleansing in Nazi-Allied Romania* (2010) as well as of a number of articles and essays on Romanian, Moldovan, and Soviet history. His research focuses on World War II in Southeast Europe and ethnic cleansing and the Holocaust. He is currently completing his second book-length project on the social history of southern Ukraine under the Romanian occupation during World War II.

Notes

1. The study of Nazi collaborators received powerful impetus from the publication of two tremendously influential works: Daniel Jonah Goldhagen, *Hitler's Willing Executioners: Ordinary Germans and the Holocaust* (New York: Knopf, 1996); and Christopher Browning, *Ordinary Men: Reserve Police Battalion 101 and the Final Solution in Poland* (New York: HarperCollins, 1992), along with the subsequent "Goldhagen-Browning" debate, for which see Daniel J. Goldhagen, Christopher Browning, and Leon Wieselter, *The "Willing Executioners"/"Ordinary Men" Debate: Selections from the Symposium April 8, 1996*, with an introduction by Michael Berenbaum (Washington, DC: United States Holocaust Memorial Museum, 2001). A useful review of the historiography on Nazi perpetrators can be found in Lynne Viola, "The Question of the Perpetrator in Soviet History," *Slavic Review* 72, no. 1 (2013): 1–9. Influential recent books on local perpetrators in the Soviet-occupied territories include Wolfgang Benz, JTM Houwink ten Cate, and Gerhard Otto, eds, *Anpassung, Kollaboration, Widerstand: Kollektive Reaktionen auf die Okkupation* (Berlin: Metropol, 1996); Ruth B. Birn, *Die Sicherheitspolizei in Estland 1941–1944: Eine Studie zur Kollaboration im Osten* (Paderborn: Schoeningh, 2006); Bernhard Chiari, *Besatzung, Kollaboration und Widerstand in Weissrussland 1941–1944* (Düsseldorf: Droste, 1998); Martin Dean, *Collaboration in the Holocaust: Crimes of the Local Police in Belorussia and Ukraine, 1941–1944* (New York: St. Martin's, 2000); Knut Stang, *Kollaboration und Massenmord: Die litauische Hilfspolizei, das Rollkommando Hamann und die Ermordung der litauischen Juden* (Frankfurt am Main: Peter Lang, 1994); Christoph Dieckmann, *Kooperation und Verbrechen: Formen der "Kollaboration" im östlichen Europa 1939–1945* (Göttingen: Wallstein, 2003); Tanja Penter, *Kohle für Stalin und Hitler: Arbeiten und Leben im Donbas 1929 bis 1953* (Essen: Klartext, 2010), 269–300; Dieter Pohl, "Ukrainische Hilskräfte beim Mord an den Juden," in *Die Täter der Shoah: Fanatische Nationalisten oder ganz normale Deutsche?*, ed. Gerhard Paul (Göttingen: Wallstein, 2002), 205–34; Alexander V. Prusin, *The Lands Between: Conflict in the East European Borderlands, 1870–1992* (Oxford: Oxford Scholarship Online, 2010), 150–76; and Michael Wildt, *An Uncompromising Generation: The Nazi Leadership of the Reich Security Main Office*, trans. Tom Lampert (Madison: University of Wisconsin Press, 2009).

2. See Claus-Christian W. Szejnmann, "Perpetrators of the Holocaust: A Historiography," in *Ordinary People as Mass Murderers*, ed. Olaf Jensen and Szejnmann (New

York: Palgrave MacMillan, 2008), 42–43. Szejnmann summarizes the findings of other scholars, in particular Michael MacQueen and Martin Dean.

3. Martin Dean, "Schutzmannschaften in Ukraine and Belarus: Profiles of Local Police Collaboration," in *Lessons and Legacies: The Holocaust in International Perspective*, ed. Dagmar Herzog (Evanston: Northwestern University Press, 2006), 7:226–29. Also quoted in Szejnmann, "Perpetrators of the Holocaust," 43.

4. Christopher Browning, "Ideology, Culture, Situation, and Disposition: Holocaust Perpetrators and the Group Dynamic of Mass Killing," in *NS-Gewaltherrschaft: Beiträge zur historischen Forschung und juristischen Aufarbeitung*, ed. Alfred Gottwald, Norberth Kampe, and Peter Klein, Publikationen der Gedenk- und Bildungsstätte Haus der Wannsee-Konferenz 11 (Berlin: Edition Hentrich, 2005), 66–84, citation is from 74.

5. Ibid., 75.

6. Alexander Prusin, "Ukrainkaia politsia i Holokost v general'nom okruge kiev, 1941–1943: deistviia I motivatsii," *Golokost I suchastnist'* 1, no. 3 (2007): 43–49.

7. Vladimir Solonari, "Hating Soviets-Killing Jews: How Anti-Semitic Were Local Perpetrators in Southern Ukraine, 1941–1942?" *Kritika: Explorations in Russian and Eurasian History* 15, no. 3 (2014): 505–34.

8. Timothy Snyder, *Bloodlands: Europe between Hitler and Stalin* (New York: Basic Books, 2010), 397.

9. Christopher Browning, *Remembering Survival: Inside a Nazi Slave Labor-Camp* (New York: Norton, 2011), 170.

10. For estimates on the number of victims, see International Commission on the Holocaust in Romania, *Final Report* (Iași: Polirom, 2005), 382. On ethnic Germans and their role in the murder of Jews in Transnistria, see Eric Conrad Steinhart, *The Holocaust and the Germanization of Ukraine*. Publications of the German Historical Institute (New York: Cambridge University Press, 2015). The Selbstschutz was under the orders of SS Einzatskommando R headquartered in the village of Landau, Berezovka County. The local police were subordinated to the Romanian gendarmerie. The term "Ukrainian police," used by some scholars, particularly Jean Ancel, is incorrect both because no Ukrainian organization was in any way responsible for setting it up and because ethnic Ukrainians were favored neither at the time of recruitment nor for promotion. In fact, Romanian authorities quite often put local ethnic Romanians (Moldovans) in charge of police units. Nor is it an original term. For these reasons I will call them "local police."

11. For more on massacres in Transnistria, see Jean Ancel, *Transnistria, 1941–1942: The Romanian Mass Murder Campaigns* (Tel Aviv: Tel Aviv University, 2003), vol. 1, esp. 87–338.

12. The work brigade was created by the executioners from among able-bodied Jews. Having been promised to spare their lives, they were forced to bring other Jews to the place of execution and to sort victims' clothes in different categories, from the most to the least usable ones, with executioners later appropriating the best and distributing the remainder among the local residents. Understandably, most members of the work brigade preferred to dwell on this latter assignment, but some of them sometimes mentioned the former, more gruesome task as well, as did other eyewitnesses and perpetrators. Two hundred people were initially selected, but some were shot during the executions that lasted from late December 1941 to April 1942, as well as afterward; survivors from this "brigade" later claimed that they also expected to be shot but were spared owing to the alleged order from above to stop executions. See depositions of Lerner Braitman, Gosudarstvennyi Arckhiv Rossiskoi Federatsii (hereinafter GARF) Fond 7021 Opis' 54 delo 1341 190 copy held in Yad Vashem (hereinafter YV) JM-19.942 (his further identity unknown); perpetrator Ivan Pastushenko

in Galuzebyi Derzhavnyi Arkhiv Sluzhby Bezpeki Ukraïny (hereinafter GDA SBU) spr.13189 tom 3, 63–64, 120 copy held in US Holocaust Hemorial Museum (hereinafter USHMM) RG-31.018M reel 17; eyewitness Nikolai Gavrilenko, ibid., tom 18, 16–18; Jewish survivors and former members of the "work brigade" Pavel Michel'son, Fel'dman Mina, Abram Bershadskii, Bibergal Mikhail, Rakhil' Veksel'man, and Kapel' Shoikhet (brigadier), in ibid., spr.13189 tom 20, esp. 3–4, 7, 11, 31, 51, 54, 56, 76–77, 101v. reel 18; Grigorii Rozenberg tom 21, 162 reel 19; Filipp Klinov ibid., spr.69, . 207 YA JM 19.765 Samuil Saifert ibid., 194–194v.

13. These files come from GDA SBU, the archive of the former KGB. I accessed microfilm copies stored at USHMM and YV JM. All in all, I researched more than 150 individual files, some of them containing many volumes devoted to different persons.
14. Solonari, "Hating Soviets-Killing Jews," 515–16.
15. Diana Dumitru, "An Analysis of Soviet Postwar Investigation and Trial Documents and Their Relevance for Holocaust Studies," in *The Holocaust in the East: Local Perpetrators and Soviet Responses*, ed. Michael David-Fox, Peter Holquist, and Alexander Martin (Pittsburgh: University of Pittsburgh Press, 2014), 142–57.
16. For more on the Bogdanovka massacre, see Ancel, *Transnistria*, 1:120–39. Ancel was not aware of the participation of the Volksdeutsche Selbstschutz in this massacre because he did not use Soviet sources. For Soviet materials on Selbstschutz participation, see in GDA SBU spr.13189 toms 1–26 in USHMM RG-31.018M reels 17, 18, 19. On the leadership of Hartung and Bichler, see esp. ibid., tom 2, 83 reel 17, deposition of Ivan Pastushenko, perpetrator.
17. See GDA SBU, spr.13189, vol. 9, 58 reel 17.
18. See Arhiva Serviciului Român de Informaţii (hereinafter ASRI), dos. 40011, vol. 20, f. 131 (USHMM RG-25.004M, reel 21; Kogan, first name illegible, 1945); ff. 73–75 v. (Iosif Bronshtein, 1945); and GDA SBU no. 13189, vol. 20, 62 v. (USHMM RG-31.018M, reel 18; Rakhil' Veksel'man, 1966). According to Rakhil' Veksel'man, at the time of her interrogation this policeman resided somewhere in Donbass, which suggests that he escaped severe punishment for his refusal to shoot. For other cases of policemen and Selbstschutz militiamen refusing to murder Jews on sites other than Bogdanovka, see Solonari, "Hating Soviets-Killing Jews," 529–31.
19. GDA SBU no. 13189, vol. 25, 280–82 (USHMM RG-32.018M, reel 19, eyewitness Vladimir Kamenskii). This deposition seems to contradict that of the defendant Anatolii Kotsiubinskii, who claimed that Andrusin assembled all his men; however, it is not clear from this text whether he meant that all of them actually went to the killing site (ibid., 218). According to Ivan Arkhipenko, some policemen were informed about the purpose of their trip, others were not (ibid., 241–44).
20. Roginskaia had only three years of schooling and due to this fact worked as an orderly with the Golta police for a very short time before being fired; afterward, she worked as a laundress for Romanian troops. See her personal form in GDA SBU spr. 914, 48–49 YV JM 23.495. She was sentenced to death and executed. See GDA SBU spr.914, 187–199 YV JM-24.495.
21. GDA SBU sprave 914, 37v YV JM 23.495. In her defense, Roginskaia claimed that "appropriation of [victims clothes] was caused by the material distress of her family, as she had to support three children while her husband was serving in the Red Army" (ibid., 55). For other depositions, see in GDA SBU spr.13189 tom 20, 74 USHMM Rg-31.008M reel 18 (Rahel' Veksel'man); ibid.,101v (Kapel' Shoihet).
22. Ibid., 55–55v.
23. This is according to Iosif (Joseph) Scheel; see GDA SBU spr.20 tom 20, 56–56v YV JM-19.763. On his Ukrainian wife, see ibid., 160 Gregor Anton.
24. GDA SBU spr.20 tom 20, 1–53 YV JM-19.763. Joseph Scheel and Gregor Anton, a perpetrator executed by a firing squad, gave evaluations of their fellow Selbstschutz

members that are quite similar to Akkerman's: see ibid., 57–67, 79–89. For the Soviet sentence, see in ibid., spr.20 tom 33, 210ff YV JM-19.762.
25. See ibid., 57–67 and 79–89. Soviet sentence, see in ibid., spr.20 tom 33, 210ff YV JM-19.762.
26. GDA SBU spr.5806s, 165–166, 256 USHMM RG-31.008M reel 22.
27. GDA SBU spr.5776, 223v-224 USHMM RG-31.008M reel 22.
28. GDA SBU spr.4603, 19-19v, 26-26v USHMM RG-31.008M reel 23.
29. USHMM A. 1076 # 276. This testimony belongs to the collections gathered in the early 1990s by the Jewish community from its members in the Ukrainian city of Chernivtsy.
30. USHMM A. 1076 #523
31. USHMM A. 1076 # 648.
32. GDA SBU spr.20 tom 20, 12 YA JM-19.763.
33. GDA SBU spr.2858, 26v27 USHMM RG-31.008M reel 23.
34. GDA SBU spr.20, 64, YV JM-19.763.
35. GDA SBU spr. 20 tom 10, 47, 60, 147–149 YV JM-19.764.
36. GDA SBU spr.13189 tom 6, 94–95 USHMM RG-32.018M reel 17 and GDA SBU arh. # (I have indicated the archival number, arh.#, in case the file number is missing) 13153 tom 10, 60, 147–149 YV JM-19.764.
37. GDA SBU Spr.13189 tom 5, 94–95 USHMM RG-31.008M reel 17.
38. See GDA SBU arh. # 13153 tom 12, 142 YV JM-19.767. This version seems to be substantiated by another eyewitness, who also attributed Rötler's release to his marriage to a Russian woman; see ibid., tom 28, 121 YV JM-19.762.
39. GDA SBU spr.13153 tom 31, 166v-167YV JM 19.763.
40. GDA SBU spr.20 tom 14, 211-211v YV JM-19.763.
41. See GDA SBU arh. # 13153 tom 21, . 130 YV JM-19.765.
42. GDA SBU arh. # 13151 tom 10, 62 and YV JM-19.764 and ibid., tom 17, 180 YV JM-19.763. Both Scheel and Vezner remembered this episode in practically identical terms.
43. GDA SBU, spr.5776, 204 USHMM RG- 32.018M reel 22. It is not clear from the source what language they used to communicate: whether Munteanu knew some Russian or Ukrainian or whether local women spoke some Romanian. Neither possibility can be precluded, since there were ethnic Romanians (Moldovans) among the locals who sometimes had Russian-sounding first and last names, while some Romanian officers might in fact have been ethnic Ukrainians from Romania with Romanian-sounding names.
44. See Lynne Viola, *Peasant Rebels under Stalin: Collectivization and the Culture of Peasant Resistance* (New York: Oxford University Press, 1996), 181–204.
45. GDA SBU spr.20 tom 17, 97 JM 19.763.
46. GDA SBU, spr.13189 tom 20, 194 USHMM RG-32.018M reel 18.
47. GDA SBU arh. # 13153 tom 16, 205 YV JM-19.763.
48. See Hannah Arendt, *Eichmann in Jerusalem: A Report on the Banality of Evil* (New York: Viking Press, 1963), and Zygmunt Bauman, *Modernity and the Holocaust* (Ithaca, NY: Cornell University Press, 1989).

Bibliography

Ancel, Jean. *Transnistria, 1941–1942: The Romanian Mass Murder Campaigns*. Tel Aviv: Tel Aviv University, 2003.
Arendt, Hannah. *Eichmann in Jerusalem: A Report on the Banality of Evil*. New York: Viking Press, 1963.

Bauman, Zygmunt. *Modernity and the Holocaust*. Ithaca, NY: Cornell University Press, 1989.
Benz, Wolfgang, JTM Houwink ten Cate, and Gerhard Otto, eds. *Anpassung, Kollaboration, Widerstand: Kollektive Reaktionen auf die Okkupation*. Berlin: Metropol, 1996.
Birn, Ruth B. *Die Sicherheitspolizei in Estland 1941–1944: Eine Studie zur Kollaboration im Osten*. Paderborn: Schoeningh, 2006.
Browning, Christopher. *Remembering Survival: Inside a Nazi Slave Labor-Camp*. New York: Norton, 2011.
———. "Ideology, Culture, Situation, and Disposition: Holocaust Perpetrators and the Group Dynamic of Mass Killing", in *NS-Gewaltherrschaft: Beiträge zur historischen Forschung und juristischen Aufarbeitung*, ed. Alfred Gottwald, Norberth Kampe, and Peter Klein, Publikationen der Gedenk- und Bildungsstätte Haus der Wannsee-Konferenz 11. Berlin: Edition Hentrich, 2005.
———. *Ordinary Men: Reserve Police Battalion 101 and the Final Solution in Poland*. New York: HarperCollins, 1992.
Chiari, Bernhard. *Besatzung, Kollaboration und Widerstand in Weissrussland 1941–1944*. Düsseldorf: Droste, 1998.
Dean, Martin. "Schutzmannschaften in Ukraine and Belarus: Profiles of Local Police Collaboration", in *Lessons and Legacies: The Holocaust in International Perspective*, ed. Dagmar Herzog. Evanston, IL: Northwestern University Press, 2006.
———. *Collaboration in the Holocaust: Crimes of the Local Police in Belorussia and Ukraine, 1941–1944*. New York: St. Martin's, 2000.
Dieckmann, Christoph. *Kooperation und Verbrechen: Formen der "Kollaboration" im östlichen Europa 1939–1945*. Göttingen: Wallstein, 2003.
Dumitru, Diana. "An Analysis of Soviet Postwar Investigation and Trial Documents and Their Relevance for Holocaust Studies", in *The Holocaust in the East: Local Perpetrators and Soviet Responses*, ed. Michael David-Fox, Peter Holquist, and Alexander Martin, Pittsburgh: University of Pittsburgh Press, 2014, 142–57.
Goldhagen, Daniel J., Christopher Browning, and Leon Wieselter. *The "Willing Executioners"/"Ordinary Men" Debate: Selections from the Symposium April 8, 1996*. With an introduction by Michael Berenbaum. Washington, DC: United States Holocaust Memorial Museum, 2001.
Goldhagen, Daniel Jonah. *Hitler's Willing Executioners: Ordinary Germans and the Holocaust*. New York: Knopf, 1996.
Penter, Tanja. *Kohle für Stalin und Hitler: Arbeiten und Leben im Donbas 1929 bis 1953*. Essen: Klartext, 2010.
Pohl, Dieter. "Ukrainische Hilskräfte beim Mord an den Juden", in *Die Täter der Shoah: Fanatische Nationalisten oder ganz normale Deutsche?*, ed. Gerhard Paul, Göttingen: Wallstein, 2002, 205–234.
Prusin, Alexander V. *The Lands Between: Conflict in the East European Borderlands, 1870–1992*. Oxford: Oxford Scholarship Online, 2010.
———. "Ukrainkaia politsia I Holokost v general'nom okruge kiev, 1941–1943: deistviia I motivatsii." *Golokost I suchastnist'* 1, no. 3 (2007), 43–49.
Stang, Knut. *Kollaboration und Massenmord: Die litauische Hilfspolizei, das Rollkommando Hamann und die Ermordung der litauischen Juden*. Frankfurt am Main: Peter Lang, 1994.
Snyder, Timothy. *Bloodlands: Europe between Hitler and Stalin*. New York: Basic Books, 2010.
Solonari, Vladimir. "Hating Soviets-Killing Jews: How Anti-Semitic Were Local Perpetrators in Southern Ukraine, 1941–1942?" *Kritika: Explorations in Russian and Eurasian History* 15, no. 3 (2014), 505–34.
Steinhart, Eric Conrad. *The Holocaust and the Germanization of Ukraine*. Publications of the German Historical Institute. New York: Cambridge University Press, 2015.

Szejnmann, Claus-Christian W. "Perpetrators of the Holocaust: A Historiography", in *Ordinary People as Mass Murderers,* ed. Olaf Jensen and Szejnmann. New York: Palgrave MacMillan, 2008.

Viola, Lynne. "The Question of the Perpetrator in Soviet History." *Slavic Review* 72, no. 1 (2013), 1–9.

———. *Peasant Rebels under Stalin: Collectivization and the Culture of Peasant Resistance.* New York: Oxford University Press, 1996.

Wildt, Michael. *An Uncompromising Generation: The Nazi Leadership of the Reich Security Main Office.* Translated by Tom Lampert. Madison: University of Wisconsin Press, 2009.

Chapter 11

Defiance and Protest
A Comparative Microhistorical Reevaluation of Individual Jewish Responses to Nazi Persecution

Wolf Gruner

Some years ago, when I was in a Berlin archive reading through police and court records, a story struck me unlike anything I had come across in twenty years of Holocaust research. In 1941, a Berlin judge evicted the 36-year-old Hertha Reis from a little room she was forced to sublet with her son and her mother. Having nowhere to go, the Jewish women, who toiled as forced laborers at the time, exclaimed in broad daylight in front of the Berlin courthouse: "I got baptized; nevertheless, I was an outcast. ... We lost everything. Because of the flaming government we finally lost our home, too. This thug Hitler, this damned government, this damned people. Just because we are Jews, we are discriminated against."[1]

After eight years of Nazi rule, a Jewish woman amazingly still had the courage, in the heart of the Third Reich, to publicly speak up in protest against the persecution. Her story strongly challenges the still widespread belief in the alleged passivity of German Jews under Nazi persecution. This former view has been shaped by two main components: a restricted research perspective and a limited source base.

Historians have discussed resistance during the Holocaust mostly in terms of organized and armed group activities, thus neglecting individual acts of opposition. In the early 1960s, Hannah Arendt, Raul Hilberg, and Bruno Bettelheim all criticized the alleged lack of Jewish resistance.[2] Israeli scholars immediately challenged this assessment as wrong. While moral and spiritual resistance played a role, the academic discussion nevertheless settled soon on the Eastern occupied territories and on armed resistance. The fact that organized resistance in ghettos and camps did not occur very often nourished the traditional perception of the passive suffering of the Jewish population.[3]

Consequently, a thorough evaluation of individual Jewish defiance is missing in almost all prominent Holocaust narratives, surprisingly even in those focusing on the integration of Jewish voices, such as books authored by Saul Friedländer or Moshe Zimmermann.[4] This situation can be explained by the fact that historians have until now only used a limited set of sources. To evaluate Jewish behavior, scholars have relied on serial political reports originated by Nazi institutions, written testimonies of survivors, and more recently diaries. Yet, in all of these materials, individual acts of opposition barely emerge.

Thus, this article will challenge the traditional picture of Jewish passivity in Nazi Germany by applying a wider concept of resistance and by employing a comparative microhistorical approach introducing the analysis of a variety of new materials.

The Applied Microhistorical Research Design

For my research I revived ideas from the 1970s developed by the Israeli scholar Meir Dworzecki, the Australian historian Konrad Kwiet, and the East German scholar Helmut Eschwege, who all tried to open up the definition of Jewish resistance toward individual activities.[5] I thus defined resistance— by expanding Yehuda Bauer's definition, which focused on group activities—"as any *individual* or group action in opposition to known laws, actions, or intentions of the Nazis and their helpers."[6] Within this broader framework, individual Jewish behavior appears worthy of examination in a larger study, since a closer analysis of Nazi society through the application of this definition at a micro level produces astonishing results, with numerous acts of individual Jewish opposition.[7]

While local studies have already played a prominent role in Holocaust research for a long time, they often seemed disconnected from larger analytical perspectives. Yet only a contextualized historical research design can change this situation, particularly in the form of an intensive investigation of small actions on the local level, but one that is different from a mere case study in that it takes the local and national contexts into close consideration, thus addressing larger questions about the impact of anti-Jewish policies and the reactions they provoked among the persecuted.

The following study thus presents research—as is often attributed to the concept of microhistory—on the individual actions of ordinary people, with the goal of challenging commonly held general assumptions.[8] By altering the scale of observation, as Giovanni Levi put it, "phenomena previously considered to be sufficiently described and understood assume completely new meanings."[9] Conducting a focused analysis on individual acts of Jewish defiance, all of which caught the attention of authorities (therefore surviving in archival records), demonstrates that each case bore much greater importance[10] and that all "historical figures are actors and have agency" according to such a historical perspective.[11]

The microhistorical approach employed for this study does not mean to criticize earlier work by historians, but serves to complement and enrich our understanding of the developments in the Third Reich. The applied twofold research design in this study shall achieve this by examining individual cases of Jewish responses within the concrete local or even sub-local setting, as in the case of Berlin and its districts, and will then analyze them as concrete reactions toward particular anti-Jewish measures, attacks, and laws, whether of sub-local, local, or national origin. This method avoids isolating these individual acts, intending instead to contextualize them; this is possible today only due to research, such as my own, that has provided over the last two decades a much more detailed picture of the complex and often contradictory anti-Jewish policies at the local, regional, and central level of the Nazi state.[12] This research has especially demonstrated the important role of municipal governments in designing and radicalizing these policies, as well as the overlooked impact of many local measures on the life of the persecuted. This acquired knowledge allows us to much better detect and understand what Jews actually responded to and to thus pursue a contextualized and integrated microhistorical study.

My research on individual Jewish defiance started in Berlin by coincidence. In the Berlin state archives, logbooks for around forty of approximately three hundred police precincts have survived the war but have barely been examined by researchers. For an older project, I used some of these diaries to explore Nazi persecution in the spring of 1943 and discovered some astonishing facts about the suicides and deportations of Berlin Jews.[13] Later, I decided to systematically investigate these sources from 1933 to 1945 for traces of anti-Jewish policies and their impact on Jews. Among thousands of reports about lost keys, stolen bicycles, drunken people, and apprehended exhibitionists, evidence of public protest and criticism expressed by Jews against anti-Jewish policies suddenly surfaced by the dozen.[14] While the individual stories were fascinating, the logbook entries written by the Berlin police officers about the arrest of protesting Jews were rather brief, simply describing the place, time, and general content of the protest and offering only the name, birthdate, and address of the arrestee. A similar problem emerged with another collection in the same archive, police precinct reports about political incidents that were based on such logbook entries. Since the Nazi state penalized political protest under a new law from December 1934, against so called treacherous attacks on the state or the Nazi Party,[15] I embarked on a search to find the respective names from the police reports in the two thousand special court (*Sondergericht*) files that had survived for approximately ten thousand cases. Most of the files, now also housed in the Berlin state archive, offer only an indictment or the judgment of the trial, usually three to five typescript pages long, and in rare instances include the interrogation as well. Although, I did not find any familiar names in these court files, many new cases emerged and revealed that historians had hitherto overlooked the fact that the special courts had widely exploited the law on treacherous attacks to punish critique, and quell protest by Jews.[16]

After such astonishing findings, the question arose as to whether these results would be representative only for Berlin—the place with the biggest German Jewish community and often praised as the refuge of anonymity—or if similar evidence of individual Jewish defiance could be found for other cities in the German Reich. I therefore started to conduct a comparative microhistorical research for Hamburg, Frankfurt, Vienna, and Leipzig. Although their local archives did not contain similar police records as those in Berlin, all of them offered access to rich portions of material produced by special courts during the Third Reich. Sifting through these trial records brought to the surface not only political incidents, with Jews being punished under the law on treacherous attacks, but also individual cases of Jewish defiance against other measures, and its subsequent treatment by special and regular local courts (*Amtsgerichte*) under various anti-Jewish or even regular legislation.

To complement this new material from the special courts and police precincts, which nevertheless was limited to two record groups, I added a thorough examination of more than three hundred survivor video testimonies from the USC Shoah Foundation in Los Angeles. Again, after my wider definition of resistance was applied, this research quickly provided evidence of many Jews who engaged in individual acts of opposition starting in 1933 but lasting well into the war. Some of the interviews confirmed results from previous archival work, while others provided astounding details of hitherto unknown types of resistance.

This comparative microhistorical study raises many questions. In what ways did Jews resist and why? Did oppositional behavior change over time, and did such changes correspond to certain stages in persecution? How do the results of this microhistorical approach modify our macro view, and finally, can they alter the traditional image of Jewish passivity under the Nazis?

How Did Jews React to Persecution?

Against the first wave of persecution, the notorious boycott of shops and expulsion from public jobs in 1933, Jews protested at the German ministries and local governments responsible for the implementation of these measures. In local and federal archives, numerous petitions can be found that have been written by individuals, representatives of Jewish organizations and communities, and even groups of Jews, such as the textile merchants in Berlin who protested against their exclusion from the public market.[17]

Yet as revealed by police and court records as well as USC Shoah Foundation video testimonies, Jews also spoke up in public against the discrimination from the very beginning. In Frankfurt am Main, a special court sentenced German Jews, as early as March and April of 1933, for publicly criticizing the beatings and murder of Jews by SA gangs and the torture of Jews in concentration camps by the SS.[18] For example, on 29 March 1933, the prosecutor at the state court in Frankfurt indicted the merchant Erich Löwenstein, who was born in 1908, for spreading rumors. Just a few days earlier, Löwenstein had spoken with some acquaintances, who happened to be members of the Nazi Party. He interrogated them about the goals of the NSDAP regarding the Jews, asking especially whether the Nazis wanted to drive the Jews out of Germany or harm them in any way. Last but not least, he discussed the rumours about frequent beatings and murders of Jews. On 1 April 1933, boycott day, he was sentenced for this to one year in prison.[19]

German Jews not only voiced verbal critique, but also actively battled Nazi propaganda and the regime itself. In Munich and Hamburg, the police arrested Jews for destroying Nazi posters or symbols, for sullying displays of the anti-Semitic newspaper the *Stürmer*, and for contesting the Hitler salute.[20] During the first years under Nazi rule, some Jews, in particular younger ones, decided to join Communist resistance groups. Diane Jacobs, who was born in 1921, conducted surveillance missions on the Nazi Party and Hitler youth gatherings for Communist cells in Frankfurt and Berlin, and Efrayim Vagner mixed explosives with three other Jews for a Communist underground group in Frankfurt.[21]

The waves of organized anti-Jewish riots instigated by the party produced, in particular, reactions on the part of the persecuted. In Berlin, storm troopers, Hitler Youth, and other Germans defiled Jewish stores and physically attacked Jews and foreigners in June and July 1935.[22] When the Berlin police did not stop the organized riots for weeks, business-card-sized fliers were found in the mailboxes of businesses with the following message: "Germany is a cultural disgrace today. I am a German Jew and loyal to the emperor. Indeed, the Germans should expel the foreigner Hitler. My father and I were born in Hamburg. I served as a private in the world war. Down with HITLER."[23] The flyer was ironically signed with the pseudonym King Cohn, the latter a common Jewish last name that Germans traditionally used in anti-Semitic poems or songs.

During the month of July 1935 alone, the Berlin police arrested more than one hundred Jews, mostly for offences against the German state and the Nazi Party. Louis Wilczyk, who was born in 1905 and was the former owner of an office supply shop, had been denounced for gravely offending Hitler and Joseph Goebbels in public. Rosalie Mielzynski, born in 1878, was sent to a concentration camp because she had publicly criticized the riots by saying that "since the German state can't succeed, the Jews are blamed and attacked." It is remarkable that in their July report for Berlin, the Gestapo emphasized that Jews were born with disrespect for state authority.[24]

However, neither arrests, new local measures, nor the notorious Nuremberg Laws could suppress Jewish opposition. On the contrary, in Cologne, Königsberg, and other cities, Jews deliberately ignored the new local prohibitions by visiting swimming pools, cinemas, theaters, and operas, as many testimonies from the USC Shoah Foundation reveal.[25] They also fought back against individual actions by anti-Semites. Henry Schuster's family rented out the store in their house to a non-Jewish merchant, who placed a "Strictly Prohibited for Jews" sign at the private entry to the apartments. One night, Henry's mother changed one letter on the sign so that it now read "Strictly Prohibited for Everybody."[26] Some still intervened at city governments, as in Hanover, where Jews collectively demanded free access to the public pool.[27] Others, such as Irmgard Herrmann, documented crimes after storm troopers beat up her son, by taking pictures and sending them to newspapers.[28] Many others went to German courts and demanded their rights—for example, suing employers for outstanding wages or fighting unfair dismissals from jobs. While during the first years Jews could still be successful in local courts, after 1935 and the enactment of the Nuremberg Laws the attitude of many judges toward Jews changed; after the pogrom of November 1938 in particular, the chances of winning a lawsuit became very slim, not least because of the increasing number of anti-Jewish national regulations and laws.[29]

Jews also spoke up in public, for instance in Frankfurt am Main, where the sales agent Ernst Meyer, born in 1873, criticized Hitler, the persecution of Jews, and especially the Nuremberg Laws during a visit to a business firm. The special court tried Meyer in November 1935 and sentenced him under the law on treacherous attacks to six months in prison.[30] Rosalie Kowalski, born in 1887, was denounced by neighbors, arrested, and punished by Frankfurt's special court in July 1937 with six months in prison. She had repeatedly used the debasing term "Hitler pack" and openly stated that Goebbels was simply telling lies.[31]

It is even more astonishing that acts of individual resistance against physical attacks emerged in numbers from these new sources. In Frankfurt, for example, Oskar Junghans, who was born in 1904, beat up some teenagers who had aimed slingshots at Jews leaving a synagogue in 1936.[32] Survivor testimonies from the USC Shoah Foundation show that men got into brawls with coworkers, Nazi neighbors, and SA men, both on the street or when the SA intruded into homes.[33] They defended their family or Jewish neighbors, as in the case of Joan Winter's father, who knocked over a Nazi neighbor in his apartment house after he had personally forbidden that the elevator be used by Jews.[34] In Berlin, nineteen-year-old Frank Theyleg provoked and beat up two SA men in his apartment building, since both tenants had frequently terrorized the two old Jewish ladies who owned the house.[35]

However, not all Jews acted with such open courage. Paul Malch, a leather product merchant from Düsseldorf, used two business trips across the border to the nearby Dutch town of Venlo in 1937 to compose, from his hotel room, letters full of fierce complaints about the persecution, which he then mailed from the Netherlands directly to his son in the United States. The regular family mail sent weekly from Germany for years did not contain any criticism.[36] A widespread fear of censorship might thus explain the apolitical tone of most contemporary letters written by German Jews until the year 1938.

To the devastating attack of the November 1938 pogrom, Jews responded in a variety of ways. Some saved religious objects or private goods; others documented the crimes by creating address lists of destroyed shops or damaged businesses, or by taking pictures of the wreckage.[37] And some criticized the events in public, such as Henriette Schäfer in Frankfurt, who entered her neighbor's shop and asked, "What are you saying about the fact that everything is being destroyed and the synagogues are being set on fire?" After the shopkeeper responded that people were outraged by the murder of a German diplomat by a Jew, Schäfer replied, "This is not the people, but the government. They are all blackguards, scamps, and criminals. Hitler is the biggest bandit. If I could, I would poison them all." The special court of Frankfurt punished her with six months in prison under the law on treacherous attacks.[38]

During the pogrom, some Jews physically resisted attackers. Sixteen-year-old Diane Jacobs, who lived in an agricultural training camp for emigration to Palestine, even stabbed an SA man. On 10 November, a gang of storm troopers raided her camp, first beating up the boys and then the girls. When it was her turn, her attacker played with a rusty knife, but Diane Jacobs head-butted him in the stomach, a trick she had learned to defend herself at the Zionist youth group Hashomer Hatzair. Taking advantage of the assailant's surprise, she twisted the knife from his hand and stabbed him in the stomach. He fell down. Fortunately the other storm troopers did not notice, so she was able to hide the unconscious body of her attacker behind a sofa with the help of some friends, before running into the fields and escaping.[39]

The violent pogrom was followed by a set of new national restrictions. On the search for personal responses in each archive in Frankfurt, Hamburg, Vienna, and Leipzig, as well as in the USC Shoah Foundation Visual History Archive, dozen of cases surfaced of Jews who disobeyed the new rules. For example, the decrees to hand over all precious metals in February 1939,[40] to deposit all liquid assets and money in frozen bank accounts,[41] or to leave all valuables behind in Germany upon emigration.[42] These Jews were punished by either special or local courts. Wilhelm Sander, a former merchant born in 1876, was arrested in 1940 before his emigration to Palestine, for hiding cash at home and smuggling money into Switzerland. The special court in Frankfurt found him guilty of two counts of foreign currency offenses and sentenced him to seven months in jail.[43] In 1942, a fifty-year-old Jewish woman from Berlin was arrested in Hamburg. Martha Frank had complained—at a special office for Jews (*Sonderdienststelle für Juden*) in the presence of other Jews—that her request to pick up her food ration cards was declined because she had been late. The Gestapo also found that she was hiding jewelry in her underwear and precious metals at home, was not wearing the yellow star, and had not registered in Hamburg. The local court penalized these offenses with six months in prison. During the investigation it came to light that Frank had already received two sentences for not showing the special identification card for Jews which demonstrates her unstoppable courage.[44]

Although the Nazi state had obliged all Jews to wear specially marked identification cards in July 1938[45] and to adopt the discriminatory middle names Israel and Sara in August 1938,[46] the local archives in Hamburg, Vienna, and Frankfurt provide many instances of Jews who resisted filing the necessary application forms.[47] In Berlin, 68-year-old painter Max Antlers repeatedly declined requests to fill out the forms; he didn't even change his mind after he was to appear at the police station in February 1939.[48] In Leipzig, 73-year-old Ida Schneider didn't apply for the identification card and refused to use the forced middle name "Sara". Once detected in 1941, she consequently received seven months in prison.[49]

If German Jews had formally adopted the forced middle names, they needed to inform municipal and other offices of these name changes. Margarete Engel, who was born in 1879 and lived in Leipzig, did not inform the civil registry, as required, of where she was born and where she got married, so that the officers in her case in Berlin and Bremen could issue new altered certificates. She was therefore arrested in mid-January 1942 by the local court, which was the legal branch responsible for this matter, and a few days later punished with two weeks in prison for neglecting the decree regarding changes in family names and first names. After serving the sentence, the court ordered that she be handed over to the Gestapo.[50] In Hamburg, chief rabbi Dr. Joseph Carlebach was interrogated for not sending an update to his local phone book company.[51]

At any time since 1939, Jews had to identify themselves in public by using the forcibly adopted middle names, yet an unknown number simply refused to do so. Following are examples from 1940 to 1942 in Hamburg: Dr. Edgar Fels and his female companion drove a private car to a music event, were stopped by the police, and did not identify themselves using the middle names.[52] Dreise Kaste had to pay 3.76 reichsmark for not using "Sara" when she was brought to a police station after walking at night with a flashlight in the street, which was forbidden since the beginning of the war by the law on air defense.[53] Adolf Katzenstein, a former chef who worked as a forced laborer in construction, wrote a petition to Nazi gauleiter Kaufmann about his economically dire situation as a result of the persecution. He did not sign the letter with "Israel," nor did he put down his special ID-card number. Katzenstein had already received a punishment for not applying for the ID.[54]

Others were turned in by private individuals and municipal officials. Caroline Falck received a jail sentence of two days for not using "Sara" in a private complaint letter to a Hamburg transport company.⁵⁵ Adolf Hermann had been already punished once in 1941 with a fine of 20 Reichsmark but continued to sign his ration cards without the name "Israel"—he worked individually for a private employer instead of as a forced laborer—for which he received a sentence of five months in prison.⁵⁶

Other actions of defiance were penalized under different laws. When Jews deliberately did not hand over their radios in the fall of 1939⁵⁷ or listened to forbidden foreign broadcasts during the war, regular courts punished them under the law against radio crimes.⁵⁸ However some Jews, such as Hannelore Noe, were not caught.⁵⁹ Others did not obey the order to hand over their handguns in the fall of 1938, such as Manfred Feldmann, who was born in Hamburg in 1908 and interned after the pogrom in Sachsenhausen concentration camp.⁶⁰ Those Jews would be tried under the German gun law.⁶¹ In Vienna, Laura Rechnitz was sent to jail for six months, by a judge employing the German penal code, after she had broken the curfew for Jews and told political jokes in the Esterhazi-Bar.⁶²

Breaking the anti-Jewish curfew introduced in September 1939⁶³ to visit forbidden bars, restaurants, cinemas, or theaters seems to have been common among Jews, regardless of age.⁶⁴ The same seems true of ignoring limited shopping hours for Jews, as introduced in Vienna or Berlin. Moreover, Berlin police logbooks show that dozens of Jews resisted or sabotaged forced labor since 1939 and were sent by the Gestapo to *Arbeitserziehungslager* (reeducation camps) or concentration camps.⁶⁵

For treason, the former real estate broker Benno Neuburger was put on trial in Munich. He had randomly sent out a dozen postcards between the fall of 1941 and the spring of 1942 with foresighted comments such as "The eternal mass murderer Hitler. Disgusting!" or "Murderer of 5,000,000." Neuburger argued that as a Jew, he hated Hitler, for the persecution since 1933, but especially for his public pronouncement to exterminate all Jews in his speech to the German parliament on 30 January 1939. He received the death sentence and was executed in September 1942 at the age of seventy-one.⁶⁶

Thus, even after the terror of the November pogrom, new radical regulations, and the beginning of the war, Jews still spoke up against the Nazi state and its anti-Jewish measures. In August 1939, the lawyer Dr. Arthur Singer, born in 1877, had loudly protested at the Vienna municipal housing office. Singer exclaimed in front of dozens of other Jews that Jews could not be forced to sublet to other people, and he cursed Hitler and the Reich commissar for Austria, Bürckel. Singer even urged the other Jews to join his protest against these Viennese orders and to storm the offices. After his arrest, the Vienna state court, functioning as a special court, sentenced Singer to one year in prison under the law on treacherous attacks; yet he was acquitted on the charge of public unrest, since the other Jews resisted to testify.[67] In Leipzig, a Jewish man was charged by the police for bringing down and destroying a Nazi flag in September of 1939.[68] In Berlin, the former tailor Alfred Lewithan, born in 1913, was punished for public comments harming the German state. He received a sentence of nine months in jail, which did not stop him either. In the spring of 1940, Lewithan smuggled letters, hidden in mail-order catalogues printed in prison, calling for an uprising and blaming Hitler for his mistake of persecuting the Jews.[69] After the deportations started, on 21 December 1941, the former actress Melanie Krohn, born in 1889, entered a Hamburg police station and shouted out loud, "Down with Hitler." Weeping, she stated that she had no will to live anymore. She received only two weeks in prison, since the judge believed that she was acting out of despair.[70] In Leipzig, the special court indicted Toba Flaschmann under the law on treacherous attacks in February 1942. The 51-year-old Jewish woman of former Polish citizenship, who had lived in Leipzig since 1901, toiled as a forced laborer for the private Hugo Luckner Company. Her husband was in a concentration camp at that time. At the end of September 1941, Toba Flaschmann got into an argument with her foreman at work, complaining that she was not receiving vacations. The foreman, Gustav May, denounced her as having claimed during the altercation, "We are deceived and betrayed by the German state."[71] Not to forget Hertha Reis from the beginning of this chapter, who shouted in the capital of the Third Reich in 1941, "This thug Hitler, this damned government, this damned people. Just because we are Jews, we are discriminated against."[72]

Employing a microhistorical approach, this study has investigated the individual behavior of Jews in Nazi Germany—by focusing on their reactions toward persecution—in order to challenge the traditional perception of their alleged passivity. Moreover, the chapter analyzed these personal reactions not as isolated incidents, but as being individually provoked by diverse and changing anti-Jewish policies in Nazi society. The actions were therefore examined in their concrete historical context and connected to specific means of persecution on the local, regional, and national level.

After the perspective of the study was changed by broadening the definition of Jewish resistance to include individual acts against Nazi measures and plans, first systematic microhistorical research in a Berlin archive—exploring the logbooks of Berlin police precincts for the years

1933–1945—yielded compelling evidence of individual protest by Jews, as did further research with similarly overlooked materials, such as police reports on political cases or special court files regarding the law on treacherous attacks. The examples that were unearthed demonstrate that Jews reacted not only to well-known national laws, but more often to specific local anti-Jewish measures and local waves of anti-Jewish violence. These spectacular findings from Berlin demonstrated the need to look for other neglected local archives and for a systematic investigation on the micro level to solidify these surprising new insights.

Based on the microhistorical research design developed for Berlin, the study here applies the contextualized method to Hamburg, Frankfurt, Vienna, and Leipzig, thus developing a comparative microhistorical approach that revealed even more forgotten actions. While police reports didn't survive in these cities, abundant material from special courts revealed not only offenses against the law on treacherous attacks, as in Berlin, but also against others Nazi regulations. These findings then triggered a successful search for Jews on trial at regular courts for offenses against a variety of national decrees and local restrictions. The new results were complemented by a close analysis of video testimonies by survivors, which confirmed the new archival insights, while adding even more surprising nuances of personal opposition by Jews to the revised picture, such as cases of physical self-defense.

The twofold strategy of dealing with an under-researched topic in overlooked archives, on the microhistorical level of individual cases, thus generated astonishing results that alter our general view of Jews' responses to persecution in Nazi Germany. A contextualized and comparative microhistory allows us to see how Jews developed changing response strategies over time: first against Nazi propaganda and exclusionary economic measures, later against violent local attacks and municipal restrictions as well as the nationwide November pogrom and radical segregationist laws, and finally against forced labor and deportation. While special courts prosecuted and punished public criticism or protest under the law on treacherous attacks as well as other offenses, regular courts penalized many other Jewish acts of defiance against laws and local measures. It is surprising that local differences between Berlin and other cities did not emerge—except perhaps in terms of numbers—as well as no age, socialization, or gender patterns. Jewish women and men of all ages and from all educational and professional backgrounds defied Nazi measures or raised their voices in protest.

Beyond mere observations about individual German Jews, these microhistorical findings change our view on macrohistory. For the first time, we can understand what the frequent mention in Gestapo and

Security Service (*Sicherheitsdienst*) reports of impudent Jews was referring to: actual opposition and protest by individual Jews. The fact that German Jews protested in public and that so many people defied Nazi measures obliterates the common view of passivity on the part of the persecuted. It instead gives agency back to ordinary Jews in extraordinary circumstances. Many German Jews thus evolve as courageous historical actors who resisted Nazi persecution. While the microhistorical research presented here unearthed numerous similar accounts of individual Jewish opposition and resistance in various local archives and many video testimonies, these courageous acts still await their incorporation into the general narrative of Nazi persecution of the Jews.

Wolf Gruner holds the Shapell-Guerin Chair in Jewish Studies and is professor of history and founding director of the USC Shoah Foundation Center for Advanced Genocide Research at the University of Southern California, Los Angeles. He is the author of nine books on the Holocaust, including *Jewish Forced Labor under the Nazis: Economic Needs and Nazi Racial Aims* (2006), and is coeditor of *The Greater German Reich and the Jews: Nazi Persecution Policies in the Annexed Territories 1935–1945* (2015). He published in Spanish the book *Parias de la Patria: The Myth of the Liberation of the Indigenous People in the Republic of Bolivia 1825–1890* (2015). His most recent study on the persecution of the Jews in the Protectorate of Bohemia Moravia appeared in German with Wallstein Verlag in 2016.

Notes

1. LA Berlin, A Rep. 355, No. 5697, no fols: Anklage, Generalstaatsanwalt beim Landgericht als Leiter der Anklagebehörde beim Sondergericht an das Sondergericht Berlin, June 7, 1941, 1–4. For the English citation, see Wolf Gruner, "'The Germans Should Expel the Foreigner Hitler': Open Protest and Other Forms of Jewish Defiance in Nazi Germany," *Yad Vashem Studies* 39, no. 2 (2011): 13–53, here 44. For the development of Berlin's policy of expelling Jewish tenants, see Susanne Willems, *Der entsiedelte Jude: Albert Speers Wohnungsmarktpolitik für den Berliner Hauptstadtbau* (Berlin: Edition Hentrich, 2002).
2. See Michael Marrus, "Jewish Resistance to the Holocaust," *Journal of Contemporary History* 30, no. 1 (1995): 86; Konrad Kwiet, "Problems of Jewish Resistance Historiography," *Leo Baeck Institute Yearbook* 24 (1979): 37. Robert Rozett added Bettelheim to the common picture of Arendt and Hilberg, both of whom neglected the existence of Jewish resistance; see Rozett's article 'Jewish Resistance," in *The Historiography of the Holocaust,* ed. Dan Stone (Houndmills, U.K.: Palgrave Macmillan, 2004), 343.
3. For a recent account of the historiography of Jewish resistance, see Gruner, "The Germans," 14–17.

4. Saul Friedländer, *Nazi Germany and the Jews*, vol. 1, *The Years of Persecution, 1933–1939* (New York: HarperCollins, 1998); Friedländer, *The Years of Extermination: Nazi Germany and the Jews, 1939–1945* (New York: HarperCollins, 2008); Moshe Zimmermann, *Deutsche gegen Deutsche: Das Schicksal der Juden 1938–1945* (Berlin: Aufbau 2008).
5. Meir Dworzecki, "The Day to Day Stand of the Jews," in *Jewish Resistance during the Holocaust: Proceedings of the Conference on Manifestations of Jewish Resistance, Jerusalem, April 7–11, 1968* (Jerusalem: Yad Vashem, 1971), 152–81; Konrad Kwiet and Helmut Eschwege, *Selbstbehauptung und Widerstand: Deutsche Juden im Kampf um Existenz und Menschenwürde, 1933–1945*, 2nd edn (Hamburg: Christians, 1986), 18–19. See also Kwiet, "Problems," 41.
6. Gruner, "The Germans," 18. For Bauer's definition, see Yehuda Bauer, "Forms of Jewish Resistance," in *The Holocaust: Problems and Perspectives of Interpretation*, ed. Donald L. Niewyk, 3rd edn (Boston: Wadsworth Publishing, 2002), 117.
7. The research presented here is part of a larger book project by the author.
8. On the development and challenges of microhistory, see, for example, Carlo Ginzburg, "Microhistory: Two or Three Things That I Know about It," *Critical Inquiry* 20, no. 1 (Autumn 1993): 10–35; Sigurdur Gylfi Magnusson, "What Is Microhistory?," *History News Network*, May 7, 2006, http://hnn.us/articles/23720.html (last accessed 09/12/2014). See also John Brewer, "Microhistory and the Histories of Everyday Life," *Cultural and Social History* 7 (2010): 87–109; and a response by Filippo de Vivo, "Prospect or Refuge? Microhistory, History on the Large Scale: A Response," *Cultural and Social History* 7 (2010): 387–97.
9. Giovanni Levi, "On Microhistory," in *New Perspectives on Historical Writing*, ed. Peter Burke, ed. (Cambridge: Polity, 1991), 97–98.
10. Ibid., 107.
11. Brewer, "Microhistory," 89.
12. For example: Wolf Gruner, *Öffentliche Wohlfahrt und Judenverfolgung: Wechselwirkungen lokaler und zentraler Politik im NS-Staat, 1933–1942* (Munich: Oldenbourg, 2002); Gruner, "Local Initiatives, Central Coordination: German Municipal Administration and the Holocaust," in *Networks of Nazi Persecution: Bureaucracy, Business, and the Organization of the Holocaust*, ed. Gerald D. Feldman and Wolfgang Seibel (New York, Oxford: Berghahn Books, 2005), 269–94; Gruner, *The Persecution of the Jews in Berlin 1933–1945: A Chronology of Measures by the Authorities in the German Capital* (Berlin: Stiftung Topography des Terrors, 2014) (German 1st edn 1996); Rüdiger Fleiter, *Stadtverwaltung im Dritten Reich: Verfolgungspolitik auf kommunaler Ebene am Beispiel Hannovers* (Hanover: Verlag Hahnsche Buchhandlung, 2006); Martin Friedenberger, *Fiskalische Ausplünderung: Die Berliner Steuer- und Finanzverwaltung und die jüdische Bevölkerung 1933–1945* (Berlin: Metropol Verlag, 2008).
13. See Wolf Gruner, *Widerstand in der Rosenstraße. Die Fabrik-Aktion und die Verfolgung der "Mischehen" 1943* (Frankfurt am Main: Fischer-Verlag, 2005).
14. See examples in Gruner, "The Germans," 13–53.
15. RGBl., 1934 I, 1269. See Bernward Dörner, *"Heimtücke". Das Gesetz als Waffe. Kontrolle, Abschreckung und Verfolgung in Deutschland 1933–1945* (Paderborn: Schöningh, 1998), 20–25, 67–84, 120–27.
16. For a first account based on Berlin examples, see Gruner, "The Germans," 13–53.
17. For a more detailed discussion of written petitions authored by Jewish organizations and communities, see Gruner, "The Germans," 21–27. For collective as well as individual response strategies of Jewish merchants in Berlin, see Christoph Kreutzmüller, *Ausverkauf: Die Vernichtung der jüdischen Gewerbetätigkeit in Berlin 1930–1945* (Berlin: Metropol, 2012), 275–323.

18. HStA Wiesbaden, Akten des Sondergerichts Frankfurt am Main, Abt. 461, No. 7277 Isaak Leser; ibid., No. 7281 Hans Oster; ibid., No. 7282 Rahel Lorsch; ibid., No. 7294 Bernhard Mannsbach, fol. 11; ibid., No. 7351 Hermann Rosenthal; ibid., No. 7306 Bertram Stern.
19. HStA Wiesbaden, Akten des Sondergerichts Frankfurt a.M. Abt. 461, No. 7273 Erich Löwenstein, fols. 2–3.
20. For example, see USC Shoah Foundation Visual History Archive (USC SF/VHA) Los Angeles, Pesach Schindler, tape 1, min. 36; ibid, Ester Scheiner, tape 1, min. 23; StA Hamburg, 213-11_01242/36, Jacob Heilbut wg. Sachbeschädigung; § 303 StGB, fol. 12.
21. USC SF/VHA, Diane Jacobs, tape 3, min. 13.30; ibid., Efrayim Vagner, tape 1, min. 28.
22. For details about the weeklong organized riots, based on different sources, see Ahlheim, Hannah: *"Deutsche, kauft nicht bei Juden!"*. *Antisemitismus und politischer Boykott in Deutschland 1924 bis 1935*. (Göttingen: Wallstein Verlag 2011), 379–90; Gruner, *The Persecution of the Jews in Berlin*, 81–84; Gruner, *Die Berliner und die NS-Judenverfolgung. Eine mikrohistorische Studie individueller Handlungen und sozialer Beziehungen*, in *Berlin im Nationalsozialismus. Politik und Gesellschaft 1933–1945*, ed. Rüdiger Hachtmann, Thomas Schaarschmidt, and Winfried Süß, Beiträge zur Geschichte des Nationalsozialismus 27 (Göttingen: Wallstein 2011), 57–87, here 60–63; Kreutzmüller, *Ausverkauf*, 145–50.
23. LA Berlin, A. Pr. Br. Rep. 030, Nr. 21640, fol. 599: Polizeibericht vom 19.7.1935.
24. Otto Dov Kulka and Eberhard Jäckel, eds, *Die Juden in den geheimen NS-Stimmungsberichten 1933–1945* (Düsseldorf, 2004), CD version, CD-Nr. 1004: Stapostelle Landespolizeibezirk Berlin. Bericht für Juli 1935 (o.D.). (For the English book version, with excerpts from 752 of the 3,744 documents, see idem, *The Jews in the Secret Nazi Reports on Popular Opinion in Germany, 1933–1945* (New Haven: Yale University Press, 2010). For more details on the arrests, see Gruner, "The Germans," 32.
25. USC SF/VHA, Gunner Lukas, tape 2, min. 6; ibid., Paula Lindemann, tape 1, min. 22; ibid., Heinz Langer, tape 2, min. 17; ibid., Irene Hofstein, tape 1 min. 28; ibid., Efrayim Vagner, tape 1 min. 42; Edith Sternfeld, tape 1 min. 22; ibid., Anita Siegel, tape 2, min. 45; ibid., No. Martha Friedmann, tape 3, min. 1–5; ibid., Kurt Liffmann, tape 2.
26. From "Für Juden strengstens verboten" to "Für Jeden strengstens verboten"; USC SF/VHA, Henry Schuster, tape 1, min. 26–28.
27. Fleiter, *Stadtverwaltung im Dritten Reich*, 142–43.
28. USC SF/VHA, Irmgard Hoffmann, tape 1, min. 24–29.
29. Regarding labor law and German labor courts, see, for example, Gruner, Wolf: *Der Geschlossene Arbeitseinsatz deutscher Juden. Zwangsarbeit als ein Element der Verfolgung 1938-1943.* (Berlin: Metropol-Verlag 1997), 98–101.
30. HStA Wiesbaden, Akten des Sondergerichts Frankfurt a.M., Abt. 461, No. 7435 Ernst Meyer, fol. 39–41RS.
31. HStA Wiesbaden, Akten des Sondergerichts Frankfurt a.M., Abt. 461, No. 7722 Rosalie Kowalski, fols 109–13. See also, for another case, USC SF/VHA, Inge Stutzel, tape 1, min. 22.
32. HStA Wiesbaden, Akten des Sondergerichts Frankfurt a.M., Abt. 461, No. 16778 Oskar Junghans, fols 7–7RS.
33. USC SF/VHA, Bert Wallace, tape 2, min. 24; ibid., Haviva Salomon, tape 1, min. 15; ibid., Helmut Gruenewald, tape 4 min. 25.
34. USC SF/VHA, Joan Winter, tape 2, min. 56.
35. USC SF/VHA, Frank Theyleg, tape 2, min. 13–18.

36. See letters from 17 April 1937 and 10 November 1937 printed in Wolf Gruner, ed., *Die Verfolgung und Ermordung der europäischen Juden durch das nationalsozialistische Deutschland 1933–1945*, vol. 1, *Das Deutsche Reich 1933 bis 1937* (Munich: Oldenbourg, 2008), 647–48, 731–32. For an English excerpt of the second letter, see citation by Gruner, "The Germans," 36.
37. USC SF/VHA, Elena Marx, tape 1, min. 25; ibid., Lea Aronson, tape 1 min. 27–31. For more examples, see Gruner, "The Germans," 38.
38. HStA Wiesbaden, Akten des Sondergerichts Frankfurt a.M., Abt. 461, No. 7925 Henriette Schäfer, fols 24–35 and 42.
39. USC SF/VHA, Diane Jacobs, tape 3, min. 10–13.
40. HStA Wiesbaden, Akten des Sondergerichts Frankfurt a.M., Abt. 461, No. 17287 Moses Rosenbaum; ibid., No. 9293 Gustav Beiersdorf; StA Hamburg, 213-11_0875/41 Hinrichsen, Carl Marcus David; USC SF/VHA, Walter Blumenthal, tape 2, min. 18.
41. Sächsisches Staatsarchiv Leipzig (StA-L), 20114 Landgericht Leipzig, No. 5627, Käthe Kanstein, and ibid., 20031 Polizeipräsidium, PP-S 1839/173 Kanstein Käthe; HStA Wiesbaden, Akten des Sondergerichts Frankfurt a.M., Abt. 461, No. 8148 Wilhelm Sander; ibid., No. 9293 Gustav Beiersdorf.
42. USC SF/VHA, Hilde Watermann, tape 1; ibid., Irene Hofstein, tape 3; StA Hamburg, 213-11_3274/40 679601, Goldschmidt, Aron.
43. HStA Wiesbaden, Akten des Sondergerichts Frankfurt a.M., Abt. 461, No. 8148 Wilhelm Sander: Urteil Sondergericht vom 10.7.1940, 4.
44. StA Hamburg, 213-11_0317/43 Martha Frank, fol. 1.
45. *Dritte Bekanntmachung über den Kennkartenzwang;* (RGBl., 1938 I) 922.
46. *2. VO zur Durchführung des Gesetzes über die Änderung von Familien- und Vornamen;* (RGBl., 1938 I) 1044.
47. For Leipzig, see, for example, StA-L, 20031 Polizeipräsidium, PP-S 1216/187 Hamel, Marie; ibid., PP-S 1839/32 Kaufmann, Julius; PP-S 2317/31 Moschkewietz, Ernestine; ibid., PP-S 2857 Johanna Quaas; ibid., PP-S 3400/80 Rosenthal, Betty; ibid., PP-S 4174 Schwartz, Karl.
48. Gruner, "The Germans," 39.
49. StA-L, 20031 Polizeipräsidium, PP-S 4173 Schneider, Ida.
50. StA-L, 20114 Landgericht Leipzig, No. 6075 Margarete Engel, fols 5 and 10–12.
51. StA Hamburg, 213-11_4095/41 Carlebach, Dr. Joseph.
52. StA Hamburg, 213-11_0282/41 Fels, Dr. Edgar.
53. StA Hamburg, 213-11_2669/42 Kaste, Dreise.
54. StA Hamburg, 213-11_5659/41 Katzenstein, Adolf David.
55. StA Hamburg, 213-11_5785/41, Falck, Caroline.
56. StA Hamburg, 213-11_4145/42 Adler, Hermann.
57. Facsimile of the decree in Irmgard Harmann-Schütz and Franz Blome-Drees, *Die Geschichte der Juden in Sundern* (Sundern, 1988), 156.
58. Jews received one year in jail for not handing over radios or for listening to foreign broadcasts: Wiener Stadt- und Landesarchiv, Sondergericht, SHv Strafakten, 5612 Irma Sara Plehn; ibid., 5770 Rudolf Konitzer; USC SFA.
59. USC SF/VHA, Hannelore Noe, tape 3, min. 62.
60. StA Hamburg, 213-11_09392/39 Feldmann, Manfred.
61. *Verordnung gegen den Waffenbesitz der Juden, 11.11.1938*; RGBl., 1938 I, 1573. See Stephen P. Halbrook, "Nazi Firearms Law and the Disarming of the German Jews," *Arizona Journal of International and Comparative Law* 17, no. 3 (2000): 483–535, here 516–21.
62. Wiener Stadt- und Landesarchiv, Sondergericht, SHv Strafakten, 5216 Laura Rechnitz.
63. StA Freiburg i. Br., Landratsamt Mühlheim, P.Nr. 365, Nr. 243, no fols: RFSS decree, 6 September 1939 in circular decree Stapoleitstelle Karlsruhe, 10 September 1939.

64. As mentioned in many memoirs of Jewish survivors. For some examples, see Wiener Stadt- und Landesarchiv, Sondergericht, SHv Strafakten 6276 Edith Weiss; USC SF/ VHA, Anita Siegel, tape 2, min. 45.
65. Gruner, "The Germans," 40–43.
66. Marion Detjen, *"Zum Staatsfeind ernannt": Widerstand, Resistenz und Verweigerung gegen das NS-Regime in München* (Munich: Buchendorfer Verlag, 1998), 258–59. See Gruner, "The Germans," 49–50. For the Hitler speech on 30 January 1939, see Max Domarus, ed., *Hitler. Reden und Proklamationen 1932–1945*, vol. 2, Untergang; 1. Halbband: 1939–1940 (Munich: Süddeutscher Verlag, 1965), 1047–67, here 1058.
67. Wiener Stadt- und Landesarchiv, Sondergericht, SHv Strafakten, No. 5067 Dr. Arthur Singer, fol. 65–66RS.
68. StA-L, 20031 Polizeipräsidium, PP-S 5004, no fols: Report Abschnittskommando Süd to Order police, 30 September 1939.
69. Gruner, "The Germans," 41–42.
70. StA Hamburg, 213-11_0648/41, Melanie Krohn, fol. 1–12.
71. She was arrested in October 1941 and held in custody until the indictment. The outcome of the trial is unknown; StA-L, 20114 Landgericht Leipzig, No. 4477: Anklage, Sondergericht Leipzig, 11.2.1942.
72. Gruner, "The Germans," 44.

Bibliography

Bauer, Yehuda. "Forms of Jewish Resistance." In *The Holocaust: Problems and Perspectives of Interpretation,* edited by Donald L. Niewyk, 3rd edn. Boston: Wadsworth Publishing, 2002, 116–132.
Brewer, John. "Microhistory and the Histories of Everyday Life." *Cultural and Social History* 7 (2010), 87–109.
Detjen, Marion. *"Zum Staatsfeind ernannt": Widerstand, Resistenz und Verweigerung gegen das NS-Regime in München.* Munich: Buchendorfer Verlag, 1998.
Domarus, Max, ed. *Hitler. Reden und Proklamationen 1932–1945.* Vol. 2, *Untergang; 1. Halbband: 1939–1940.* Munich: Süddeutscher Verlag, 1965.
Dörner, Bernward. *"Heimtücke". Das Gesetz als Waffe. Kontrolle, Abschreckung und Verfolgung in Deutschland 1933–1945.* Paderborn: Schöningh, 1998.
Dworzecki, Meir. "The Day to Day Stand of the Jews", in *Jewish Resistance during the Holocaust: Proceedings of the Conference on Manifestations of Jewish Resistance, Jerusalem, April 7–11, 1968,* Jerusalem: Yad Vashem, 1971, 152–81.
Fleiter, Rüdiger. *Stadtverwaltung im Dritten Reich: Verfolgungspolitik auf kommunaler Ebene am Beispiel Hannovers.* Hanover: Verlag Hahnsche Buchhandlung, 2006.
Friedenberger, Martin. *Fiskalische Ausplünderung: Die Berliner Steuer- und Finanzverwaltung und die jüdische Bevölkerung 1933–1945.* Berlin: Metropol Verlag, 2008.
Friedländer, Saul. *The Years of Extermination: Nazi Germany and the Jews, 1939–1945.* New York: HarperCollins, 2008.
———. *Nazi Germany and the Jews: The Years of Persecution, 1933–1939.* New York: HarperCollins, 1998.
Ginzburg, Carlo. "Microhistory: Two or Three Things That I Know about It." *Critical Inquiry* 20, no. 1 (Autumn 1993), 10–35.
Gruner, Wolf. "Die Berliner und die NS-Judenverfolgung. Eine mikrohistorische Studie individueller Handlungen und sozialer Beziehungen", in *Berlin im Nationalsozialismus. Politik und Gesellschaft 1933–1945,* edited by Rüdiger Hachtmann, Thomas

Schaarschmidt, and Winfried Süß, Beiträge zur Geschichte des Nationalsozialismus 27. Göttingen: Wallstein 2011, 57–87.

———. *Der Geschlossene Arbeitseinsatz deutscher Juden. Zwangsarbeit als ein Element der Verfolgung 1938-1943*. Berlin: Metropol-Verlag, 1997.

———. "'The Germans Should Expel the Foreigner Hitler': Open Protest and Other Forms of Jewish Defiance in Nazi Germany." *Yad Vashem Studies* 39, no. 2 (2011): 13–53.

———. "Local Initiatives, Central Coordination: German Municipal Administration and the Holocaust", in *Networks of Nazi Persecution: Bureaucracy, Business, and the Organization of the Holocaust*, edited by Gerald D. Feldman and Wolfgang Seibel, New York, Oxford: Berghahn Books, 2005, 269–94.

———. *The Persecution of the Jews in Berlin 1933–1945: A Chronology of Measures by the Authorities in the German Capital*. Berlin: Stiftung Topography des Terrors, 2014.

———. *Widerstand in der Rosenstraße. Die Fabrik-Aktion und die Verfolgung der "Mischehen" 1943*. Frankfurt am Main: Fischer-Verlag, 2005.

———. *Öffentliche Wohlfahrt und Judenverfolgung: Wechselwirkungen lokaler und zentraler Politik im NS-Staat, 1933–1942*. Munich: Oldenbourg, 2002.

———, ed. *Die Verfolgung und Ermordung der europäischen Juden durch das nationalsozialistische Deutschland 1933–1945*. Vol. 1, *Das Deutsche Reich 1933 bis 1937*. Munich: Oldenbourg, 2008.

Halbrook, Stephen P. "Nazi Firearms Law and the Disarming of the German Jews." *Arizona Journal of International and Comparative Law* 17, no. 3 (2000), 483–535.

Kreutzmüller, Christoph. *Ausverkauf: Die Vernichtung der Jüdischen Gewerbetätigkeit in Berlin 1930–1945*. Berlin: Metropol, 2012.

Kulka, Otto Dov, and Eberhard Jäckel, eds. *The Jews in the Secret Nazi Reports on Popular Opinion in Germany, 1933–1945*. New Haven, CT: Yale University Press, 2010.

Kwiet, Konrad. "Problems of Jewish Resistance Historiography." *Leo Baeck Institute Yearbook*, 24 (1979), 37–57.

Kwiet, Konrad, and Helmut Eschwege. *Selbstbehauptung und Widerstand: Deutsche Juden im Kampf um Existenz und Menschenwürde, 1933–1945*, 2nd ed., Hamburg: Christians, 1986.

Levi, Giovanni. "On Microhistory", in *New Perspectives on Historical Writing*, edited by Peter Burke. Cambridge: Polity, 1991, 97–119.

Marrus, Michael. "Jewish Resistance to the Holocaust." *Journal of Contemporary History* 30, no. 1, (1995), 83–110.

Rozett, Robert. "Jewish Resistance." In *The Historiography of the Holocaust*, edited by Dan Stone. Houndmills, U.K.: Palgrave Macmillan, 2004, 341–63.

Vivo, Filippo de. "Prospect or Refuge? Microhistory, History on the Large Scale: A Response." *Cultural and Social History* 7 (2010), 387–97.

Willems, Susanne. *Der entsiedelte Jude: Albert Speers Wohnungsmarktpolitik für den Berliner Hauptstadtbau*. Berlin: Edition Hentrich, 2002.

Zimmermann, Moshe. *Deutsche gegen Deutsche: Das Schicksal der Juden 1938–1945*. Berlin: Aufbau, 2008.

CHAPTER 12

THE MURDER OF THE JEWS OF OSTRÓW MAZOWIECKA IN NOVEMBER 1939

Markus Roth

From the very first day of the invasion of Poland, civilians were killed, among them many Jews. Military units of the *Wehrmacht,* especially *Einsatzgruppen* (operation groups) of the *Sicherheitspolizei* (Security Police) and the *Sicherheitsdienst* (Security Service), killed members of the Polish and Jewish elite, mostly politicians, doctors, lawyers, and teachers, among others. According to Hitler's orders, the measures aimed to deprive Poland of any chance of ever rising again as a state.

These first executions were still very different from those committed in the occupied territories of the Soviet Union from the summer of 1941 onward, when the Einsatzgruppen proceeded to successively and systematically kill all Jews. However, there had already been incidents where entire Jewish communities in Poland were annihilated in the fall of 1939. One of the earliest incidents took place in November 1939 in the small town of Ostrów Mazowiecka, in northeastern Poland. Before the war, the town counted 20,500 inhabitants, of whom 7,600 were Jews. In the spring of 1940, not a single Jew lived in Ostrów Mazowiecka.[1]

As a first step, I will attempt a microhistorical reconstruction of the murderous events that happened in Ostrów Mazowiecka in November

1939, especially with regard to the perpetrators' behavior and motivations. What really took place in November 1939? What did the prehistory of mass murder resemble, and does it explain the eruption of violence? How did policemen act that day, and how did they react to the orders of murder? The example of Ostrów Mazowiecka will serve as a basis for a short discussion of microhistory's role in the history of the Holocaust and as a source for possible explanations for the perpetrators' behavior.

The First Weeks of German Occupation

Already in the first days of September, the coming war could be felt in Ostrów. Large numbers of Jewish refugees from the regions located further to the west had escaped the invading German troops and fled into town, where they waited and discussed what steps to take next. On 9 September, only one day after the first German soldiers had been spotted, SS men, who might have been members of *Einsatzkommando* 2 of *Einsatzgruppe* V, came to Ostrów.[2] They broke into Jewish houses and apartments and detained all men near the Polish secondary school. During the day, the anti-Semitic mob triumphed over the victims: Poles, some from neighboring areas, walked through the streets and pointed out to the German soldiers which houses, apartments, and shops were the property of Jewish inhabitants. The doors were then forced open, with German approval, and the mob robbed the victims.[3]

At nighttime, the Jews of Ostrów found themselves exposed to a wave of terror again. The German occupiers forced themselves into homes and ravaged them, ruthlessly killing; several people were ruthlessly killed in the aggressive frenzy.[4] On the morning of 10 September, the *Sicherheitspolizei* summoned Rabbi Singer and Tuwia Makower, the secretary of the Jewish community. When both arrived at the headquarters, the Germans used physical violence to force them to cut off each other's beards. After this humiliation, they were ordered to guarantee, on their own authority, that all Jewish men aged sixteen to sixty would assemble before the town hall by noon.

Those who did not follow the orders, they told Singer and Makower, would be shot. When the considerable crowd arrived at the marketplace, they were made to wait for hours with their hands raised above their heads. The elderly in particular were not able to withstand the exertion over a long period of time and collapsed. Soldiers regularly patrolled the area, beat people at random, and searched them for weapons. Soldiers armed with machine guns were positioned on the balconies in the vicinity.[5]

The waiting crowd was escorted in the aftermath to the yard of the Polish secondary school, where they were made to sit down. Around six o'clock, one of the Germans took the floor and announced that the town would be destroyed if any Germans were shot. No Jew could walk through the streets after six o'clock. He then ordered the crowd to go home. As people got up to obey the orders, they were fired upon. Some witnesses reported that on their way home, they ran into an unknown army group that had just arrived, which immediately opened fire on them. Panic-stricken people tried to run for safety and evade the attackers. It remains unclear how many people lost their lives that day, but according to reports, the numbers vary between twenty-one and three hundred victims.[6] After the bloody incidents, many inhabitants were determined to flee to the east; even those who were tentative about doing so had the decision made for them, as daily violence and looting continued. These refugee movements eastward were typical of the border regions in the east of occupied Poland. In some invaded areas, the local authorities now in charge even tried to aggressively accelerate these migration movements, in order to get rid of a high number of Jews at an early stage. This also applies for the areas adjacent to the southern part of East Prussia, which were considered to be the prospective territory of the *Reich*. County chiefs from East Prussia, along with the police, the *Wehrmacht*, and SS troops were therefore very eager to act according to the objectives of this goal.[7]

The county of Ostrów was one of the specific districts that was planned for annexation to the German province of East Prussia in the near future. This is why from mid-October 1939 onward, Ostrów was controlled by Heinrich von Bünau, a County Chief from Allenstein, immediately after it turned out in the end of September that the county would not become part of the Soviet-occupied territories of Poland.[8] This decision resulted in a mass exodus of refugees trying to reach the Soviet-occupied parts of Poland. The German administration, with von Bünau at the head, aimed to accept the fewest possible number of Jews in the county, instead expelling as many of them as possible. At the beginning of November, things changed again, for it was decided that the district of Ostrów would not be annexed to East Prussia, but would instead be a part of the General Government, founded on October 26. Moreover, the few hundred Jews who had stayed in Ostrów until then no longer had the opportunity to flee, because the previously open escape route to the Soviet-occupied regions of Poland was barred when the Soviets closed the border.[9]

The Mass Murder

At the beginning of November 1939, the situation became critical. In the prior weeks, the occupiers had created an atmosphere marked by violence. Jews were regarded as outlawed; their lives counted for nothing. Their property, along with the belongings of the Polish population, were declared free for looting. Already in the second half of October, County Chief von Bünau had conjured up a scenario fraught with danger: he claimed that state authority was endangered and that the police presence was too light, because there were not enough police forces at his disposal. Furthermore, he stated that the constant stream of refugees posed a danger, because they were uncontrollable.[10] He also remained suspicious of the Polish population, although, as he put it, faced with the threat of a Soviet invasion, the Poles considered the Germans as the lesser of two evils. Nevertheless, von Bünau stated:

> The efforts to get rid of the lesser evil can be observed, especially among the intelligentsia, and wherever Polish officers operate clandestinely. These people hope that in time Germany will also lose this war and that the time will then come to have the Germans make up for the injustice done to them. This is why, from the German perspective, the question of possible riots should be given maximum attention.[11]

On the same day, after von Bünau had reported his safety concerns to Warsaw, it seemed as if they had proved to be true: on 9 November, a fire broke out in the marketplace in the center of town and spread instantaneously, because the houses were mainly made of wood. Soldiers of the 217th Division were able to quickly detect the source of the fire and extinguish it, but when they left, leaving behind only Hans-Joachim Timm of *Reserve-Polizeibataillon* 11, the fire rekindled, and more houses burned down. County Chief von Bünau immediately knew who the culprits were; he neither awaited nor did what he could to further investigations on the cause of the fire. He reported the fire to Warsaw and blamed the Jews for causing it. He claimed to have been informed that "the Jews had murmured in advance that Ostrów would burn very soon."[12]

Regardless of the cause, the fire provided the police and the German administration with a welcome pretext for striking their decisive blow against the few remaining Jews of Ostrów. On the same night and the following day, the police and *Reserve-Polizeibataillon* 11 arrested all Jews they could get hold of.[13] Meanwhile, in Warsaw and Kraków, the Jews' fate was decided, and their murder organized. Senior SS and Police Leader Krüger is said to have given the order over the phone to Karl Brenner, commander of the *Polizeiregiment* of Warsaw and commander of the *Ordnungspolizei* (Order Police) in the district of Warsaw, to have all Jews of Ostrów shot.[14] Brenner ordered the attending officer, Kurt Kirschner, to go to Ostrów the next day and supervise the execution. He then called for company commander Hans Hoffmann and instructed him to accompany Brenner and to recruit the firing squad in Ostrów. Theodor Pillich, a hardened Nazi functionary from the *Technische Nothilfe* (Technical Emergency Service), happened to be present and asked if he would be allowed to come to Ostrów too to watch the execution, a request that was granted.[15] After the war, Pillich testified that he had simply been curious, because he "had never before seen a man being shot. This is why I was interested in attending such an event."[16]

Since they were running out of time, Hoffmann immediately set to work and instructed a chief police officer to select thirty men who "possessed the necessary hardness" and to undertake all practical preparations.[17] Hoffmann went off to his room and a little later was joined by Kirschner, Pillich, and the regimental adjutant. The group consumed an excessive amount of alcohol and then called for Lieutenant Otto Franke, who had joined the unit only four days earlier. Hoffmann told Franke that he was expected to attend to the "execution" of Jews the next day. Franke was appalled but was derided by the others with roaring laughter. He asked to be exempted from the operation, but Hoffmann harshly rejected his request and indicated that this would be considered an act of insubordination.[18]

On the following day, the men assembled and were informed by Hoffmann that they would leave for a highly confidential special deployment. At that point, Hofmann was still concealing that the men were to murder several hundred people. Everybody left for Ostrów by bus and car, where Captain Timm probably met them. He informed Kirschner that he had had all Jews arrested and that burial pits outside of Ostrów had also been prepared the day before. According to the findings of the public prosecutor's office in Wiesbaden, it was only at this point that Kirschner was informed that more than half of those arrested were women and children.

Feeling uneasy with this, he went to County Chief von Bünau, together with Hoffmann, Pillich, and Timm, and made a call to Warsaw. Kirschner reached the commander of the *Ordnungspolizei,* Max Daume, on the phone, who unequivocally ordered that women and children were to be killed as well. Kirschner, Hoffmann, Pillich, Timm, and von Bünau had an informal meeting and discussed the details of the impending mass murder.[19]

A little later, they asked Franke to come. Hoffmann told him that a military court had come to the conclusion that the Jews were responsible for the fire in Ostrów and had sentenced them to death. Hoffmann also claimed that the regiment had already confirmed the verdict. Franke's company was designated to enforce the judgment, and he was designated to command it. When Franke again asked to be exempted from the operation, Hoffman responded very indignantly, telling him to "pull himself together" and not to "hit the wall." Hoffmann concealed that women and children were to be shot as well.[20]

Another member of the *Polizeibataillon* testified after the war that Hofmann had told the police that the Jews had lit several houses of so-called *Volksdeutsche* (ethnic Germans) on fire, killing the inhabitants.[21] In front of the assembled policemen, Hoffmann declared that a military court had just imposed the death penalty and that they were expected to enforce the judgment.[22]

That same morning, the firing squad from Warsaw was summoned to line up at the execution site, where Timm's unit formed a protective cordon around the three prepared pits. Others led the men and later the women and their children, who had been brought by bus near the execution site's pits.[23] Franke was instructed to give the order to fire, but when the first victims were escorted to the pit, the command was not given. Instead Franke, who confessed that he had never seen a dead body before, asked to be exempted from his position again. Hoffmann and Pillich shouted Franke down and threatened him with the serious consequences that would result from his insubordination. Only then did Franke comply and eventually gave the order to fire.[24]

From the very beginning, the order to kill the Jews of Ostrów turned out to be a crucial test for the policemen, who had never before been in a comparable situation. If it is to be believed what the policemen later testified to, there were a few among them who felt reluctant to shoot at the crowd of defenseless people. It seems as if Hoffman's adoption of a firm stance along with Pillich's vigorous intervention made it easier for the men—who were accustomed to clear commando structures—to obey and kill the Jews rather than to remain steadfast in their refusal, particularly in view of the enraged Hoffman and Pillich. Franke's unsuccessful attempt to be exempted from the orders may also have had a powerful effect on the men.

The policemen of both units who were involved obviously still lacked the routine surrounding mass murder, which many of them were to develop at a later stage. The executions repeatedly came to a halt, because longer periods of time passed as each new group was led to the pits. Hoffmann and Kirschner drove back to town more than once to determine the cause of the delay and to arrange for an unobstructed sequence of operations. This resulted in a new problem, because larger groups of victims arrived at the execution site, and the policemen were not able to shoot all of them at once. More and more persons were therefore shot individually, and the situation not only grew increasingly uncoordinated, but also endangered the perpetrators. Franke, who was in charge of giving the order to fire, at this point also had to coordinate the execution so that no policemen inadvertently shot a comrade.[25]

By then complete chaos had set in at the open grave. One of the men of the firing squad stated that "there were often cases where Jews who had been positioned at the edge of the pit were fired at just as members of the execution squad ran to the edge to bring back the Jews who had tried to escape. All of our officers were screaming all at once."[26] During the preliminary investigation, another policeman recalled that "after approximately the second or third order to fire, thus after three groups of Jewish men had been shot, outright panic broke out among us. My explanation for the panic is that we all lost our nerves at the sight of the first victims."[27] The men were armed with carbines and fired at the victims from a distance of several meters. This is why several people were often only wounded and others were not hit by a bullet. In the course of the examination, Pillich testified:

> During a break, when the shootings came to a halt while awaiting the arrival of new groups of victims, I had a conversation with one of the men from the firing squad in the vicinity of the pit. Suddenly I saw a Jew, it was a middle-aged man, jump out of the open grave; he tried to escape into the adjacent bushes. The policemen also noticed his attempt. Obviously the escapee was a man who had not been hit by a bullet and who had let himself fall into the pit in order to pretend to be dead. Surely, he wanted to use an unobserved moment of the break to save his life.[28]

One of the policemen caught up with the escapee and brought him back to the hole, and the latter had to climb into it to check if the others were indeed dead. The man was later shot.[29] A policeman who was involved reported another incident to the public prosecutor: "A Jew who was uninjured had let himself fall into the pit, feigning to have been hurt. A little later, this man gave himself away. I was able to observe him as he suddenly jumped out of the pit and called out: 'Kind Sir, cigarette, cigarette!' In accordance with the order, he was shot soon afterward."[30] From then on the policemen regularly fired into the pit at random to ensure that none of the victims had fallen into the grave lightly wounded or untouched.[31]

Toward the end of the morning, all of the detained men, the majority of them elderly, had been shot, and the policemen took a break. Hoffmann and Kirschner only now informed them that they were to shoot women and children at the other pit. Furthermore, they had deliberated with Timm on the question of how the logistics could be carried out more smoothly than before. Now the members of the firing squad were to use pistols instead, and it was ordered that they kill women and children by shooting them in the back of the neck. This new level of escalation generated great unease among the policemen. Pillich, who was not authorized to give any instructions, responded to the critical voices that arose questioning the lawfulness of the operation. With reference to the failed assassination attempt on Hitler in the *Bürgerbräukeller* in Munich, he berated the Jewish children by calling them "a brood" that needed to be annihilated. Moreover, he threatened that anyone who refused to obey would be shot. Hoffmann and Kirschner joined him in the threats. However, the ones who steadfastly continued to disobey were assigned the task of transporting the victims to the execution site. Apart from that, refusal did not lead to any further consequences.[32]

The women and children were brought out of town by bus and had already heard the sound of gunfire, either there or during the bus ride over. The bus driver reported that "there was a great clamor in the bus, emotionally draining scenarios happened."[33] Right in the middle of the street, they had to get off the bus in groups, had to hand over their valuables, and were led to the edge of the pit, where they were shot in the neck. Although it seems as if the protests against Hoffmann's and Pillich's orders had successfully been suppressed, the policemen remained reluctant while carrying out the murder and showed signs of fatigue. Some of them snuck away from the pit, went to the street, and helped "to lead the people to be shot to the execution site and to at least get away from the shootings."[34] When more and more men shirked their duties, Franke convinced Hoffmann to replace them with policemen from Timm's company. Some of them were troubled by the task itself, and the execution became even more burdensome by the attendance of Pillich, who indulged in tirades against the victims, killing some of them and especially taking photographs of the execution.[35]

In the afternoon, after they had accomplished their murderous deed, all of the policemen assembled in a restaurant in Ostrów. Most of them had lost their appetite and drank alcohol in silence, among them many men who were still indignant at the nature of the operation and the circumstances under which it had been carried out. Meanwhile, Timm's company was busy removing all traces of what had taken place. They covered the bodies with lime and filled up the pits. Throughout the day, the soil around the mass graves had turned into blood-soaked earth. The men in charge poured oil on the earth and set it alight; the fire was visible even from a great distance.[36] The policemen from Timm's company kept the area under surveillance for a longer period of time, until the mass graves were no longer discernible at first sight.[37]

On the very same day, County Chief von Bünau, who himself had watched the shootings,[38] informed the public about the mass murder. He had an informational panel put up, which read: "By judgment of the military court of Warsaw, all people found guilty of having caused the arson fire in Ostrów, their accomplices, and confidants were executed today. I hereby point out that any act of sabotage will be punished by death."[39] For the first time, ordinary men had annihilated an entire Jewish community—including men, women, and children—and taken photographs and informed the public afterward.

At that point in time, during the fall of 1939, acts like these were not yet considered a normality of the war, a fact that was to change only one and a half years later. Furthermore, the distribution of tasks and responsibilities, as well as the collaboration of the *Wehrmacht*, SS, and the police, was not clarified in detail and did not always work without impediments. In the course of the invasion of Poland and the crimes committed by *Einsatzgruppen* of the *Sicherheitspolizei*, conflicts between the *Wehrmacht* and the SS arose, triggered by the army's fears that their morality might be undermined and by the fact that the SS and police formations were not yet sufficiently well-informed about the wide-ranging orders.[40]

The murders in Ostrów generated investigations and reports, hardly any of which are available today. The operation had been observed very closely within the *Wehrmacht*, with some of its members even present at the execution site, including the local regimental adjutant.[41] On 15 November, only four days before the crime, Lieutenant General Max von Schenckendorff composed an extensive statement to the *Oberost* (commander in chief), reporting on the events leading up to the execution and how it was carried out. Schenckendorff referred to the details provided by local members of the Wehrmacht, as well as those given by Timm and von Bünau; he ended his report by emphasizing that "the troops were not involved in the execution."[42] The occurrences at Ostrów came to be known by high-ranking members of the Wehrmacht. During meetings in January and February 1940, von Brauchitsch remonstrated with Himmler regarding the mass murders in Ostrów and two of the latter's other "misdemeanors." This did not lead to any further consequences, and there are no known details of the conversation.[43] Six days after the execution, on 17 November, Himmler himself told Hitler about what had happened in Ostrów, either to boast or to retroactively legitimize the mass murders.[44]

After the Mass Murders

Apart from a few Jews dispersed among the area and living in hiding, the town of Ostrów was considered completely "free of Jews." Soon after, County Chief von Bünau was redeployed to East Prussia, and in December 1939 he was replaced with Gerhard Littschwager. Littschwager promoted vigorous action against the five hundred remaining Jews in the area. He threatened to concentrate them in one place, where they would "be allocated purposeful work."[45] The directive produced the desired effect, as most Jews quickly left the county, with the rest doing so by the end of April 1940. On taking stock of the results of the first months of German occupation, Littschwager proudly emphasized that "Ostrów is the only county of the Generalgouvernement that shows no signs of Jewish settlement anymore."[46] Yet it took more time until the last remaining traces of the mass murders were covered. Only in 1944 did SS men, possibly members of the so-called *Sonderkommando 1005*—accompanied by Jewish inmates from Treblinka who had arrived in Ostrów—open the mass graves, burn the human remains, and plant trees to disguise the execution site.[47]

Although the traces had been removed, it was impossible to conceal the mass murders of Ostrów from anyone at that point in time. By the fall and winter of 1939, what had happened in Ostrów had already transpired far beyond the borders of the town. Proof of the wide circulation of information is the fact that in Warsaw, Emanuel Ringelblum noted in his diary at the beginning of December 1939 that six hundred Jews from Ostrów are said to have been shot with machine guns outside of the town.[48] The Polish underground composed a report about the period of occupation until the end of October 1940 and sent it to the government-in-exile. In their publication, Ostrów is only one example in a list of German mass crimes committed in Poland. It further described how a Jewish warehouse in Ostrów containing confiscated goods had burned down and that six hundred Jews had consequently been driven out of the town and shot, with the wounded being buried alive.[49] In London, the Polish government-in-exile published several "Black Books" in order to inform the global public.[50]

Through Polish smugglers from the region, news about the murder of the Jews of Ostrów also reached those who had fled into Soviet-occupied areas by September or October 1939.[51]

For most of the perpetrators involved, Ostrów was just an "episode" in their lives. Only the members of the *Polizeibataillon* remained in the area for a longer period of time. This battalion later became part of the genocide of the Jews in the Soviet Union and the war against the civilian population, which was often camouflaged as *Bandenkampf* (fighting bandits).⁵²

However, for most of the policemen in *Polizeibataillon* 91, Ostrów was only a one-day operation. Like many other *Polizeibataillon,* they were later involved in the murder of Jews, as well as in the war against the civilian population in other places, especially in the Soviet Union.⁵³

It is difficult to determine the extent to which the mass murders in Ostrów in the autumn of 1939 served as an initiation to killing and whether they propelled the severe brutalization of individuals or groups as a whole. This difficulty results from the fact that there are gaps in the sources concerning individual policemen as well as military units. No Jewish eyewitnesses survived, and there are no Polish eyewitness accounts.

Owing to the fact that the sources are incomplete, a microhistorical study of the murders in Ostrów is limited, because it can only be based on the accounts of the culprits, which were composed and submitted after the war as part of the prosecution of the main perpetrators. This context strongly influenced the reports, which are marked by attempts at justification, omissions, and lies. Yet at the same time, not evaluating these problematic sources means silencing the murders of the Jews of Ostrów and overlooking the crime.

The case also raises questions concerning the perpetrators. Why did ordinary policemen shoot men, women, and children? Why apparently did none of them refuse obedience to their superiors? What role did ideology and especially anti-Semitism play? These questions to some degree need answers other than those provided by Christopher Browning in his explanation of the mass murder committed by the policemen of *Reserve-Polizeibataillon* 101.⁵⁴ Unlike the *Einsatzgruppen* and the *Polizeibataillon* in the summer of 1941, in Ostrów there was no routinization of killing or brutalization, like the one undergone by "ordinary men." The setting in Ostrów was quite different. The policemen arrived a few days before the mass murder; there was no time for a deeper radicalization in the face of local circumstances or for a long-lasting racial war. The police unit in Ostrów, unlike *Reserve-Polizeibataillon* 101, had recently been formed, and its members did not share common experiences in violence and anti-Jewish acts. It seems that in Ostrów the superiors exerted a great deal of pressure; a familiar atmosphere conducive to dissenting from orders, as one may see in the *Reserve-Polizeibataillon* 101, did not exist. It remains uncertain whether the reference to the failed assassination attempt on Hitler or the fire allegedly caused by the Jews was of special importance to the policemen. The case of Ostrów took place over a year before the beginning of the Final Solution and its mass murder. The policemen in Ostrów did not do what many policemen did in the East, as in 1942. They did what nearly no other policeman had done at that time: they killed all of the Jewish men, women, and children in a certain city. Hence, the case of Ostrów raises more questions than research can answer.

Markus Roth, Ph.D., is a historian and since 2010 the deputy head of the Arbeitsstelle Holocaustliteratur at the University of Gießen (Centre for Holocaust Literature). From 2008 to 2012 he was researcher at the Herder-Institut in Marburg. His recent publications include *"Ihr wißt, wollt es aber nicht wissen". Verfolgung, Terror und Widerstand im Dritten Reich* (C.H. Beck Verlag, 2015); *Judenmord in Ostrow Mazowiecka. Tat und Ahndung* (with Annalena Schmidt; Metropol Verlag, 2013); Konrad Heiden. *Eine Nacht im November 1938. Ein zeitgenössischer Bericht* (coedited; Wallstein Verlag, 2013); Friedrich Kellner. *"Vernebelt, verdunkelt sind alle Hirne". Tagebücher 1939–1945* (coedited; Wallstein Verlag, 2011).

Notes

1. Population figures are quotes from Marcin Urynowicz, "Ludność żydowska w Jedwabnem. Zmiany demograficzne od końca XIX wieku do 1941 roku na tle regionu łomżyńskiego" [The Jewish population in Jedwabne: Demographic changes since the end of the nineteenth century until 1941 in the region Lomza], in *Wokół Jedwabnego* [Around Jedwabne], vol. 1, ed. Machcewicz Paweł and Krzysztof Persak (Warsaw: Instytut Pamięci Narodowej, 2002), 87f.
2. Klaus-Michael Mallmann, Jochen Böhler, and Jürgen Matthäus, *Einsatzgruppen in Polen. Darstellung und Dokumentation* (Darmstadt: Wissenschaftliche Buchgesellschaft, 2008), 52; Maria Wardzyńska, *Był rok 1939. Operacja niemieckiej policji bezpieczeństwa w Polsce Intelligenzaktion* [The year was 1939: Operation of German Security Police in Poland] (Warsaw: Instytut Pamięci Narodowej, 2009), 54. According to Wardzyńska, Einsatzgruppe V did not come to Ostrów before September 15, whereas Mallmann et al. state that the exact date is not known.
3. Jakob Widelec, "A Diary of Four Weeks with the Nazis in Ostrow," in *Memorial Book to the Jewish Community Ostrów Mazowicka*, accessed 18 October 2011, http://www.jewishgen.org/yizkor/ostrow/ost409.html.
4. Ibid. See also the report by Tuwia Makower, "Surviving the War (Under the Nazis)", in *Memorial Book to the Jewish Community Ostrów Mazowicka*, accessed 7 July 2016, http://www.jewishgen.org/yizkor/ostrow/ost409.html#Page415.
5. On the events of 10 September 1939, see also the reports by Jakob Widelec, Tuwia Makower, Benjamin Goldsztejn, Abraham Jakubowski, Noach Laska, Chana Lewitt, Chaim Ciechanowiecki, and Szmul Konopiaty in *Memorial Book to the Jewish Community Ostrów Mazowicka*, accessed 18 October 2011, http://www.jewishgen.org/yizkor/ostrow/ost429.html; Losy Żydów Ostrowi-Mazowieckiej podczas okupacji niemieckiej. Relacja Helena Najmark, 14.8.1945, Archiwum Żydowskiego Instytutu Historycznego (AŻIH) 301/738, Bl. 3.

6. Ibid. Martin Gilbert, *Endlösung. Die Vertreibung und Vernichtung der Juden. Ein Atlas* (Reinbek: Rowohlt, 1995), 33 (map 29).
7. Michał Grynberg, *Żydzi w rejencji ciechanowskiej 1939–1942* [The Jews in Ciechanów District 1939–1942] (Warsaw: Państwowe Wydawnictwo Naukowe, 1984), 28f.
8. Report of the County Chief, November 11, 1939, Archiwum Państwowe m.st. Warszawy (APW), Kreishauptmannschaft Ostrow 16, 18v.–19v.
9. Report of the County Chief, 28.10.1939, APW, 3v. The exact number of Jews remaining in the town is unknown. It is assumed that there were at least 370 people.
10. Report of the County Chief, 21.10.1939, APW, 1.
11. All translations from the German are by the author. Report of the County Chief, 9.11.1939, APW, 20.
12. Höheres Kommando z.B. V. XXXV an Oberost, Bericht über die Vorgänge in Ostrow-Mazowiecka am 9.11., Abschrift, 15.11.1939, Bundesarchiv-Militärarchiv (BA-MA), RH 20-18/14, 2.
13. Ibid., 31; Höheres Kommando z.B. V. XXXV an Oberost, Bericht über die Vorgänge in Ostrow-Mazowiecka am 9.11., Abschrift, 15.11.1939, BA-MA, RH 20-18/14, 2.
14. Interrogation of Kurt Kirschner, 2.3.1960, Hessisches Hauptstaatsarchiv Wiesbaden (HHStAW), Abt. 468, Nr. 403/2, 216; Auszug aus der Gegenüberstellung, 9.6.1960, ibid., Nr. 403/5, 589.
15. Der Oberstaatsanwalt Wiesbaden an das Landgericht Gießen, Anklageschrift, 27.12.1961, Bundesarchiv Ludwigsburg (BAL), B 162/4670, fol. 1, 31f.
16. Interrogation of Theodor Pillich, 20.12.1961, HHStAW, Abt. 468, Nr. 403/10, 165.
17. Interrogation of J.K., 16.2.1960, HHStAW, Abt. 468, Nr. 403/2, 159.
18. Interrogation von Otto Franke, 22.2.1960, HHStAW, Abt. 468, Nr. 403/2, p. 1987; Der Oberstaatsanwalt Wiesbaden an das Landgericht Gießen, Anklageschrift, 27.12.1961, BAL, B 162/4670, fol. 1, 32–34.
19. Der Oberstaatsanwalt Wiesbaden an das Landgericht Gießen, Anklageschrift, 27.12.1961, BAL, B 162/4670, fol. 1, 35f.
20. Ibid., 36f.
21. Interrogation of H.H., 23.3.1960, HHStAW, Abt. Nr. 468, Nr. 403/3, 302.
22. Interrogation of R.D., 5.4.1961, HHStAW, Abt. Nr. 468, Nr. 403/8, 1005; Vernehmung von E.T., 5.2.1960, BAL, B 162/4852, 101f.
23. Interrogation of H.D., 23.3.1960, HHStAW, Abt. Nr. 468, Nr. 403/3, 299.
24. Interrogation of E.T., 5.2.1960, BAL, B 162/4852, Bl. 102; Der Oberstaatsanwalt Wiesbaden an das Landgericht Gießen, Anklageschrift, 27.12.1961, BAL, B 162/4670, fol. 1, 38f.
25. Der Oberstaatsanwalt Wiesbaden an das Landgericht Gießen, Anklageschrift, 27.12.1961, BAL, B 162/4670, fol. 1, 39.
26. Interrogation of R.D., 8.11.1961, HHStAW, Abt. 468, Nr. 403/10, 120.
27. Interrogation of G.T., 9.11.1961, HHStAW, Abt. 468, Nr. 403/10, 128.
28. Interrogation of Theodor Pillich, 6.10.1961, HHStAW, Abt. 468, Nr. 403/10, 50f.
29. Ibid.
30. Interrogation of G.T., HHStAW, Abt. 468, Nr. 403/10, 129.
31. Der Oberstaatsanwalt Wiesbaden an das Landgericht Gießen, Anklageschrift, 27.12.1961, BAL, B 162/4670, fol. 1, 44.
32. Der Oberstaatsanwalt Wiesbaden an das Landgericht Gießen, Anklageschrift, 27.12.1961, BAL, B 162/4670, 40f.
33. Interrogation of H.D., 13.12.1960, HHStAW, Abt. 468, No. 403/6, 857.
34. Interrogation of W.Sch., 13.12.1960, HHStAW, Abt. 468, No. 403/6, 854.
35. Der Oberstaatsanwalt Wiesbaden an das Landgericht Gießen, Anklageschrift, 27.12.1961, BAL, B 162/4670, fol. 1, 41f.

36. See interrogation of F.P., 12.12.1960, BAL, B 162/4854, 462; interrogation of Theodor Pillich, 6.10.1961, HHStAW, Abt. 468, Nr. 403/10, 51; interrogation of R.D., 5.4.1961, HHStAW, Abt. 468, Nr. 403/10, 1006.
37. See interrogation of Hans-Joachim Timm, 27.2.1962, HHStAW, Abt. 468, Nr. 403/11, 244.
38. See interrogation of Heinrich von Bünau, 28.3.1961, HHStAW, Abt. 468, Nr. 403/7, 953.
39. Bekanntmachung, 11.11.1939, quoted from: Urteil des Landgerichts Gießen, 3.12.1963, in *Justiz und NS-Verbrechen*, 566.
40. For more information, see Mallmann, Böhler, and Matthäus, *Einsatzgruppen*, 54–69.
41. Interrogation of Heinrich von Bünau, 28.9.1961, HHStAW, Abt. 468, Nr. 403/8, 1120.
42. Höheres Kommando z.B. V. XXXV an Oberost, Bericht über die Vorgänge in Ostrow-Mazowiecka am 9./11.11., Abschrift, 15.11.1939, BA-MA, RH 20-18/14, 2.
43. Wilhelm Krausnick, *Hitlers Einsatzgruppen. Die Truppen des Weltanschauungskrieges 1938–1942*. (Frankfurt am Main: Fischer, 1985), 81.
44. Besprechungsnotiz RFSS vom 17. November 1939, Bundesarchiv Berlin (BAB), NS 19/1447.
45. Report of the County Chief, 17.2.1940, APW, Kreishauptmannschaft Ostrów 16, 38.
46. General report of the County Chief, 28.6.1940, APW, Kreishauptmannschaft Ostrów 16, 47.
47. Der Oberstaatsanwalt Wiesbaden an das Landgericht Gießen, Anklageschrift, 27.12.1961, BAL, B 162/4670, fol. 1, 46.
48. Emanuel Ringelblum, *Kronika getta warszawskiego. Wrzesień 1939—Styczeń 1943* [Chronicle of the Warsaw Ghetto, September 1939–January 1943], ed. Artur Eisenbach (Warsaw: Czytelnik, 1983), 36.
49. Działalność władz okupacyjnych na terytorium Rzeczypospolitej w okresie 1 IX 1939–1 XI 1940. Raport z archiwum politycznego prof. Stanisława Kota, Janusz Gmitruk and Jerzy Mazurek (Warsaw: Muzeum Historii Polskiego Ruchu Ludowego, 1999), 216.
50. *The Black Book of Poland* (New York: G.P. Putnam's Son, 1942), 224.
51. E.g., the reports of Chaim Słomka (AŻIH 301/4099/B), Ida Słomka (AŻIH 301/4094/B), and Mosze Surowicz (AŻIH 301/4096/B).
52. See, for instance, Stefan Klemp, *"Nicht ermittelt". Polizeibataillone und die Nachkriegsjustiz. Ein Handbuch* (Essen: Klartext, 2005), 108–11; Wolfang Curilla, *Die deutsche Ordnungspolizei und der Holocaust im Baltikum und in Weißrussland 1941–1944* (Paderborn: Schöningh, 2006), 151–81.
53. Klemp, *"Nicht ermittelt,"* 206–11; Curilla, *Der Judenmord in Polen und die deutsche Ordnungspolizei 1939–1945* (Paderborn: Schöningh, 2011), 544–48; Curilla, *Ordnungspolizei*, 644–49.
54. Christoper Browning, *Ordinary Men: Reserve Police Battalion 101 and the Final Solution in Poland* (New York: HarperCollins, 1998), 159–89.

Bibliography

Browning, Christopher. *Ordinary Men: Reserve Police Battalion 101 and the Final Solution in Poland*. New York: HarperCollins, 1998.

Curilla, Wolfang. *Der Judenmord in Polen und die deutsche Ordnungspolizei 1939–1945*. Paderborn: Schöningh, 2011.

———. *Die deutsche Ordnungspolizei und der Holocaust im Baltikum und in Weißrussland 1941–1944*. Paderborn: Schöningh, 2006.

Gilbert, Martin. *Endlösung. Die Vertreibung und Vernichtung der Juden. Ein Atlas*, Reinbek: Rowohlt, 1995.
Grynberg, Michał. *Żydzi w rejencji ciechanowskiej 1939–1942* [The Jews in Ciechanów District 1939–1942]. Warsaw: Państwowe Wydawnictwo Naukowe, 1984.
Klemp, Stefan. *"Nicht ermittelt". Polizeibataillone und die Nachkriegsjustiz. Ein Handbuch*. Essen: Klartext, 2005.
Krausnick, Wilhelm. *Hitlers Einsatzgruppen. Die Truppen des Weltanschauungskrieges 1938–1942*. Frankfurt am Main: Fischer, 1985.
Mallmann, Klaus-Michael, Jochen Böhler, and Jürgen Matthäus. *Einsatzgruppen in Polen. Darstellung und Dokumentation*. Darmstadt: Wissenschaftliche Buchgesellschaft, 2008.
Ringelblum, Emanuel. *Kronika getta warszawskiego. Wrzesień 1939—Styczeń 1943* [Chronicle of the Warsaw Ghetto, September 1939–January 1943]. Edited by Artur Eisenbach. Warsaw: Czytelnik, 1983.
Urynowicz, Marcin. "Ludność żydowska w Jedwabnem. Zmiany demograficzne od końca XIX wieku do 1941 roku na tle regionu łomżyńskiego" [The Jewish population in Jedwabne: Demographic changes since the end of the nineteenth century until 1941 in the region Lomza]. In *Wokół Jedwabnego* [Around Jedwabne], vol. 1, ed. Machcewicz Paweł and Krzysztof Persak, Warsaw: Instytut Pamięci Narodowej, 2002, 83–104.
Wardzyńska, Maria. *Był Rok 1939. Operacja niemieckiej policji bezpieczeństwa w Polsce Intelligenzaktion* [The year was 1939: Operation of German Security Police in Poland]. Warsaw: Instytut Pamięci Narodowej, 2009.

Chapter 13

ÉCHIROLLES, 7 AUGUST 1944
A Triple Execution

Tal Bruttmann

On 9 August 1944, the obituary column of the *Petit Dauphinois,* the most important daily newspaper in Grenoble and the surrounding area, informed readers that "the Parti Populaire Français [French People's Party, or PPF[1]] and the Jeunes de l'Europe Nouvelle [Youth of New Europe, or JEN] wish to announce the death of René Tirolle, assassinated in cowardly fashion on 7 August 1944." Two of the most active ultra-collaborationist[2] groups in Grenoble were paying homage to the man who had been shot by a cyclist in broad daylight in the city center at 13:15 PM, as recorded in a memo from the office of the prefect, which added that the deceased was an "agent of the German police," which was already present at the scene.[3]

The man executed in this way by the French Resistance was in fact a central leader of ultra-collaborationist teams working for *Sicherheitspolizei-Sicherheitsdienst* (Sipo-SD, German police/intelligence). As recently as the previous day, he and other Sipo-SD agents had interrogated a Resistance member, whom he had arrested.[4] The decision to execute Tirolle appears to have stemmed from his role in the 6 May arrest of Albert Séguin de Reyniès, chief of the Armée Secrète (Secret Army). In fact, Tirolle was a member of both the PPF and the SD, as well as close to Guy Eclache, the JEN leader.

Committed Militants

The JEN, which was founded on a national level by Marc Augier as a youth section of the *Groupe Collaboration,* held a singular position in Grenoble. It was closely linked to Eclache, a main local ultra figure with numerous political affiliations (the PPF and the Milice française).[5] He also held a number of positions, including regional director of the JEN, where he led the protection group, which in 1944 consisted of two *Beaux Arts* (fine arts) students: 20-year-old Jean Delphin and 21-year-old Jean-Pierre de Cayeux. Eclache also worked as a recruiter for the Waffen-SS and was a member of the Grenoble Sipo-SD. After several months working for the Second Service of the Milice, which fought against Jews and the Resistance alongside the Germans, he formed his own unit in early June 1944, at the age of twenty-six. Adopting the name "Lieutenant Luc Siffer," he assembled a group of men, including members from the JEN protection group he commanded and from the protection unit of the collaboration group, which was led by Georges Morel, a 24-year-old intelligence specialist. The unit totaled approximately twenty young men, most of whom had previously participated in the Jeunesse de France et d'Outremer (Youth of France and Overseas, or JFOM), of which Morel was the secretary for Grenoble. The JFOM, which was founded in 1941, was one of Vichy's most radical youth organizations and had anti-Semitism as one of its founding tenets. In 1943 the JFOM served as the foundation of the Avant-Garde, the youth branch of the newly created Milice. Eclache's men were not new to activist collaboration, either in the ranks of the JFOM, the Milice, or the other groups and movements that were part of the collaboration; nor were they new to anti-Semitism, as most had demonstrated repeatedly since 1940, in increased acts of violence against both property and people.[6]

Eclache's unit took shape within a few days and became a veritable paramilitary unit equipped by the Germans. German contributions included navy blue uniforms and caps featuring the SS *Totenkopf.* This was not the only symbol borrowed from Nazism by the JEN, whose uniforms were also decorated with the *Lebensrune,* the "life rune," which Marc Augier adopted for his movement. Each man was supplied with a pistol and a rifle, and several submachine guns and even a machine gun were also provided. The unit was garrisoned in a building next to

Sipo-SD headquarters, which paid a monthly salary of 3,000 francs to the group's members[7]—and probably more to its leaders. One of these members summarized the tasks of the JEN: "My job consisted of conducting arrests with other comrades. Eclache was almost always there, along with Morel."[8] Beginning in mid-June, the unit launched its first operations in the city and quickly made itself known to the local population, not so much for their brutality, which was ultimately on about the same level as other groups working alongside the Germans, as for their visibility and disregard for discretion. Eclache's group acted in broad daylight and in less than three months developed such a fierce reputation that even after liberation the population of Grenoble used the term *Waffen* to refer generically to collaborationists, attributing most of the ultra's crimes to the JEN.

The unit's core group consisted of a half-dozen men. Georges Rochas and the twenty-year-old student Jean Dumas were Eclache's trusted men. There were also his bodyguards, Jean Delphin and eighteen-year-old Claude de Cayeux, who was the brother of Jean-Pierre and who until that time had been a high school student.[9] Morel focused on developing intelligence activities with some of the men. The JEN also cooperated regularly with the other French units working within the SD, especially two units originating from the PPF, of which Tirolle was one of the prominent figures.[10]

The Reprisals

Word of the execution arrived at about 2:00 PM hours on 7 August 1944, just as the JEN were finishing lunch. Eclache immediately decided to conduct reprisals.[11] According to Jean-Pierre de Cayeux, "Eclache told me to get in uniform and stand guard over the body."[12] The rest of the group left their headquarters for one of Grenoble's major squares, the Place Grenette, arriving at about 2:30 PM. André Boujet, the owner of the Café du Commerce, which was located on the square, described the scene:

> At around 2:30 PM, three black Citroën *Traction Avant* [front-wheel drive] cars arrived at the Place Grenette and stopped in front of my café. Fifteen or so individuals armed with machine guns and wearing Waffen-SS uniforms (except for two of them) got out of the vehicles. While some surrounded the square, others entered the cafés and forced the customers to leave. Once all of the consumers and passersby were grouped in the popular city square, Eclache, wearing civilian clothes, came inside my café accompanied by four Waffen, among whom I recognized Delphin, whom I had often seen in the

neighborhood. They began checking documents, followed by a search of some individuals. Everyone caught in the roundup was led, one by one, into my café to present their identity cards to Eclache. They entered on the Place Grenette and left through a door leading to the Passage des Jacobins. During this time, Delphin was searching passersby.[13]

In the course of this operation, four men were taken to the rear of the café, where Jean Delphin and Claude de Cayeux guarded them at pistol-point. Three Jews and a Spaniard had been "selected." With the operation over, the four men were loaded into the Citroëns, which left the city center and headed for the aerodrome in the municipality of Échirolles, on the city's outskirts.

The four men were taken to one of the hangars at the aerodrome, where a firing squad was formed under Eclache's command. According to Claude de Cayeux, in addition to himself there were also present Jean Dumas, André Guillot-Sestier, Delphin, Rochas, Jacques Bureau, and a certain Marcellin.[14] According to Delphin, the firing squad was made up of de Cayeux, Georges Pillet, Rochas, and three figures named as Marcellin, Le Moine, and Boiron.[15] According to de Cayeux and Delphin, one or more JEN remained outside "to guard the cars,"[16] but it is more likely that they conducted surveillance and ensured that no one approached the area.

Eclache decided to spare the Spanish prisoner. Only the three arrested Jews were shot. Two of their identities are known: Mordka "Maurice" Grinwald, an eighteen-year-old apprentice furrier born in Krasnik, Poland, who had fled Paris with his family in 1942 to seek refuge in Isère; and Maurice Brzezinski, an apprentice leather worker who was also eighteen and was also born in Poland, in the city of Brzeziny.[17] The identity of the third victim, however, a man of approximately forty, remains unknown. After the three men had been executed, the JEN stripped their bodies of any identifying signs and left the aerodrome, returning to their headquarters at approximately 4:00 or 5:00 PM.[18] The entire operation lasted less than three hours.

While the JEN was engaged in this act of "revenge" in the Place Grenette, the *Service d'ordre* of the PPF of Grenoble was also conducting its own reprisals at the Café du Capitole on the cours Jean-Jaurès, one of Grenoble's main streets. All of the café's customers were rounded up and taken to German police headquarters to have their documents checked, while the café owner and two unidentified Jews were detained. The café owner was freed twelve hours later, but we do not know the fate of the two Jews. A postwar inquiry concluded that the "two Jews were apparently shot. No specific information or testimony was discovered or gathered regarding the arrests of these two Jews."[19] This lack of any trace is unquestionably attributable to a method developed by the ultras, especially the PPF, for getting rid of bodies: "[The members of the Barbier team] also assassinated an entire series of Jews whom they threw into the Isère ... I heard them saying several times that they would attach a grenade around their victims' necks after knocking them unconscious, and then throw them into the water."[20]

Tirolle's death was thus simultaneously doubly avenged. The triple execution in Échirolles, along with the two additional likely murders, is an illustration of a greatly underestimated—if not entirely neglected—phenomenon, that of the level of anti-Semitic violence in Occupied France and the ways in which the "Final Solution" was implemented.

Beyond the Example

These two operations were by no means isolated, nor were they the first or last reprisals in which Jews were killed. They are in fact part of a long list of assassinations of Jews in response to Resistance actions. In the department of Isère alone, between the spring of 1944 and liberation (in late August 1944), roughly 120 Jews were summarily executed after being arrested or were assassinated after being detained in SD or ultra jails.[21] This includes six men in Voiron on 21–22 April 1944, two in Saint-Étienne-de-Crossey on 2 July, six in Bourg-d'Oisans on 15 August, as well as a family of four, including two women and a child, in Grenoble on 18 August 1944, without even mentioning dozens of individual executions. This was not an isolated phenomenon unique to the men occupying positions in Grenoble, as several hundred Jews were killed in Lyon during the same period. Similar atrocities were committed throughout French territory over the course of 1944, some well known; seven people were executed, for example, in Rillieux-la-Pape on 29 June 1944, in reprisal for the assassination of Philippe Henriot, and thirty-six Jews were executed in the pits of Guerry in the Cher.

The twin reprisals conducted to avenge Tirolle's death highlight a particular aspect that is a recurring question with regard to the massacre of Jews in Eastern Europe,[22] but one that is rarely discussed for France. In fact, although the triple execution at Échirolles is well documented (witnesses, reports recording the facts, interrogations of the perpetrators), nothing whatsoever is known about the second reprisal operation of the double execution by the PPF, neither the location nor the identities or bodies of the victims. As a matter of fact, numerous executions in France and other locations did not leave the faintest trace of evidence.

These summary executions, whose traces hardly extend beyond the context of local history, are seldom referred to or taken into consideration within the historical record of the Holocaust in France or more generally that of the French Occupation. Although the total number of Jewish victims assassinated on French territory is relatively low (probably two thousand to three thousand people), it is of crucial historical importance for a number of reasons.

First, they reveal the prominence of ideology and anti-Semitism among militant ultra-collaborationists, whose reputation has long been (and continues to be) more that of thugs, members of the mob, or individuals completely separated from ideological commitments (whose model is the fictional title character of Louis Malle's *Lacombe Lucien*). Militants in every country in German Europe—including members of the Hungarian Arrow Cross, the Slovak Hlinka Guard, and the Romanian Iron Guard—not only shared the ideology of the Nazis, but actively participating in the implementation of the Final Solution. France was seemingly the only country where such individuals did not strike. The hundreds of summary executions of Jews, committed by Frenchmen working for the Germans in the context of reprisals, clearly contradicts this.

One aspect of the executions in Échirolles is especially revealing. During the interrogations, the perpetrators referred to a "firing squad." The report issued by the gendarmes after the bodies were discovered, however, reveals that the murders took place in a very different way. Each of the victims bore only three bullet wounds. Mordka Grinwald and Maurice Brzezinski were executed by two bullets to the chest, near the heart, and a third to the temple. The third, unknown victim was shot once beneath the eye and once in each temple. The wounds to the victims' temples, which could not have resulted from shots fired from the front, are revealing. Far from a "firing squad," which implies a certain physical distance between executioners and their victims, as well as a dilution of the responsibility among various participants in the shooting, these executions were carried out much more cold-bloodedly, each perpetrator "offering himself" his own victim, executing "his" Jew.

These kinds of summary executions, which increased beginning in the spring of 1944, also demonstrate another integral aspect of the history of the occupation and cast doubt on the idea that there was a fundamental difference between the Eastern Front and the situation in the West. The year 1944 was marked by a repressive crackdown by the German occupation apparatus in France. Although this intensification never reached the same level of brutality as it did in Eastern Europe, it followed a similar pattern. The massacres at Oradour-sur-Glane and Tulle are the two best-known examples, yet several dozen other killings also took place, albeit with smaller death counts. As the year 1944 advanced, only the rapid liberation of French territory brought an end to this wave of repressive violence, which grew increasingly apparent as war returned to metropolitan France after four years of relative calm. This transformation of the military situation had a direct impact on behavior. The equation of Jews with the Resistance, and more broadly with the war, structured the anti-Semitism of the Nazis as well as that of ultra-collaborationists. It was one of the mechanisms, if not the primary one, at work in this explosion of violence targeting Jews. As the activity of the Resistance intensified on French soil in 1944, reprisals targeting Jews developed and multiplied and to a certain extent partially transformed how the Final Solution was implemented in France. In 1944, the Holocaust in France was not simply deportations to Auschwitz, where victims were sent to be killed, but also took place on French soil, in the form of escalating numbers of murders.

These executions ultimately shed light on a memorial bias that for seventy years has anchored Holocaust history in France, as well as how this history is understood. At a time when the implementation of the Final Solution in France and its number of casualties is being evoked, it is through the distorting lens of "deportation" that the subject is often conceived and evoked.[23] Yet deportation was not a policy but rather a means of implementing the assassination of Jews by systematically directing them toward their place of death. Emphasizing this fundamental difference makes it possible to better understand the distortion that is thereby induced. The casualty count of the Holocaust—the Nazi project to destroy the Jews—is not limited in France only to "deportees" (with all of the memorial confusion that this word carries), but includes all of the Jews assassinated in France as they were elsewhere in Europe, regardless of the way in which they were killed. Whether they were transported outside of France (i.e., "deported") or not, assassinated by bullets or by gas, it is the end result itself that must be taken into account: their death.

Translated from the French by John Angell and Arby Gharibian.

Tal Bruttmann is a researcher. He worked for the City of Grenoble from 2001 to 2011 on a project on the "Aryanization" in the Isère Départsement during the Vichy period. His works focus on the various anti-Jewish policies implemented in France between 1940 and 1944 and the "Final Solution." He has published several books on the French and German administrations. His study *Auschwitz* was published in 2015 (La Découverte).

Notes

1. Created in 1936 by Jacques Doriot, a former senior official in the French Communist Party, the PPF quickly became the most important Fascist party in the country. Its members nevertheless numbered only a few tens of thousands. In the summer of 1940, it became one of the main Parisian parties asserting total collaboration with the Reich, one that went well further than that put in place by the Vichy regime.
2. The term "ultra-collaboration" indicates parties and movements that found Vichy policy too moderate and that demanded more radical policies, as well as greater collaboration with the Nazis. Ultra-collaboration was made up essentially by "Parisian parties" such as the PPF—which were named thus because they were based in the capital, in the occupied zone, and because they did not hold back in their criticism of the Vichy government—as well as by the Milice française (French Militia).
3. Departmental Archives of Isère (ADI), 13R 945.
4. ADI, 7291W 140, dossier 50 337, deposition of Jules Reynaud, 1 March 1945.
5. Founded in January 1943, the Milice française (French Militia) represented the hard-liners among those who supported the Vichy regime. The organization was placed under the authority of the state and sought to be a kind of French SS, giving itself multiple missions (e.g., propaganda, social matters) and equipping itself with an intelligence service as well as an armed wing in order to fight against the "enemies of the Marshall" and France. The Milice became the embodiment of ultra-collaboration in the eyes of the French population, and *milicien* (militia member) became a generic term designating all ultra-collaborationists.
6. See Tal Bruttmann, *La logique des bourreaux, 1943–1944* (Paris: Hachette littératures, 2003).
7. This represents approximately three times the minimum wage. Aside from the salary, the members shared a part of the spoils collected during the arrest of Jews, transferring another part to the Germans and to their movement's treasury (see Bruttmann, *La logique*).
8. ADI, 20U 86, dossier 984, testimony of Gilbert Quillon, 16 May 1945.
9. ADI, 20U 86, dossier 984, testimony of Exertier et Moulin-Ollagnier, without date, and interrogation of Jean-Pierre de Cayeux, 21 June 1945.
10. See Bruttmann, *La logique*.
11. Musée de la Résistance et de la Déportation de l'Isère, 92.91.01.85, testimony from the interrogation of Jean Dumas.
12. ADI, 20U 86, dossier 984, interrogation of Jean-Pierre de Cayeux, 21 June 1945.
13. ADI, 7291W 320, dossier 89352, testimony of André Boujet.
14. ADI, 20U 86, dossier 984, interrogation of Claude de Cayeux, 2 July 1946.
15. ADI, 20U 86, dossier 984, statement by Jean Delphin, 23 July 1946.
16. Ibid.
17. ADI, 20U 86, dossier 984, report to the police commissioner, chief of the judicial section, 4 March 1946 and 2973W 691, dossier Mordka Grinwald.
18. ADI, 20 U 86, dossier 984, interrogation of Jean-Pierre de Cayeux, 21 June 1945. The gendarmes, alerted by the aerodrome guard, who estimated that the shootings took place around 5:00 PM, noted the assassinations at 6:30 PM (ADI, 13 R 980, Commune de Grenoble).
19. ADI, 7291W 140, dossier 55528, report to the police commissioner, chief of the judicial police section of Grenoble, 17 March 1946.
20. ADI, 20U 34, dossier 499, Depoix interrogation.
21. Bruttmann, *La logique*.

22. See, for example, Jan T. Gross, *Neighbors: The Destruction of the Jewish Community in Jedwabne* (Princeton, NJ: Princeton University Press, 2001).
23. See Tal Bruttmann, Laurent Joly, and Annette Wieviorka, eds, *Qu'est-ce qu'un déporté ? Histoire et mémoires des déportations de la Seconde Guerre mondiale* (Paris: CNRS Editions, 2009).

Bibliography

Bruttmann, Tal. *La logique des bourreaux, 1943–1944*. Paris: Hachette littératures, 2003.
Bruttmann, Tal, Laurent Joly, and Annette Wieviorka, eds. *Qu'est-ce qu'un déporté? Histoire et mémoires des déportations de la Seconde Guerre mondiale*. Paris: CNRS Editions, 2009.
Burrin, Philippe. *Ressentiment et apocalypse. Essai sur l'antisémitisme nazi*. Paris: Éditions du Seuil, 2007.
———. *La France à l'heure allemande, 1940–1944*. Paris: Editions du Seuil, 1997.
Dean, Martin. *Collaboration in the Holocaust: Crimes of the Local Police in Belorussia and Ukraine, 1941–1944*. New York: St. Martin's Press, 2000.
Delperrié de Bayac, Jacques. *Histoire de la Milice, 1918–1945*. Paris: Fayard, 1969.
Gross, Jan T. *Neighbors: The Destruction of the Jewish Community in Jedwabne*. Princeton, NJ: Princeton University Press, 2001.
Klarsfeld, Serge. *Mémorial de la déportation des Juifs de France*. Paris: B. et S. Klarsfeld, 1978.
Meyer, Ahlrich. *Die deutsche Besatzung in Frankreich 1940–1944. Widerstandsbekämpfung und Judenverfolgung*. Darmstadt: Wissenschaftliche Buchgesellschaft, 2000.

Chapter 14

The Beginning— First Massacres against the Jews in the Romanian Holocaust
Level of Decision, Genocidal Strategy, and Killing Methods regarding the Dorohoi and Galați Pogroms, June–July, 1940

Alexandru Muraru

Today, after more than seventy years, the Romanian retreat from Bessarabia and North Bukovina in 1940 is still an insufficiently analyzed event. The administration, army, and civilians were retreated in only four days, from a territory that represented one-sixth of Romania's surface area, comparable to that of today's Slovakia. This was a key event in the chronology of the Romanian Holocaust, generating a huge number of Jewish victims. This chapter will attempt to answer a number of strategic questions. What was the historical context in Romania and Bessarabia before the start of the war? What was the situation of the Romanian Jewish community? What was the "story" of the retreat from Bessarabia and North Bukovina immediately after the Soviet ultimatum? How did the persecution and terror against Jews during retreat operations take place? What were the main institutional actions of premeditated and coordinated terror and crimes against the Jews? How did the phenomenon of crime in trains take place as a method for killing Jews during the retreat? What was the main form of criminal conduct during the pogrom in Dorohoi, and using what methods? What were the strategies and actions directed toward military and civilian killings? How were the institutional details of the massacre in Galați prepared? How were the government and military used to kill Jews in transit? What do the retreat and killing of those days represent within the larger phenomenon of the Romanian Holocaust?

Before the beginning of the war, the Jewish community in Romania was the fourth largest Jewish community in the world. After two decades of aggressive anti-Semitic attitudes, Romania toward 1940 was in a state of domestic and foreign political bankruptcy. King Carol II had installed a dictatorship based on crimes and political intrigue. With no parliament or political parties, the extremists enjoyed exaggerated power, and the signs sent by foreign allies to Romania grew increasingly feeble. Romania was an inoperative state: from a military perspective it lacked a defensive structure and strong military alliances and also had a "disordered economic structure."[1] Anti-Semitic propaganda, encouraged by the far-right movement as well as by political and cultural personalities, was intensified at the end of the 1930s. Three years before the retreat, the citizenship of Jews was revoked, with 225,000 Jews thereby losing the state's protection. Romania was the first state to take this step after Nazi Germany.

Bessarabia had been subject to numerous Russian invasions over the centuries, and in 1918, after the Great War, it had become part of Romania. Bessarabia was the key to Romanian-Soviet relations. In twenty years, two hundred military incidents were recorded at the shared border, resulting in deaths and injuries. The Soviet Union used to openly speak about its legitimate right over the province between the Dniester and the Prut. On the other hand, Romanian leaders, from the party leadership to the king, would state that the province would not be yielded without war. The official proposals for retreat were rejected in April–May 1940, for reasons of political prestige.

Bessarabia was in an unprecedented situation during the interwar period. Though officially it represented a national ideal, it became a neglected, peripheral province. It was the "French Guyana of Bucharest," as the administration was "ethnically Romanianized" with corrupt or incompetent public servants.[2] Ethnic and religious minorities (e.g., Russians, Jews, Ukrainians, Ruthenians) were completely neglected, and even the majority was hostile to central authorities.

The capitulation of France was a clear signal for the Soviet Union that the invasion of northeastern Romania could no longer be delayed. The Soviet Union had massed, starting in the summer of 1940,[3] over one hundred divisions at the Romanian border.[4] Beginning in 1939, Romania had mobilized about 65 percent of its military effectives along its eastern border, representing 1.2 million men.[5]

After receiving Germany and Italy's assent, the USSR sent Romania an ultimatum on 26 June 1940 regarding the ceding of territory. Identical developments took place as part of the Ribbentrop-Molotov Pact in Finland, Poland, and the Baltic States. The ultimatum focused on two major points, the ceding of Bessarabia and North Bukovina. The Romanian answer was a hesitant one, but it quickly gave up without fight. Moreover, the refusal of the Romanian ambassador to Moscow to take the map made by the Soviets would lead to indescribable chaos, as Romania did not actually know what precise area of territory it had ceded until the retreat was over.

Though ill-prepared and weakly organized, and decapitated by Stalin's purges, the Red Army brutally entered the two provinces. The Soviets passed the Romanian border before the established date, occupying five strategic points. Numerous incidents prove that the Soviet troops opened fire, took prisoners, disarmed retreating troops, and confiscated war materials and equipment.

Romania met serious problems because of the fast pace of retreat it was forced to undertake and because of the "breaking" of military and civilian lines by the Soviets after they penetrated deep into the claimed territories. One of the most difficult problems was the ceding of a larger territory than the one established by the ultimatum and the connected debates, that is, North Bukovina and the Hertza region. Even the Nazis were surprised by this decision, which was not part of the Ribbentrop-Molotov Pact.

As a result of the Soviet Union's occupation of the two territories, Romania lost over fifty thousand square kilometers of territory and 3.7 million inhabitants from its population. Ethnic minorities represented half of the population, with almost 300,000 Jews living there.

The persecution and terror against the Jews started before the retreat proper. The authorities decided in May 1940 that in the event of the territory's evacuation, the "unsympathetic minority population would remain at the location." This statement clearly referred to Jewish communities. Romanian Jews were thus abandoned to the Soviets in advance and with premeditation. Civilians began discussing the possibility of evacuation and, implicitly, the hostile attitude of the authorities toward Jews. On the day of the retreat, the authorities reinforced the decision indicating that "no Jew is allowed to pass"[6] and warned, at about the same date, that "more serious anti-Semitic manifestations from the army are not excluded." An official warning actually announced the implication of the army.

In Bessarabia and Bukovina, German propaganda (one hundred thousand ethnic Germans lived there) wreaked havoc in favor of alignment with the Reich's politics. Thus, in the months before the war started, an important number of ethnic Germans (illegally) enrolled in the Wehrmacht and the Waffen-SS. Anti-Semitic actions were also well known. Military informational periodicals and journals were distributed constantly within the Romanian army in Bessarabia and Bukovina. *Information Journal about German Action in Romania* had been published monthly. Further proof is provided by the implication of German minority leaders: according to the informative notes of the police and secret services, Emil Strobel, Alexander Bross, Oskar Kehrer, and Ernst Bohnet were frequently accused of aggressive German propaganda. In the context of Soviet danger, public guardians in many localities often refused to erase the messages drawn in public places by pro-Nazi groups. At the beginning of July 1941, military documents mentioned a specific case in Chișinău, where the message "Long live Hitler, Come to us too!" was discovered, with the authorities refusing to erase it. Moreover, the retreat from Poland had brought in many Jews, and the stereotype of their affiliation with communism continued to grow.[7]

The retreat was a complete chaos. The soldiers were asked not to respond to possible aggressions or to destroy anything. Aside from the terrible propaganda, Soviet military and secret agents humiliated, robbed, and killed dozens of Romanian soldiers and officers.[8] The number of desertions in connection with the retreat was huge, numbering fifty thousand. Romanian authorities blamed Jewish paramilitary groups for the soldiers who were killed or wounded or who had disappeared. The propaganda and terror of those days, along with the national failure and widespread disorder, make it almost impossible today to make a fair evaluation of the number of people who were killed or who deserted.

The army spoke of acts of violence, agitation, instigation to violence, destruction, and robbery committed by the "Communist Jews" in several cities (Cernăuți, Chișinău, Vijnița, Storojineț, Hotin, Soroca, Bălți, Tighina, Comrat, Cetatea Albă, Ismail) or in other smaller villages on the Bessarabian bank of the Prut. It is clear from the hundreds of documents I consulted that in the majority of cases, everything was made up to cover the disaster of the retreat, which was caused by the chaos of withdrawal orders from the central authorities or by the betrayal of officers who abandoned their units. The easiest way to avoid penalties or even military court sanctions was to emphasize the Jews in reports or retreat documents, and Jews thus became scapegoats for everything.

For the "tens of thousands of Communist Jews" in Moldova, there are no names or evidence, nor even exact data. It is obvious that the interwar Romanian Communist Party, which counted several hundred members and was considered illegal, could not have organized such attacks against the Romanian authorities.[9]

In other cases, the civilian population took advantage of the authority vacuum (from several hours to one to two days) to rob the institutions and valuables left behind in the retreat. In many situations, the ethnic majority of Romanians were taking revenge against those who were supposed to defend them from the Russians and thus received the Romanian troops with hostility. In other cases, ethnic Russians, Ukrainians, Bulgarians, Jews, and Gagauz manifested their frustration from years and years of humiliation at the hands of the Romanian state.

The bureaucratic system of the Romanian state was unable to organize an effective retreat; contradictory orders, long wait times, and last-second changes to the retreat plans led to a collapse. The detachments that did not wait for new orders had the most effective retreat; these troops reported almost no aggressions by the Jews.[10] Many officers fled from the Russians' path, abandoning their troops, and thus the so-called aggressions of the "Communist Jews" were nothing but pure invention to mask the inefficiency and failure of the retreat. Official Romanian propaganda even mentioned fourteen-year-old children with grenades in their pockets[11] and small groups of Jews who managed to stop regiments of thousands of armed soldiers.[12]

Their religious and political leaders confirmed the institutional premeditation of terror and crimes against the Jews. Minister of the Interior Mihail Ghelmegeanu indirectly warned them when they were called to the Home Office the day before the retreat. Chief Rabbi Alexandru Şafran recounted in his memoirs:

> In reality, at the very time when the secretary received us, the orders were already given for the Jews to be thrown out from running trains and for pogroms to be started in the villages and cities of North Moldavia and Bukovina. A few hours later, just as we arrived at our homes, we learned that our people were being massacred everywhere.[13]

The phenomenon of the crimes in trains was a method for killing Jews during the retreat, with or without the implication of the authorities.[14] Many murders were committed all over the railways of Moldova. The presence of Jews in these trains was apparently unexpected, but with each case the situation grew more common. According to the decision taken in May 1940, mentioned earlier, Jews were not allowed to be part of the retreat operations. In many cases, these orders were not respected, or because of the chaos generated by the retreat, Jews tried to use trains in order to return to their community or families in the Old Kingdom or simply in an attempt to flee from the Soviets. There were cases when Jews were traveling under false identities or had paid bribes to board trains. In other cases, when passenger railroad cars were no longer available, Jews traveled in freight train cars, sometimes doing so with Romanians. From the moving trains, with refugees and dislocated troops, the victims or the dead bodies were thrown out the windows. This barbaric method helped the killers avoid criminal liability (the crimes were taking place in territory that was going to be occupied by the Soviets, thus the trace would be lost in the chaos). The conniving authorities ignored these massacres. Many such cases took place on running trains in between stations, so that the Jews died in agony or remained with severe disabilities.[15] Some of the Jews were called to their regiments and killed, and subsequently buried by the locals.

Civilians, some of them members of the social elite,[16] sometimes perpetrated crimes on the trains, and the victims were often robbed (there are reports listing the violence, aggressions, and robberies, ranging from one case up to eighty cases in a single train). Two more observations can be made here. First, the crimes and acts of violence took place in trains retreating from Bessarabia and Bukovina, as well as in trains leaving Romania for these destinations. The second aspect concerns the proportion of robberies and their victims, who were children, women, the elderly, soldiers, and civilians. Some of the railroad cars carrying Jews were marked on the outside with different messages ("Kill the Jews, for they destroyed our country"),[17] so that the aggressors would be aware of their passing.[18] Jews were identified because they often spoke in Yiddish, and rabbis were easily recognized by their specific dress. In some cases, Jews were recognized by neighbors, acquaintances, work colleagues, or the army, and in some cases there were lists of passengers boarding the train. The phenomenon of train violence and crimes also affected Jewish military and religious leaders. The rabbis were shot or beaten to death.

Aside from these murders, in Moldova, Bucharest, or in the cities of Transylvania the Jews were submitted to numerous instances of persecution and acts of violence. In the months of July and August, ravages and robbery became commonplace. Damage to Jewish shops, stores, restaurants, or private property was significant; members of the military, railroad employees, and locals participated in the robberies and acts of violence.

Aside from the crimes in trains and individual murders, the most significant instances of violence were the massacres at Dorohoi and Galați. Both Romanian military and civilians perpetrated the pogrom of Dorohoi on 1 July 1940. Dorohoi was a provincial town, with 40 percent of its inhabitants being Jews (5,800 Jews according to the 1938 census). It was the only railway and road junction connecting North Bukovina to the Old Kingdom, so it became one of the retreat roads toward Romania. Retreating Romanian troops used language to create an atmosphere of terror, fear, and general panic and managed to change the general climate of the area and to create unprecedented tension.[19] The pogrom started at the funeral of a Jewish soldier, who had died at Hertza while attempting to defend his Romanian superior. The Jewish soldiers were disarmed by the retreating Romanian military and then executed near the cemetery. The civilians who were attending the funeral—women, children, and the elderly—were executed in the mortuary where they had taken refuge.

The atmosphere in town was carefully prepared. Civilians spread rumors that the Jews had all of a sudden become Bolsheviks and, knowing about the retreat of the troops, advised Romanians to adorn their houses with crosses or to place icons in windows or Romanian flags on doors. "He probably hasn't learned the order about the Jews," an officer said about a soldier who tried to defend a Jew.[20]

Besides the 110 murders in Dorohoi (50 at the town cemetery, the rest in the most important streets and areas of the town) and tens of others in the vicinity of town, quite significant in terms of atrocity and speed, the extent of the destruction was huge, including the vandalizing of almost all Jewish shops and homes (many instances just for the soldiers' fun) and the raping of women. The witnesses say that locals and then retreating troops appropriated (the latter crowding their wagons) a great deal of goods stolen from the Jews of Dorohoi.[21] Phrases like the "Bolshevik Jews" were spread in the streets by civilians, who were used as guides by the military to identify Jewish houses (the military was coming from tens of kilometers away). Jews were shot with machine guns or pistols, including from the official army cars patrolling the town. The victims, aged between two and ninety-six, died from beating, stabbing, shooting, mutilation, or torture.

There was no trial of war criminals after 1944 for the Dorohoi pogrom that took place on 1 July 1940. Civil authorities under Ion Antonescu concluded that no Jews had been killed and that there were no weapons found on the dead bodies. The disciplinary military investigations covered up the facts. The commanding officers of the units lied, invoked the panic caused by rumors that the "Russians were coming," and spoke about acts of violence committed by the Jews. No army officer was brought before the military court.[22]

The biggest massacre during the 1940 Romanian retreat took place at Galați. This was a port on the Danube, a railway and naval junction between Bessarabia and the Old Kingdom of Romania. On 30 June 1940, there were over ten thousand refugees in the town, some of them going to Bessarabia, others coming back to Romania. Sources mention that a large number of these refugees were locals from Reni City (Bessarabian harbor city near Galați) or Jews from Galați released on 30 June from Romania and who had already arrived at Reni. These refugees were forced to stay by local authorities, and a transit camp was improvised next to the railway station. Without specific conditions for such a difficult organization, the authorities decided that these refugees, who wanted to be repatriated to Bessarabia, should be gathered in this transit camp, a kind of a former marketplace surrounded by a fence. This was created on an enclosed plot of land, where the refugees were kept under the pretext that there were not enough means for their movement and that specific new orders were expected regarding their repatriation. It was known that the army coordinated withdrawal operations and that the refugees were kept there without food or water until the day of 30 June.

I studied the criminal investigation file from 1950–51, and I can say that the massacre was premeditated through local decisions. The preparation of the massacre was made with the collaboration of the army, the railway administration, the navy, and the gendarmerie. Leaders from the police, the Galați gendarmerie, the army, and the general staff established the details of the massacre one day before: machine guns were brought and set up, two infantry detachments from the neighboring city of Brăila were taken there, including a machine gun company, and orders were given for the ammunition to be prepared and the weapons to be set up.[23] The soldiers in charge were selected and placed, as was the railway station guard. The ones chosen were those who had served in Bessarabia and had been humiliated by the Soviets during the retreat. On the morning of 30 June 1940, the security of the concentration camp where the refugees were confined was reinforced with a navy detachment.

At 2:30 PM the machine guns started the massacre. A few hundred of the three thousand refugees in the concentration camp (90 percent Jews; the rest Russian or Gagauz)[24] were shot down in thirty minutes. The military leaders took great care with the massacre and personally ran after those who tried to escape. The officers urged soldiers to pursue those who had fled the bullets. Civilians in the vicinity also participated, killing refugees with crowbars and clubs. The victims were shot or beaten with the stock of a gun so violently that many of the weapons were destroyed in the process. The leaders of the authorities participated, and civilians subsequently robbed the dead bodies. Their extermination continued under the official pretext that this was all due to an attack by Jewish Communists, a spontaneous riot that would have eventually reached the town.[25] The refugees were searched, and the possession of weapons was forbidden.[26]

The German consul at Galați reported to the Reich authorities on 4 July 1940 that the massacre had not ended in the improvised transit camp next to the railway station but had continued late into the night, as well as in the following days. The consul, Alfred Lorner, recounted how the survivors from the railway station tried to hide downtown and in the neighborhoods inhabited by foreign diplomats. Other spontaneous executions took place during the night in many parts of town. The Nazi official reported, "The pursuit and brutal killing of the three hundred to four hundred escaped persons who were missing, hiding in houses and gardens, continued all through that night." Moreover, according to the official, on 3 July several tramcars with Jews coming from the city were driven to the tramline terminus, in a poor neighborhood of Galați, where they were exterminated during the night.[27]

The investigation of 1940 was falsified. The prosecutor dictated the witness declarations, and nobody answered for the massacre until 1950, when the number of deaths was indicated as one thousand,[28] and not the three hundred claimed up to that point.[29] The victims were buried in a common grave the next night, near the Eternitatea cemetery in Galați. The witnesses say that the municipality's public health cars carried dead bodies to the grave for twelve straight hours.[30] This mass grave has not yet been investigated to this day.

Another unknown pogrom related to the context of the retreat from Bessarabia and North Bukovina occurred in the village of Zaharești, in the county of Suceava. Thirty-four Jews from the counties of Rădăuți and Storojineț were executed there under the command of Major Valeriu Carp.[31] Aside from the genocidal actions presented above, according to Radu Ioanid, there were also reprisals in the months of July and August 1940 in the area of Moldova.[32] For instance, in the communes of Drânceni and Răducăneni, Jews were deported to Huși, from where they were subsequently sent to labor camps.

According to Jean Ancel, although the annexation of Bessarabia and North Bukovina was rather welcomed by a number of Jews, for most of them this moment was a painful turning point in history. The life of the Jewish community in the first year of Soviet occupation was almost destroyed, and relations between Zionist organizations and groups with their counterparts across the world were censored. On 13 June 1941, thousands of Jews from all over Bessarabia, including community leaders and Zionist activists, were arrested and deported to Siberia, while their property and wealth were immediately confiscated. No Jews were allowed to keep their property or businesses.

The retreat was used by the Romanian state to build anti-Jewish propaganda. The Jewish community tried, through desperate attempts, to convince the authorities and public opinion of the huge mistake of ascribing general blame. All Jews from the Old Kingdom of Romania suddenly became Communists from the national viewpoint, and the ones in the provinces were "traitors." The rumors were fed by state institutions and political and military leaders. The retreat without a fight and the humiliation at the hands of the Soviets led to an artificial image of the fictitious culprit. The Jewish minority, which became the major "political lightning rod" meant to channel all popular frustrations generated by the retreat, embodied this fictitious culprit.[33]

The massacres of Dorohoi and Galați were clearly premeditated. They took place in the territory that Romania had not ceded and represented a way of testing the killing measures that would be used in the pogroms of Iași and Bucharest in 1941. The techniques used at Dorohoi (drawing crosses on Jewish houses, rumors that the Jews were attacking with arms or communicating with Soviet troops) and Galați represented clear aspects of carefully prepared plans. The primary order has not yet been identified in the archives, and the absence of such a document should not be surprising. Yet this does not mean that such an order did not exist, at least on a local level. During the Holocaust, most genocidal orders were not written.[34] As Christopher Browning has shown, formal laws and rulings melt into a powerful opaque and tacit network of secret, vaguely authorized, and orally communicated directives, with little further explanations. Such innuendo put the local simple bureaucrat in a position of power. Clear orders were replaced with a "problem of consonance and synchronization." The local decision makers put the implied consensus in practice, but the parameters and objectives of the genocidal actions originated from the center, where the main lines were mapped out.[35] Other historians, like Mark Roseaman[36] or Raul Hilberg, argued the relentless clockwork of bureaucracy, when "ordinary men thus came to perform extraordinary tasks," as Roseman excellent observes. For example, Hilberg explained the bureaucrats' behavior who, receiving a vague target, "displayed a striking path finding ability in the absence of directives, a congruity of activities without jurisdictional guidelines, a fundamental comprehension of the task even when there were no explicit communications."[37]

Moreover, in our case, the most important archives, those of Antonescu's secret service, which was the intermediary for the general staff, disappeared after 1944.

The involvement of the army and other public services in massacres is confirmed by many archival documents. If the orders at Dorohoi originated from the commanding officers of a legion of gendarmes and border guards, at Galați the navy and the royal resident were involved in addition to the army and the gendarmerie.

This chapter for the first time brings to light an important number of details regarding the act of genocide. The report of the Wiesel Commission for the Study of the Holocaust in Romania concluded that the number of deaths during the retreat from Bessarabia and North Bukovina in 1940 was somewhere between 136 and several hundred.[38] Relying on documents, I have shown that there were over 1,000 deaths: 200 at Dorohoi and the vicinity, dozens on the trains, and between 800 and 1,000 in the massacre of Galați, including a common grave that has not yet been investigated. Difficult access to Romanian archives until 2005–6 resulted in a lack of information regarding the real number of victims from different massacres or pogroms. In many cases, the former Communist regime selectively or completely destroyed a large number of documents to protect many secret agents who after 1944 became part of the new regime. In other situations, the opening of the archives revised the number of victims, especially in some specific cases. For example, the real number of victims for Iasi pogrom[39] (one of the biggest pogroms from the Eastern Front at the beginning of the war) is still a historiographical issue; different official documents (produced by secret services, the police, the gendarmerie, or even by German authorities) present major differences regarding the death count. Moreover, the International Commission for the Study of the Holocaust in Romania concluded in 2004, after a close study of the archives, that "between 280,000 and 380,000 Romanian and Ukrainian Jews were murdered or died during the Holocaust in Romania and the territories under its control";[40] this means that many massacres, victims, or pogroms were not sufficiently investigated given the absence of archives. Since it was a massacre that took place before the war started, it is very possible that the file of the Galați investigation has not been found until now.

The USSR invasion in 1941 was made under the banner of revenge against the Jews. Archival documents, trial testimonies, and Antonescu's official declarations confirm it.[41] It was an occasion to take revenge on Jews "in the name of the humiliations that the regiment was submitted to during the 1940 evacuation";[42] it is in these terms that the commanding officers of Romanian divisions addressed their own soldiers upon the reconquest of Bessarabia at the end of June 1941, exterminating tens of thousands of Jews in the villages of Bessarabia and Bukovina. Furthermore, one of the official argumentative pillars of Antonescu's policy of ethnic purging was revenge for the retreat. Civilians have always used this cliché—that Jews were the main guilty party. This strategy on the part of authorities ensured popular support and the population's participation in the massacre of Jews.[43] In fact, most of the Jews in Bessarabia and North Bukovina were deported and exterminated in Transnistria.

Alexandru Muraru, Ph.D., is researcher and associate professor in political science within the Alexandru Ioan Cuza University of Iasi, Romania. He was Tziporah Wiesel Fellow 2010–11 at the Center for Advanced Holocaust Studies at the United States Holocaust Memorial Museum (Washington, DC). He also received scholarships/fellowships in Jewish and Holocaust studies, political science, and nationalism and attended programs granted by or organized by prestigious universities or advanced studies centers in Europe and North America. He has published two academic books and dozens of articles and studies in Jewish and Holocaust studies, political science, and history. Since 2005 he has held important public and governmental dignities for the Romanian state.

Notes

This study was made possible through a Tziporah Wiesel Fellowship at the Center for Advanced Holocaust Studies, United States Holocaust Memorial Museum.
1. Alex Mihai Stoenescu, *Armata, mareşalul şi evreii. Cazurile Dorohoi, Bucureşti, Iaşi, Odessa* [The army, the marshall and the Jews: Dorohoi, Bucharest, Iaşi, Odessa cases] (Bucharest, 1998), 10.
2. Ibid.
3. Radu Ioanid, Tuvia Friling, and Mihail Ionescu, eds, *The Final Report of the International Commission for the Study of the Holocaust in Romania* (Iaşi, 2006), 77.
4. Raoul Bossy, *Amintiri din viţa diplomatică, 1918–1940* [Memories of the diplomatic life, 1918–1940] (Bucharest, 1993), 2:248.
5. Ioanid, Friling, and Ionescu, *The Final Report*, 81.
6. Lya Benjamin, ed., *The International Commission for the Study of the Holocaust in Romania: Documents* (Iaşi, 2005), 65.
7. Mihai Pelin, *Adevăr şi legendă* [Truth and legend] (Bucharest, 1994), 24–25.
8. Ioanid, Friling, and Ionescu, *The Final Report*, 84.
9. Pelin, *Adevăr şi Legendă*, 54–55.
10. Ibid., 42–43.
11. Response letter sent by Ion Antonescu to William Filderman, the leader of the Romanian Jewish community on 19 October 1941. Paul Goma, *Săptămâna roşie 28 iunie–3 iulie 1940 sau Basarabia şi evreii* [The Reed Week, June 28–July 3, 1940 or Bessarabia and the Jews] (Author`s Publishing House, electronic edition, 2007), 331–332.
12. Pelin, *Adevăr şi Legendă*, 52–53.

13. Stoenescu, *Armata, mareşalul şi evreii*, 101.
14. Radu Ioanid, *The Holocaust in Romania: The Destruction of Jews and Gypsies under the Antonescu Regime, 1940–1944* (Chicago, 2008), 57.
15. Matias Carp, *Cartea neagră. Suferinţa evreilor în România 1940–1944* [Black book: Jewish suffering in Romania 1940–1944], vol. 3 (Bucharest, 1996), 28.
16. The report of the case of an artist who beat up and threw a Jew from the train; for details, see *Evreii din România între 1940–1944*, vol. 3, *1940–1942: Perioada unei mari restrişti* [The Jews from Romania between 1940–1944, vol. 3, 1940–1942: The period of great tribulation] (Bucureşti, 1997), 46.
17. USHMM, RG-25.004M, reel 7, Romanian Information Service-Bucharest (SRI) records, [State Security Council, folder 2716], 422.
18. *Evreii din România între 1940–1944*, 3:40.
19. Marius Mircu, *Ce s-a întâmplat cu evreii din România?* [What happened with the Romanian Jewry?] (Bat Yam, 1996), 2:21.
20. Ibid., 2:28.
21. Ibid., 2:28–34.
22. Ioanid, Friling, and Ionescu, *The Final Report*, 92.
23. USHMM, RG-25.004M, reel 7, Romanian Information Service-Bucharest (SRI) records, [Ministry of Internal Affairs, operative archive, file 4087], 103.
24. Dennis Deletant and Ottmar Traşcă, eds, *Al III-lea Reich şi Holocaustul din România: 1940–1944: documente din arhivele germane* [The Third Reich and the Holocaust in Romania: 1940–1944: Documents from German archives] (Bucharest, 2007), 137–43 (Politisches Archis des Auswärtingen Amtes Berlin, R 103611, Pol. IV Politische Bezienhungen zwischen Rumänien und Russland, E. 387868-387879; Deutsches Konsulat Galatz, Paket 3, Heft 1, Berichterstattung Bessarabien 1939–1942).
25. USHMM, RG-25.004M, reel 7, Romanian Information Service-Bucharest (SRI) records, [Ministry of Internal Affairs, operative archive, file 4087], 29.
26. USHMM, RG-25.004M, reel 7, Romanian Information Service-Bucharest (SRI) records, [Ministry of Internal Affairs, operative archive, file 4087], 112–13.
27. Deletant and Traşcă, *Al III-lea Reich şi Holocaustul*, 137–43.
28. USHMM, RG-25.004M, reel 7, Romanian Information Service-Bucharest (SRI) records, [Ministry of Internal Affairs, operative archive, file 4087], f. 115. (and 600–700 victims in the Nazi official's report—Deletant and Traşcă, *Al III-lea Reich şi Holocaustul*, 137–43).
29. Ioanid, Friling, and Ionescu, *The Final Report*, 92.
30. USHMM, RG-25.004M, reel 7, Romanian Information Service-Bucharest (SRI) records, [Ministry of Internal Affairs, operative archive, file 4087], 279.
31. *Martiriul evreilor români, 1940–1944* [The martyrdom of the Romanian Jewry, 1940–1944] (Bucharest, 1991), 36 (see Bucharest State Archive, Ministry of Justice, County Branch, file 22-1940, f. 756–57; in the same document, as an official report, it was sent by the head of police to the Suceava prosecutor office); Aurelian Căruntu, *Bucovina în timpul celui de-al doilea război mondial* [Bukovina during World War II] (Iaşi, 2004), 145.
32. Ioanid, *The Holocaust in Romania*, 42–43.
33. Ioanid, Friling, and Ionescu, *The Final Report*, 92.
34. Deletant and Traşcă, *Al III-lea Reich şi Holocaustul*, 68.
35. Christopher Browning, *Nazi Policy, Jewish Workers, German Killers* (Cambridge, 2000), 116–18.
36. See for example, Mark Roseman, "Beyond Conviction? Perpetrators, Ideas, and Action in the Holocaust in Historiographical Perspective, in Frank Biess, Mark Roseaman, Hanna Schissler, *Conflict, Catastrophe and Continuity: Essays on Modern German History*, New York, Oxford: Berghahn Books, 2007, 86–87.

37. Raul Hiberg, *The Distruction of European Jews*, 3rd Edition, New Haven: Yale University Press, 2003, 1059–1060.
38. Ioanid, Friling and Ionescu, *The Final Report*, 381–82.
39. For a general image of this event, see Jean Ancel, *Pogromul de Iași 28–30 iunie 1941—Prologul Holocaustului din România* [Iași Pogrom 28–30 June 1941—Romanian Holocaust prologue] (Iași, 2006).
40. Ioanid, Friling, and Ionescu, *The Final Report*, 92–93.
41. For example, see Ion Antonescu, "Marshal Antonescu's response to the letter of Professor I. Găvănescu," *Curentul Newspaper* 14, no. 4928, 3 November 1941, Bucharest, 3; response letter sent by Ion Antonescu to William Filderman, the leader of the Romanian Jewish community on 19 October 1941 (Paul Goma, *Săptămâna roșie*, 331–32).
42. USHMM, RG-25.004M, reel 128, Romanian Information Service-Bucharest (SRI) records, [State Security Archive, Prosecutorial Fund, file 64472], 4.
43. Ioanid, Friling, and Ionescu, *The Final Report*, 93.

Bibliography

Ancel, Jean. *Pogromul de Iași 28–30 iunie 1941—Prologul Holocaustului din România* [Iași pogrom 28–30 June1941—Romanian Holocaust prologue]. Iași: Polirom, 2006.
Antonescu, Ion. "Marshal Antonescu's response to the letter of Professor I. Găvănescu." *Curentul Newspaper* 14, no. 492, 3 November 1941, Bucharest, 3.
Benjamin, Lya, ed. *The International Commission for the Study of the Holocaust in Romania: Documents*. Iași: Polirom, 2005.
Bossy, Raoul. *Amintiri din vița diplomatică, 1918–1940* [Memories of the diplomatic life, 1918–1940]. Bucharest: Humanitas, 1993.
Browning, Christopher. *Nazi Policy, Jewish Workers, German Killers*. Cambridge, 2000.
Carp, Matias. *Cartea neagră. Suferința evreilor în România 1940–1944* [Black book: Jewish suffering in Romania 1940–1944]. Bucharest: Diogene, 1996.
Deletant, Dennis, and Ottmar Trașcă, eds. *Al III-lea Reich și Holocaustul din România: 1940–1944: documente din arhivele germane* [The Third Reich and the Holocaust in Romania: 1940–1944: Documents from German archives]. Bucharest: Elie Wiesel National Institute for Studying Holocaust in Romania publishing House, 2007.
Evreii din România între 1940–1944. Vol. 3, *1940–1942: Perioada unei mari restriști* [The Jews from Romania between 1940–1944. Vol. 3, 1940–1942: The period of great tribulation]. Bucharest: Hasefer, 1997.
Goma, Paul. *Săptămâna roșie 28 iunie–3 iulie 1940 sau Basarabia și evreii* [The Reed Week, June 28–July 3, 1940 or Bessarabia and the Jews]. Author's Publishing House, electronic edition, 2007.
Ioanid, Radu. *The Holocaust in Romania: The Destruction of Jews and Gypsies under the Antonescu Regime, 1940–1944*. Chicago: Ivan R. Dee, 2008.
Ioanid, Radu, Tuvia Friling, and Mihail Ionescu, eds. *The Final Report of the International Commission for the Study of the Holocaust in Romania*. Iași: Polirom, 2006.
Martiriul evreilor români, 1940–1944 [The martyrdom of the Romanian Jewry, 1940–1944]. Bucharest: Hasefer, 1991.
Mircu, Marius. *Ce s-a întâmplat cu evreii din România?* [What happened with the Romanian Jewry?]. Bat Yam: GLOB; Holon: Papyrus, 1996-1997.
Pelin, Mihai. *Adevăr și legendă* [Truth and legend]. Bucharest: Edart, 1994.
Stoenescu, Alex Mihai. *Armata, mareșalul și evreii. Cazurile Dorohoi, București, Iași, Odessa* [The army, the marshall and the Jews: Dorohoi, Bucharest, Iași, Odessa cases]. Bucharest: Rao, 1998.

Part III

The Material for Shifting Scales
Sources between Testimonies and Archives

CHAPTER 15

THE HOLOCAUST AND POSTWAR JUSTICE IN POLAND IN THREE ACTS

Andrew Kornbluth

The seldom wieldy, sometimes rusty, and often clogged machinery of the modern justice system would, at first glance, hardly seem to be the stuff of microhistories. Yet all of the major revelations about the Holocaust in Poland over the last fifteen years—beginning with the notorious case study of the Jedwabne massacre in Jan Gross's *Neighbors,* and continuing with the microhistorical work of authors like Barbara Engelking and Jan Grabowski—have depended on the records of individual trials of war criminals and collaborators conducted after the war under the auspices of the new, Soviet-backed Polish government, commonly referred to as "People's Poland."[1] However, less light has been shed on the trials themselves. That is unfortunate, because in contrast to the crudity of the trials taking place in the Soviet Union, where unqualified or barely competent military tribunals were empowered to mete out draconian punishments, the process of postwar retribution in Poland was a scrupulously legal affair entrusted to civilian jurists.[2] Every defendant was required to be represented by an attorney, trials took place in open court according to the prewar code on criminal proceedings, and the presumption of innocence was genuine—up to half of those accused may have been acquitted.[3]

But precisely because it was the rare venue not conquered by the Stalinism overtaking all other areas of public life, the law in Poland rapidly became a site of contestation not just for criminal responsibility, but also for a broader range of issues haunting postwar reconstruction. Trials for wartime crimes against Jews were especially susceptible to this dynamic, threatening as they did the national myths that many relied on to assuage their anxieties during a period of Soviet colonial subordination. Then as now, Poland prided itself on having been the only occupied country in Europe "without a Quisling." Lacking a collaborationist government, Poland had mounted one of the most sophisticated and tenacious armed resistance efforts of the war, a distinction for which it had suffered terribly. But the narrative of implacable opposition also served to obscure less heroic aspects of the occupation.

Emanuel Ringelblum, the historian of Jewish life under occupation who was himself betrayed to the Germans in 1944, considered prewar Poland as the "leading anti-Semitic country in Europe, second to Germany alone."[4] The corrosive effect of years of both popular and official anti-Semitism in independent Poland was acutely felt after the Nazi invasion. Jan Karski, the government-in-exile's famed emissary in London, who traveled through occupied Poland on intelligence-gathering missions, reported that hatred of Jews was a rare "bridge" on which the "Germans and a large part of Polish society meet willingly."[5]

No definitive numbers exist, but it is presently estimated that between 120,000 and 200,000 Polish Jews, representing 75 to 80 percent of all those who escaped the major deportations to the death camps and went into hiding, did not live to see the end of the war.[6] While the most rudimentary estimates admit that "tens of thousands" of ethnic Jews were betrayed or killed by Poles, painstaking microhistories like that of Jan Grabowski, who determined that 65 percent of the more than 300 Jews hiding in just one rural county fell victim to local people, give a terrifying hint of how widespread the indigenous contribution to ethnic cleansing may have been.[7]

Given that the issue of the murder of Polish Jews by their neighbors is considered tantamount to treason in Poland to this very day, one can imagine how delicately the postwar authorities had to tread in handling prosecutions of the accused. This sensitivity was reflected in both the unusually low rates of conviction for anti-Jewish persecution—in some courts as low as 15 percent—as well as the government's unsettled and evolving stance on postwar retribution.

Using three representative cases from the three distinct phases of the retribution, this chapter proposes to examine the exchange between the "macro" and "micro" levels, looking at how the intricacies of the crimes perpetrated against Jews informed judicial policies made at a national level and how those same policies in turn affected the outcome of the trials.

The "Rabbit Hunt"

The postwar rulers of Poland faced a delicate balancing act in their early years. Weak and confronted by open rebellion, they could not afford to ignore the high expectations that Poland's long-standing tradition of state life had inculcated in the populace. Moreover, below the level of the Politburo, the upper echelons of officialdom were more diverse than the Soviet pedigree of the leadership might suggest; they included not only fanatical true believers and agents of the Kremlin, but also various fellow travelers and left-wing adherents who remained committed to the web of institutions, not least among them the courts, that had distinguished interwar Poland from its poorer, less developed neighbors. As a result, although "tied to the Soviet chariot" and led by Stalinists, the regime did not attempt, at least initially, to slavishly imitate the Russian example.

In the aftermath of the devastation wrought by the Nazis, the punishment of collaborators and war criminals was the political equivalent of low-hanging fruit. To capitalize on the widespread appetite for revenge, the government hastily unveiled the Decree of 31 August 1944, better known as the August Decree (and hence the shorthand of "August cases" to describe crimes of collaboration), at a time when much of the country was still under German occupation. The decree was modeled on the Soviet Union's own (secret) legislation on war crimes, first promulgated in 1943, but redrafted and stripped of its ideological content to make it more palatable.[8] Left deliberately vague to allow for prosecution of the widest range of collaborators, the wording of the decree, regardless of its origins, was not really that different from the special laws passed elsewhere in Europe; its main innovations were the inclusion of lay judges in the "Special Criminal Courts" that were to hear crimes of collaboration, and the death penalty mandated in Article 1 for "taking part" in murder or contributing to the capture of persons "sought or persecuted" by the German occupiers.[9] The first step was meant to ensure the "popular" character of the new special courts—only one of the three judges would be a professional, meaning that the lay judges could theoretically outvote him—while the second, an act unprecedented in modern Polish jurisprudence, was meant to give vent to popular fury. But popularizing the courts also meant asking laymen to condemn not just Gestapo informers and German policemen, but ordinary civilians who could claim to have been following the occupier's laws regarding the country's most unloved minority.

The trial of Aleksandra Mrozowska was a perfect illustration of the tension between the populist aspirations of the new law and the realities of prosecution. In the banality of her person and the crime of which she was accused, Mrozowska, a 26-year-old farmer's wife from the small settlement of Bezek, could have stood in for any number of postwar defendants. Her offense differed little from thousands of other such cases throughout rural Poland: she had denounced a group of eight Jews, including her neighbor Szloma Ziserman and his children, who were hiding in an abandoned quarry on her property. Jews in hiding during the war in Poland almost inevitably depended on either active aid—typically paid for and rarely altruistic—or at the very least the willingness of local people to turn a blind eye to their presence. When that presence became an inconvenience, whether because the Jews could no longer pay, the locals wanted to seize their belongings, or the fear of exposure grew too great, denunciation to a third party was a well-established mechanism to resolve the "problem." What greatly complicated so many of these cases was that the denunciation was not made to the Germans, but to the long-standing institutions of rural self-government.

The evil genius of this German-instituted method was that it piggybacked on the existing structure of village administration. The traditional village head (*sołtys*), a man usually elected by popular vote, was required to arrange the transport and, if necessary, apprehension of Jews denounced to him by his constituents. Sometimes policemen would be fetched to carry out the task; more commonly the *sołtys* would send members of the village watch or fire brigade to seize the captives and guard them during their transport to the German or wartime Polish police, known as the "blue" police, for execution. The watchmen and firemen could and did carry out executions too. This meant that many a Jew was denounced, detained, and executed without seeing a single German. Thus, the postwar courts would be tasked with assigning guilt for crimes of genocide that not only took place in the physical absence of the thinly stretched occupiers, but that also implicated numerous, well-respected villagers in a confusingly diffuse chain of responsibility.

Despite the pleas and promises of the fifty-year-old Ziserman that his group would leave immediately, they were surrounded that night by the *sołtys,* the village militia, and local peasants armed with pitchforks and shovels. Mrozowska, who had known Ziserman since she was a child, reportedly laughed as they were taken prisoner. At daybreak they were put on carts and sent to the authorities in Chełm, a journey of about thirteen kilometers, but Ziserman and one of his children jumped off in the forest and escaped.[10]

In contrast to the numerous people implicated in Mrozowska's actions, Jewish victims like Ziserman were very much alone. Ziserman was a rare creature twice over: he had been one of Poland's small class of Jewish farmers, and he had survived the war. No statistics exist on exactly what percentage of the thirty-two thousand August trials involved crimes against Jews, but some limiting factors can be identified with certainty. To begin with, few victims had survived the war inside Poland, and most emigrated rapidly, first internally—to escape the immediate danger of murder in rural areas at the hands of nationalist partisans or local people determined to take hold of formerly Jewish property—and then externally—as they made their way to Western Europe, the United States, and Israel to seek a new life away from reminders of the terrible tragedy and the pervasive atmosphere of anti-Semitism. More than a few trials were torpedoed when it turned out that key Jewish witnesses had left the country during the sometimes long period between the end of the investigation and the convening of the court, and painful choices had to be made, even for those who remained. For Ziserman, it was a matter of not rocking the boat in the insular community of Bezek. He explained to the authorities that he had waited until June 1945 to accuse Mrozowska because he had initially returned intending to "stay on [his] farm and live among the people." Only when he "gave up" did he go to the police.[11]

Even before the trial, the solidarity of the village made itself felt. Eighty-one villagers signed a testimonial—a document commonly solicited by defense lawyers to present to the court—in support of Mrozowska, a mother and guardian of two orphans, who had relied on the kindness of neighbors while her husband, a reservist, was a German prisoner of war.[12] Mrozowska never denied contacting *sołtys* Michał Gregoruk about the Jews, instead claiming in the run-up to the trial that she had tolerated their presence for weeks after spotting their tracks in the snow and only asked Gregoruk to remove them when complaints from local "Ukrainians" and their threats of denouncing her became intolerable. Gregoruk, she alleged, had released the Jews outside of the village after receiving a bribe. Although the Ukrainian villagers, including Gregoruk, would be cast in a sinister light at the trial, none of the witnesses suggested that there was anything unusual about their conduct, nor had any of them known that there were Jews hiding in the settlement until that day. Mrozowska, in a carefully worded, typewritten request from prison to have the charges against her dropped, emphasized the legality and propriety of her action in alerting the "local *sołtys*, elected by a normal vote." Indeed, the captives had been held overnight at the house of Maria Czerniakiewicz, a Pole, and guarded by "two Poles and two Ukrainians."[13]

At trial at the Special Criminal Court of Lublin, however, in a pattern recognizable from any number of other August cases, the witnesses—that is, the defendant's fellow villagers—closed ranks around Mrozowska, revising or recanting their earlier testimonies in favor of an entirely new and previously unaired version of events. Taking the stand, Mrozowska now testified that an imminent "rabbit hunt" by the Germans had been the immediate impetus for removing the Jews from her property. She had warned the Jews, but they were resigned to their fate: "They responded that it was all the same to them whether they died here or somewhere else." In any event, she claimed that the Ukrainians had released the Jews after Ziserman bribed them.[14] Naturally, none of these details had been in the lengthy, self-justifying memorandum that she had filed before the trial. Similarly, witnesses who had made no mention of it in their initial testimony suddenly "remembered" corroborating details of the rabbit hunt.[15]

When the trial reached the sentencing phase, lay judges Szydłowski and Widelski showed that their sympathies indeed lay with the common people. Wholeheartedly accepting the story of the "rabbit hunt" and the "release" of the captives, they overruled Judge Łanowski and voted to impose the minimum possible sentence of three years on Mrozowska for depriving the victims of their hiding place. Judge Łanowski, in his dissenting opinion, vigorously protested:

> It was common knowledge to all residents of the village that *sołtysi* were obliged to capture hiding Jews and deliver them to the Germans. On the basis of the very admission of the accused, it was necessary to recognize that she committed the crime laid out in [Article 1] and sentence her to death. The fact that the trial did not clearly establish where the persons taken captive by the *sołtys* were sent, and what fate they met, is completely immaterial for the qualification of the act.... In these circumstances the qualification of the act by the lay judges ... and the assigning of the lowest punishment appears to be in blatant contradiction with the conclusions of the trial.[16]

Not only did Mrozowska enjoy the forbearance of the lay judges, whose presence was prescribed by the August Decree, she also benefited from a backlash created by the decree's theoretical severity. The mandatory death penalty provided for in Article 1 had been highly controversial from the start. In early 1945, protests by judges and reports from the field that courts preferred to acquit defendants, rather than sentence them to death for relatively "minor" crimes, persuaded the Ministry of Justice to add a new, second article for crimes "other than [those] foreseen in Article 1."¹⁷ Article 2, under which Mrozowska was sentenced, was, in essence, a catchall article designed as an escape hatch from Article 1. This, in essence, was the compromise required to ensure that defendants like Mrozowska served any time at all, instead of going scot-free.

"As If Going to a Gala"

Just as the new government had maintained the prewar legal architecture, it retained the services of the surviving members of the prewar judiciary. The latter found themselves in an awkward marriage of convenience: on the one hand, these judges and prosecutors were conscientious professionals who, like most of the country, remained loyal to the government-in-exile in London and to Polish sovereignty; on the other hand, their help was needed by the Soviet-aligned regime to rebuild a system decimated by the war and to maintain an image of continuity vital to the legitimacy of the "new order." Hence the Ministry of Justice became the "only ministry in reborn Poland" to rely "exclusively on the old cadre."[18] The contradiction was all the more glaring because not only had the prewar judiciary been tasked with prosecuting members of the then-illegal Communist Party, but much of the remaining legal class were graduates of the law schools of the 1930s, which had been hotbeds of ultranationalist and anti-Semitic agitation. The relative freedom given the judiciary was therefore more than just a chance to uphold the integrity of their profession. For some, it was also an opportunity to resist the imposition of Soviet Communism on Poland, a process they blamed squarely on Poland's annihilated Jewish minority.

To complicate matters, the immediate postwar fervor for punishment was declining precipitously. In October 1946, the Special Criminal Courts were abolished, and jurisdiction for the August trials was transferred to Poland's ordinary district courts. While 18 percent of Special Criminal Court verdicts resulted in death sentences, their ultimate punishment was handed down in only 5 percent of the August cases heard in 1947 by the district courts.[19] Amid evidence that the courts were still unwilling to convict defendants who were clearly guilty under Article 1, the August Decree was revised yet again in December 1946; the original provision appearing in Article 5, which prohibited the courts from taking into consideration the possibility that a defendant was acting under duress or orders, was this time amended to permit the consideration of mitigating factors.[20] If punishing "ordinary" anti-Jewish perpetrators like Mrozowska was difficult enough, prosecuting actual patriots who had distinguished themselves in the service of Polish independence would be even harder.

For Apolinary Sokołowski, arrested in April 1948, it was a fortuitous conjuncture. A well-known figure in the town of Burzec, where he ran a grocery store and served as the regional fire brigade chief, Sokołowski was seen by several residents in late 1942 as he led an exhausted Jewish boy on a rope to the *sołtys* for transport to the Germans. Zygmunt Bosek, a fellow fireman who later reproached Sokołowski and was fired for his pains, recalled that Sokołowski, dressed in his ceremonial uniform "as if going to a gala," had pulled the Jew along "with great pride." Witness Aleksander Ciołek described the boy's appearance as so haggard that "it was simply horrible to look at him." Even earlier, in 1941, Sokołowski had waved down a German patrol on a local road to arrest a man he had detained, shouting, "You mangy Jew, you won't wander about here."[21]

But Sokołowski, who was said to have received a house formerly belonging to Jews, had not confined himself to seizing individual stragglers. In the spring of 1942, he and three other firemen had, "with great pomp," transported the town's Jewish families on their carts to the designated collection point in the county seat of Wojcieszków, where they then got drunk with the German police. He had also organized an alarm system in the surrounding villages, providing them with noisemakers made of sheet metal to sound in the event Jews appeared. He himself frequently set off the alarms and was seen amid the assembled villagers armed with an iron bar and a flashlight.[22]

Sokołowski was hardly the image of a "renegade," as postwar Polish newspapers sometimes referred to collaborators. A founder of the local parish, he had fought in the Polish-Soviet War of 1918–21—in the same unit in which Father Ignacy Skorupka was famously killed delivering last rites on the battlefield—and again during the German invasion in September 1939. His neighbor Ciołek and *sołtys* Edward Sady, even as they delivered damning testimony about his crimes, insisted simultaneously that he was a "good Pole" who had interceded with the Germans, who frequently lunched at his store, in order to prevent the arrest of several Poles, including Ciołek.[23]

His patriotic background could not have been lost on the prosecutor, Władysław Grzymała, or the presiding judge, Czesław Kosiński, at the district court in the town of Siedlce, both of whom had been part of the judiciary before the war. Neither man could be expected to feel much affinity for Poland's new, postwar reality. Recalling his legal training, Grzymała wrote in his unpublished memoirs that the "majority" of his fellow law students were active in the "radical-nationalist camp," while

Kosiński had graduated from the law faculty in Wilno in 1932, a year marked by open and fatal conflict between ethnic Polish and Jewish students.[24] An ardent anti-Communist who had been a member of the underground Home Army during the war, Grzymała was deeply skeptical of postwar accusations of anti-Jewish crimes. In his view, "only a few exceptions" among Poles had betrayed Jews, "most often for fear of their own lives," and survivors were not to be trusted, since all of the "more honest Jews" had died in the war, and only the "scum" remained. Instead, the real crime was the supposed "massive enrollment" of Jews in the security forces of the Soviet-backed state.[25] As such, Grzymała described colluding with judges to exonerate defendants whom he felt had been unfairly accused.[26]

There is no way to tell whether Grzymała and Kosiński did the same for Sokołowski, but they were certainly indulgent. Despite the mutually corroborating testimony of prosecution witnesses, Grzymała called on the court to apply leniency under Article 5 in his closing statement. Judge Kosiński went one better; he downgraded the charge from Article 1 to Article 2, reasoning that since no one had actually seen Sokołowski *physically apprehend* the Jewish boy or give him over to the Germans—*sołtys* Sady and a carter had transported him to the blue police—his crime did not correspond to the act of "capture" laid out in the more severe article.

The whole conveyor-belt mechanism of rural denunciation and capture of Jews—the negotiation between the original captor and the *sołtys*, the designation of guards to transport the prisoner, and the handover to the Germans or blue police, with death as virtually the only possible outcome—was completely ignored. As for the other charge regarding the Jew seized by the roadside, the court accepted the claims of the defense and ruled that the matter was "undoubtedly the result of a coincidence." Regarding his punishment, the court kept in mind that the defendant was "acting under the ... orders of the German authorities to arrest 'wandering' Jews on pain of death," although no Germans had been involved at any time in the incident with the boy on the rope. Zygmunt Makuła, one of the witnesses called by the defense on short notice, whose story about Sokołowski feeding a Soviet escapee was credited by the court, was also mooted by several prosecution witnesses as the original denouncer of the Jewish boy. In an oft-repeated formula, the court wrote that given his "heretofore impeccable behavior, level of intellectual and moral development, as well as help rendered during the occupation to members of the underground and Soviet POWs," Sokołowski was to be sentenced to two years in prison with time served, as well as the loss of his civil rights for two years and the loss of all his property.[27]

Though the latter point might seem devastating, it proved to be a punishment rarely enforced in practice.

"Many People Flew Out from All the Surrounding Villages"

In 1949, a year after the verdict in the Sokołowski trial, the court in Siedlce received a letter from the Office of Prosecutorial Oversight at the Ministry of Justice, excoriating their handling of the case. The construction of the indictment had been faulty, no investigation had been launched into Sokołowski's other alleged crimes, and the *sołtys* and carter had not been charged despite their admitted involvement. Worse yet, if one were to accept the court's logic that the standing orders to arrest Jews could be considered a mitigating factor despite the absence of Germans at the crime scene, then every collaborator who had obeyed standing orders to hand over members of the Resistance to the Gestapo should also be treated with leniency, in which case "sentencing of August cases as mandated by the law would be *a priori* impossible."[28]

The letter was but one in a long series of indications—communicated privately and publicly since 1945—in which ministerial authorities expressed their displeasure with the work of the courts. Mild sentences and "incorrect" verdicts, both for August crimes and in general, were singled out as the "sore point" of the "catastrophic state" of criminal justice in the country, alternatively blamed on the judiciary's alleged "passive resistance," "legal ossification," "anti-Soviet and anti-Semitic instincts," and "liberalism."[29] Demonstrating the dualistic nature of Poland's Stalinist government, the "most important part of criminal sentencing"—that is, cases of anti-Communist resistance—were entrusted to the dreaded military courts, while the government resigned itself to the years-long project of slowly educating a "new cadre" that could supplant the prewar civilian judiciary.[30]

As we have seen, a certain number of judges and prosecutors were indeed secretly hostile or in "internal emigration," but to some extent, the government's disappointment was the inevitable result of its own "penal populism" and "campaign mentality" toward criminal justice, according to which there could never be enough punishment. It was also due to the fact that the government itself, painfully aware of its unpopularity, was never actually sure of what outcome it desired. The archival documentation from the early years of People's Poland is fragmentary, but evidence indicates that the state took a pragmatic approach to the trials from the very beginning, carefully weighing the benefits and risks to its authority. Only three days before the German capitulation in May 1945, Leon Chajn, nominally the deputy minister of justice but widely reputed to be the real head of the department, sent a memo to Bolesław Bierut, the *de facto* leader of People's Poland, urging clemency in the case of a teenaged Slovak who had been sentenced to death for, among other things, killing Jews while serving as an SS volunteer. Because the condemned had defected to the Polish Communist partisans and fought with distinction, Chajn successfully argued that sparing him would serve as an example to others that "social integration" could "erase the results of the greatest crimes."[31]

No definitive proof has been found, but there are hints that the government may have actively sought to soft-pedal prosecutions of anti-Jewish crimes. In his memoirs, Janusz Bardach, a Polish Jew who survived the war as a prisoner in the Soviet gulag, recalled an admission made in 1947 by a childhood friend, Jacek Grębecki, then a prosecutor in the city of Łódź and Communist Party member:

> One month ago I got a directive from the Minister of Justice to mitigate the prosecution of Poles who collaborated with the Nazis if the only crimes they committed were against Jews, with the exception of murder. The new regime is taking great pains to avoid antagonizing the Poles. They want to quell any public outcry that the Jewish communists now in power are taking revenge on Poles.... We [party members] must try to win over the Poles, not antagonize them further.[32]

It is impossible to know how accurate the anecdote is—Bardach, a pioneering maxillofacial surgeon, died in 2002—and, if such an order did exist, whether it was in written form and whether it was distributed nationwide. Certainly, one wonders why the ministry would have bothered upbraiding Grzymała for his conduct of the Sokołowski trial if it had really been so disinterested.

By the same token, the government and judiciary alike, each for its own reasons, were clearly interested in striking a balance between the theoretical severity of the law and the more forgiving reality of its execution. In practice, this meant that legality ever more frequently gave way to a performance of legality, a transformation that was reflected in debates over the role and work of the Supreme Court. The high court's role was doubly important not only because it was the court of appeal for most August trials, but also because it was relied upon by lower courts to interpret the rudimentary, sparsely worded August Decree. It turned out, however, that the Supreme Court was no less squeamish about the harsh character of the decree; correspondence from the high court to the ministry described the judges' reluctance to impose the death sentence on defendants whom the lower courts had deliberately convicted on lesser charges by "stretching" the categorization of their crimes.[33] From the beginning, the Supreme Court's rulings hewed conservative, narrowing the meanings of "capture" and "murder" to an extreme degree that arguably contravened the intent of the legislators. In the case of Aleksandra Mrozowska above, for example, the Supreme Court eventually acquitted her of all charges on appeal, deciding that there was "no basis" for assuming that the captured Jews had been sent to the Germans or that she had reported their presence with that intent. In the high court's view, Mrozowska had not "denounced" her victims, but merely refused them shelter.[34]

Presiding over the decision in the Mrozowska case was Judge Kazimierz Bzowski, who, as chief judge of the criminal section of the Supreme Court, issued a number of appeals decisions favorable to defendants. Although much of the internal documentation from the era has been lost, it seems probable that Bzowski, a Supreme Court judge before the war who became an outspoken supporter of People's Poland afterward, enjoyed the regime's confidence and to an extent represented its will on the court; of the nine judges who had been most involved in the restrictive interpretations of the August Decree, he was the only one to still have his job by 1949. His advocacy for a new hard line in August trials in that year was followed two years later by an abrupt retreat, suggesting that he was merely transmitting a shaky commitment at higher levels of the government to punishing defendants.

By the end of the 1940s, the new government could finally feel that it had consolidated its power; the armed resistance had been effectively suppressed by 1948, and 1949 was the year when the percentage of new cadre in the judiciary reached the 50 percent mark, as young candidates graduated from abbreviated law schools and prewar professionals were retired. Indicative of the renewed severity was the percentage of death sentences, which jumped from around 8 percent of all sentences in 1948 to almost 14 percent in 1949.[35] The capstone to the year was a new, wide-ranging interpretation by the Supreme Court of what constituted "capture" under Article 1 of the August Decree; once and for all, it seemed to dispel all the ambiguity over the issue by categorically stating that capture was a "lasting crime," which implicated everyone who took part not just in the seizure of the victim, but in his or her handing over to the occupier.[36]

For Władysław Sidor and Bolesław Lemiech, the timing was infelicitous. Although the two were eventually convicted of murder, not capture, they clearly had the misfortune of being sentenced—in July

1950—during a period in which the crimes of the decree were subject to expansive readings. That was not, of course, to say that their crimes were not odious in themselves. Sidor, a decorated veteran of the Polish-Soviet war, had been appointed head of the watch in the village of Domaszewska in April 1942 by *sołtys* Szymon Droś; in May he had traveled the eight kilometers to attend a meeting of village watch commanders in the town of Łuków, where the Germans instructed them to keep an eye out for Jews and all other suspicious persons. That same month, the conveyor belt that the occupiers had erected in this tiny hamlet sprang to life when watchman Antoni Ścioch reported to Droś that there were Jews in his barn. Droś gave the order, and Sidor and half a dozen other watchmen detained five members of the Pryzant family, driving them to the blue police in Łuków. Along the way, the Jews complained that they had given 10,000 złotys to Ścioch for their upkeep, which he had instead used to build himself a new house.[37]

Later that month, another watchman spotted Jews near some haystacks in the field of a large estate several hundred meters from the town limits. Droś wanted to summon the Germans, but Sidor insisted that he could "take care of it himself." Each participant in the chase gave conflicting accounts of what ensued, but all agreed that around ten watchmen, led by Droś and Sidor, had raided the haystacks, then pursued several Jews into the forest, reinforced by workers from the estate and onlookers who "flew out" from the surrounding villages. Two Jews were killed with rocks, and possibly a shovel or pitchfork—a witness described seeing a corpse with a smashed jaw—while one was captured and transported to Łuków.[38]

Sidor and Bolesław Lemiech had been in that section of the raiding party that broke away to chase the two Jews who were ultimately killed. Although the Lublin Appellate Court—the appellate courts having become the court of first instance for August crimes in 1949—had found it impossible to establish who struck the fatal blows—each accused the other—under the August Decree's expansive understanding of "taking part in murder," they were convicted and sentenced to death, while five of their confederates were given terms of between six and ten years.[39]

But Sidor and Lemiech's luck had not run out. In February 1951, less than a year and a half after it had enlarged the August Decree's scope, the Supreme Court suddenly reversed itself, declaring that the crime of capture ended "at the moment" when the victim was "deprived of liberty," and affirming that all subsequent actions—guarding, restraining, or transporting the captive—"could be" punished under the catchall Article 2 "depending on the circumstances." The Supreme Court explained that lower courts, despite the influx of new blood, had continued to acquit defendants or to unjustifiably resort to mitigating factors in order to avoid the harsh implications of the 1949 interpretation.[40]

Several days later, in a ruling highly reminiscent of the new resolution, insofar as it restricted the concept of murder, the Supreme Court rejected out of hand the possibility that Sidor and Lemiech "intended at any moment" to kill the Jews, simply because the first Jew they captured—who surrendered immediately—was not killed out of hand. Thus, "any excess [i.e., murder] arising from the large number of participants in the chase ... cannot be the basis for ascribing guilt" to the two defendants, who were responsible only for "what was actually proved, that is, the attempt to catch the Jewish complainants."[41] Sidor and Lemiech were reassigned penalties of fifteen and twelve years of imprisonment—still stiff sentences for a Polish court of the period—and all of their accomplices had their sentences reduced.

Behind the scenes, even as they fretted about the "disturbingly large" number of acquittals and "striking liberalism" of the lower courts, Supreme Court representatives admitted at meetings of the Ministry of Justice that they had sent conflicting messages, "tighten[ing] the screws sharply" in August cases and then relaxing them suddenly.[42] Perhaps the real reason for the pullback was the realization on the part of both the government and the upper echelons of the judiciary that, in the end, a hard line was politically counterproductive. A month after the 1951 resolution, Bzowski had written to the ministry in support of revising the August Decree to remove the mandatory death penalties; while the high court was doing its best to "blunt ... the cutting edge" of the decree, the fact remained that its specter risked alienating the "laboring peasantry," from which most defendants came, and sowing anti-government feelings in the "widest masses of the people." But the ministry brushed off the suggestion. The Supreme Court, it replied, was already doing a good job "effectively avert[ing]" the "negative repercussions" of the August Decree by suspending "unjust verdicts," and in any case, the "present international situation"—namely the need to not appear lax at a moment when the Western powers were forgiving and reenlisting their former enemies—dictated that the August Decree be maintained in its present form.[43] In short, the courts would continue to pretend to be uncompromising in their treatment of wartime misdeeds, and People's Poland would continue to pretend that it was nothing like the "Anglo-Saxon imperialists."

In a sense, the interventions of the Supreme Court were redundant, because it was unlikely that the death sentence for Sidor and Lemiech would have ever been carried out anyway; fifteen of the sixteen death sentences issued between 1949 and 1951 by a single venue, the Lublin Appellate Court, were commuted by President Bolesław Bierut, suggesting that the government had already more or less decided to retire the ultimate punishment. Nor was a commutation to a life sentence any reason to despair; an October 1951 law on parole, followed by a partial amnesty in 1952, shortened many sentences significantly and reduced the required time served before parole—which was granted virtually automatically—to half of the sentence or to ten years in the event of a life sentence.

The penalties for participating in the conveyor belt of genocide fell to such low levels that Apolinary Sokołowski, the fire chief of Burzec and a free man since 1950, wrote to the Council of State in 1954 to request that the still-unexecuted confiscation of his property, an obligatory but unevenly enforced part of every sentence under the August Decree, be commuted. Aside from the standard invocations of his misfortune at having "collided with criminal justice due to the express orders of the German occupier" and his otherwise blameless conduct, Sokołowski also appealed to the state's sense of fairness; although he had served only two years in prison, he noted that "presently, verdicts for this kind of act are significantly lighter."[44]

The winding down of postwar retribution was capped by the amnesty of 1956, which, following Bierut's sudden death in the wake of Soviet premier Nikita Khrushchev's earth-shaking anti-Stalinist "Secret Speech," effectively put an end to all further investigations into August crimes and led to the rapid release of the majority of those still serving sentences. Władysław Gomułka—the advocate of a "Polish road" to socialism who was carried into office that year on a wave of popular enthusiasm—commented regarding an earlier amnesty that a "wise politics knows how to forget."[45]

The question of whether justice was done remains, sadly, a matter of perspective. From the point of view of the Jewish victims, it would be hard to give an affirmative answer. From the perspective of a traumatized Polish society, counting its own losses, eager to move on, and in no mood to confront the collaboration of many ordinary people in the Nazi project of ethnic cleansing, retribution had probably been "excessive." For the unpopular, Soviet-imposed government, which had permitted the prosecution of collaborators for twelve years even as its commitment, never great to begin with, noticeably flagged over time, it was probably justice enough.

Andrew Kornbluth is a doctoral student in history at the University of California, Berkeley. He received his BA from Columbia University. His last article, "'Jest wielu Kainów pośród nas.' Polski wymiar sprawiedliwości a Zagłada, 1944–1956," was published in *Zagłada Żydów: Studia i Materiały*, no. 9 (2013).

Notes

1. For the sake of brevity, I will refer to the Soviet-sponsored Polish government—whose official title changed multiple times before settling on *Polska Rzeczpospolita Ludowa* (PRL) in 1952—as "People's Poland" in the text. The use of the term is not, however, intended to detract from the dictatorial nature of that regime.
2. It should be noted that the law on collaboration was used under false pretenses in only a small number of cases against the anti-Communist Resistance, most notably against General Emil Fieldorf, in trials held in the handpicked "secret section" of the Regional Court for the City of Warsaw in the early 1950s. The vast majority of politically motivated trials were sent to the military court system. For trials in the USSR, see the work of historians Nathalie Moine, Tanja Penter, and Vanessa Voisin. According to Tanja Penter, only 18 of the 134 "leading and operational staff" of the Soviet military tribunals in the Ukrainian SSR had a higher legal education; Tanja Penter, "Local Collaborators on Trial: Soviet War Crimes Trials under Stalin (1943–1953)," *Cahiers du Monde russe* 49, nos. 2/3 (2008): 346.
3. This article is derived from research that forms part of the author's forthcoming dissertation "Poland on Trial: Postwar Courts, Collaboration, and the Holocaust, 1944–1956." The author also wishes to thank the Takiff Family Foundation at the Center for Advanced Holocaust Studies of the United States Holocaust Memorial Museum and the Saul Kagan Fellowship in Advanced Shoah Studies of the Conference on Jewish Material Claims against Germany for their support.
4. Emanuel Ringelblum, *Polish-Jewish Relations during the Second World War* (Jerusalem, 1974), 10.
5. Jan Karski, *Zagadnienie żydowskie w kraju* (London, 1940), 10. Retrieved from the website of the Museum of the History of the Jews of Poland.
6. Krzysztof Persak, "Wstęp," in *Zarys krajobrazu: Wieś polska wobec Zagłady Żydów 1942–1945*, ed. Barbara Engelking and Jan Grabowski (Warsaw, 2011), 26; Grabowski, *Hunt for the Jews: Betrayal and Murder in German-Occupied Poland* (Bloomington, 2013), 2–3.
7. Persak, "Wstęp," 27; Grabowski, *Hunt for the Jews,* 61.
8. For the full text of the Soviet decree, see the Russian *Wikipedia* entry: Указ_«О_мерах_наказания_для_немецко-фашистских_злодеев...».
9. *Journal of Laws of the Polish Republic* (Dziennik Ustaw, DzU), 1944, nr. 4, poz. 16.
10. United States Holocaust Memorial Museum (USHMM), Specjalny Sąd Karny w Lublinie (SSKL), case 98, reel 4, slide 319.
11. Ibid.
12. Ibid., slide 286.
13. Ibid., slides 300, 290, 321.
14. Ibid., slide 318.
15. Ibid., slides 320, 321.
16. Ibid., slide 332.
17. DzU 1945, no. 7, poz. 29.
18. "Zagadnienia Resortu Sprawiedliwości," *Demokratyczny Przegląd Prawniczy* (DPP), nos. 5–6 (1946): 52.

19. Archiwum Akt Nowych (AAN), Ministerstwo Sprawiedliwości (MS), file 859, 19.
20. DzU 1946, no. 69, poz. 377.
21. Archiwum Państwowe w Siedlcach (APS), Sąd okręgowy w Siedlcach (SOS), case 695, 17 *verte*, 15 *verte*, 11.
22. Archiwum Państwowe w Siedlcach (APS), Sąd okręgowy w Siedlcach (SOS), case 695, 17 *verte*, 14 *verte*, 4.
23. Archiwum Państwowe w Siedlcach (APS), Sąd okręgowy w Siedlcach (SOS), case 695, 3, 111 *verte*, 23–24.
24. Władysław Grzymała, *Wspomnienia rozpoczęte w dniu 17 kwietnia 1982*, unpublished manuscript in author's collection, 84; AAN, MS, folder 13/636, Czesław Kosiński.
25. Of roughly four hundred "leading" positions in the Ministry of Public Security between 1944 and 1954, it has been calculated that 37 percent were occupied by ethnic Jews. But away from Warsaw and in the countryside, Jews were few and far between in the ranks of the political police [*Urząd Bezpieczeństwa*, UB]. In early 1946 in Lublin province, the heart of both the anti-Communist insurgency and a former center of Jewish life in eastern Poland, less than 2 percent of UB personnel were Jews. See Krzysztof Szwagrzyk, ed., *Aparat bezpieczeństwa w Polsce: Kadra kierownicza, Tom I, 1944–1956* (Warsaw, 2005), 63; Adam Kopciowski, "Zajścia antyżydowskie na Lubelszczyźnie w pierwszych latach po drugiej wojnie światowej," *Zagłada Żydów: Studia i Materiały*, no. 3 (2007): 183.
26. Grzymała, *Wspomnienia*, 61–62 and 74–76.
27. APS, SOS 695, 128–29.
28. APS, SOS 695, 143–44 *verte*.
29. Leon Chajn, "Sądy a społeczeństwo," *DPP*, no. 2 (1945): 8–9; Chajn, "Trzeci rok," *DPP*, no. 7 (1946): 7; AAN, MS 372, 139.
30. Chajn, "Trzeci rok," 7.
31. USHMM, SSKL 34, reel 2, slides 229–31.
32. Janusz Bardach, *Surviving Freedom: After the Gulag* (Berkeley, 2003), 166.
33. AAN, MS 4852, 1.
34. USHMM, SSKL 98, reel 4, slides 350–53.
35. Leszek Kubicki, *Zbrodnie wojenne w świetle prawa polskiego* (Warsaw, 1963), 182; AAN, MS 854, 129.
36. AAN, Sąd Najwyższy (SN), case K 1519/49, file 2/8695, 6–10.
37. USHMM, Sąd Apelacyjny w Lublinie (SAL), case 97, reel 18, slide 48.
38. Ibid., slides 14, 64, 105.
39. Ibid., slide 402.
40. AAN, SN, case K 1076/50, file 2/11793, 64–67.
41. Ibid., slide 443.
42. AAN, MS 456, 183.
43. AAN, MS 1972, 13–15.
44. APS, SOS 695, 152.
45. Leon Chajn, *Kiedy Lublin był Warszawą* (Warsaw, 1964), 209.

Bibliography

Bardach, Janusz. *Surviving Freedom: After the Gulag*. University of California Press, 2003.
Chajn, Leon. *Kiedy Lublin był Warszawą* [When Lublin was Warsaw]. Czytelnik, 1964.
Grabowski, Jan. *Hunt for the Jews: Betrayal and Murder in German-Occupied Poland*. Indiana University Press, 2013.

Karski, Jan. "Zagadnienie żydowskie w kraju" [The Jewish Question in the Country]. London, 1940.
Kopciowski, Adam. "Zajścia antyżżydowskie na Lubelszczyźnie w pierwszych latach po drugiej wojnie światowej" [Anti-Jewish Incidents in the Lublin region in the First Years after World War II]. *Zagłada Żydów: Studia i Materiały* [The Holocaust: Studies and Materials], no. 3 (2007).
Penter, Tanja. "Local Collaborators on Trial: Soviet War Crimes Trials under Stalin (1943–1953)." *Cahiers du Monde russe* 49, nos. 2/3 (2008).
Persak, Krzysztof. "Wstęp" [Foreword], in *Zarys Krajobrazu. Wieś polska wobec Zagady, 1942–1945* [The Contour of a Landscape: Rural Poland and the Holocaust, 1942–1945], edited by Barbara Engelking and Jan Grabowski. Warsaw, 2011.
Ringelblum, Emanuel. *Polish-Jewish Relations during the Second World War.* Jerusalem, 1974.
Szwagrzyk, Krzysztof, ed. *Aparat bezpieczeństwa w Polsce: Kadra kierownicza, Tom I, 1944–1956* [The Security Apparatus in Poland: Leading Cadre, Volume I, 1944–1956]. Warsaw, 2005.

CHAPTER 16

THE SMALL AND THE GOOD
MICROHISTORY THROUGH THE EYES OF THE WITNESS—A CASE STUDY

Hannah Pollin-Galay

Morris P., born in Vilkaviškis, Lithuania, in 1922, testified for the USC Shoah Foundation in 1998 in Houston, Texas.[1] His testimony is abundant with details—what he heard, said, saw, and thought. After calling a break, and unaware that the camera was still rolling, the interviewer congratulated Morris on his testimonial style, saying, "You're doing really well. You're giving me a lot of *good detail*." Providing "good detail" is perhaps the goal of every microhistorian. But what does this entail? Once a small-scale historical approach is adopted, how does one determine which details are relevant and why? In turning away from national, military, *longue durée,* or diplomatic histories, we may be tempted to consider microhistory a more natural conduit to reality. And yet, in examining microhistory from the perspective of the Jewish witness, we find different ways of "thinking small."

Overall, one could characterize the "era of the witness"[2] as a series of massively scaled attempts to archive small-scale perspectives on the Holocaust. In the USC Shoah Foundation interviewing guidelines, the word "detail" appears repeatedly, as in "Describe your home in detail,"[3]

"Ask detailed questions about changes in Jewish life before the establishment of the ghettos,"[4] or "Were the laws of kashrut observed? How? Describe in detail."[5] These same guidelines indicate that the interviewer should aim "to elicit complete descriptions of experiences." Since this ideal of complete experience is impossible to attain, the details that do surface are always partial, in both senses of the word. In sorting through the vast number of micronarratives amassed at this stage of Holocaust research, we should attend to the normative notions that make certain kinds of particulars relevant, as well as to their conceptual implications.

To investigate this topic, one could mine institutional protocol further, as some researchers have done.[6] But here I will adopt a vernacular approach, looking carefully at the notions of "micro" that emerge from a select number of witness testimonies. I will also approach this matter comparatively. Almost all of the major testimonial institutions, including the USC Shoah Foundation, the Fortunoff Archive, and the United States Holocaust Memorial Museum, exported their projects into a wide range of contemporary geographic and linguistic contexts, where institutional notions of proper description encountered local, unofficial ones. When interviewers and witnesses worked together to negotiate a testimonial approach—including notions of truth telling, biography, and historical reflection—they drew from conventions that had accumulated over years of conversation, as well as broader discursive concerns in their shared environment.[7]

This chapter explores culturally distinct notions of "the micro" through the testimonies of Lithuanian Jews born between 1918 and 1935, who share similar life stories but testify to the Holocaust in two different contexts—in English in North America, and in Yiddish in contemporary Lithuania. All of the testimonies were recorded between 1985 and 2005.[8] In both contexts, witnesses move between micro- and macroscopic types of recollection. Sometimes witnesses summarize entire years in one sentence or report what happened in Lithuania as a whole. Here, however, I focus on two different microhistorical possibilities, one found in the Yiddish-Lithuanian corpus and one in the English-language American corpus. In order to underscore what is so meaningfully different about these two different types of micronarration, I propose we think of them as two different genres of historical narrative: *collective-forensic* microtestimony, a narrative strategy employed by Yiddish-speaking witnesses in Lithuania, and *personal-allegorical*, found among English-speaking witnesses in North America. At the end of this essay, I will briefly explore how these historical genres also appear in the works of two professional microhistorians—Christopher Browning and Jan Gross.

Personal-Allegorical Testimony

In the personal-allegorical mode of recollection, witnesses speak the truth about events by focusing on individual perception. A "good detail" is one that the witness saw, heard, or felt and that lingers in the psyche for one reason or another. As a possible further outcome, this sensual and emotional detail may enable the listener to envision him- or herself in the witness's shoes. Because this type of personal detail can be transported into a variety of settings, the story becomes a stage for contemporary or universal moral reflection. To explore this genre, we can look to the testimony of Esther A., who in 1998 testified in English in New York City with the USC Shoah Foundation.[9] Esther was born in 1924, in the north-central town of Radviliškis (Radvilishek) in the Šiauliai (Shavl) region of Lithuania. She remained on Lithuanian soil for the duration of the war—first in the small ghetto established in Radviliškis, and then in the Šiauliai ghetto, the nearby Linkaičiai work camp, and finally in hiding in a Lithuanian household until liberation.[10]

Consider the way in which Esther recalls the outbreak of war: "It was the last day [of school]. I went to pick up my diploma without realizing that war is on. I went to pick up my diploma and I had a hard time coming back home. With a freight train, somehow I managed. The war was on. That's when my family decided we have to run." She goes on to recount that her family managed to board an eastbound train in hopes of fleeing Lithuania. However, her father was uneasy about leaving his brother's family behind. As a result of his misgivings, he took his wife and children off the train with him in the town of Panevėžys, in order to bring these family members along. In Panevėžys, Esther's family was caught and returned to Radviliškis. In this decisive early segment, Esther shapes her microcosm of relevance around herself and her family members. She contextualizes the chronological moment in terms of her life story and personal development, emphasizing that the German invasion coincided with her milestone achievement of completing her gymnasium studies. Internal family dynamics are crucial for understanding causality in this framework.

Of course the witness does not present the war as a mere domestic drama. Esther does describe the actions of people far from her intimate circle, including those of perpetrators. She recounts that upon return to Radviliškis, she and her family, along with all of the remaining local Jews, were rounded up and imprisoned in former army barracks. There, she relates, Lithuanian guards used to line up the Jewish prisoners every night and give them a speech: "'You parasites, you nothing, you bastards. Now we're going shoot you.' With machine guns in front I always had marks in my hand from my father's nails, trying to control himself." The effect of this detail is not to assign guilt to individuals or to explore the reasons for their heinous deeds. Instead, Esther views the moment through the private sensory world, which registers the impact of events on those nearest to her.

Much later in her testimony, when the Linkaičiai prisoners were gathering for deportation, Esther recalls being separated from her parents. "I panicked and a whole group of us started to run. I was barefoot and I started to run. I had a little dress on. I was in a trance and I started to run from house to house." Supplying details about her clothing, her state of mind, her movement, Esther once again invites the listener into her sensual world. She stresses her position as an individual actor in this moment, repeating, "I panicked," "I started to run." Later in her testimony, Esther meditates on the impact that this personal choice may have had on her parents, saying, "I lived all my life with the guilt that if I didn't run, somehow I would have been able to help [them]." Such delicate, intimate reflection makes sense—sounds appropriate and comprehensible—thanks to her earlier micro-description: she has reconstructed the moment of personal initiative, the sensation of changing one's fate and possibly that of others. The scene's sensual details derive their power from their ability to ignite moral reflection of a lasting, personal nature.

After telling of her escape, Esther goes on to portray the gentile woman who finally took her in, whose name is Polina Seskavičiene. In the specific manner in which she depicts this woman, Esther creates a conceptual bridge between private self-reflection and broader moral allegory. She describes Polina as a devout Catholic, who prayed for the safety of Esther and her brother Lusik, beseeching, "Please, Maria, save the children, for you were once Jewish yourself." Twice Esther quotes Polina saying, "What will happen to my children will happen to you. You're both staying here." Esther ponders the woman's bravery with amazement, saying, "She risked the life of her own children to save us. I wonder if I would be able to do that." The portrait of Polina initiates an open-ended chain of comparisons: Polina asks Saint Mary to compare herself to the Jewish children; Polina compares her children to Esther and Lusik; Esther compares herself to Polina; and following this comparative momentum, the listener is invited to compare him- or herself to Polina or to Esther.

At the end of her testimony, Esther affirms the allegorical possibilities toward which she alluded throughout her testimony. She says that as a result of her Holocaust experience, "I hate wars. I don't want to see wars. I don't want people to hate each other because of color or religion.... I think I instilled this in my children." This final reflection sounds fitting, well justified, based on Esther's method of narration and the comparative thinking she has initiated for her listeners. Esther has focused on the autonomous perceiver, the decision maker, and his or her ability to do right and wrong for other people. This type of microcosm is a decidedly transportable one. In limiting the amount of detail regarding her geographic or social environment, she makes room for analogies across cultures and time periods. Esther's memories are not tied down to Lithuania during 1941 to 1945. Her broadly inflected ideals regarding child-rearing, "hate," "wars," "race," and "religion" correspond to the type of detail work she has done throughout.

Another English-speaking American witness, named Jack A., adopts a similar microtestimonial approach, particularly in his representation of space.[11] He delimits the borders of perception, and therefore relevance, not as a town, a city, or a neighborhood, but as the intimate domestic realm. In depicting interwar Vilna, Jack mentions several institutions and public locales: "Jewish teacher's seminaries,"[12] the "Perlman's *cheder*" where he studied, "Beitar," "the Real Gymnasium." But Jack and his interviewer quickly zoom in on his house, which he locates on "Subotch Street 7." Taking the listener on an almost cinematic tour, Jack describes the courtyard at the entrance to the building, then the staircase and the apartment. He finally arrives at the house's center: "My sister and I shared a bedroom when we were little. The windows in the back of the apartment faced into a garden and a Russian church." As he is describing the flora and fauna that was visible from his window, Jack recalls looking out onto a Russian Orthodox church from that same viewpoint. The interviewer encourages this type of description: "And what about the other side of the apartment, what could you see out the front?" From that lookout spot, Jack describes friends, neighbors, and other relations. What ties the natural and the human world together—defining both of them as objects of truthful and relevant memory—is that they are perceptible from within the personal domestic space.

In particular, it is Jack's view from the bedroom window, the most intimate of all lookouts, that the interviewer finds compelling. In fact, he asks Jack to return to this visual frame after a short detour through the city. "You described the view from your room as being of gardens and an Orthodox church. What was your relationship to the Orthodox church?" "Absolutely wonderful," Jack answers, recounting how one priest, Father John, would rest a ladder on his window in order to let him down to play in the monastery. This depiction of interethnic friendship gains legitimacy when considered from the right vantage point, from the inside looking out. Jack's imagery in this scene also carries powerful allegorical possibilities: the ladder leads directly from the private sphere to the natural one, with the garden bypassing the divisive social scene of the street. In the garden, unencumbered by ethnic and political identities, people may freely befriend one another.

Toward the end of his testimony, Jack reflects on the universal and contemporary implications of his story: "We have to be alert. We have to tell the story to all the students, as uncomfortable as it is.... But, we have to stand on guard. And it has happened. It has manifested itself again in Yugoslavia, the former Yugoslavia. It has manifested itself in ethnic cleansing. It has manifested itself in Africa one tribe against another." As was the case with Esther A., such comparative reflection does not come as a surprise. It sounds like a justified conclusion to Jack's testimony. His focus on personal perception, which is transferable to the individual perceiver almost anywhere, supports this process of analogy and open identification.

Collective-Forensic Testimony

As a contrast to the personal-allegorical genre, we find a different detail-intensive method of testifying among witnesses who remained in Lithuania and offer their testimony in Yiddish, which we can call collective-forensic. In this mode of testimony, witnesses delineate their microcosm of relevance as their town or city, an entity that is at once social and geographic. Here, witnesses tend to remember in panorama, recalling details about other people and events that they did not see directly. A wide cast of characters and long lists of local names are often striking features of such testimonies. In this sense, these testimonies resemble the earlier genres of Jewish communal history, *Pinkasim* or *Yizkor bikher* (memory books).[13] Together with the task of communal chronicling, these testimonies also display a forensic aim—of "attacking or defending someone" and "proving guilt or innocence."[14]

We can explore these generic dynamics in the testimony of Shmuel S.[15] He was born in the same region as Esther A., in a section of the northern city of Šiauliai. He too survived the war entirely on Lithuanian territory. After working and living on the Zokniai (Zokne) military airfield, he was sent to perform forced labor on a local farm owned by Lithuanians. He was later imprisoned in the Šiauliai ghetto and then transferred to the nearby Akemenė lime pits, before escaping to take shelter in various Lithuanian houses until liberation. In sum, the basic facts about his wartime experience are quite similar to Esther's. However, his context of remembering differs from hers greatly; he delivered testimony both to the USC Shoah Foundation (1995) and to me (2004) in Yiddish in Kaunas, Lithuania.

While Esther framed the outbreak of war in the context of her educational achievement and family life, note how very differently Shmuel recalls this same moment:

> That bloody Sunday is when the war broke out. The twenty-second at eight o'clock in the morning. The first one that they killed was Simkhele Luria. He used to always pass by our house. He had cows.... And on the last day of his life, he passed through our field with his cows. On the road from Konigsberg to Riga, the Soviet army was then on its way, fleeing. A soldier's vehicle stopped and asked him for directions to Riga. He knew the way to Riga. So, the soldier drove away. At that very moment, a neighbor drove up, a Lithuanian, Jankunis.... And with the tool you use to bind cattle, the flatiron, he smashed his head to pieces, took his cattle, and off he went.[16]

Shmuel locates the moment not on a trajectory of his personal development, but in an atmosphere of everyday neighborly activity. We also note that Shmuel is bent on naming names. He identifies the first victim of violence as his neighbor Simkhele Luria, a cow farmer with an adjacent lot. He also names another neighbor, Valodke, a witness to the crime. Continuing to expand his cast of characters, Shmuel later singles out the killing of "Faynberg the chemist," "Traystman," and the "Shavler Rabbi Nachamovski." Shmuel directs the listener's attention to these town figures, identifying them by profession and sometimes even by street address. Adopting the role of community chronicler, Shmuel gives equal attention to his fellow townspeople as to his nuclear family. Events that he did not see firsthand, such as the killings of Faynberg, Traystman, and Rabbi Nachamovski, are nonetheless legitimate memory details according to this framework. As a member of the micropolity of Šiauliai, of Jewish Shavl, he is a credible witness to events that occurred to this collective.

But Shmuel's evocative detail goes beyond the ritual chronicling of a lost community. He is as attentive to local enemies as he is to friends. He names the policeman "Braijeris" as the leader of mass shootings (*der glavner shiser*) in his neighborhood of Kalniuk. He also singles out "the bloody bandit, the thief, Marcinkus," an overseer at the Akmenė work site. His criteria for identifying these perpetrators are both ethnic, placing blame squarely on local non-Jewish Lithuanians, as well as individual, as if it were possible to seek out these guilty parties even today.

Not only does Shmuel make an effort to identify guilty parties by name, he also tries to explicate the means by which they committed their crime. In his depiction of the events of 22 June 1941, he specifies that Jankunis killed Luria with a flatiron. When discussing Marcinkus of Akmenė, he mentions that this perpetrator killed "with his bare hands." Shmuel attempts the same level of forensic precision when situating the event chronologically: he asserts that Jankunis killed Luria on "the twenty-second of June at eight o'clock in the morning" and that Marcinkus killed ten Jewish prisoners "the morning of October tenth" (1941).

Further connecting his micronarrative to the legal tradition, Shmuel tries to establish concrete motivations for the violence he recounts. The interviewer asks him why, at the outbreak of war, Jankunis would kill Simkhele Luria. The witness finds the question of individual motivation perfectly reasonable and answers without hesitation, "Because he gave directions to a Russian soldier." Aside from conflicting political alliances, Shmuel points to material gain and ethnic rivalry as possible motivations for local violence. He recounts, for example, how the Lithuanian baker Šnaris had shot his rival Jewish baker, Masevetksii, in the first week of the war, ostensibly out of jealousy. Here too, he emphasizes that Masevetksii was a neighbor; to live near Shmuel is a prime criterion for inclusion in his microhistory. Masevetskii's "crime was that he baked better bread than Šnaris." As his narrative progresses in time, Shmuel seems to find it harder to articulate such concrete motivations for perpetration, though he does not dwell on this type of inexplicable violence. He is more interested in detailing that which he can understand and explain.

To be clear, Shmuel's legalistic style does guarantee that his account is more accurate than Esther's or Jack's from the American context. One could argue that he deemphasizes the German military's role in inciting and organizing local killings at the beginning of the war, and even their presence in the Šiauliai ghetto and surrounding camps.[17] Like Esther's and Jack's accounts, Shmuel's testimony is highly accurate and aligns with information from other sources regarding these events. Like them, Shmuel's testimony is partial in the details it presents.

At the end of his testimony, Shmuel indicates one of the purposes of his forensic recounting—that of settling the local score, seeking justice or revenge in the local microcosm. He tells of how he enlisted immediately in the Red Army in August 1944, after his region of Lithuania was liberated. Once armed and in uniform, Shmuel remembers tracking down one particular perpetrator, the local mistress of a German officer who had released her dogs on Shmuel's mother. Likewise, he dwells on the fates and current whereabouts of other local perpetrators. He recounts that many were arrested and tried in the postwar years, but that many fled to the woods or escaped to Australia or Canada. Shmuel's preoccupation with guilty parties—his attempt to say "*j'accuse*" decades after the fact—seems to express, on the one hand, a sense of confidence that the Holocaust is explicable, recordable, and justiciable and, on the other, an ongoing dissatisfaction that the event remains an open case.

Unlike in the English-language American testimonies, it would be very difficult to read his testimony allegorically, because the memory world he depicts is rooted at every angle in the particulars of an ethnic, geographic, and linguistic microcosm. His graphic portrayals of Jankunis or Marcinkus are irreducible to a message about hatred at large. Indeed, Shmuel adds that it is the name "Marcinkus" that he hopes his "children and children's children will always remember."[18] In his two interviews, Shmuel expresses a range of views about contemporary Lithuanian memory-politics—shifting between the poles of bitter and conciliatory stances. But, crucially, his reflections always bring him back to this geographically and temporally bound setting, to the history of its polity, and never to abstract values at large.

Other witnesses in Shmuel's environment share his interest in the local Jewish body politic—some focusing more on its members than on its violators, on the *collective* rather than the *forensic* side of the genre. Such is the case with Doba R., born in Jurbarkas (Yurberik), Lithuania, in 1928 and interviewed by the USC Shoah Foundation in Kaunas in 1996.[19] Doba recollects the outbreak of war through the lens of the "Yurberiker" collective. In a manner that strikingly resembles what might be found in a *Yizkor bukh* entry, she recalls what happened to a long list of town figures, such as "my mother's brother Uncle Faivel" and "my father's brother Uncle Max." Amid this communal chronicling, she does make extra room for her nuclear family; she takes time to provide an up-close account of the capture of first her father and then her mother. But she quickly expands her lens of recollection to focus on more distant kin who became foster parents. She is precise in identifying the man who took her in as "the neighbor, my mother's cousin's husband—Abe Vailes."

While Doba's emphasis is on the Jewish collective, she too provides detail about guilty parties. In the days following the outbreak of war, Doba specifies that it was "Reloška," "a simple worker," who led her father away from their house. Likewise, she later relates that "two Lithuanian policemen, Kelikovitch and Almonaitis, ... dragged me out to the courtyard and pushed me with my head against the window, so that I would tell them where the gold and silver is. I didn't even know."[20] As in Shmuel's testimony, Doba assigns these perpetrators a concrete motivation—theft. One can envision these local perpetrators in the town scene, just as clearly as Doba's friends and family. The outcome is a micronarrative that could be found not only in the pages of a *Yizkor bukh,* but also in the files of a local war-crimes investigation.[21] What drives Doba's selection of detail is her investment in Jurbarkas as a social entity, one that includes both guilty and innocent elements.

The Personal and the Forensic in Professional History

Now that we have searched for the notions of relevance that help Jewish Holocaust witnesses select the right information to be shared, what happens if we attempt the same procedure with professional microhistorians? Looking to Christopher Browning's seminal work *Ordinary Men: Reserve Police Battalion 101 and the Final Solution in Poland* as an example, we find a very specific notion of what makes a small story relevant.[22] The kinds of details that interest Browning most are those that animate the personal perceptual and psychological worlds of these "ordinary" reservists—their processes of brutalization, their relationships to each other as peers, the choices each one faced, what each one would have heard and known at each moment. Starting with prominent passages in his opening chapter, Browning trains his reader to think personal, as in the following: "Pale and nervous, with choking voice and tears in his eyes, Trapp visibly fought to control himself as he spoke."[23] Browning incorporates psychological assessments as strategic or causal explanations throughout the chapters: "There was a constant tendency to assign the actual shooting duties to these units, in order to shift the psychological burden from the German police to their collaborators."[24] Even when simply stating that an action took place, Browning often incorporates the sensory world of an individual observer: "Heilmann watched while the Jews who had been incarcerated in the cellar prison of Security Police headquarters were hauled out and led away."[25]

In his introduction and conclusion, Browning explains his focus on the personal realm of these low-level perpetrators: "The policemen in the battalion who carried out the massacres and deportations, like the much smaller number who refused or evaded, were human beings. I must recognize that in the same situation, I could have been either a killer or an evader—both were human—if I want to understand and explain the behavior of both as best I can."[26] By way of analogy and comparison, the narrative of these policemen ought to enable personal moral reflection for the contemporary reader. Cumulatively, if enough "I's" read about these ordinary anti-heroes, the book should offer insight into human ethics at large: "Within virtually every social collective, the peer group exerts tremendous pressures on behavior and sets moral norms.

If the men of Reserve Police Battalion 101 could become killers under such circumstances, what group of men cannot?"[27] As in the cases of Esther A. and Jack A., Browning's final reflections are about *the human*. The type of detail and interpretive lens that appear throughout Browning's work supports and enables this type of final analysis.[28] Having learned what these policemen heard their superiors say, what they watched their victims do, and the psychological strategies employed to propel them into violence, we can indeed put ourselves in their shoes and engage in comparative reflection. In other words, there is a noticeable affinity between the vernacular notions of personal-allegorical microhistory found among the North American witnesses we studied and this scholarly work by Christopher Browning from this same setting.

Browning implements his model of small-scaled, human history in a consistent and thoughtful manner. But that does not imply that his model is neutral or self-evident. We can look to the book *Neighbors* by Jan Gross to note a profoundly different notion of what makes a small-scale historical account valuable.[29] In his statement of purpose, Gross does not reflect on the moral realm of the individual-human anywhere, but that of the body politic, specifically the Polish one. He opens his work with the question "After all, *how can the wiping out of one-third of its urban population be anything other than a central issue of Poland's modern history?*" (italics in the original).[30] The borders of Jedwabne, as a social and geographic entity, are those that define his microcosm of relevance. The town becomes a collective witness, both the producer and container of history, in passages such as this one: "According to folklore preserved in Jedwabne to this day, it was a very cruel affair. The Jedwabne pharmacist ... repeats almost verbatim the words we have already heard from the lips of another witness."[31] Not only does Gross name the names of locals, as in the witness testimonies from Lithuania that we discussed, he speaks directly about the importance of the *nameability* of perpetrators as an element of the event: "Ninety-two participants were singled out by name. These were all adult men, residents of the town of Jedwabne."[32] For Gross, this familiarity between victim and perpetrator is further reason for indictment.

Gross concludes the book with an open assessment of collective guilt, on the local and then national scale: "As we now know beyond reasonable doubt, and as Jedwabne citizens knew all along, it was their neighbors who killed them."[33] He is not speaking to humans everywhere but to Polish society. The violent reactions to this work in Poland show the effectiveness of his rhetoric.[34] His readers understood that this history carries forensic weight, that its telling invites accusation or defense, rather than comparison or allegory. An intellectual product of Eastern

Europe, Gross's scholarly concerns closely approach the vernacular ones of Shmuel S. or Doba R., lifelong citizens of nearby Lithuania. In defining good detail, Browning and Gross contribute to different historiographical and ethical projects—related to their respective environments of training and expected audiences.

We may contextualize these contrasting genres of microhistory in the intellectual currents of Eastern Europe and North America in the 1990s. Historian Dan Diner proposes that following the collapse of the Soviet Union, Eastern and Central Europe turned to the traditional interpretive trope of "the totality of ethnos."[35] Accordingly, the Holocaust represents the extreme result of centuries-old ethnic conquest. By contrast, since the 1990s, American culture has strengthened its tendency to frame history, the Holocaust in particular, as "a struggle over values."[36] Diner's schema helps explain the microhistorical lenses I have explored here: the collective-forensic genre seems to combine contemporary concerns of ethnic competition with various traditions of community chronicling, maintained in the original environment and languages of the event. Likewise, personal-allegorical microtestimony coheres with Diner's observation about an American values-narrative, while also incorporating a psychological idiom, one that prioritizes individual internality and private sensation as the basis of authentic recollection.

There is a conventional way to diminish the effect of these testimonial genres: cross-checking. By comparing and contrasting the testimonies of witnesses with differing contemporary viewpoints, we may theoretically arrive at some unencumbered reconstruction of small-scale events. But there are problems with such efforts to circumvent the witness's approach to microhistory. The first is simply a matter of "missing out" on an important dynamic of our research object. The witness's notion of truth, concretized in perspectival lens and selection of detail, is an inherent, fascinating, and highly human element of the source. It enlightens us about the specific meaning-making process into which the event entered from the moment it happened. As a second point of concern, the historian who avoids the witness's microcosmic lens often naturalizes his own method of "zooming in the lens." As arbiter of good detail, the professional microhistorian also instructs us in how to read the past ethically. Narrative analysis is one way to recognize this slippage between professional and vernacular modes of historical understanding and to make the procedure of detail selection into an object of historical study, rather than an invisible norm.

Hannah Pollin-Galay completed her Ph.D. in history at Tel Aviv University in the fall of 2014 and has held fellowships at Columbia University, University of Pennsylvania and the United States Holocaust Memorial Museum. Her publications have appeared or will appear in journals such as *Jewish Social Studies, Holocaust and Genocide Studies, Prooftexts* and *Dapim: Studies on the Holocaust.* She teaches at the University of Massachusetts, Amherst, in the Department of English and the Institute for Holocaust, Genocide, and Memory Studies and is currently working on a book entitled *Ecologies of Witnessing: Language, Place and Holocaust Testimony.*

Notes

1. Morris P., interview 38035, Visual History Archive (VHA), USC Shoah Foundation, Texas, 1998.
2. Annette Wieviorka, *The Era of the Witness* (Ithaca, NY: Cornell University Press, 2006).
3. "Topical Questions," USC Shoah Foundation Institute Organizational Archives, Los Angeles, CA, documents updated April 2004, 4.
4. Ibid., 6.
5. Ibid., 25.
6. Jessica Wiederhorn, "Holocaust Testimony," in *Oxford Handbook of Oral History*, ed. Donald Ritchie (Oxford: Oxford University Press, 2011), 248–51. For an analysis of institutional policy from a media-centered perspective, see Noah Shenker, *Reframing Holocaust Testimony* (Bloomington; Indiana University Press, 2015).
7. Linguist Ruth Wajnryb calls this process the "co-creation of meaning," in *The Silence: How Tragedy Shapes Talk* (Crows Nest, N.S.W.: Allen and Unwin, 2001), 174. Her approach is based on "relevance theory," which claims that human conversation is guided by the mutual aim to make oneself relevant to an interlocutor. See Dan Sperber and Deirdre Wilson, *Relevance Theory: Communication and Cognition* (Oxford: Blackwell Press, 1986).
8. I studied testimonies from three collections: (1) a set of forty-four interviews I conducted in Lithuania in 2004–5; (2) the USC Shoah Foundation Visual History Archive (seventeen in Yiddish from Lithuania and nineteen in English from North America); (3) the Fortunoff Video Archive for Holocaust Testimony (fifteen testimonies in English from North America). I examined more testimonies from the Yiddish-Lithuanian setting, as there was no previous work done on this group of witnesses.
9. Esther A., interview 43872, VHA, USC Shoah Foundation, New York, 1998.
10. On the small enclosure for Jewish prisoners in Radviliškis, see Guy Miron, ed., *The Yad Vashem Encyclopedia of Ghettos*, vol. 2, (Jerusalem: Yad Vashem, 2009), 639. Linkaičiai was one of the work camps around Šiauliai; ibid., 708; Christoph Dieckmann, *Deutsche Besatzungspolitik in Litauen 1941–1944* (Gottingen: Wallstein Verlag, 2011), 1306.
11. Jack A., interview 19111, VHA, USC Shoah Foundation, New York, 1996.
12. For more on these institutions, see Cecile Kuznitz, *YIVO and the Making of Modern Jewish Culture: Scholarship for the Yiddish Nation* (Cambridge: Cambridge University Press, 2014), 38.
13. Annette Wieviorka discusses these genres as precursors to contemporary testimony in *The Era of the Witness*, 27.
14. Aristotle, *Rhetoric and Poetics* (New York: Random House, 1954), I.3.1–42 (here 32).

15. Shmuel S., interview with the author, Kaunas, Lithuania, 7 February 2005; and Smuelis S., interview 13033, VHA, USC Shoah Foundation, Kaunas, Lithuania, 1995. All quotations are from the VHA testimony, unless marked "Shmuel S. HPG," indicating interview with the author.
16. Shmuel S. HPG.
17. For further considerations on this point, see Christoph Dieckmann and Saulius Sužiedėlis, *The Persecution and Mass Murder of Lithuanian Jews during Summer and Fall of 1941* (Vilnius: Margi Raštai, 2006).
18. Shmuel S. HPG.
19. Doba R., interview 9896, VHA, USC Shoah Foundation, Kaunas, Lithuania, 1996.
20. The names of these local perpetrators are hardly familiar beyond the specific region of the events, let alone on a worldwide, historical stage. Their inclusion has a cumulative, aesthetic effect on the testimony—emphasizing culpability and agency outside of the Western European and American field of vision. In "Mapping Western Conceptions of Evil," Steven Ascheim proposes that Western European perpetrators and atrocities dominate Western memory in part because of the familiar aesthetic of their names. In Helmet Dubiel and Gabriel Motzkin, eds., *The Lesser Evil: Moral Approaches to Genocide Practices* (New York: Routledge, 2004), 77.
21. See Alfonsas Eidintas, *Jews, Lithuanians and the Holocaust* (Vilnius: Verseus Aurelius, 2003), 336–84, on war-crimes trials in Lithuania.
22. Christopher R. Browning, *Ordinary Men: Reserve Police Battalion 101 and the Final Solution in Poland* (New York: HarperCollins, 1992).
23. Ibid., 2.
24. Ibid., 25.
25. Ibid., 108.
26. Ibid., xix.
27. Ibid., 189.
28. In this volume, Jeff Wallen reflects on Browning's method in *Remembering Survival: Inside a Nazi Slave Labor Camp* (New York: Norton, 2011).
29. Jan Tomasz Gross, *Neighbors: The Destruction of the Jewish Community in Jedwabne, Poland* (Princeton, NJ: Princeton University Press, 2001).
30. Ibid., 9.
31. Ibid., 88.
32. Ibid., 87.
33. Ibid., 168.
34. Janine P. Holc, "Working through Jan Gross's *Neighbors*," *Slavic Review* 61, no. 3 (2002): 453–59.
35. Dan Diner, "Problems of Periodization and Historical Memory," *New German Critique* 53 (1991): 167.
36. Ibid., 165.

Bibliography

Aristotle. *Rhetoric and Poetics*. New York: Random House, 1954.
Browning, Christopher R. *Remembering Survival: Inside a Nazi Slave Labor Camp*. New York: Norton, 2011.
———. *Ordinary Men: Reserve Police Battalion 101 and the Final Solution in Poland*. New York: HarperCollins, 1992.
Dieckmann, Christoph. *Deutsche Besatzungspolitik in Litauen 1941–1944*. Gottingen: Wallstein Verlag, 2011.

Dieckmann, Christoph, and Saulius Sužiedžlis. *The Persecution and Mass Murder of Lithuanian Jews during Summer and Fall of 1941.* Vilnius: Margi Raštai, 2006.

Diner, Dan, "Problems of Periodization and Historical Memory." *New German Critique* 53 (1991), 163–174.

Dubiel, Helmet, and Gabriel Motzkin, eds. *The Lesser Evil: Moral Approaches to Genocide Practices.* New York: Routledge, 2004.

Eidintas, Alfonsas. *Jews, Lithuanians and the Holocaust.* Vilnius: Verseus Aurelius, 2003.

Gross, Jan Tomasz. *Neighbors: The Destruction of the Jewish Community in Jedwabne, Poland.* Princeton, NJ: Princeton University Press, 2001.

Holc, Janine P. "Working through Jan Gross's *Neighbors*." *Slavic Review* 61, no. 3 (2002), 453–59.

Kuznitz, Cecile. *YIVO and the Making of Modern Jewish Culture: Scholarship for the Yiddish Nation.* Cambridge: Cambridge University Press, 2014.

Miron, Guy, ed. *The Yad Vashem Encyclopedia of Ghettos.* Vol. 2, Jerusalem: Yad Vashem, 2009.

Shenker, Noah. *Reframing Holocaust Testimony.* Bloomington: Indiana University Press, 2015.

Sperber, Dan, and Deirdre Wilson. *Relevance Theory: Communication and Cognition.* Oxford: Blackwell Press, 1986.

Wajnryb, Ruth. *The Silence: How Tragedy Shapes Talk.* Crows Nest, N.S.W.: Allen and Unwin, 2001.

Wiederhorn, Jessica. "Holocaust Testimony", in *Oxford Handbook of Oral History*, edited by Donald Ritchie, 248–51. Oxford: Oxford University Press, 2011.

Wieviorka, Annette. *The Era of the Witness.* Ithaca, NY: Cornell University Press, 2006.

CHAPTER 17

THE WITNESS AGAINST THE ARCHIVE
TOWARD A MICROHISTORY OF CHRISTIANSTADT

Jeffrey Wallen

Christopher Browning, at the end of a conference in Jena in 2011 featuring Hayden White, Saul Friedländer, and himself (in honor of the "Probing the Limits of Representation" conference at UCLA twenty years earlier), suggested that the microhistorical case study is now the main frontier of research for Holocaust historians and that we need to go "down to the village level ... to see this as human experience, and to understand how all this could have happened."[1] This echoes his recent book *Remembering Survival: Inside a Nazi Slave-Labor Camp*, where he states that the "microhistorical approach offers one way to explore the history of the Holocaust from below, as experienced by the victims and involving multiple actors."[2] A major driving force today is to fill in the blank spaces on the map of Holocaust historiography, so to speak. Now that the main concentration camps, extermination centers, ghettos, and other sites of mass killing and mass grouping of Jews have been well studied, the smaller labor camps—of which there were a staggering number—along with villages and other small units of space and social organization provide the best terrain for understanding the *lives* of Jews during the Holocaust. The details of a little-known place that perhaps even today is not marked by any form of memorial can be investigated and brought to light, and the variety and depth of personal experiences can be partially recuperated, providing at least a measure of restoration against what has been lost and erased. Such studies can also displace the more common images and evocations of the Holocaust. "Typical" (which seems an inappropriate word) survivors of Auschwitz (which was itself a large network of main camps and sub-camps) often spent much of their time in many other places dominated by the Nazi powers, places that often have little or no place in the popular imagination or collective memory.

Before sketching some possible directions and goals for a microhistory, I want first to address a central question posed by the conference organizers, about "how the choice of a microscale contributes to our macro comprehension of the history of the holocaust."[3] My contrarian suggestion is that the answer is usually "not much." But this is not necessarily a bad thing. It is a worthwhile enterprise to illuminate, and thus to honor, the "human experience" of the victims and also to interrogate the experiences of the onlookers and perpetrators as well. Investigations that inform us about the factors that influenced the chances of survival (which is really at the heart of Browning's book) or that construct the cultural history of these spaces add to our knowledge and are important gestures of bringing attention to the lives of the murdered. But the belief that exploring some poorly mapped terrain in detail will necessarily affect our broader comprehension of the Holocaust is misguided. It assumes that our understandings of the Holocaust are lacking because we have paid insufficient attention to the texture of events at the more comprehensible and intimate scale of the village, small space, or cluster of people (and which happens to be the researcher's particular area of interest). This is not to say that recent research on hundreds of little-known killing sites has not had any effect on views of the Holocaust. Research after the fall of the Soviet Union in the Ukraine, for example, about what some have called the "Holocaust by bullets," is slowly starting to change popular as well as scholarly understanding: it is now more widely known that many Jews were killed very near where they lived, that their neighbors knew about the killings, and that they were shot and not killed in gas chambers.[4]

The desire to *turn* from the "macro" to the "micro"—and also from the archival document to the voice of the victim, from "above" to "below" and "outside" to inside," from the better known to the overlooked and largely forgotten—derives in large part from the topic of the Holocaust itself, the murder of millions of people. Timothy Snyder, who disparages the current popularity of the "micromode" in Holocaust studies,[5] nevertheless ends his book *Bloodlands* with the following appeal: "The

Nazi and Soviet regimes turned people into numbers.... It is for us as scholars to seek these numbers and to put them into perspective. It is for us as humanists to turn the numbers back into people."[6] The desire to "turn the numbers back into people" haunts much Holocaust scholarship, but it no longer carries the sort of corrective force to the dominant historical approaches that it did a few decades ago, before "the era of the witness," when Elie Wiesel could complain that for most Holocaust historians, "human beings were less important than paper."[7]

For the humanist attempting to understand the Holocaust, the harder task today is to work to comprehend dehumanization, which one might describe as a movement in the other direction, from "human beings" to "paper." I want to suggest that this shift to the more human scale of the "micro" can also work *against* our ability to understand the Holocaust. In adopting a microscale, a key goal is usually to move (borrowing Saul Friedländer's words) from "the history of the administrative and murderous measures ... with its abstract statistical expression" to "concrete history ... carried by personal stories" and the "narration of individual fates."[8] Yet a turn to "personal stories" and the "narration of individual fates" can inhibit our ability to grasp what took place, as it suggests that the path for understanding is to assert our own sympathy, imagination, and capacity for intersubjectivity, when what we are trying to understand is in fact the breakdown of these "humanistic" forces and the radical reshaping and transformation of the human subject under extreme circumstances. Paradoxically, in order to better understand the Holocaust, we need to move continually in opposing directions: from "paper" to "human beings" (as Wiesel urged historians to do), but also from "human beings" to "paper."

The challenge of microhistory is usually presented as a tension between "big" and "small," between a panoramic perspective and a narrow focus. Timothy Snyder, in dismissing the current trend toward microhistory, asserts that "when you get that intimate and that small," you cannot "really catch the big things" and have "full explanations."[9] I am arguing that we need to consider a different challenge in our efforts to explain the Holocaust: how to look at things at the micro level without thereby embracing a perspective that privileges the individual over the mass, the personal over the bureaucratic, the autonomous instead of the systemic.

Microhistory has the potential to change the pictures we have of the Holocaust: not only to substitute a finer and more complex understanding for the set of better-known names, places, and events, but to help us rethink the boundaries and oppositions that structure our understanding. In the second half of this essay, I will begin to describe some of the reasons why a microhistory of Christianstadt, a munitions factory and slave labor site, would be especially promising. But first I want to foreground and address this problematic of working at the micro level, without turning away from what is hardest to confront and comprehend about the Holocaust: processes of systematic destruction that deny human subjectivity.

One of the major transformations in Holocaust scholarship in recent decades, and one of the great resources for microhistory, has been the explosion in the collection of eyewitness testimony. The widespread use of individual testimony by scholars also characterizes an important shift in perspective: from the contemporaneous written bureaucratic document to the experience remembered (often forty or fifty years later) in (often oral) recorded form; from the archive to the witness; and from the perpetrator to the victim. A means to problematize this optic of the witness, which privileges interiority and gives us the lure of unmediated access to experience, is to read testimonies against archival documents, to read them as opposing modes of discourses rather than for complementarity (one filling in the holes of what was not noted or could not be seen by the other) or competition (which view [German or Jewish] and which perspective [bureaucratic or individual] is to dominate).

Bearing witness is a transformative act. It reasserts the individual voice against the forces that negate any individual worth and claims authority over one's identity, struggling against the portrait of oneself created by others. Anne-Lise Stern, a survivor of Birkenau and a participant in an earlier French conference on the Shoah in 1996, described the dismay of another survivor at being treated by historians as a "document," musing:

> Document: paper is also made from rags, from scraps.... What are we? What am I? the survivor asks. All those who were deported in truth bear witness to that, to the scraps they have become. Knowledge of the deportation is that—knowledge of waste, of scraps. But when they speak of it, testify to it, they are no longer scraps.[10]

Testifying is also a negation and a reversal of what one testifies about, of the scrap one had become.

Archival documents created for administrative purposes, which "remain the bread of the historian," as Annette Wieviorka put it, present us with a different model of knowing and remembering.[11] A document is not only a container of information; it too carries out an action, transforming the people it places within a system for managing them into objects of attention, classification, and organization. One can glean "facts" from bureaucratic documents, but they are not neutral or objective, in contrast to the subjectivity or bias or unreliability of survivor testimony. Contemporaneous documents often present a polar contrast to witness testimony: impersonal rather than personal, multiple rather than singular or unique, shaped and organized by the functions of an administrative system rather than by the living memories and storytelling demands of a narrating "I."

Scholars today often read (or listen to) testimonies not exclusively for the "facts," but equally for what is not said, attending to the pauses and hesitations, and treating the witness account as a "speech act," as a "performative" utterance rather than a "constative" one that merely reports or describes a state of affairs. One might read archival documents with a similar, almost literary attentiveness and bring out the ways in which the discourse is *shaped* by the archive.[12] Here is a small example (which pertains to the shooting of Jews in the Ukraine):

> Lviv, 22 August 1942
> 5th Commissariat of
> Ukrainian Police in Lviv
> No. 2826/43
>
> Subject: Jewish action carried out on 21 August 1942
> Reference: Order of Ukrainian Police Commandant
>
> to Commandant of Ukrainian Police in Lviv
> I hereby report that on 21 August 1942, 805 Jews were delivered to the assembly point from the 5th Ukrainian Police Commissariat area.
>
> | Revolver shots fired | |
> |---|---|
> | 1/ Viytovich, Mikhailo fired | 1 shot |
> | 2/ Zherebukh, Andriy " | 1 " |
> | 3/ Krivistky, Lev " | 2 " |
> | 4/ Petruschevksy, Lev " | 2 " |
> | 5/ Kalimum, Ivan " | 2 " |
> | 6/ Borukh, Roman " | 4 " |
> | 7/ Fitjo " | 4 " |
> | 8/ Leskiv, Mykola " | 4 " |
> | 9/ Stakhiv, Timko " | 6 " |
> | Total shots fired | 26 |
> | Killed 12 Jews, wounded 3 | |
>
> A total of 1,095 zlotys were taken from the Jews as bribes, and at the direction of [Lieutenant] Lehmann [German Order Police] are enclosed herewith.
>
> Enclosures: 2
> Head of Commissariat[13]

Each shot fired is registered and each shooter identified, but what we would ordinarily see as the more consequential act—who was killed and wounded—is summed up in one line, giving us only the gross total ("Killed 12 Jews, wounded 3"). The priorities of the accounting are clear: what needs to be reported most are the number of shells expended. The gap between who is named (the Ukrainian shooters) and who is not (the 805 Jews who were rounded up and the 15 who were shot) is radical: it is the gap between the usual bureaucratic processes directed toward regulating life and their perverse redirection toward the destruction of life. What is recorded in this report seems an extreme antithesis to "witnessing," presenting a perspective antithetical to the expression of what it was like to see and live through these events. Yet its focus on accounting becomes entirely ordinary; its sense derives from it being one of a series of similar documents, responding to a request for reports of similar information. The paper document preserves here that which would not be remembered (the number of shots fired by each person) and which would escape memory altogether if it were not written down and transmitted. It is a knowledge that is located elsewhere, not in particular memories but in an archive. In contrast, the survivor's testimony springs from what is burned into memory.

While focusing on a highly delimited terrain of investigation, Holocaust microhistory can—and I think should—actively juxtapose contrasting modes of knowing and memory, such as the archive and the witness, rather than seeking primarily to penetrate ever deeper into the "human experience" or approach ever closer to a "human" scale. An archival document can yield an even harsher "knowledge of waste, of scraps" than the narration of the witness. But a microhistory need not lead to a micro-mode of viewing that encourages us to believe that we can better grasp the Holocaust by turning each number back into a person or by trying to understand "what it felt like to be there."[14] A microhistory of Christianstadt, where more than a thousand Jewish women worked as slave laborers during the last half of 1944, might be especially promising in bringing out some of the ways in which a microhistory can contribute to addressing the challenges we still face in understanding the Holocaust.

Christianstadt—which before the war was in Germany but today is the Polish Krzystkowice, less than fifty kilometers east of what is now the border with Germany—was the site of a huge explosives factory (code named "Ulme"), for which planning and construction began shortly before the start of the war.[15] Some of the largest German industrial concerns were involved: Dynamit-Actien-Gesellschaft (DAG; formerly Alfred Nobel & Co.) ran the facility, and Siemens was responsible for the construction and other facets. Many thousands of people worked there, the majority of whom were prisoners of war, forced laborers, and slave laborers from many different countries, and in 1944 a sub-camp of Gross Rosen (more than 130 kilometers away) was opened, in which Jewish women worked both in the munitions factory and in road building and other outdoor construction activities. Altogether more than one thousand Jewish women were sent there, most coming directly from Auschwitz-Birkenau beginning in July 1944.[16] If people have heard of Christianstadt at all, it is usually from a chapter in Ruth Kluger's book *Still Alive*.[17] Today the site is completely overgrown, almost impossible to find without a guide, and parts of it are still occupied by the Polish military and are strictly off-limits to visitors.[18] The surrounding population is entirely different from that during and before the war. At the end of the war the German population was expelled westward, and it was repopulated with Polish nationals, many of whom had been expelled from what had been eastern Poland, so the discontinuity between past and present is even greater there than in many other places.

Here are four ways in which a "micro" focus might push outward as well as inward and in which an account of Christianstadt would deepen our knowledge and perhaps challenge our thinking. Firstly, it would disturb and add complexity to the more commonly known patterns and images. The Jewish women arrived there *after* Auschwitz—spending about six months in Christianstadt after six or so weeks in Auschwitz. We usually think of Auschwitz as the end point and summation of Holocaust horror. Moreover, both in the munitions factory and in road and railroad construction, women performed the hardest labor there. It also would bring attention to the juxtapositions and interactions between groups of people, going beyond the dominant dualistic portrait of SS guard and Jewish prisoner. Thirdly, a study of Christianstadt could highlight connections and networks, such as the ways in which Christianstadt was thoroughly intertwined with the changing landscapes of what was happening elsewhere during the war. Working to trace, for instance, the shipment of goods—what munitions were manufactured there, where they were deployed, and with what effects—would help us to see how this remote place was crucially interconnected to the German war effort. And lastly, it should encourage us to consider not only the spatial but also the temporal dimensions of this place. Microhistory is an act that affects the present, not just one that restores a forgotten or suppressed past. One reason for a microhistory of Christianstadt is to push against the state-sponsored forgetting and to foreground the many layers of intervening history that colluded in continuing to camouflage this zone.

Perhaps the most iconic image of the Holocaust is of the railroad tracks leading into Birkenau. Yet one rarely thinks of these tracks leading people out of the camp. Of course far more people entered than left, but for many, Auschwitz-Birkenau was not the last transport point, and exploring the multitude of trajectories of Jews during the Holocaust adds to our understanding of German aims and Jewish experiences. In interviews with women who survived Christianstadt, from the USC Shoah Foundation Visual History Archive, the interviewers usually ask a lot of questions about Auschwitz, where the person spent six weeks, but show little or no interest in Christianstadt, where they spent the next six months.[19] The structural limitations of these interviews—such as the ways in which a onetime interview with someone previously unknown to the interviewee tends to direct testimony along the more familiar and conventional patterns of public Holocaust knowledge—need to be actively brought out, interrogated, and perhaps to some extent resisted.

Following these women's trajectories also illuminates the factors that led to the movement of people, such as the tension among some of the German hierarchy between killing Jews and exploiting them for their labor. Mapping the *movements* of Jews in the period 1939–45 can add greatly to our understanding. For the women arriving at Christianstadt from Auschwitz, the first impression was often one of pleasant surprise: "It was impossible not to register the beauty and fragrance of the summertime forest ... [we] couldn't get over our amazement: there were bunks in each room and they had straw mattresses."[20] But these impressions quickly gave way to the hardship and poisonous danger of the work, filling and cleaning grenades, and walking five or six kilometers each way to the factory. The work with the explosives turned the women's hair orange. Although recently there has been more attention paid to the experiences of Jewish women during the Holocaust, an exclusively Jewish women's slave labor camp opens up many important questions about gender. Ruth Kluger states that the "women guards of Christianstadt were more moderate in their authoritarianism" and argues that "the Nazi evil was male, not female."[21]

Christianstadt, as a major industrial military enterprise, brought together the entire spectrum of workers and slave laborers, with German civilian managers (men) at the top, and the Jewish women, who did the most hazardous and unhealthy work, at the bottom. Fences are dominant images of the Holocaust: of camps and ghettos, with Jews and SS guards on the inside and all others on the outside. A study of the explosives factory at Christianstadt necessarily pushes against this image of stark separation. There were continual crossings of boundaries, between different spaces (daily movement from one place to another), between groups (frequent contact between civilians and the enslaved, between locals and workers from elsewhere, between people of many different ethnicities occupying different places on the social hierarchy), and also between sexes (the anomaly of the Jewish slave labor here being exclusively women, working primarily among men). There were of course many forms of division and separation, including fences, only some of which were enforced by the Germans.[22] An investigation of *spaces* in Christianstadt would highlight the ways in which many different "realities" continually came into contact with each other. The broad categories of perpetrator, bystander, and victim do not really get at the complexity of the interactions between people over time at a place such as Christianstadt, and a microhistory could help refine and rethink these terms.

A Czech forced laborer who worked in the power plant at Christianstadt also played guitar in the company orchestra (there was a *"Betriebsorchester"* [company orchestra] composed mainly of forced laborers) and took many documents with him, such as the schedule of performances (including the amount paid for each performance), throughout the complex from November 1943 to November 1944.[23] His one refuge and joy during his time there was the orchestra. The Jewish women, of course, did not attend these concerts (such as for the "Kundgebung NSDAP [Nazi Party rally]" on 18 September 1944, though far more common are performances simply noted as "evening concert"), but a juxtaposition of these archival documents and accounts of life in the labor camp disturbs our perspectives. The document is ordinary yet also extraordinary, and haunting from a postwar perspective. It sharpens the contrast between seemingly routine activities and the extreme circumstances in which enslaved people from several parts of the world made music together for the enjoyment of other workers far from home and occasionally for party functionaries. A microhistory of Christianstadt would be less an act of penetration into a hidden space than of mapping and attending to movements within and across spaces.

A focus on Christianstadt can also open up a window into the complexity of the far-flung German labor and industrial system during the war. The Christianstadt site was a military secret, but it was integrated into the main networks of German society and was critical for the German war effort (it was most important for the production of "Hexogen," an explosive more than twice as powerful as TNT). A study of Christianstadt should trace and explore these networks, movements, and connections and not be restricted to the spatial borders of the geographic site.

The temporal boundaries and layers of Christianstadt are as complicated as the spatial ones, and microhistory can be especially useful for examining and working against the postwar forgetting and erasure of the industrial complex at Christianstadt, which is much less well-known than other major German armaments sites. It did not have the "glamour" of producing V-1 and V-2 rockets, although some women claimed in their testimony that they were being manufactured at the site,[24] and after the war many people and several countries (Germany, Poland, the USSR) had an interest in forgetting its existence and in letting the area return mostly to a "wild" state of overgrown forest with scattered industrial ruins.[25] The history of Christianstadt before the arrival of the Jewish women is also essentially connected to Holocaust history, and a few Jewish slave laborers did work there earlier on, such as in 1942.[26]

In concluding, rather than sketch out further the importance of including the postwar period in a microhistory of Christianstadt, I want to briefly turn to two of the very few explorations of Christianstadt, both by artists: the photographer Yishay Garbasz and the writer Jan Faktor (their mothers were both there).[27] What is most striking in each of their work, in very different ways, is the pursuit of and extreme attention to some of the remaining artifacts: ruins in the landscape, documents, and also memories from people who were there. Each detail and nuance that they make visible holds the promise of providing access to many further threads that have been lost, forgotten, suppressed, and overgrown. But the power of the details is in part that they are orphaned—that they do not belong (yet) to a well-known terrain, even as they are situated within the history of the Holocaust and the Third Reich.

What might the (micro) historian learn from the artist about the treatment and framing of the detail? Garbasz's approach, in her book *In My Mother's Footsteps,* seems relatively straightforward: photographs of the ruins of Christianstadt and of the "Am Schwedenwall" women's camp (as it was named) are juxtaposed on facing pages with her excerpts from her mother Salla's memoir (written before Yishay took the photos). This work highlights the gap between past and present, text and image, personal recollection and traces of evidence. But as Garbasz notes, "I am not trying to illustrate her words," which would have "been a much simpler and quicker process." Rather, "the things she would not speak were the most important parts of the text. The silences ... spoke volumes."[28] These photographs, taken with a large-format camera (which takes a great deal more time and preparation than a digital snapshot), begin to inhabit the places where they are taken and can help us to meditate on, think through, and especially learn from the words and their silences.

Faktor's work (which includes sections from a novel as well as a television documentary, a newspaper essay, and other documentary pursuits) is driven by what is no longer seeable and what is not known. Each moment of looking, asking, and exploring is an act of resistance against the discontinuity between past and present. His penetration of the thickets around Christianstadt, interviews of those with knowledge of the place, extensive photographing of what is there today, and collection of documents pursue the double task of seeing what remains of the places that correspond to his memories of his mother's stories of Christianstadt and of bringing what had been remembered and talked about only privately back into the realm of the public. On the one hand, he completes the private journey that he never undertook with his mother and provides a physical correspondence for the harrowing, surreal, and at times comic stories he grew up with; and on the other hand, there is a refusal of the "private" (this munitions factory, central to the Nazi war effort, was secret but never private) in an attempt to push what should be "public" knowledge into view.

For these artists, the question of how to relate the detail to a larger picture haunts and drives their work. The common trope of synecdoche, of a part standing in for the whole, does not supply their operative logic. Each detail is powerful in relation to the objects and people that are no longer present, and the artists foreground the tension between knowing and not knowing in which they find themselves. A dynamics of knowing and not knowing should be at the heart of any engagement with the Holocaust.

Jeffrey Wallen is dean of the School of Humanities, Arts, and Cultural Studies and professor of comparative literature at Hampshire College, in Amherst, Massachusetts. He has taught as a visiting professor at the Free University Berlin and at the University of Toulouse and is the director of Hampshire's semester-long study abroad program in Berlin. He has published widely on nineteenth- and twentieth-century European literature; on biography and literary portraiture; on eyewitness testimony, Holocaust literature, and Berlin Jewish history; and on debates about education. He is currently working on a study of the archive in contemporary thought and art.

Notes

1. Norbert Frei and Wulf Kansteiner, eds., *Den Holocaust erzählen: Historiographie zwischen wissenschaftlicher Empirie und narrativer Kreativität* (Göttingen: Wallstein Verlag, 2013), 246.
2. Christopher Browning, *Remembering Survival: Inside a Nazi Slave-Labor Camp* (New York: W. W. Norton & Co., 2010), 291.
3. H-Net: Humanities and Social Sciences Online, "Call for Papers: Exploring the micro history of the Holocaust." https://www.h-net.org/announce/show.cgi?ID=190022.

4. Patrick Desbois's work and his book *The Holocaust by Bullets: A Priest's Journey to Uncover the Murder of 1.5 Million Jews* (New York: Palgrave Macmillan, 2008) have been instrumental in bringing to light numerous killing sites in the Ukraine and elsewhere. For an indication of the (very slowly) growing penetration of this research in the popular imagination, see Alison Smale, "Shedding Light on a Vast Toll of Jews Killed away from the Death Camps," *New York Times*, 27 January 2014, http://www.nytimes.com/2014/01/28/world/europe/a-light-on-a-vast-toll-of-jews-killed-away-from-the-death-camps.html?_r=0.
5. David Mikics quotes from his conversation with Snyder: "The field now is in a very micro-mode," he [Snyder] said. "And what I think about the micro-mode is that it's a little bit self-indulgent, because you talk about Poles and Ukrainians and Jews, and it ends up confirming your own view about Poles and Ukrainians and Jews." See David Mikics, "The Diplomat of Shoah History," *Tablet*, 26 July 2012, http://www.tabletmag.com/jewish-arts-and-culture/books/107382/diplomat-of-shoah-history?all=1.
6. Timothy Snyder, *Bloodlands: Europe between Hitler and Stalin* (New York: Basic Books, 2010), 408.
7. The "era of the witness" is Annette Wieviorka's term, from her book *The Era of the Witness*, trans. Jared Stark (New York: Cornell University Press, 2006); Elie Wiesel, "Twentieth Anniversary Keynote," in *What Have We Learned? Telling the Story and Teaching the Lessons of the Holocaust: Papers of the Twentieth Anniversary Scholar's Conference*, ed. Franklin Littell (Lewiston: Edwin Mellen Press, 1993), 5–6.
8. Saul Friedländer, *Nazi Germany and the Jews*, vol. 1, *The Years of Persecution* (New York: Harper Perennial, 1998), 5.
9. David Mikics, "The Diplomat of Shoah History," *Tablet*, 26 July 2012.
10. Wieviorka, *The Era of the Witness*, 126. Wieviorka is quoting from Anne-Lise Stern's essay "Sois déportée ... et témoigne! Psychanalyser, témoigner: double bind?," in *La Shoah: témoignages, savoirs, oeuvres*, ed. A. Wieviorka and C. Mouchard (Vincennes: Presses Universitaires de Vincennes, 1999), 17. I have used Jared Stark's translation from Wieviorka's book but translated a few additional words from Stern's text that precede the passage quoted by Wieviorka.
11. A. Wieviorka, introduction to *La Shoah: témoignages, savoirs, oeuvres* (Vincennes: Presses Universitaires de Vincennes, 1999), 12, my translation.
12. I mean here both the "literal" archive to which the report is destined, as well as the "archive" in the much broader sense used, quite differently, by Jacques Derrida, Michel Foucault, and Pierre Nora. See my essay "Narrative Tensions: The Eyewitness and the Archive," *Partial Answers* 7, no. 2 (2009): 261–78.
13. This document is transcribed in Raul Hilberg's *Sources of Holocaust Research: An Analysis* (Chicago: Ivan R. Dee, 2001), 149. Hilberg in turn is quoting from Michael Hanusiak, *Lest We Forget* (New York, 1975), 92–93. In the edition of *Lest We Forget* that I consulted (Toronto: Progress Books, 1976), the cited material is on pages 122–23.
14. In his concluding remarks at the "Den Holocaust erzählen" conference, Hayden White, in speaking about witness literature generally and about Primo Levi in particular, stated, "Primo Levi does not try to add to the factual information about the Holocaust in *If This Is a Man*. He does not try to contribute new data. What he tries to do is to tell us, to give us a sense of *what it felt like* to be there." Frei and Kansteiner, *Den Holocaust erzählen*, 249.
15. The largest study of Christianstadt is Martina Löbner's dissertation, "'Geheime Reichssache' Christianstadt" (Ph.D. diss., Universität Hannover, 2002). I have relied heavily on research done by Jan Faktor, some of which can be viewed in a short television documentary with Christhard Läpple broadcast on ZDF in September 2010, *Das Geheimnis von Christianstadt*. In this television episode Faktor states

that Christianstadt was three to four times the size of Peenemünde. He writes about his explorations of Christianstadt in the article "Das vergessene Konzentrationslager Christianstadt: Tarnname Ulme," *Frankfurter Allgemeine Zeitung*, 27 August 2010, http://www.faz.net/aktuell/feuilleton/themen/das-vergessene-konzentrationslager-christianstadt-tarnname-ulme-11027861.html, and I have benefited greatly through correspondence with Faktor. Articles about Christianstadt can be found in two encyclopedic projects: Barbara Sawicka, "Christianstadt," in *The United States Holocaust Memorial Museum Encyclopedia of Camps and Ghettos*, ed. Geoffrey Magergee, vol. 1, part A (Bloomington: Indiana University Press, 2009), 722–23; and Andrea Rudorff, "Christianstadt (Krzystkowice)," in *Der Ort des Terrors: Geschichte der nationalsozialistischen Konzentrationslager, Band 6, Natzweiler, Groß-Rosen, Stutthof*, ed. Wolfgang Benz and Barbara Distel (Munich: C. H. Beck, 2007), 270–75. A volume of memoirs about Christianstadt (including a piece by Jan Faktor's mother) is Ela Fischerová et al., *The World without Human Dimensions: Four Women's Memories* (Prague: State Jewish Museum in Prague, 1991). There are numerous testimonies that mention Christianstadt, some at length, in the USC Shoah Foundation's Visual History Archive.
16. The USHMM *Encyclopedia* article states that in "September 1944, two transports of Jewish women from the Auschwitz concentration camp" were "the first known transports to Christianstadt" (722), but several testimonies speak of arriving in July 1944, such as Frantiska Faktorova-Schornsteinova, in Fischerová et al., *The World without Human Dimensions* (208), and Anna Hyndrakova and Esther Weiss, in their Visual History Archive (VHA) interviews (interviews 2058 and 2210, VHA, USC Shoah Foundation). The German encyclopedic article by Rudorff states that the first transport from Auschwitz arrived 9 July 1944 ("Christianstadt [Krzystkowice]," 271).
17. Ruth Kluger, *Still Alive: A Holocaust Girlhood Remembered* (New York: Feminist Press, 2003). She discusses Christianstadt in the chapter "Forced Labor Camp," 113–31, and states that they left Auschwitz "in late June" (113).
18. A photograph of this restricted area can be seen on Christhard Läpple's website, http://www.christhard-laepple.de/archiv-christianstadt.html.
19. An example of the interviewer's lack of interest in Christianstadt is the interview with Rosa Rachlin (interview 3407, VHA, USC Shoah Foundation).
20. Vera Hájková-Duxová, in Fischerová et al., *The World without Human Dimensions*, 101.
21. Kluger, *Still Alive*, 116, 115.
22. In several testimonies people spoke of a hierarchy among the Jewish women, with the Czech and Austrian German-speaking Jews, who arrived earlier, looking down at the "shtetl" Jews from farther east who arrived later.
23. Karel Fucík, interviewed by Jan Faktor.
24. For example, Helen Shonberg, interview 1640, VHA, USC Shoah Foundation.
25. In the 1980s Krzystkowice was incorporated into the neighboring Nowogród Bobrzanski, so even the place name has in a sense disappeared.
26. Moniek Baumzecer (interview 5724, VHA, USC Shoah Foundation) speaks of being sent to work at a factory there in 1942. He was badly beaten by the Gestapo after being accused (accurately) of sleeping with a German girl and was later sent to Matthausen and Auschwitz. Rudorff also mentions Jews (presumably men) working there as well in 1942 ("Christianstadt [Krzystkowice]," 271).
27. Yishay Garbasz, *In My Mother's Footsteps* (Ostfildern: Hatje Cantz, 2009); and Jan Faktor's novel *Georgs Sorgen um die Vergangenheit, oder im Reich des Heiligen Hodensack-Bimbams von Prag* (Frankfurt: Fischer Taschenbuch Verlag, 2011).
28. Garbasz, *In My Mother's Footsteps*, 9.

Bibliography

Baumzecer, Moniek. Interview 5724. Visual History Archive, USC Shoah Foundation.
Browning, Christopher. *Remembering Survival: Inside a Nazi Slave-Labor Camp*. New York: W. W. Norton & Co., 2010.
Desbois, Patrick. *The Holocaust by Bullets: A Priest's Journey to Uncover the Murder of 1.5 Million Jews*. New York: Palgrave Macmillan, 2008.
Faktor, Jan. *Georgs Sorgen um die Vergangenheit, oder im Reich des Heiligen Hodensack-Bimbams von Prag*. Frankfurt: Fischer Taschenbuch Verlag, 2011.
———. "Das vergessene Konzentrationslager Christianstadt: Tarnname Ulme." *Frankfurter Allgemeine Zeitung*, 27 August 2010. http://www.faz.net/aktuell/feuilleton/themen/das-vergessene-konzentrationslager-christianstadt-tarnname-ulme-11027861.html.
Fischerová, Ela, et al. *The World without Human Dimensions: Four Women's Memories*. Prague: State Jewish Museum in Prague, 1991.
Frei, Norbert, and Wulf Kansteiner, eds. *Den Holocaust erzählen: Historiographie zwischen wissenschaftlicher Empirie und narrativer Kreativität*. Göttingen: Wallstein Verlag, 2013.
Friedländer, Saul. *Nazi Germany and the Jews*. Vol. 1, *The Years of Persecution*. New York: Harper Perennial, 1998
Garbasz, Yishay. *In My Mother's Footsteps*. Ostfildern: Hatje Cantz, 2009.
Hanusiak, Michael. *Lest We Forget*. Toronto: Progress Books, 1976.
Hilberg, Raul. *Sources of Holocaust Research: An Analysis*. Chicago: Ivan R. Dee, 2001.
Hyndrakova, Anna. Interview 2058. Visual History Archive, USC Shoah Foundation.
Kluger, Ruth. *Still Alive: A Holocaust Girlhood Remembered*. New York: Feminist Press, 2003.
Läpple, Christhard. *Das Geheinmis von Christianstadt*. ZDF, Mainz, September 2010.
———. http://www.christhard-laepple.de/archiv-christianstadt.html.
Löbner, Martina. "'Geheime Reichssache' Christianstadt." Ph.D. diss., Universität Hannover, 2002.
Mikics, David. "The Diplomat of Shoah History." *Tablet*, 26 July 2012. http://www.tabletmag.com/jewish-arts-and-culture/books/107382/diplomat-of-shoah-history?all=1.
Rachlin, Rosa. Interview 3407. Visual History Archive, USC Shoah Foundation.
Rudorff, Andrea. "Christianstadt (Krzystkowice)", in *Der Ort des Terrors: Geschichte der nationalsozialistischen Konzentrationslager, Band 6, Natzweiler, Groß-Rosen, Stutthof*, edited by Wolfgang Benz and Barbara Distel, Munich: C. H. Beck, 2007, 270–75.
Sawicka, Barbara. "Christianstadt", in *The United States Holocaust Memorial Museum Encyclopedia of Camps and Ghettos*, edited by Geoffrey Magergee, vol. 1, part A, 722–23. Bloomington: Indiana University Press, 2009.
Shonberg, Helen. Interview 1640. Visual History Archive, USC Shoah Foundation.
Smale, Alison. "Shedding Light on a Vast Toll of Jews Killed away from the Death Camps." *New York Times*, 27 January 2014. http://www.nytimes.com/2014/01/28/world/europe/a-light-on-a-vast-toll-of-jews-killed-away-from-the-death-camps.html?_r=0.
Snyder, Timothy. *Bloodlands: Europe between Hitler and Stalin*. New York: Basic Books, 2010.
Stern, Anne-Lise. "Sois déportée ... et témoigne! Psychanalyser, témoigner: *double bind*?" In *La Shoah: témoignages, savoirs, oeuvres*, edited by A. Wieviorka and C. Mouchard. Vincennes: Presses Universitaires de Vincennes, 1999, 15-22.
Wallen, Jeffrey. "Narrative Tensions: The Eyewitness and the Archive." *Partial Answers* 7, no. 2 (2009), 261–78.
Weiss, Esther. Interview 2210. Visual History Archive, USC Shoah Foundation.

Wiesel, Elie. "Twentieth Anniversary Keynote", in *What Have We Learned? Telling the Story and Teaching the Lessons of the Holocaust: Papers of the Twentieth Anniversary Scholar's Conference,* edited by Franklin Littell. Lewiston: Edwin Mellen Press, 1993, 1–14.

Wieviorka, Annette. *The Era of the Witness,* translated by Jared Stark. New York: Cornell University Press, 2006.

———. Introduction to *La Shoah: témoignages, savoirs, oeuvres,* edited by A. Wieviorka and C. Mouchard. Vincennes: Presses Universitaires de Vincennes, 1999, 11–14.

INDEX

A

Adamowicz, Ludwik, 183, 188
Adana, 20
AE Wassermann, 20, 21
affidavit, 34
Africa, 89, 290
agency, 3, 8, 76, 185, 191, 202, 211, 221
agricultural training camp, 216
Akkerman, Peter, 195-6, 199, 206
Allach, 163
allgemeine Treuhand-Stelle für jüdische Auswanderung GmbH, 20
allied bombings, 47, 51, 53
Almeidas, Mihail, 72, 82
Alsace, 164
Alsoviso, 56
Alter, Miriam, 162, 169
Aly, Götz, 11, 91, 110
Amsterdam, 20-21
Amtsgerichte, 212
Andreasik, Andrzej, 180, 188
Andriiasova, Niura, 199
Andrusin, Afanasii, 194-5, 205
Angoulême, 89
Ankara, 20
Anschluss, 29, 30, 35
anti-Jewish, 211-12, 214-15, 218-20, 237, 260, 268, 273, 275, 277
anti-Semitism, 19, 29, 76, 95, 116, 184, 191, 202, 237, 243, 247-48, 268, 271
Antlers, Max, 217
Antoniów, 175

Arbeitserziehungslager, 218
arbitrariness, 8, 103, 107-8
Arendt, Hannah, 202, 206-7, 210, 221
artists, 309-310
aryanization, 36, 87, 91- 92, 106
Athens, 73
Atlasz, Eugen, 55, 57
Atlasz, Tomas, 55, 57
attacks, 211-12, 215-16, 219-20, 255
Auden, W.H., 171
Augier, Marc, 243
Augsburg, 156, 165
August Decree, 269, 272-73, 277-81
Augustyn, family, 180
Augustyn, Józef, 180
Auschwitz, 4, 6, 44-48, 50-51, 60, 61, 74, 91, 106, 154, 158-61, 165, 248, 301, 306-7
Australia, 30-33, 292
Austria, 4, 19, 33, 35-36, 39, 155, 218
Avion, 90, 92

B

Bad Arolsen, 8, 45
Bajorek, Stanisław, 181
Bălți, 254
Baltic States, 253
Bandman, Hersz, 55
Bardach, Janusz, 277, 283
Baron, Léon, 102
Basel, 18
Bauer, Yehuda, 210, 222

Bauman, Zygmunt, 202, 206-7
Belarus, 2
Belgium, 85, 87-88, 91, 104-5, 160
Bełżec, 137, 140, 147
Bendhem, Elise, born Frank, 25-26
Berezovka, 193, 197, 201
Bergen-Belsen, 144
Berger, Jeno, 55, 57
Berkowits, Alexander (Srulik Bercovics), 48, 62, 64-66
Berlin, 6, 17-21, 23-24, 57, 69, 80, 90, 113, 153, 209, 211-20
Berman, Tibor, 51
Berman, Wilhelm, 51
Bessarabia, 193, 198, 251-54, 256, 258-62
Béthune, 88-90, 92-93, 95, 101-2
Bettelheim, Bruno, 210, 221
Bezek, 270-1
Białystok, 6
Bierut, Bolesław, 277, 281
Birkenau, 6, 44, 46-50, 60, 303, 306-7
Birnbaum, Sidney, 151, 159, 165, 167, 169
Blatman, Daniel, 184, 188
Bloch, Marc, 8, 12
Block, 45-61, 64, 115, 153, 191
Bobrowa, 183
Boder, David, 43, 51-52, 54, 62, 65
Bogdanovka, 193, 195, 197, 199, 201
Bohemia, 133, 221
Bohnet, Ernst, 254
Bohrer, Eva, 165, 169
Bordeaux, 89
Bosek, Zygmunt, 274
Boujet, André, 244, 249
Boulogne-sur-Mer, 89
Bourg-d'Oisans, 246
Brăila, 258
Bremen, 217
Brenner, Karl, 230
Brnik, 146, 147, 148
Brody, family, 117-119, 121
Broikos, Athanassios, 72, 78-79, 83
Bross, Alexander, 254
Browning, Christopher, 7, 11-12, 23, 27, 110-111, 186, 188, 191-2, 203-4, 207, 237, 240, 260, 263-4, 286, 294-6, 298, 300-1, 310, 313
Brunner, Alois, 80
Brzeziany, 180
Brzezinski, Maurice, 245, 247
Brzóza (Brzuza), 181
Bucharest, 252, 256, 260

Buchenwald, 4, 6, 44-46, 48-53
Budapest, 5, 6, 46, 113-18, 120-2
Buenos Aires, 80
Bukovina, 251, 253-7, 259, 261-2
Buna, 6, 44, 46, 47, 48, 49, 50, 51, 53, 54, 55, 56, 57, 58, 60, 62
Bünau, Heinrich von, 229-31, 235-6, 240
Bürckel, Josef, 218
Bureau, Jacques, 245
Burzec, 274, 281
Butrimonys, 177
bystander, 8, 133-4, 308
Bzowski, Kazimierz, 278, 280

C

Calw, 159
Canada, 31, 32, 36-37, 148, 292
Carlebach, Emil, 58
Carlebach, Joseph, 217, 224
Carol II, king, 252
Carp, Valeriu, 259
Cayeux, Claude de, 244-245
Cayeux, Jean-Pierre de, 243-4
cemetery, 7, 68-81, 102, 148, 257, 259
census, 87, 89, 91, 95, 103, 106, 115, 257
Central Office for Jewish Emigration, 19
Cernăuți, 254
Cetatea Albă, 254
Chajn, Leon, 277, 283
Chełm, 270
Cher, 246
Cherniavskaia, Efrosin'ia, 201
Chișinău, 254
Cholovskii, Safran, 201
Christianstadt, 10, 300, 303, 305-10
Chrysochoou, Athanassios, 69, 77-78
Chrząstów, 181
Cin, Sam (Samu Cin), 48, 52, 55, 57
Ciołek, Aleksander, 274
Cognac, 89
collaboration, 73, 134-5, 181, 190, 235, 242-4, 247-8, 258, 268-9, 281
collective memory, 86, 301
Cologne, 6, 214
Comlausa, 49, 62-63
communist, 8, 53-54, 58-59, 135, 190, 193, 214, 254-5, 259, 260-1, 273, 275-7
comparative microhistory, 220
Comrat, 254
concentration camp, 44, 52, 60, 144, 147, 152-3, 156, 161, 174, 192, 197-8, 213-4, 218-9, 258, 300

convoy, 2, 7, 91
Costa Rica, 32
courageous acts, 221
crimes against humanity, 190-1
Curfew, 87, 119, 121, 218
Czajka, family, 179
Czechoslovakia, 5, 45, 48-49, 51, 62-63, 157, 159, 165
Czelatyce, 176
Czen, Salomon, 48, 51-52, 55, 57, 62
Czermno, 179
Czerniakiewicz, Maria, 272
Czernowitz, 6
Czerwonek, family, 177

D

Dąbie, 177, 178
Dąbrowa Tarnowska, 135, 137-9, 143, 145-6
Dachau, 37, 151, 153
Daume, Max, 231
Davidson, Shamai, 61, 66-67
Dawidowicz, family, 89-95, 99, 101-2
Dawidowicz, Jakob, 55
Dawidowicz, Jean, 93, 110
Dawidowicz, Joseph, 88, 99
Dawidowicz, Mendel, 55
Dawidowicz, Moïse, 90
Dębica, 180, 183
defiance, 209
Delestrez, family, 101
Delphin, Jean, 243-245, 249
Denmark, 90
deportation, 6, 17-18, 21-23, 36-37, 68, 76-77, 79-80, 85, 88-89, 92-93, 103-4, 113, 115-6, 137, 140, 154, 173, 184, 211, 219-20, 248, 268, 288, 294, 303
deported, 5, 18, 22, 34, 44, 49, 87, 91, 94, 103-104, 106, 137, 140, 154, 174, 192, 198, 248, 259-60, 262, 303
Dernau, 165
deutsche Golddiskontbank, 23
diaries, 38, 210-211
Dilg, Adolf, 163
Diner, Dan, 296, 298-9
Dniester river, 192, 198, 252
Domanevka, 193, 199
Domaszewska, 279
Dorohoi, 7, 251-2, 257, 260-1
Douai, 90, 92, 102
Drânceni, 259

Droś, Szymon, 279
Dudek, family, 176, 187
Dumas, Jean, 244-5, 249
Dumitru, Diana, 193, 205, 207
Düsseldorf, 215
Dworzecki, Meir, 210, 222, 225

E

East Prussia, 229, 236
Échirolles, 6, 242, 245-7
Eclache, Guy, 243-5
Eichmann, Adolf, 19, 25, 46, 69, 80-82, 84, 206-7
Einsatzgruppen, 227, 235, 237
Eleu-dit-Leauwette, 102
Eliahu, rabbi, 52
Ellenbogen, Marianne, 113
Ellenbogen, Zoltan, 48, 60, 62, 64
emigration, 4-5, 7, 17-20, 22-23, 30, 32-36, 38, 216, 276
Engel, Margarete, 217, 224
Engelking, Barbara, 267, 282, 284
England, 33, 90
Erben, Peter, 159, 168
Erlich, Berek, 62
Erlich, Yehuda, 176
Ermolaev, Nikolai, 197
Eschershausen, 56
Eschwege, Helmut, 210, 222, 226
Ettersburg, 45
Europe, 1, 6, 17, 30, 35-36, 39, 53, 68, 85, 90, 133-4, 166, 171, 190, 203, 242, 246-8, 262, 268-9, 271, 296
Evian Conference, 19
exodus, 89, 91, 93, 98, 102, 229
eyewitness, 8, 72, 193-7, 199, 201, 237, 303, 310

F

Faktor, Jan, 309, 311-3
Falck, Caroline, 217, 224
Feldmann, Manfred, 218, 224
Fels, Edgar, 217, 224
Fereński, Jan, 179, 187
Final Solution, 1, 2, 6, 8, 46, 69, 80, 134, 154, 237, 246-8, 294
Finland, 253
Fischböck, Hans, 23
Fischman, Harry, 55, 62, 65
Flaschmann, Toba, 219
Florida, 61
Flossenbürg, 6, 151, 153, 159, 163

forced middle names, 217
France, 5, 6, 8, 47, 51, 63, 85, 87–88, 90, 93–97, 104–5, 148, 156–7, 160, 243, 246–8, 253
Frank, Gertrud (born Munk), 21
Frank, Hans, 174
Frank, Martha, 216–7, 224
Frank, Miriam, 162, 169
Frank, Richard, 5, 17, 18, 20–27
Franke, Otto, 231–4, 239
Frankfurt am Main, 213, 215
Freiberg, 160, 163, 165
Friedländer, Saul, 1, 10, 12, 24, 27, 132, 149–50, 171, 185–6, 189, 210, 222, 225, 300, 302, 311, 313
Frommer, Benjamin, 133, 149–50
Fruchter, Zehava, 162, 169
Frydrich, Szmul, 55, 57

G
Galați, 7, 251, 252, 257–61
Gamratka, 179
Garbasz, Yishay, 309, 312–3
Garofallou, Periklis, 73, 82
gas chambers, 301
gendarme/gendarmerie, 7, 140, 146–7, 172–6, 178–182, 197, 201, 247, 258, 261
General Government, 9, 134–5, 153, 155, 162, 173, 177, 181, 184–5, 229
Gennadios, bishop, 79
Geography, 114, 122
German propaganda, 254
Germany, 5, 17–23, 29, 34–36, 38, 44–47, 56, 90, 151–2, 154–7, 160, 165–6, 175, 179, 210, 213–6, 219, 220, 230, 252–3, 268, 305, 309
Gertner, Jakob, 200
Gertner, Johannes, 200
Gestapo, 23, 144, 147, 163, 177, 179, 180–2, 214, 216–8, 220, 270, 276
Geva, Agnes, 159, 168
Ghelmegeanu, Mihail, 255
ghettoization, 76, 114–122
ghettos, 1, 9, 15, 17, 46, 74, 114, 116, 118, 153, 171, 174–5, 181, 184, 192, 210, 286, 300, 307
Gild, Liudmila, 200
Ginzburg, Carlo, 3, 6, 11–12, 122, 126, 222, 225
Gipner, Vladimir, 194, 199
Gitgaru, Efim, 195

Giventer, Roza, 198
Givon, Miriam, 160, 161, 168–9
Gleiwitz, 44, 47, 49, 51, 61
Glicksman, Sara, 90
Gniewczyna Łęczycka, 172
Gniewczyna Tryniecka, 172
Gniewczyna, 132
Goebbels, Joseph, 214–5
Goldberg, Albert, 101–102
Goldfinger, József, 177
Goldman, family, 172
Goldman, Sabina, 137, 139–40, 149
Golembowski, family, 177
Golta, 193–5, 197
Gomułka, Władysław, 281
Göring, Hermann, 19, 153, 167
Gorlice, 179
Görlitz, 162
Gotha, 57
Gottlieb, Abraham (Abraham Ahuvia), 54, 65, 67
Gottlieb, Chaim Meir, 54
Gotzamanis, Sotirios, 73, 82
Grabka, József, 146–7
Grabka, Wojciech, 147
Granchak, Ivan, 201–2
Grębecki, Jacek, 277
Greece, 70, 77
Greenwood, 31
Gregoruk, Michał, 271
Grendi, Edoardo, 4, 11–12
Grenoble, 6, 101, 242–6
Grinwald, Mordka "Maurice", 245, 247, 249
Grochowe, 179
Gross Rosen, 306
Gross, Alex (Szandor), 47, 51, 54, 59, 62, 64–65, 67
Gross, Jan T., 11, 192, 250, 267, 286, 295–6, 298–9
Gross, Samu (Sam Gross), 47, 54, 62
Gross, Ted (Tibor), 49, 51, 62, 64
Grossman, Chaim Hersz (Henry Grossman), 48–49, 52, 56, 62, 64
Grossman, Vasily, 1, 10, 13
Grüner, Miklos, 56
Grzymała, Władysław, 274–5, 277, 283
Guatemala Transfer, 20, 22–23
Guatemala, 20–23
Guerre, Martin, 113, 122, 127
Guerry, 246
Guillot-Sestier, André, 245

Gurs, 102
Guttman, Istvan, 50

H
Haavara Transfer, 20
Halberstadt, 56, 58
Hamburg, 90, 212–214, 216–20
Hartung, Rudolf, 194, 205
Harz mountains, 56
Haske, Nathan, 179
Hauch, Karl, 180
Heinkel aircraft factory, 151
Heinkel, Ernst, 151, 153–6, 158, 162–3, 167–70
Heinz, Tecklenburg & Co, 21–23
Henriot, Philippe, 246
Hermann, Adolf, 218
Herring, Alfons, 20–22
Herrmann, Irmgard, 214
Herskovicz, Josef, 55
Heydrich, Reinhard, 19
Hilberg, Raul, 1, 8, 10, 12–13, 210, 221, 260, 311, 313
Hils, 56
Himmler, Heinrich, 17, 23, 153, 162, 167, 235
Hirsch, Imre, 50–52, 55, 60
Hirsch, Istvan (Stefan Guttman), 50–52, 55, 60, 62
Hirsch, Paul, 50–52, 55, 60, 62
Hitler youth, 214
Hitler, Adolf, 24, 28–29, 145, 154, 203–4, 207, 209, 213–6, 218–9, 221, 225, 227, 234–5, 237, 240–1, 254, 311
Hoffmann, Hans, 231–4
Holland, 47, 157
Holzen, 56
Horenburg, 161
Horwitz, Gordon, 116, 124
Hotin, 198, 254
Houston, 285
Hugo Luckner Company, 219
Huși, 259
Huszt, 46, 48, 56, 62

I
Iasi, 261–262
Iatropoulos, Petros, 74, 82
identification cards, 217, 245
IG Farben, 47
immigration, 23, 29–34, 36, 37–38

individual Jewish resistance, 9, 210, 219, 221
International Tracing Service (ITS), 8, 45
internment, 87
interview, 51, 54, 55, 62, 64, 93, 120, 158, 193, 213, 285–6, 289, 292–3, 307, 310
Ioanid, Radu, 259, 262–4
Isaacson, Lena, 29, 32, 34
Isaacson, Rudolf, 29, 32, 34
Isakovics, Samuel, 51, 52, 54, 62, 65
Isère, 132, 245–6, 248
Ismail, 254
Israel, 45, 159, 217, 218, 271
Italy, 47, 79, 101, 157, 160, 253
Izsak, Sam, 49, 51, 52, 55, 62

J
Jacobs, Diane, 214, 216, 223–4
Jaki, Wilhelm, 180
Jakubowitz, Samuel, 48, 52, 55, 62–64
Janinagrube, 48
Jasło, 178, 180–181
Jedwabne, 267, 295
Jewish identity, 59, 93, 96
Jewish opposition, 210, 214, 221
Jewish World Congress, 19
Jonus, Alexander, 200
journey, 23, 31, 34, 38, 52, 120, 140, 270, 310
Judenhaus, 21
Judenreferat, 133
Junghans, Oskar, 215, 223

K
Kalina, Antonin, 53, 58–59
Kammler, Hans, 154
Kapo, 47–49, 53, 163–4
Karski, Jan, 268, 282, 284
Kassau, 55, 57
Kaste, Dreise, 217, 224
Kaszovitz, Paul (Paul Kassy), 50, 62, 65
Kaszów, 177
Kaszyce, 176
Katz, Andor, 56
Katz, family, 4, 29–30, 35, 38–39
Katz, Grete, 29, 39–42
Katz, Philip, 29, 31, 39–42
Katzenstein, Adolf, 217, 224
Kaunas, 291, 293
Kehrer, Oskar, 254
Khrushchev, Nikita, 281

Kielce, 135
Kiew (Kiev), 191
Kinderblock, 53–55, 59, 61, 64
Kirschner, Kurt, 231–4, 239
Klausner, Heinrich, 21
Kluger, Ruth, 306–7, 312–3
Kmieć, Adam, 146, 149
Koch, Florian, 200
Kommandos, 47, 60
Königsberg, 214, 291
Konusz, 56, 62
Koretz, Zvi, 71–72, 79, 82
Kornblum, Wolf (William Kaye), 55, 62
Kosiński, Czesław, 274–5, 283
Kotula, Franciszek, 178, 182, 185, 187–9
Kowalski, Rosalie, 215, 223
Kozlov, 54
Kozlova, Akulina, 199
Kraków, 135–6, 144, 151, 184, 230
Krohn, Melanie, 219, 225
Krüger, Friedrich-Wilhelm, 230
Krzystkowice *see* Christianstadt
Kur, Zofia, 179, 187
Kwiet, Konrad, 210–2, 226
Kyriakidis, Stilpon, 79, 83

L
Łańcut, 172
Langenstein-Zwieberge, 56–58
Lau, Israel Meir, 64
law on treacherous attacks, 212, 215–6, 219–20
Leipzig, 156, 212, 216–7, 219–20
Lemiech, Bolesław, 278–80
Lens, 5, 6, 87–96, 98–99, 101–9, 132
Les Mureaux, 157
Leszega, Mikołaj, 180, 188,
Letsas, Alexandros, 79, 82–83
letter collections, 36, 38
letters, 29–31, 33–38, 72, 95–96, 118, 215, 219
Lévai, Jenö, 117, 125
Levi, Giovanni, 3, 11, 13, 123, 126, 211, 222, 226
Levi, Primo, 45, 64, 67, 311
Lewithan, Alfred, 219
Libusza, 179
Liebermann, Martha, 23, 28
Lipose, 55
liquidation action, 137, 184
Liszki, 177
Lithuania, 10, 285–7, 289–96

Littschwager, Gerhard, 236
local courts, 212, 215–7
Łódź, 116
London, 33, 37, 236, 268, 273
Łopuszka Wielka, 176
Lorimer, Hayden, 113, 123, 126
Lorner, Alfred, 259
Lorraine, 165
Los Angeles, 212
Löwenstein, Erich, 213, 223
Lower Saxony, 56
Lublin, 2, 6, 272, 279, 281
Luchterhand, Elmer, 60, 66–67
Łuków, 6, 132
Luria, Simkhele, 291–2
Lviv, 304
Lyon, 89, 246

M
Macedonia, 71, 75–76, 78–79
Magdeburg, 21
Majdanek, 6, 51
Makower, Tuwia, 228, 238
Makuła, Zygmunt, 275
Malachyt, 56
Malakis, Georgios, 73
Malch, Paul, 215
Malines, 91
Malinie, 182
Mangarten, David, 62
Markkleeberg, 159–60, 162
Markowa, 172, 176
Matteoli Commission, 8
Mauthausen, 152–3, 164–5
May, Gustav, 219
Meisner, Anton (Anton Mason), 50–52, 58, 60, 62, 65
Mendelsohn, Daniel, 6, 11, 13, 91, 111–2, 131, 148, 150
Merkouriou, Konstantinos, 73, 82
Merten, Maximilian, 70–73, 77–78, 82
Metz, 89
Metzger, Chaja, 147
Metzger, Estera, 137, 145–7
Metzger, family, 145–6
Metzger, Tolka, 147
Meuse, 90
Meyer, Ernst, 215, 223
Michelis & Co, 23
microhistory, 1–6, 24, 46, 88, 114, 122, 131–132, 135, 148, 154, 157–158, 165–166, 171–3, 184–5, 191, 211,

220, 228, 285, 292, 295–6, 300–3, 305–6, 308–9
Miednoje, 174
Mielec, 6, 140, 151, 153, 162–3, 176, 178–9, 181–2
Mielzynski, Rosalie, 214
Milch, Erhard, 153, 163, 169
Miller, Ioannis, 70
Mińsk Mazowiecki, 179
MM Warburg & Co, 20–21
Moldova, 6, 193, 255–6, 259
Molho, Michael, 72–74, 78, 80, 82–84
Monowitz *see* Buna
Montevideo, 31
Moraczow, 151
moral, 77, 81, 86, 94, 131, 172, 174, 185, 190–192, 195, 198, 202, 210, 235, 275, 287–8, 294–5
Morel, Georges, 243–4
Moskovic, Alex (Sandor), 45, 50–51, 53–55, 59, 61–62, 64–66
Moskovic, David, 48, 56, 62, 64
Moskovic, Zoltan, 53–54
Moskovics, Gyula (Julius Moskowits), 50–51, 55, 59, 62, 66
Moździeż, Weronika, 146
Mrozowska, Aleksandra, 270–3, 278
Mühldorf, 165
Munich, 213, 218, 234
municipal/municipality, 71, 73–76, 118, 134, 211, 217–8, 220, 245, 259
Munkacs, 46–47, 51, 55–57, 63

N
Nagykarola, 50–51, 62
Nancy, 90
national socialism, 68
nationality, 88, 90, 93–96, 104–5, 108
naturalization, 87, 92
naturalize, 105, 296
Nazi gauleiter, 217
Nazi regime, 18–19, 36, 38
neighbor, 6, 24, 50, 88, 91–93, 98, 99, 102, 117–9, 121, 139–40, 145–6, 172, 177, 190, 192–3, 215–6, 228, 245, 256, 258–9, 267–1, 274, 289, 291–3, 295, 301
Netherlands, 23, 85, 90, 215
network, 93, 99–102, 114, 117–8, 120, 182, 260, 301, 306, 308
Neuburger, Benno, 218
Neue-Amerika, 194–5, 199–200

Neumann, Simon (Tommy Newman), 48, 60, 62
New York, 31, 287
Nice, 89
Niederorschel, 162
Noe, Hannelore, 218, 224
Nœux-les-Mines, 101
Noisy-le-Grand, 89
Nord, 87, 92
North America, 10, 38, 286, 295–6
November pogrom, 18–19, 220
Nuremberg laws, 214–5
Nutovits, David, 57
Nyirbator, 48, 62
Nyirigyhaza, 46

O
occupied zone, 87, 100–2, 106
Odessa, 192, 200
Ohrdruf, 57
Ołpiny, 180
Operation Reinhard, 9, 173
Oradour-sur-Glane, 247
oral histories, 38
Oranienburg, 153, 155–6, 162
Oschersleben, 21
Ostaszków, 174
Ostrów Mazowiecka, 6, 7, 227–8
Ostrowiec, 55, 57
Owsiak, Franciszek, 146–7, 149
Oxford, 77

P
Pająk, Michał, 176
Palestine, 49, 216
Panama Canal, 37
Pankowski, Itzchak, 163, 169
Panou, Dimitrios, 79, 83
Pantalowice, 176–177
Parczew, 6
Paris, 5–6, 31, 81, 95, 100–1, 148, 245
Pas-de-Calais, 87–89, 92
Pau, 89, 102
Pawłosiów, 177
Pelekanidis, Stylianos, 77
Penn, Morris, 285, 297
Périgueux, 5
perpetrators, 8, 24, 129, 132, 184–5, 190–6, 198–200, 202, 228, 233, 236–7, 246–7, 273, 287, 291–5, 301
physical self-defense, 220
Pielach, Jan, 177–8, 187

Pillich, Theodor, 231–4, 239, 240
Pinsk, 6
Pinsker, Josef, 161–2, 169
Plaszow, 159
Podborze, 176–7, 184
Podoleanka, 201
pogrom, 7, 18–19, 21, 135, 215–6, 218, 220, 251–2, 255, 257, 259–61
Poitiers, 5
Poland, 5, 9, 36, 53–55, 62–63, 74, 90, 131, 133–5, 148, 151, 172–3, 227, 229, 235–6, 245, 253–4, 267–1, 273–4, 276–8, 280, 294–5, 306, 309
Poliakov, Léon, 1, 10, 13
police, 7, 9, 21, 23, 89, 91–101, 119, 132–4, 139–40, 142–3, 145–8, 172–80, 183–4, 191, 193–5, 197–201, 209, 211–4, 217–20, 227–35, 237–8, 242, 245, 254, 258, 261, 270–1, 274–5, 279, 291, 293–5, 304
Pollak, Michael, 85, 110, 112
Poni, Carlo, 3, 6, 12, 122, 126
Pont-Rémy, 90
postcards, 218
Prague, 18, 133
prison/prisoner, 37, 44–47, 49, 51–54, 56–61, 90, 134–5, 144, 163, 173, 181, 213, 215–9, 245, 253, 270–1, 275, 277, 280–1, 287–8, 290, 292, 294, 306
propaganda, 79, 166, 202, 213, 220, 252, 254–5, 260
protest, 7, 77, 201, 209, 212–3, 218–21, 234, 272
Protter, Bogdan, 181–2, 188
Prusin, Alexander, 191, 203–4, 207
Przeworsk, 172, 179
punishment, 134, 163, 202, 217, 267, 269, 272–3, 275–6, 281
Pustków, 183

Q
quantitative analysis, 4, 86, 94, 99, 103, 108–9

R
Rączyna, 176
Radom, 47, 180
Radomyśl Wielki, 140–1, 145
Răducăneni, 259
Radviliškis (Radvilishek), 287
Raguhn, 162
Raidolino, 197

ration cards, 134, 216, 218
Rechnitz, Laura, 218, 224
Red Army, 1, 45, 193, 253, 292
Red Cross, 45, 54–55, 92, 101
red triangles, 59
Reich commissar, 218
Reich Flight Tax, 19
Reich Ministry for Economics, 22
Reich Security Main Office, 17, 22
Reichsbank, 19, 22–23
Reim, Edith, 154
Reitlinger, Gerald, 1, 10, 13
Reni, 258
resistance, 9, 94, 162, 210, 212–215, 219, 221, 242–3, 246, 248, 268, 276, 278, 310
revenge, 245, 255, 261–2, 269, 277, 292
Ribbentrop-Molotov Pact, 253
Riga, 2, 291
Rillieux-la-Pape, 246
Ringelblum, Emanuel, 11, 13, 236, 240–1, 268, 282, 284
Rochas, Georges, 244–5
Roginskaia (Rolinskaia), Anna, 195
Rokietnica, 176
Romania, 5, 44, 62–63, 192, 201, 251–4, 256–62
room to maneuver, 108
Roseman, Mark, 24, 28, 110, 112–3, 123, 127, 260, 263
Rosenblatt, Chaja, 137, 140–2, 144, 146, 148–9
Roth, Cecil, 77, 83, 84
Roth, John, 114, 123–4, 126, 127
Rötler, Joseph, 200, 206
Rozental, Jakob (Jack Rosenthal), 49, 51–52, 55, 63
Ruggiero, Guido, 12, 166, 169–170
Russia, 160
Rydzewski, Stanisław, 175, 186
Rzepiennik Strzyżewski, 181
Rzeszów, 7, 145, 164, 172, 178

S
Saar, 5
Sachsenhausen, 153, 155, 218
Sady, Edward, 274–5
Şafran, Alexandru, 255
Saint-Étienne-de-Crossey, 246
Salamonovics, Josef, 63
Salamonovics, Max (Max Sands), 57–58, 63, 66

Sallaumines, 90–92, 102
Samuliak, Khristofor, 201
San Cristobal, 20
Sander, Wilhelm, 216, 224
satellite camps, 44, 46, 56–57, 61, 63
Satmar, 46, 49, 54–55, 57, 62–63
Saur, Karl Otto, 153
Saxony-Anhalt, 56
Schäfer, Henriette, 216, 224
Scharfman, William, 108, 111
Scheel, Joseph (Iosif), 196, 205–6
Scheel, Peter, 200
Schenckendorff, Max von, 235
Schiller, Gustav, 53, 58
Schneider, Ida, 217, 224
Schuster, family, 214
Schuster, Henry, 214, 223
Ścioch, Antoni, 279
segregation, 5, 114, 116–118, 122, 220
Séguin de Reyniès, Albert, 242
Seifert, Rafael, 200
Selbstschutz, 193–4, 196, 199–201
self-declaration, 87, 93, 95–96, 99, 103
self-declared, 96, 103–4, 106
Sergeev, Alexei, 197
Seskavičiene, Polina, 288
Shanghai, 34
Shenker, Rivka, 137, 139, 142, 144, 146, 148–9
Shwiatowitz, Tzipora, 162, 169
Šiauliai, 287, 290–2
Sicherheitsdienst, 221, 227
Sicherheitspolizei, 227–8, 235
Sidor, Władysław, 278–80
Siedlce, 6, 274, 276
Siegmeyer, Karl, 58
Sighet, 44, 46, 48, 50–52, 55, 58, 62–63
Simonidis, Vassilios, 71–72, 78–79, 82–83
Singer, Arthur, 218–9, 225
Singer, rabbi, 228
Skorupka, Ignacy, 274
Skowroń, Jan, 183, 188
Skrzyniarz, Piotr, 147, 149
Slatinsky Doly, 45–46, 48
slave labor, 56, 69, 71, 151–5, 157–8, 161–2, 165–6, 300, 303, 305–9
Slomovics, Samuel, 51, 55, 57
Slovakia, 50, 160, 251
smuggle, 219, 236
Snyder, Timothy, 191–2, 204, 207, 301–2, 311, 313
Sobrance, 45, 50, 54, 62

socioeconomic status, 106–8
Sokołowski, Apolinary, 274–7, 281
Somme, 90
Sonderdienststelle für Juden, 216
Sontag, Walter, 58
Soroca, 254
South America, 32
Southern Buh River, 192
Soviet Union
spaces of possibilities, 108
special court, 134, 212–3, 215–6, 219–20, 269
Speer, Albert, 26, 28, 153, 221, 226
SS (Schutzstaffel), 37, 44, 47–49, 59, 153–6, 159, 161–5, 173, 194, 213, 228–30, 235–6, 243–4, 254, 277, 306–7
Stachowicz, Jan, 142–3
Starachowice, 55, 62, 192
Steinberg, Franz, 55
Steinhart, Eric Conrad, 204, 208
Stern, Anne-Lise, 303, 311, 313
Stern, Mark, 163, 169
Sternberg, 165
Storojineț, 254, 259
Straszęcin, 183
Strobel, Emil, 254
Strząpka, Michał, 177, 184, 188
study of perpetrators, 132, 190
Studzinskii, Ivan, 197
Stuhl, Ferencz, 57
Stuhl, Herman, 57
Stuhl, Sruly (Israel), 45, 48, 52, 55, 63–64
Stuhl, Vilmos, 52, 55
Stürmer, 213
Subcarpathian Ruthenia, 46
Suceava, 259
Sumners, Hatton, 34, 41
survive, 18, 29, 46, 58, 60, 68, 86, 91, 107, 134–5, 140, 142, 144, 146, 148, 161, 176, 180, 193, 211–2, 220, 237, 271, 277, 290, 307
survivor, 8–9, 45, 51, 56, 61, 85–86, 91, 132–3, 135, 147, 152, 158–161, 163, 166, 190, 192, 193–8, 201, 210, 212, 215, 220, 259, 275, 301, 303–5
survivor's testimony, 305
Süss, Hela, 137, 142–3, 148–9
Süss, Salomea, 137, 142–3, 148–9
Switzerland, 5, 17, 23, 79, 100–1, 216
Sypko, Edward, 181, 188
Szarwark, 146–7
Szczebrzedzyn, 6

Szejnmann, Claus-Christian W., 190, 204, 208
Szerzyny, 180
Szynkarzyzna, 181

T
Tarnobrzeg, 175, 182
Tarnów, 137, 140, 144, 147, 177, 181
Taub, Martin, 57
testimonials, 9, 102
testimony, 62, 86, 92–93, 99, 133, 143, 152, 176, 178, 180, 245, 272, 274, 275, 285–8, 290–3, 296, 303–5, 307, 309
Thekenbergen, 56
Theresienstadt, 18
Thessaloniki, 7, 68–71, 73–81
Theyleg, Frank, 215, 223
Tiercelet, 159, 165
Tighina, 254
Timm, Hans-Joachim, 230–5, 240
Tirolle, René, 242–4, 246
Tisa River, 46
Todesco, Emilio, 55, 58
Todt organization, 69
Toulouse, 5, 310
Transnistria, 190, 192–193, 197–198, 201, 262
transport, 15, 18, 44–47, 49–50, 52–63, 68, 74, 76, 90, 159–60, 164–5, 180, 200, 218, 234, 248, 270, 274–5, 279, 287, 289, 307
Transylvania, 44, 46, 49, 256
trauma, 60, 157, 281
treason, 218, 268
Treblinka, 1, 181, 236
trial, 9, 78, 134–135, 184, 193, 212, 218, 220, 257, 261, 267, 268–73, 276–8
Trivellato, Francesca, 3, 11, 13
Tulle, 247
Turk Transfer Scheme, 20
turning point, 3, 109, 259

U
Ukraine, 7, 192, 301, 304
Ulma, family, 172, 176
Ulma, Józef, 172, 186, 189
Ulma, Wiktoria, 172
Ungvar, 46, 50, 55, 57
United Kingdom, 21, 23
United States, 30–31, 34–35, 215, 262, 271, 286, 297

Uriage, 89
USC Shoah Foundation Visual History Archive, 9, 216, 307
USHMM, 92
USSR, 253, 261, 309
Uzhorod, 58, 62–63

V
Vagner, Efrayim, 214, 223
Vancouver, 32
Vasdravelis, Giannis, 79, 83
Venice, 55
Venlo, 215
Veselinovo, 197
Vichy regime, 92, 106–7
victims, 7, 8, 85, 87, 93, 108, 129, 132, 135, 148, 185, 191–5, 198–200, 228, 229, 232–4, 246–248, 251, 256–9, 261, 271–2, 278, 281, 295, 300–1
Vienna, 6, 23, 29, 30–32, 34–38, 163, 212, 216–20
Vijnița, 254
Vilkaviškis, 285
village, 46, 89–90, 132, 137, 140, 142, 144–47, 172–81, 183, 193–4, 196–7, 199–201, 254–5, 259, 262, 270–2, 274, 276, 279, 300–1
violence, 7, 23, 162, 172, 175–7, 184–5, 220, 228–30, 237, 243, 246, 248, 254, 256–8, 291–2, 295
Visa, 23, 31–36, 39
Voiron, 246
Vojnatina, 48, 62
Vradievka, 197, 201
Vuich, Iosif, 199

W
Waffen SS, 243–4, 254
Wannsee Conference, 17
Wannsee, 17, 21, 24
Warsaw, 5, 6, 51, 62, 133, 173, 181, 230–2, 235–6
Warthegau, 174
Węgrów, 181
Węgrzyn, Feliks, 146
Wehrmacht, 155, 227, 229, 235, 254
Weimar, 44, 53
Weiner, Abby, 63, 65
Weiser, Sigmund (Zsigismund), 49, 51, 53–54, 63–66
Weiss, Emil, 57, 63, 66
Weiss, Josef, 164, 169

Weissenberg, Melania, 135–6, 139, 142, 148
Weisz, Zoltan, 57
Weitzen, Lajos (Louis Weitzen), 50–51, 55, 59, 63, 65
Wesserling-Urbès, 164
White, Hayden, 300, 311
Wieliczka, 151
Wielopole Skrzyńskie, 180
Wiesel, Lazar Eliezer, called Elie, 4, 44–52, 55, 59, 61, 63–67, 302, 311, 314
Wieviorka, Annette, 11–13, 110–112, 250, 297, 299, 303, 311, 313–4
Wilczyk, Louis, 214
Winter, Joan, 215, 223
Wisliceny, Dieter, 80
witnesses, 147, 157–158, 163, 219, 229, 246–57, 259, 271–2, 275, 286–7, 290, 293–6
Wojcieszków, 274
Wojko, Stanisław, 183, 188
Wojnar, Franciszek, 178, 187
Wólka Ogryzkowa, 179

Y

Yacoel, Yomtov, 69–73, 77–84
Yad Vashem Institute, 92
yellow star/star of David, 17, 21, 87, 92, 114, 117, 120–1, 216
Yiddish, 10, 133, 182, 256, 286, 290–1

Z

Zahareşti, 259
Zemon Davis, Natalie, 113, 122, 127
Zentralstelle für jüdische Auswanderung, 19
Ziment, Leopold (Lipot Ciment), 63
Zimmermann, Moshe, 25, 28, 210, 222, 226
Zimna Woda, 178
Ziserman, Szloma, 270–2
Zittau, 160–1
Zolf, Rachel, 160, 168
Zulang, Szlama (Sol Culang), 51, 62, 65
Zurich, 22–23
Zylberberg, Izek, 180, 187
Zyskind, Jerzy, 56, 63